AF361579

PUSHKIN'S MONUMENT AND ALLUSION

Poem, Statue, Performance

Pushkin's Monument and Allusion

Poem, Statue, Performance

SIDNEY ERIC DEMENT

UNIVERSITY OF TORONTO PRESS
Toronto Buffalo London

Library and Archives Canada Cataloguing in Publication

Title: Pushkin's Monument and allusion: poem, statue, performance /
Sidney Eric Dement.
Names: Dement, Sidney Eric, 1978– author.
Description: Includes bibliographical references and index.
Identifiers: Canadiana 20190087560 | ISBN 9781487505523 (hardcover)
Subjects: LCSH: Pushkin, Aleksandr Sergeevich, 1799–1837 – Monuments –
Russia (Federation) – Moscow. | LCSH: Pushkin, Aleksandr Sergeevich,
1799–1837 – Allusions. | LCSH: Pushkin, Aleksandr
Sergeevich, 1799–1837 – Criticism and interpretation.
Classification: LCC PG3353.D46 2019 | DDC 891.71/3—dc23

Publication of this book was made possible, in part, by a grant from
the First Book Subvention Program of the Association for Slavic, East
European, and Eurasian Studies.

University of Toronto Press acknowledges the financial assistance to its
publishing program of the Canada Council for the Arts and the Ontario
Arts Council, an agency of the Government of Ontario.

Funded by the   Financé par le
Government   gouvernement
of Canada   du Canada

Canadä

To Deena

Contents

Figures

Acknowledgments

I am grateful to a long list of patient and thoughtful colleagues who have shaped and reshaped my understanding of Pushkin's Monument and its place in Russian culture. From the beginning, Tat'iana Vladimirovna Tsiv'ian has been a constant source of inspiration as a scholar, mentor, and friend. Marcus Levitt, David Bethea, Carol Any, Anindita Banerjee, and Edith Clowes provided encouragement and criticism at crucial turning points in the project. Maria Carlson first saw the potential in my initial idea, and for that I am especially grateful. At Binghamton University, respected colleagues have been readers, mentors, and friends: Donald Loewen, Nancy Tittler, Marina Zalesski, Zoja Pavlovskis-Petit, Carl Gelderloos, Harald Zils, Neil Christian Pages, Ingeborg Majer-O'Sickey, Rosmarie Morewedge, Scott Henkel, Kelly Kinney, Jeroen Gerrits, Dina Danon, John Havard, Tina Chronopoulos, and Adam Laats. Students in my courses on Moscow and St Petersburg and Activism in Russia also deserve credit as enthusiastic interlocutors on various aspects of the project.

The annual conferences of the Association for Slavic, East-European, and Eurasian Studies and the American Association of Teachers of Slavic and East European Languages have been important fora in which to test and refine my ideas. I would like to thank Alison Annunziata, Katya Hokanson, James Rann, Nina Wieda, Diane Nemec-Ignashev, Carlotta Chenoweth, Kat Scollins, Clint Walker, Karen Rosenflanz, Keith Gessen, and Katherine Bowers for important conversations along the way. Miranda Jakiša at Humboldt University in Berlin and Alexei Hegai at the State Bulgakov Museum in Moscow significantly shaped the direction of the project by inviting me to lecture on it at an early stage. A writing group with Heather DeHaan, Paul Shovlin, Giovanna Montenegro, and Ana Candela added some much-needed refinement in finalizing the manuscript.

Binghamton University has provided generous support for the project through research leaves and financial support: a fellowship in the Institute for Advanced Studies in the Humanities (Spring 2015), a Dean's Research Semester (Spring 2016), funding for travel to and work in the archives of the Shchusev Museum of Architecture (2013), and a publishing subvention. The Association for Slavic, East-European, and Eurasian Studies also helped to make publication possible through a subvention. The first chapter of this book was published in a slightly different version as "The Lifelike Statues of Ovid and Pushkin's Orthodoxy" in *Pushkin Review* 18–19 (2015–16): 85–105. A translation of that article was invited for publication in Russian translation as "Жизнеподобие статуй Овидия и православие Пушкина" in *Итоги и перспективы экфрастической теории* (Siedlce, Poland: State University of Siedlce, 2018): 168–90. I would like to thank the anonymous reviewers and the editors (Ivan Eubanks, Emily Wang, and Tat'iana Evgen'evna Avtukhovich) of these publications for their insightful comments. The English-language chapter is reprinted here in modified form with the kind permission of *Pushkin Review*.

At the University of Toronto Press I would like to thank Stephen Shapiro for his support of and insight into the project. Thanks also to Suzanne Rancourt for some much-needed counsel and to Kathleen Lynch for the stunning cover design. I am deeply indebted to three anonymous reviewers who gave involved and insightful readings that significantly improved the organization and accessibility of my arguments.

On a personal note, I owe a great deal to my first professor of Russian literature, Harley Wagler, who also introduced me to the Pushkin Monument in Moscow for the first time. His moving performance of Pushkin's poem "Monument," standing at its pedestal on a windy January evening in 2000 was one of my first and most memorable experiences of Russia, when I still knew nothing of Pushkin and could just barely decipher Cyrillic. Anastasiya Makarycheva's thought-provoking photographs of the Pushkin Monument have added a creative visual dimension to the book. My father-in-law, Chester Moore, earned my sincere gratitude for his fearless and careful proofreading of the entire final manuscript. I am daily thankful for my children, Maya and Everett, who "teach me English" and remind me that "I'm not broken" even at this early stage of their lives when they are blissfully unaware of the Pushkin Monument in Moscow. Finally, the project has been faithfully supported and shaped above all others by my wife, Deena, to whom I dedicate this book.

PUSHKIN'S MONUMENT AND ALLUSION

Poem, Statue, Performance

Dimensions of the Pushkin Monument

Alexander Pushkin (1799–1837) is Russia's most venerated poet. In part, this is because of his contributions to literary language. At a critical moment in early-nineteenth-century Russian culture, Pushkin made choices about Russian literary style in poetry and prose that set the stage for Russia's greatest contributions to world literature: the novels of Ivan Turgenev, Fedor Dostoevskii, and Lev Tolstoi and the short stories and drama of Anton Chekhov. In part, Pushkin is venerated for political and ideological reasons. His death in 1837 came just before the split between the Slavophiles and Westernizers in the 1840s. He never had to choose a side and wrote with such a unique mixture of clarity and complexity that both sides could claim to be his heirs. On the one hand, he faced intense censorship from both church and state, and therefore became an inspiring hero to generations of intelligentsia who have found themselves in similar sorts of political precarity. On the other hand, he managed to choose his words with enough ambiguity and sophistication so as to move in the intimate social circle of the Tsar while maintaining his status as poet. For all of these reasons, and quite a few more besides, Pushkin continues to hold significance for Russian society across political, social, and class divisions.

Monuments to Pushkin in Russia testify to the ubiquity of the cult of Pushkin. If ever Pushkin lived in, visited, or wrote about a place, the fact is likely marked at least by a commemorative plaque or a bust, if not a stand-alone monument. There are plenty of monuments to Pushkin in places of which he may never have heard and that he certainly never saw. Pushkin monuments in Russia are undeniably a cliché – a material expression of an official cult whose lexicon is limited to the superlative, simultaneously exaggerating and obscuring the poetic depth of Pushkin's life and work. These monumental clichés, however, do not diminish the aesthetic riches of the first – the Pushkin Monument in Moscow, designed by Alexander Mikhailovich Opekushin (1838–1923) and erected in 1880. It has its own story and active role in generating aesthetic trends that intersect with Russia's grand narratives, especially the official cult and the national myth of Pushkin.

At first glance the Pushkin Monument seems simple enough: in Moscow's Pushkin Square, a metallic likeness of a man with impeccably coiffed sideburns stands on a pedestal and contemplates the flow of traffic in one of Moscow's busiest intersections of pedestrian, auto, and subway routes (figure I.1).

The simplicity is deceptive.

When a viewer is contemplating the Pushkin Monument for the first time, the statue of Pushkin might seem to dominate the design of the monument. Upon closer inspection, however, it becomes apparent that the statue is in dialogue with the excerpts from Pushkin's 1836 ode, "Monument," that adorn the sides of the pedestal. This is the naive viewer's first clue that there is much more to this monument than its visual depiction of Pushkin: what exactly is the relationship between this verbal poem and the visual statue? The tension between the statue and the poem, the visual and the verbal, the elevated visual focus and the grounded material base defines the monument. To unpack its meaning, however, demands considerable knowledge of literary history; Pushkin's life, works, and worldview; and the history of the monument itself. In this regard, the monument is an invitation to learn something new as much as to remember something already known.

Turning from the tension between the visual and verbal elements within the monument to their interaction with the surrounding built environment presents a similar puzzle. Why was the first Pushkin Monument erected in this Moscow square? Does the Pushkin Monument make meaningful sense when juxtaposed with the movie theatre behind it, the entrance to the Metro at its feet, or the McDonald's restaurant off to one side? A brief tour of the history of Pushkin Square reveals the complexity of the Pushkin Monument's interaction with its environment.

Originally the first Pushkin Monument was intended neither for Moscow nor for Pushkin Square but rather for Moscow's rival city, St Petersburg. When the monument was erected in 1880, St Petersburg had been the centre of political, cultural, and literary life since it was founded in 1703. Pushkin was born in Moscow in 1799, but his literary career unfolded in and around St Petersburg. From his education at the Lyceum in one of Petersburg's suburbs, Tsarskoe Selo (1811–17), to his 1836 cycle named for Petersburg's "Stony Island" composed just a few months before his death, Pushkin's literary output reflects his biographical and symbolic

I.1 The visual and verbal dimensions of the Pushkin Monument in Moscow,
2010. This 2010 photograph of the monument gives a sense of the balance between
the verbal poem and the visual statue. Photograph by Anastasiya Lvova, made
available through Wikicommons (CC BY-SA 3.0): https://ru.wikipedia
.org/wiki/Памятник_А._С._Пушкину_(Москва,_Пушкинская_площадь)#/media/
File:PushkinMskVblizi.jpg. (last accessed 3 November 2018).

connection to Russia's imperial capital. While Pushkin was born in the pre-Petrine capital, he died in St Petersburg, and the Pushkin Monument is in many ways more closely connected to his death and legacy than to his birth and heritage. Pushkin's most prominent urban allusions in the poem "Monument" are to other Petersburg monuments, and the poem itself was written as part of a Petersburg cycle. Nonetheless, for reasons that will become clear later in this study, the Pushkin Monument ended up in Moscow. St Petersburg has not relinquished its claim on Pushkin's Monument, however. The strong connection of the poem to St Petersburg continues to conflict with the physical presence of the statue in Moscow – a Petersburg poem on a Moscow monument.

The question of where exactly to put the Pushkin Monument was not settled by the decision to erect it in Moscow. Currently, the Pushkin Monument stands on the northeast side of Moscow's Tverskaia Street and looks to the southwest, but that is not its original location or orientation in Pushkin Square. Just beneath the surface of its pedestal still lie the foundations of a different structure – the bell tower of Strastnoi Monastery, one of Moscow's oldest and most cherished pre-revolutionary monastic communities. From its dedication in 1880 until the destruction of the bell tower in 1937, the Pushkin Monument directed its gaze to the northwest, towards this architectural and spiritual landmark, from its location on the southwest side of Tverskaia Street (figure I.2).

The first viewers of the monument interpreted Pushkin's contemplation of the bell tower as pivotal to the monument's meaning. The statue seemed to venerate this symbol of Russian Orthodoxy and therefore to comment on Pushkin's spiritual life. For some twenty-first-century observers acquainted with all of Pushkin's writings such a biographical interpretation poses significant problems, but in the late nineteenth century such nuances went largely unexamined. The bell tower also recalled Pushkin's burial near a different monastic community close to his inherited estate, relatively far from the urban centres of Moscow and Petersburg and inaccessible to his average reader for many years.

The October Revolution and the militant atheism of the first decade of the Soviet Union reshaped this landscape and, with it, the meaning of the Pushkin Monument. The Strastnoi Monastery officially ceased to function as a monastic community in 1919, and the bell tower became a billboard for Soviet propaganda (figure I.3).

Instead of Orthodoxy and mortality, the Pushkin Monument was made to interact with the literary history of the surrounding built environment. The building that housed the *Izvestiia* news agency along with the many theatres on Tverskoi Boulevard drew out the literary

I.2 A pre-revolutionary postcard of Tverskaia Square, indicating the original location and orientation of the Pushkin Monument in Pushkin Square (referred to as Tverskaia Square on the postcard). Pushkin faces the bell tower of the Strastnoi Monastery across Tverskaia Street with his back to Tverskoi Boulevard. Anonymous late-nineteenth-century postcard, public domain. Reproduction number: LC-DIG-ppmsca-03850, made available by the Library of Congress, Prints and Photographs Division, Photochrom Prints Collection, through Wikicommons: https://ru.wikipedia.org/wiki/Памятник_А._С._Пушкину_(Москва,_Пушкинская_площадь)#/media/File:Strastnoy.jpg (last accessed 3 November 2018).

I.3 The Pushkin Monument during the celebration of the twentieth
anniversary of *Pravda*, 1932. The title of the newspaper, which means "truth,"
can be seen displayed on the bell tower of the Strastnoi Monastery along with
a slogan: "The press must serve as a weapon of socialist construction." The
building of the newspaper *Izvestiia*, which means "news," can be seen between
the bell tower and the Pushkin Monument. The use of the Strastnoi bell tower
as a billboard for propaganda can also be seen as an allusion to Maiakovskii's
agitational propaganda that suggested removing Strastnoi Monastery so that
Pushkin could better read the news (i.e., the *Izvestiia* building). In this photograph,
Pushkin is reading the "truth." The original photograph is held in the Shchusev
Museum of Architecture, file KPof 5694–1. Reprinted with permission.

culture of the square, and the propaganda displayed on the bell tower frequently had a literary theme. In 1931, Strastnaia Square was renamed Pushkin Square to emphasize the Pushkin Monument and Pushkin as a new architectural and ideological dominant. In 1937, the 100th anniversary of Pushkin's death was marked with a large poster of Pushkin hung on the bell tower (figure I.4), accompanied by several lines of his poetry that were seen to fit the theme of another anniversary that year, twenty years of the Revolution (1917–37). The Pushkin Monument was transformed from its humble contemplation of God and mortality to a proud prophecy of the Bolshevik Revolution.

At the same time, the monument itself was significantly modified in preparation for the 1937 anniversary of Pushkin's death. The text of Pushkin's poem "Monument" on the pedestal was altered in preparation for the Jubilee. When the Pushkin Monument was erected in 1880, only the censored version of Pushkin's poem was known and, consequently, the censored text appeared on the pedestal of Opekushin's monument. The Soviets replaced the censored text with Pushkin's original and included more of the poem itself: two whole stanzas instead of two lines.

Architectural modifications followed soon after. The bell tower of Strastnoi Monastery was removed later in 1937, so the Pushkin Monument faced a void filled with various place holders (figure I.5). Something permanent and significant was needed to replace the memory of Strastnoi Monastery and the Orthodoxy that it symbolically represented.

In 1950, the Pushkin Monument was moved to fill the void, which it has occupied since. Significant symbolism accompanied the relocation. From an ideological perspective, one could argue that the move symbolizes how art and the cult of Pushkin replaced the tradition of Orthodoxy. From a literary point of view, one could find parallels between the literal "movement" of the Pushkin Monument and one of Pushkin's favourite devices – the monument that comes to life. Architecturally, the move made the Pushkin Monument the architectural dominant of the square, casting it as a palimpsest, a text written over an erased but still legible predecessor. As a continuation of this history, the Pushkin Monument interacts with its current built environment in important ways. The aesthetic domain of cinema (the movie theatre behind it), the technological advances of Soviet industrialization (the Metro in front of it), and the ideology of Western market capitalism (McDonald's) all create meanings through proximity to the Pushkin Monument, even as various voices advocate for either innovative new buildings or the restoration of the pre-revolutionary square and the rebuilding of Strastnoi Monastery. One of the unique features of the Pushkin Monument is its unstable

I.4 The cover of *The Construction of Moscow* from February 1937 expertly
frames the Pushkin Monument. On the left side of the photograph, the
viewer reads one stanza from Pushkin's 1836 poem "Monument" engraved
on the pedestal of the monument. On the right, the viewer observes the
poster of Pushkin hanging from the bell tower of Strastnoi Monastery. The
image of Pushkin on the poster stands in for Opekushin's statue of Pushkin,
excised by the photographer. By splitting statue and pedestal in this way,
the photograph incorporates the *Izvestiia* newspaper building and the Soviet
masses celebrating the 100th anniversary of Pushkin's death into Pushkin's
monumental legacy. Poem, statue, and performance are integral components
of the monument. Photograph from the collections of the State Pushkin
Museum in Moscow, with thanks to Monika L'vovna Spivak.

I.5 The monument to Prometheus standing in place of the recently destroyed
Strastnoi Monastery, ca 1938. The monument occupies the spot where the bell
tower of the monastery once stood. The figure of Prometheus in this context
signifies not only the Titan who crafted humans from clay, but also the rebel
who stole from the gods to better the lives of humans. Replacing a significant
symbol of Russian Orthodoxy with the symbolic figure of heroic rebellion
against the gods alludes to the campaign against religion in the 1920s
and 1930s. See Melikhova and Tsekhanskii's discussion of this monument
to Prometheus and its context in *Strasti i nadezhdy Pushkinskoi (Strastnoi)
ploshchadi i strastnogo monastyria* (48–51). In 1950, the Pushkin Monument was
moved across Tverskaia Street to take Prometheus's place. Given Pushkin's
interest in the lifelike statue and the significant role that Prometheus plays
as the first to create humans as living statues in Ovid's *Metamorphoses* (see
chapter 1), this monument to Prometheus provides a rich layer of allusion to
the better-known architectural relationship between the Strastnoi Monastery
and the Pushkin Monument. The original photograph is held
in the Shchusev Museum of Architecture, file KPnvf 491–9.
Reprinted with permission.

relationship to its location: should the Strastnoi Monastery be rebuilt, the Pushkin Monument might once again move back across Tverskaia Street. The question of just what exactly the Pushkin Monument should be contemplating is one of the defining features of its current location.

Photographer Marina Volosevich's 2017 photograph (figure I.6) of the Pushkin Monument reveals how complicated the palimpsest of Pushkin's statuesque contemplation has become. Volosevich recounts how, while searching for an unexpected vision of Moscow's beauty, she stumbled upon the combination of this advertisement and the monument to Pushkin.[1] When she saw the frame she had captured, she immediately thought of one of Pushkin's unpublished poems (variously dated 1831 and 1835), in which the poet had thought that his heart had lost the ability to experience passion (*stradat'*). "Delight," "sorrow," and "naive dreams" had seemed fated to remain in the past. But, the poet writes, they have once again stirred before the forceful power of beauty.[2] Volosevich's photograph and experience of the Pushkin Monument reveal the way it continues to speak to aesthetic minds: her performance as a photographer engages with both the visual dimension of the monument and its deeply rooted verbal connection to Pushkin's poetry.

The composition of Volosevich's image can also be interpreted in the context of the contradictory meanings that the gaze of Opekushin's statue has been made to express in various historical moments. If in pre-revolutionary Russia Pushkin contemplated a convent with humility, in this contemporary photograph he is distracted by the sensuous image hanging from the nearby building. The image plays on the polysemy of Strastnaia (Passion) Square, the former name of Pushkin Square: "passion" (*strast'*) is etymologically related to suffering (*stradanie*) but can also refer to sexual desire. When interpreted as a palimpsest, the photograph captures both the serious side of Pushkin's work that some have interpreted as religious devotion and several irreverent episodes in Pushkin's work that blend eroticism with blasphemy. Furthermore, it recalls the fundamentally erotic nature of the myth of the statue that comes to life and the problematic gender dynamics, especially in light of current gender politics, that accompany its manifestations in Pushkin's poetic biography.[3] When this angle of the statue's gaze is interpreted against a poem like "No, I do not prize stormy pleasure," in which Pushkin expresses how much he values his power to bring his statue-like wife to sexual arousal, the photograph becomes more complex: just who has the power to bring whom to life in this photograph?

Still there is more. While this photograph can create associations based on the interaction of Pushkin's poetry and the statue, it can also create associations with the performances of another poet who interpreted

I.6 Contemplating poem, statue, and performance as dimensions of
the Pushkin Monument, 2017. The photograph is from the archive of
Russkaia Gazeta, published in 2017 with an article about O.A. Davydova's
new account of sculptor Alexander Mikhailovich Opekushin's works related
to Pushkin (Vasil'eva, "Igry s Pushkinym") (last accessed 3 November 2018).
Photograph by Marina Volosevich. Reprinted with permission.

Pushkin's contemplation of the Strastnoi Monastery, a monastic community of women, in a blasphemous way. Claiming a shortage of paper in 1919, Sergei Esenin and several other imagist poets used the walls of Strastnoi Monastery to "publish" quotations of their poetry. Esenin cited one line from his poem "Transfiguration," "Lord, bear a calf!," which was immediately perceived as an affront to the women of the monastic community.[4] Esenin's performance foreshadows the later Soviet use of the Strastnoi bell tower as a sort of billboard for things that Pushkin should be contemplating, while also harking back to Pushkin's blasphemous portrayal of the doctrine of Mary's virginity and the Incarnation in his satirical poem *The Gabrieliad*.

As the Esenin episode suggests, the complexity of the history of the built environment with which the Pushkin Monument interacts is matched by the tradition of performance near it. Some of these performances are private. People walk by the monument every day: some contemplate it, others ignore it. Some read on the benches near it. People meet up with friends or dates in the centre of the city at its base. At least one soccer fan has climbed the statue to celebrate a victory on Pushkin's shoulders. These sorts of informal performances coexist alongside others that are organized, public, and highly visible. Protests are staged under the statue's gaze. Anniversaries of Pushkin's birth and death are commemorated here by huge crowds. Among poets, Esenin is certainly not alone. Other poets and novelists have also given significant performances at the Pushkin Monument. Some claim to enhance Pushkin's legacy while others seek to overthrow it. Regardless of the attitude of these writers to Pushkin, the monument provides a setting for their poetic performances that is saturated with tradition and meaning. Each new performance interacts not only with Pushkin's poem and Opekushin's statue but with a host of previous performances, giving the square an accumulated performative significance that augments its visual and verbal dimensions.

So, yes, the Pushkin Monument may appear to be a simple statue at first glance, but it is actually a complex aesthetic object that exists simultaneously as a poem, a statue, and a performative space. That is not to say, however, that these three elements always coexisted in creative tension as they do today. The poem came first. In August of 1836, Pushkin (1799–1837) wrote the ode now popularly known simply as "Monument." He died a few months later in January of 1837. In the decades following his death, the poem "Monument" was transformed into a statue in central Moscow: The Pushkin Monument, designed by Opekushin. At the dedication of the monument in 1880, the interaction between the verbal text and the visual, material form it assumed in urban space generated a performative dynamic that subsequent generations of passersby, protesters, admirers, artists, and thinkers have amplified. This tradition continues, and in this sense, the story of the Pushkin Monument remains open-ended.

Analysing the interpenetration of the monument's three hypostases tells the story of one of Russia's significant aesthetic objects while at the same time making discoveries about the texts and performances in which it is conceptualized and transformed. One of the reasons that Moscow's Pushkin Monument is unique, even among monuments to Pushkin more generally, is that its story informs other important developments in the Russian literary tradition – both aesthetic trends and historical-cultural trends, such as Russia's expanding readership, censorship, and ideology. For this reason, it is impossible to interpret the Pushkin Monument without telling another important story along the way. This second story is about allusion, the aesthetic device by which writers reference select elements of cultural history (texts, people, places, events, ideas) to enrich the meaning of their new creation and invite their reader into the shared experience of tradition.

On the level of form, the increasing number of dimensions makes allusions to the Pushkin Monument more complex. When Pushkin wrote his poem, he drew on many other "Monument" poems by authors of antiquity, such as Horace (65 BCE–8 BCE) and Ovid (43 BCE–17 or 18 CE), as well as his eighteenth-century Russian predecessors Mikhail Vasilievich Lomonosov (1711–1765), Alexander Nikolaevich Radishchev (1749–1802), and Gavriil Romanovich Derzhavin (1743–1816). Opekushin's Pushkin Monument added a dimension of visual art to this long tradition of verbal art. Both poem and statue became a fixture in Moscow's urban space – the stage for significant performances by artists who are keenly aware of how poets before them have defined themselves in the space of the monument. By the twentieth century, both writers and readers negotiated increasingly complex allusions to all of these interrelated dimensions.

On the level of meaning, allusions to the Pushkin Monument reflect the changing relationship between the artists who make the allusions and the readers who reconstruct them. Already in his 1836 poem "Monument," Pushkin differentiated between the naive masses and the future poets among his readers. As the population of newly literate Russians grew in subsequent generations, images of the future poet and the naive reader became crucial signifiers of the most meaningful allusions to the Pushkin Monument in the work of every subsequent generation of Russian writers.

By the beginning of the twenty-first century, allusions to the monument consistently relied on its unique interplay between poem, statue, and performance. Within this cultural space, the monument reflects the core antinomies in the study of allusion, which often attempts to reconcile "anxiety of influence" (the temporal, personal, psychological aspect of allusion that privileges the author) with "intertextuality" (the spatial, depersonalized, linguistic aspect that privileges the reader). The verbal, visual, and performative dimensions of the Pushkin Monument allow for a close look at how allusive practice evolves through the interaction of both time and space, through the work of both author and reader, through the forces of both anxiety and objective linguistic fact.

One of the great ironies here is that the Pushkin Monument's allusive complexity so frequently bypasses the general reader. As allusion to the monument evolved over generations of poetic innovation, it was accompanied by an ever-larger but increasingly naive readership. When Pushkin himself first wrote about monuments and allusion in the early nineteenth century, he wrote for a small, educated elite. By the 1980s the Soviet Union boasted universal literacy. However, as works like Mikhail Bulgakov's *Master and Margarita*, Vladimir Toporov's theory of monumental sculpture, and Tat'iana Tolstaia's *Slynx* show, twentieth-century authors recognized the challenges that the Pushkin Monument as a trope poses to poets and their readers alike. Writers who allude to the monument can quickly lapse into cliché. Readers who interpret these allusions, especially naive readers, can easily miss the layers of cultural memory that a writer triggers by re-creating the space of the monument. The story of the Pushkin Monument emphasizes the key moments of poetic innovation that gave rise to an increasingly complex practice of allusion, while also highlighting the anxiety of making a meaningful connection with future audiences whose frames of reference may differ so greatly as to make those allusions inaccessible.

Two Contemporary Case Studies

As a transition from this general discussion of the Pushkin Monument and its cultural history to more detailed definitions of its unique relationship to the practice of allusion, I present two contemporary case studies that will make the discussion that follows less abstract and theoretical. Both of these events derive much of their meaning from the Pushkin Monument, exemplifying the connection between the monument's verbal, visual, and performative dimensions and the practice of allusion. Interpreting how they interact with the monument gives a contemporary snapshot of the Pushkin Monument, while also providing some concrete examples of allusion. In 2013, two architects published their vision for the reconstruction of the Strastnoi Monastery and the restoration of the historical Pushkin Square. In 2007, a poet passed his self-published manuscripts to an American translator and editor at the foot of the Pushkin Monument. The architects' approach emphasizes the necessity to preserve the meanings of the Pushkin Monument and its surroundings for the naive masses who move through the square daily but mostly fail to recognize its historical and cultural significance. The poet's performance seems unconcerned with any audience at all, regardless of whether or not readers are capable of attending to the rich literary, cultural, and historical significance of the performative act. Reading these two events together accomplishes two tasks. First, their contrasting approaches interact with different aspects of the history of the Pushkin Monument and exemplify its contemporary relevance. Second, each event demonstrates the Pushkin Monument's contribution to the study of allusive practice.

In their recent (2013) study of the architectural ensemble that historically dominated Pushkin Square (Strastnaia Square in pre-revolutionary Russia), architects Aida Aleksandrovna Melikhova and Roman V. Tsekhanskii argue that the renaissance of the Strastnoi Monastery, second only to the Church of Christ the Saviour in its cultural and spiritual significance, will lead to no less than the "stilling of human suffering" and the "cessation of discord in society."[5] Their utopian claims for this future hinge on the idea that, "quite literally, we propose not so much to bring back to life (*vozrodit'*) monuments or their ensemble in Pushkin Square, but historical memory."[6] Undertaken by the "Old Moscow Commission," the work is in part a response to fears that the empty space of Pushkin Square will succumb to the "temptations of the interests of big business," with new buildings geared towards twenty-first-century consumerist ideology and architectural utility.[7] The authors assume the task of preservation, aiming to protect the architectural heritage of the square from "historically foreign innovative structural changes" and leaving to future generations the possibility of reconstructing one of Moscow's most culturally significant squares with its list of intangible values: spiritual, cultural, and historical.[8]

Their vision for the immediate future of the square reflects the extent to which they invest its urban space with cultural and spiritual meaning. For example, even before the rebuilding of the Strastnoi Monastery would commence, the authors argue that jumbo-sized advertisements on the roofs and facades of buildings should be removed and that the thematics of the films and advertisements of the movie theatre "Russia" should be reoriented to reflect historical, spiritual, and cultural values.

These preparations in advance of the reconstruction would make Push-kin Square "even more attractive for Muscovites and guests of the capi-tal, who will be informed of the spiritual-cultural significance of this tourist attraction in Moscow and of the future changes connected with the restoration of its historical appearance."[9]

The future of the square becomes a point of education in its Russian sense of *obrazovanie*, which has at its root the word for image (*obraz*). The architects catalogue the grievances (*bezobrazie*) they perceive in the present culture of the square, much of which has to do with the Push-kin Monument, the only remaining physical structure of the historical square. Deprived of its historical surroundings, the statue of the "Poet" seems awkward, out of place, empty.[10] That emptiness contributes to the culture of disrespect (in the opinion of Melikhova and Tsekhanskii) that has grown up around it: its chains have been stolen on occasion; street performers dance in front of the thoughtful poet; and a soccer fan climbed the statue and sat on Pushkin's shoulders in his enthusiasm over a Russian victory. Furthermore, Pushkin Square, according to the authors, is the only one in the centre of Moscow that is not guarded by police at night.[11] As an unguarded, unprincipled void, in their interpre-tation, the square is a reflection of the twentieth-century destruction of spiritual and cultural values that does not suffice as a warning to future generations of the dangers of radical revolution. The void must be filled with the original content of the square as a way to move forward into a future Russia with its spiritual and cultural history intact.

The architects' interpretation of the square looks almost entirely to its past, which, nearly lost, defines the future of what it means to inhabit and interact with Russian cultural space. The vision is selective, how-ever. Only certain aspects of the history of Pushkin Square deserve a place in the future. When justifying their suggestions for the near future of the square, the authors argue for the rebirth of a proper atmo-sphere as an inviting place for pedestrian recreation instead of a place of crowded protests and picketing.[12] Their vague reference alludes to a strong tradition of protest against censorship and a rigged legal system that coalesced around the monument during the trial of authors Sinia-vskii and Daniel' in the Soviet era. Instead, Melikhova and Tsekhan-skii suggest that the square should invoke the spirit of sacred memory, listing the acts of violence committed against the Russian populace in the square: during the Napoleonic invasion of Moscow in 1812, during the Stalinist purges (they specifically refer to members of the Strastnoi monastic community who were executed at the Butovo Firing Range), and in the terrorist attack in the underground walkway of Pushkin Square in 2000.[13]

Emphasis on the reconstruction of the Strastnoi Monastery as the architectural dominant of the square has implications for the Pushkin Monument. The authors frequently note the connection between the Pushkin Monument and Strastnoi Monastery as integral to the design of the monument.[14] As proof of the compositional unity, they cite the well-documented tradition of photographing the Pushkin Monument from behind, with the bell tower of the Strastnoi Monastery as its background – the perspective in the pre-revolutionary postcard and the photograph on the cover of *The Construction of Moscow*, pictured above (figure I.4).[15] Deprived of all but the Pushkin Monument, Pushkin Square has become an "empty landscape" and has "almost completely" lost its "wholeness."[16] Or, referencing a different metaphor, the authors describe how the addition of the Pushkin Monument in 1880 turned the intersection of the Boulevard Ring and Tverskaia Street into "the most interesting, 'multivoiced' (as later historians will call it) of Moscow's ensembles, fully formed by the centuries out of diverse objects."[17] Their architectural focus reflects the importance of the Pushkin Monument for the square as a poem, a statue, and a performative space that gives meaning to the surrounding architecture. Historically, Pushkin Square certainly deserved the epithet "multivoiced"; but, with most of these voices silenced (the average person probably does not know about the buildings that have been destroyed or significantly altered in the square), the authors make the case that only through restoration can the aesthetic dimensions of Pushkin Square be preserved. The ideology of conservation, preservation, and memory that animates the efforts of architects Melikhova and Tsekhanskii represents one set of voices that can be heard in Pushkin Square.

A brief interaction between a poet and an editor at the Pushkin Monument highlights some of the allusions Melikhova and Tsekhanskii might prefer to avoid. In his introduction to *It's No Good: Poems/Essays/Actions*, editor and translator Keith Gessen describes meeting poet, essayist, and activist Kirill Medvedev at the Pushkin Monument in 2007.[18] A few years earlier, Medvedev had rejected copyright to his works, which were published anyway (and without asking the author's permission) by the respected and established *New Literary Review* (*NLO*). By 2007, Medvedev had created his own publishing forum, the Free Marxist Press, outside of the system. He undertook the translation and publishing of various Western Marxist thinkers as well as his own work; when he met Gessen, he was carrying in a large gym bag the entire print run of his book, published by his own independent press. He gave Gessen a copy at the foot of the Pushkin Monument. A pregnant understatement in Gessen's introduction, the allusions triggered by his exchange with

Medvevev beg for interpretation. The history evoked by Medvedev's action differs from the history recalled in the work of Melikhova and Tsekhanskii; therefore, it signals a different paradigm for the future of the Pushkin Monument.

Evidence from Medvedev's poetry about monuments and protest in central Moscow supports the idea that his understated, private performance at the Pushkin Monument draws on its verbal, visual, and performative dimensions. Moscow's symbolic geography plays a significant role in several works. For example, the poem "if you're having some problems" recounts a demonstration of young people protesting fascism. Medvedev recommends that the reader join a group of antifascists as they walk along a politically suggestive route through central Moscow. They start on Miasnitskaia Street, move past Lubianka (the Federal Security Service [Federal'naia Sluzhba Bezopasnosti – FSB] headquarters and prison), continue down Kuznetskii Most, and exit onto Tverskaia Street. Once they reach Tverskaia Street, the protesters turn towards the Kremlin and block half of this major thoroughfare before scattering near Okhotnyi Riad. Protesters shout slogans like "Freedom to Denis Solopov!" and "Don't stop antifa," while the lyrical voice of the poet comments on the architecture of political oppression ("one day we'll pass by this rotten citadel [i.e., Lubianka] in such a way that *nothing* will be left of it").[19] Medvedev alludes to the absence of the monument to Felix Edmundovich Dzerzhinskii, the man credited with creating the Soviet secret police. The poet's description of this emptiness in front of the FSB building at Lubianka ("beautiful empty square") and his careful charting of the protesters' progress through central Moscow (just down the street from the Pushkin Monument) reveal his attention to the same logic of symbolic geography that gives meaning to the Pushkin Monument. In that context, his choice to pass his text to a New York-based translator and editor at the foot of the Pushkin Monument seems like a political and cultural performance. The reputation of the Pushkin Monument as one of the most clichéd places to meet someone in the centre of the city only increases the semantic charge.

His other poetry aside, Medvedev's choice to stage his action at the Pushkin Monument alludes to many episodes from its cultural history. First, the Pushkin Monument encodes church and state censorship – originally a censored version of Pushkin's poem "Monument" was engraved on the pedestal of the statue. Medvedev's choice to publish his own works and circulate them through personal connections has a long history in Russia, from Radishchev and Pushkin in the early nineteenth century through the Soviet tradition of *samizdat*. Secondly, Medvedev's many calls for art to have political consequences resonates loudly in Pushkin Square; the emptiness that Melikhova and Tsekhanskii describe can be interpreted as the partial result of the agitational propaganda of leftist poet Vladimir Vladimirovich Maiakovskii, who advocated for the destruction of Strastnoi Monastery as early as 1928.[20] Finally, passing along a text to be published abroad (known in Russian as *tamizdat*) invokes the tradition of protesting the 1965 trial of Siniavskii and Daniel', prosecuted for publishing their texts in *tamizdat*. In this light, Medvedev's action reads like the inverse of Melikhova and Tsekhanskii's proposals.

A binary reading would be simplistic, however: the two projects are similarly concerned with the future of international capital. Just as Melikhova and Tsekhanskii urgently argue for preserving Pushkin Square from investors, Medvedev often resists the commodification of art. By denying copyright and founding his Free Marxist Press, Medvedev rejects the ethical quandaries of leftist authors publishing works with presses owned by multinational corporations that Gessen describes in his introduction to Medvedev's work.[21] Passing along these texts to Gessen near the Pushkin Monument also invites comment on Pushkin's thoughts about the commodification of art in poems like "Conversation between a Book-Seller and a Poet" (1824).[22]

On the aesthetic level, both the architectural conservation of the square and the progressive *samizdat/tamizdat* ritually enacted in its space recognize the power of the urban space (emptiness) surrounding the Pushkin Monument to generate references to that which is not literally there in the present, to refer – to allude – to a tradition, historical events, performances, and texts both visual and verbal. It is the *space* that facilitates the *allusions*.

Cultural Myth, Literary Politics, and the Aesthetics of Allusion

Allusions in Pushkin Square relate powerfully to the cultural myth of Pushkin. Pushkinist Stephanie Sandler introduces her analysis of the Pushkin myth in the twentieth century by describing a cultural split around Pushkin in the 1990s, noting that, at the end of the twentieth century, some Russians (like the conservative critic Stanislav Rassadin) see in Pushkin "all they hope to be, they see the integrity, creativity, and spiritual values they hold dear, and they see a dynamic, liberating mind that challenges all that seems stultifying or intolerant elsewhere in their culture."[23] To this version of the Pushkin myth Sandler juxtaposes the Petersburg poet Elena Shvarts, who sees myth making not as a positive process for ordinary people or for the projection of a healthy national identity, but rather as an inescapable trap for the poet at his death. Myth making, in the view of Shvarts, makes the poet a mortal (dead) man rather than the "godlike figure imagined by Rassadin."[24]

Sandler elucidates the various meanings of myth, all of which help to describe the Pushkin phenomenon in Russia – as an explanatory narrative for Russian culture's "emergence into modernity," as a narrative of the sacred origins of the nation, and as an explanatory system that is inherently false.[25] This set of definitions and the various ways that Sandler uses them to map the development of the Pushkin phenomenon in twentieth-century culture explain several aspects of twenty-first-century interest in Pushkin Square. Melikhova and Tsekhanskii engage with the Pushkin myth as an explanatory narrative for the preservation of Pushkin Square as well as a myth of sacred origin, the type of official Pushkinolatry that many poets have long denounced. Medvedev's action, shaped as it is by his general political message, corresponds more to the tradition of debunking the official myths of Pushkin employed by the state to validate their agenda: Medvedev's art cuts through the ideology and propaganda of the rich and powerful.

Political thought also has a role to play in explaining the future of Pushkin Square. Marcus Levitt's analysis of the literary politics of the 1880 Jubilee recounts political quarrels on both left and right leading up to the celebration and contextualizes the political atmosphere that finally allowed the Pushkin Celebration and dedication of the Pushkin Monument to emerge as a cultural neutral zone.[26] At its very beginning, the Pushkin Monument became a proxy for conservative, liberal, and nihilist political agendas, a role it continues to play in the twenty-first century. Levitt's analysis of the anticipation of the Pushkin Celebration of 1880 and its immediate aftermath is strikingly contemporary. Melikhova and Tsekhanskii's complaint that Pushkin Square is the only one of its kind in central Moscow with no police detachment at night contrasts sharply with the destruction of Lubianka and altercation with an FSB agent described by Medvedev in his poem about the antifa demonstration. However, in both projects the Pushkin Monument expresses agency by evoking allusions to the long traditions of these two very different political orientations.

In addition to the mythic and political dimensions of the Pushkin Monument, Medvedev and the architects provide concrete examples of the aesthetic layer of what happens in Pushkin Square. Alongside the mythic nature of Pushkin's role in negotiating national, cultural, and spiritual identity and the political nature of rhetoric inspired in the space of his monument, there exists the aesthetic question of how this urban space came to be so potently charged with accumulated significance. How is it that Gessen's nonchalant reference to the Pushkin

Monument as the backdrop for his meeting with Medvedev can trigger a host of verbal, visual, and performative associations? How did it come to pass that the Strastnoi Monastery would become so fundamental to the meaning of the Pushkin Monument, or that a culture of protest should be inappropriate, or that the thematics of advertisements or a movie theatre in Pushkin Square should be restricted because the poet doffs his hat before them?

The answer to these questions requires expanding accepted definitions of allusion so as to grasp how the verbal, visual, and performative dimensions of the Pushkin Monument function. Once again, the examples of Melikhova, Tsekhanskii, Gessen, and Medvedev constellate the issues. Melikhova and Tsekhanskii suggest that Pushkin Square must be preserved and reconstructed for posterity so that future generations can appreciate its spiritual and cultural value; they see in the "empty landscape" of its current configuration an allusion to destroyed spiritual values and anarchy – a void that must be filled with rightful contents, with correctly arranged signifiers, lest the many demons of multinational business rush to fill it. These architects are acutely aware of the "naive readers" who visit the square every day and, with some urgency, express the need to initiate the naive passersby into the correct interpretation of the square.

Medvedev's performance reveals a different set of issues. Postulating that he might feel the same about the emptiness of Pushkin Square as about the emptiness of Lubianka Square, in his private performance as a poet and publisher he alludes to a tradition of protest and iconoclasm, a way to resist official culture and complicity in the commodification of art. For Melikhova and Tsekhanskii, the "readers" of Pushkin Square should be made explicitly aware of the foundations of the architectural monuments that still lie beneath the landscaped parks of Pushkin Square; Medvedev, who may or may not have known that Gessen would include a description of their meeting in his introduction, seems not to care if any of his readers understand or really even know that he gave a copy of his book to Gessen at the Pushkin Monument.

The architects' and Medvedev's attitudes towards both the Pushkin Monument and their audiences reflect the definitive markers of allusion as an aesthetic device. Allusion is a deliberate act by the creative individual (in this case poet and architects) – differentiating it from intertextuality – and it must be recognizable to an audience, even though no source is cited (quotation) and the allusive material is not claimed as original to the author (plagiarism). The allusions that the Pushkin Monument makes available to the creative individual begin to merge into the aesthetic category of *topos*, or a frequently cited combination of words that always appear together and refer to a common usage as opposed to a single source.[27] But allusions to and around the Pushkin Monument differ from *topoi* in that they are facilitated not only by a combination of words but by the site specificity of the Pushkin Monument itself. The Pushkin Monument is a unique cache of cultural memory such that at times it appears to work together with the poet to evoke allusion – a sort of collaboration that complicates the notion of allusion as a deliberate act by the poet. Alluding to the Pushkin Monument also complicates the notion of audience: it reinforces the reality that not every member of an audience will recognize an allusion even when they are standing right in front of it.

While it is clear that allusion works deeply in the semiotic space of Pushkin Square to mediate the interaction of poet and audience, its unique type of spatialized allusion does not fall into well-established categories of allusive practice. Traditionally, allusions are broadly categorized according to their target or form. For example, topical allusions refer to historical events; personal allusions refer to aspects of autobiography; formal allusions reference other devices like rhyme or metaphor; metaphorical allusions deepen the meaning of the new text through a metaphorical relation to an older text; imitative allusions borrow a genre or style; and structural allusions recall the organization of the target text.[28] The Pushkin Monument facilitates allusions that can fall into these categories, but the difference is that the allusion is motivated spatially. To analyse the spatialized allusions of the Pushkin Monument that accrue during the decades of its existence demands a closer look at how allusion interacts with the universal categories of time and space.

Allusion and Time

Not all tropes configure the categories of time and space in the same way. On the metapoetic level, for example, metaphor evokes new meanings by placing a word in a new context with which it seems to be at odds.[29] Even in its Greek meaning of "transference," metaphor privileges the spatial over the temporal. Similarly, the metapoetic meanings of metonymy (substitution) and synecdoche (contiguity) privilege spatial notions: both the substitution of a part for the whole and one thing for another based on a conceptual or material connection reveal the fundamental spatiality of the trope. By contrast, however, allusion as trope balances both time and space. Temporally, for a text to allude to another work of art (visual or verbal), a historical event, or a person, the thing alluded to must exist before or at least at the same time as the alluding text, suggesting that allusion is heavily marked for the past. Even in those cases where a poet alludes to some aspect of her contemporary moment, the allusion only reinforces the sense of how that contemporaneity becomes the past ever so swiftly. It is difficult or impossible to conceptualize an allusion to a specific future event. In such cases, most likely a different trope is in play: foreshadowing and prophecy differ from allusion in fundamental ways. Understood in this traditional sense, allusion has a dramatically restricted capacity to look to the future.

Harold Bloom's notion of influence, one influential twentieth-century theoretical paradigm for allusion, builds on that sense of allusion as a historically oriented device. The son must overcome the father (the past), in order to assert originality and transform inherited tradition. Frequently criticized for reductively limiting allusion to a Freudian struggle that leaves no room for understanding allusive practice as collaboration, instruction, or gratitude, Bloom is also frequently cred-ited with restoring a sense of authorial intent and psychic drama to the study of allusion.

One aspect of Bloom's theory that is often corrected with regard to the study of Pushkin's allusive practice is specifically this privileging of the past over the future – the emphasis on what the father has to tell us about the son as opposed to what the son tells us about the father. In his 2013 study of the literary relationship between Dostoevskii and Pushkin, Gary Rosenshield expresses the need to restore the future of allusion, or as he calls it, "backward influence," to literary studies.[30] Rosenshield highlights the insight that Dostoevskii brings to us as read-ers of Pushkin – we can read more out of Pushkin by reading the two authors together than we can by reading Pushkin alone. Dostoevskii finds in Pushkin's works new layers of meaning, and by so doing enters into a creative rather than combative relationship with him.

In an article on Pushkin and Virgil, Juan Christian Pellicer, while not explicitly mentioning Bloom, also implies that any allusion worth studying illuminates both the precursor and the successor. His main concern is "to discuss whether the perceived allusion renders the Latin and the Russian passages mutually illuminating – whether it can help us to discern distinctive aspects of Virgil's poem as well as Pushkin's that might otherwise have escaped appreciation."[31] In the work of both Pellicer and Rosenshield, allusion transcends a temporally restricted notion of the precursor's influence on the successor to become a key that unlocks both past and future understandings of a work of art.

Allusion is central to what an artist does in the process of recasting the rich tradition of motifs and ideas in the national artistic traditions around the world, but it is also central to the concept of poetic legacy. In textual culture, allusion is the mechanism, the technology, of immortality and its related emanations. Should a society stop reworking its geniuses, stop adapting them for film and stage, stop dealing with the ways its great poets conceptualized the enduring themes of love, death, good, and evil that animate the collective humanity for which art is a crucial forum, then those great poets will cease to live, their clay feet crumbling under the mountain of scholarly effort it would require to make their language and images comprehensible to an audience no longer concerned with what a poet had to say or how they said it in some past century. Concepts of immortality, legacy, canon, medium, and genre rely on an understanding of allusion as a device by which references to other texts, events, and people can be *reconstructed* and *understood* by an audience that, in relation to a given work of art, moves ever farther into the future.

Pushkin's Monument raises these questions about the future of allusion. Firstly, its cultural history demonstrates an evolving relationship between art and its technology of distribution, between art's medium and its consumption, between patronage of the arts and a work's market value. A core component of allusion is its recognizability; only when recognized can it add meaning to a work of art. In various periods of Russian history, allusion can be seen as a sort of measure of the relationship between a work of art and those who will consume it. For example, when writing for an individual patron, an author can tailor allusion to that individual's frame of reference; but when writing for an anonymous readership that has an uneven and, when considering a future readership, shifting frame of reference, an author is faced with a more complex aesthetic dilemma.

Pushkin's Monument also raises the question of the rapidly expanding readership in the nineteenth and early twentieth centuries that brought the realm of high art into the realities of the common person. As the system of private patronage gave way to the commercial reader it changed the nature of allusion while at the same time raising considerable anxiety about the fate of high art in the hands of the newly semiliterate. Censorship and the bad reader in this relation are two sides of a coin that only the highly educated have historically had the right to spend. On the one hand, high art has become more and more accessible to a general reader; but that poses certain problems as well as benefits. What if allusions are ignored or misunderstood? Can an audience without the necessary frame of reference participate in productive dialogue with a highly contextual work of art?

Secondly, Pushkin's Monument presents an opportunity for considering the vexed question of allusion and intentionality from a different perspective. When Pushkin envisioned the future of allusion, he did so intentionally, but in such a way as to open up future meanings unknown and *unintended* by him. In other words, he intentionally recognized that the confluence of texts he brought together would have unforeseen and unforeseeable consequences, consequences that only a future genius would recognize. The past is knowable and the future is predictable, but only to a certain degree. Returning to Rosenshield's corrective to Bloomian influence, it is possible to go one step further: Pushkin the father conceptualized the transformative genius of a future poet like Dostoevskii as the precondition of his legacy. Pushkin submitted himself to the transformations of his successors in order to enable a dynamic future for his works as opposed to the ossified stagnation of canonicity. Pushkin created the image of future collaborator-geniuses who could find in his works new dimensions of meaning, much as he did for his precursors, and so guarantee the future life of his poetry.

As Rosenshield and Pellicer suggest, the restricted futuricity of allusion begs for transgression. Allusion *does* look to the future, but articulating just how it does so requires that combination of innovation and poetic insight that has made Pushkin such a unique linguistic and cultural phenomenon.

How exactly, then, did Pushkin innovate a future of allusion? Chapter 1 answers this question. Analysis of Pushkin's allusions to monumental sculpture unlock an innovative metapoetics of allusion in his 1836 imitation of Horace's well-known "Monument" poem. Firstly, Ovid's sculptural metaphors in *Metamorphoses* provide a crucial conceptual tool for understanding Pushkin's concept of allusion as the device by which a future poet would bring his works, his "monument," to a higher level of refinement. The evidence for Pushkin's reliance on Ovid is strengthened through discussion of the classical sculptural metaphor that the Cappadocians – thinkers who critically shaped the Orthodoxy Pushkin encountered in nineteenth-century Russia – incorporated into their theology of the Incarnation and *theosis*. Monumental sculpture helps to explain why so many critics have found in "Monument" a productive tension between pagan and Christian concepts of pride and humility, apotheosis and kenosis. Consequently, the role of the future poet in Pushkin's vision for a dynamic future of his works reveals a new understanding of Pushkin's sculptural motifs in texts written at the end of his life. Specifically, monumental sculpture provides the vehicle for Pushkin to reflect on the abstract notions that contribute to a metapoetic understanding of allusion: time and space, genre, patronage, tradition, originality, and audience.

Space and the Expanding Dimensions of Allusion

When Pushkin articulated a *future* for allusion in "Monument," he laid the groundwork for an expanding *spatialized* notion of allusion in subsequent generations of Russian art. This is not to say that allusion was not spatial before Pushkin's innovation: the incorporation of some part of a work into another can be just as spatial as metaphor or metonymy and, in an important sense, is a metonymical practice. Texts reconfigure the meanings of the texts they allude to, often collapsing temporal categories by placing texts from radically different epochs side by side.

In contrast to Bloom's emphasis on the temporal dimension of allusion, the other most influential twentieth-century theory of allusion privileged this spatial aspect of allusion – intertextuality. The prefix of Julia Kristeva's neologism "intertext" itself indicates a spatial relationship; but, in privileging space over time, intertextuality has been susceptible to criticisms that it depersonalizes the text. In contrast to Bloom's deeply psychological and personalized approach to the *author* of an allusion, "intertextuality" projects the word as a depersonalized spatial object the surface of which directs myriad vectors of connection to other texts regardless of their temporal relationship – past, contemporaneous, or future. In this sense, intertextuality privileges not only the spatial aspect of allusion, but the reader as the active agent who makes the spatially motivated juxtapositions legible.

Rosenshield highlights the connection between the atemporal extremes of intertextuality and the "death of the author" in contributions of scholars Julia Kristeva and Roland Barthes:

> The author is not a personality, an agent, but a site of dialogue, a space in which innumerable quotations are implicitly cited, and in which texts clash with and engage one another in intertextual play. The writer exists only in the present, in the time of writing. He is born simultaneous with the text; he has no past or future. The author vanishes; words take over.[32]

Rosenshield's choice of spatial terms like "site of dialogue" and "space" juxtaposed against the lack of a past or future succinctly represent the radical spatialization of allusion that intertextuality implies. Against this theoretical extreme, Rosenshield argues persuasively that the agency of the author is critical to the study of literature, while at the same time accepting the theory and practice of intertextuality to bolster his own agency as a reader of a literary relationship that illuminates both Pushkin and Dostoevskii.

In this regard, Pellicer's observations about Pushkin's allusive practice with regard to Virgil are also helpful. He writes, "Allusions are not objective facts but cognitive events."[33] He says this in another way later in the same essay: "It is as well to admit that an allusion's persuasiveness, or its claims to interpretive validity, will not be settled by forensics alone. Critics sometimes argue too positivistically, as if allusions were not figures of instability but could be hardened to the consistency of fact by the mere pressure of circumstantial evidence."[34] His observations reiterate the elusiveness of allusion; it reaches not only into the mind, the cognition, of the author/agent but to an equal extent into the mind of the critic/reader. While intertextuality proved to be an indispensable step towards explaining the formal, linguistic nature of the interrelatedness of textual culture, in privileging space and the reader over time and the author it inevitably excludes significant aspects of the aesthetics of allusion.

The argument of chapter 1 documents Pushkin's vision for the future of allusion. Pushkin's allusions to and metaphors of monumental sculpture balanced space/time and author/reader binaries. By opening up his work to unpredictable and unforeseen (unintentional) innovations by future poets, he laid the groundwork for Opekushin's statue and the many performances that would take place around it.

Having outlined the development of Pushkin's monumental concept of allusion in chapter 1, in the second chapter I analyse the cultural dynamics that lead to literalizing and visualizing Pushkin's poem. The poet Vasilii Andreevich Zhukovskii, who prepared Pushkin's papers for publication after the poet's tragic death in 1837, censored Pushkin's poetics of allusion in "Monument." His intervention highlights Pushkin's nationalism and the utility of his poetry and downplays Pushkin's sophisticated notion of allusion as the poetic transformation that ensures his immortality, tipping the carefully balanced aesthetics of reception in "Monument" towards the naive reader, the "people" (*narod*). As a result, the image of the naive reader dominated the decades-long process of designing a literal monument to Pushkin that eventually led to Opekushin's famous Pushkin Monument in Moscow. The addition of the material monument to Pushkin's verbal "Monument" resulted in yet a third dimension of allusion, a performative one. At the dedication of Opekushin's Pushkin Monument in 1880, Fedor Dostoevskii (1821–1881) performed a speech that reinstated the role of the future poet as a counterbalance to the dominance of the "people." In performing the role of the future poet envisioned by Pushkin, Dostoevskii sets a precedent for other poets who would also define their poetic roles through performance at the feet of the monument in Pushkin Square.

The chapter ends with an analysis of how the visual and verbal dimensions of Opekushin's design made Dostoevskii's performance possible and legible to future generations of poets, and what the implications of that performance were.

Between the 1880 Celebration and the commemoration of the 100th anniversary of Pushkin's death in 1937, allusions to Pushkin's "Monument" continued to accumulate. However, by the 1930s, debates about the place of the classics in Soviet society and the needs of the rapidly expanding population of newly literate readers relegated complex allusion to a hallmark of elitist, bourgeois art. The central argument of chapter 3 conveys how Mikhail Bulgakov (1891–1940) resisted this official "aesthetics of simplicity" in *Master and Margarita* through a complex network of allusions to the Pushkin Monument. Bulgakov's innovation is two-fold. First, he conflates the future poet and the naive reader of Pushkin's "Monument" in the hack poets Ivan Homeless and his double, Sasha Riukhin. Using verbal, visual, and performative allusion to the Pushkin Monument, Bulgakov poses a critical question: what happens when the future poet *is* a naive reader? No other work of this period can match the complexity of allusion that Bulgakov uses to recreate the Pushkin Monument. The naiveté of readers like Riukhin and Homeless ensures that they misunderstand such allusion. Their failure as future poets leads to one of the core tensions in the novel: what future can the Master's novel have if no poet exists to respond to it? Of all the works that addressed the Pushkin Monument during the 1937 Centennial, Bulgakov's *Master and Margarita* most thoroughly demonstrates the evolution of allusion in a society that keenly felt a crisis of the future of poetry and poetic response. Even as Pushkin achieved unprecedented recognition among scholars, artists, and the masses in 1937, he also entered the domain of cliché, or dead allusion, ironically as a tool of political oppression, which he had opposed in his lifetime.

Master and Margarita represents the culmination of an iconic tradition that interprets the poem, the statue, and performances in the space around it as separate but indivisible dimensions of Pushkin's Monument. Not surprisingly, there is also an iconoclastic tradition that rejects or disfigures one or more of the hypostases of the Pushkin Monument and thereby opens up new interpretations of the relationship between the future poet and the naive reader. Chapters 4 and 5 analyse two iconoclastic approaches to the Pushkin Monument that emerged in the 1990s. Given the tension that already exists in the Pushkin Monument between the Petersburg poem "Monument" and its incarnation in Moscow, it is perhaps both logical and unexpected that both of these iconoclastic innovations engage significantly with the tradition of writing about Petersburg.

Chapter 4 presents Vladimir Toporov's *Petersburg Text* (published posthumously in 2009), a semiotic theory of literature and urban space, as the first case study of the iconoclastic approach to the Pushkin Monument. After the Pushkin Jubilee in 1937, official cliché silenced poetic innovation in the space of the Pushkin Monument for decades. Toporov did not address this cliché in his writings on the *Petersburg Text* throughout the late 1960s, 1970s, and 1980s. However, when the time came to end his *Petersburg Text* in the 1990s, Toporov responded to the offical cliché of the Pushkin Monument by developing Pushkin's thoughts about the future poet and the future reader in the poem "Monument" to create a theory of the dynamic context of monumental sculpture. In two scholarly articles, one about Falconet's monument to Peter I and the other about Montferrand's Alexander Column, Toporov theorized the performances of a creative viewer (like Pushkin's future poet) and a naive viewer (like Pushkin's naive reader) around the same St Petersburg monuments that Pushkin alludes to in his poem "Monument." In doing so, Toporov creates a different sort of monument to Pushkin – not a visual statue in Moscow but his theory of the "Petersburg Text," the verbal tradition of writing about Petersburg urban space that Pushkin initiated. Thus Toporov's contribution to the cultural history of the Pushkin Monument is to rescue it from cliché, to propose a compelling alternative to it, while at the same time illuminating its place in the triumvirate of Russia's sculptural "firsts": the Bronze Horseman, the Alexander Column, and Opekushin's Pushkin Monument.

Chapter 5 interprets the evolution of Tatiana Tolstaia's innovative approach to the Pushkin Monument from her late-Soviet stories to her post-Soviet novel *Slynx* (2000). In contrast to Toporov's discovery of the potential of allusion as a pervasive spatial notion throughout Russian literature, Tolstaia explores the power of pervasive misquotation to generate new forms and meanings and to raise questions about the future of complexly allusive literary art in a society that has forgotten the basic technologies of the word and its tropic uses. Engaging with early responses to Toporov's writings on Petersburg as well as other iconoclastic approaches to Pushkin's Monument, such as Abram Tertz's *Strolls with Pushkin* (1975) and Viktor Pelevin's *Chapaev and the Void* (1996), Tolstaia's novel relates the story of a future Moscow that has been made unrecognizable because of a nuclear blast that resulted in biological and cultural degradation. The plot revolves around the attempt by characters in the novel to recreate the Pushkin Monument, resulting in iconoclastic distortions of Pushkin's poem, Opekushin's statue, and the surrounding performative space. Those distortions, however, have an unexpected aesthetic function: the future poets and naive readers in *Slynx* that disfigure the Pushkin Monument also highlight its aesthetic complexity and unique agency in preserving cultural memory for the future.

Monumental Sculpture and Allusion Studies

The year of publication for Tolstaia's novelistic destruction of the temporal-spatial dimensions of allusion corresponds to a much broader international scholarly trend that articulated the need to somehow hybridize the landmark theories of influence and intertextuality. Recognizing the valuable contributions of both models, scholars sought a way beyond the extremes of personalized (psychological) and depersonalized theoretical accounts of allusion. In 1999, Pushkinist Oleg Proskurin, acknowledging his debt to intertextuality, rejects its capacity for depersonalizing textual culture, writing that, "Where post-structuralists see either an ominous or carnivalesque drama of the swallowing of the subject by language, [I] tend to see a miracle of the transformation of the 'structured' into the individual, 'textuality' into texts."[35] Pushkin's sensitivity to the dual nature of the lifelike monument indicates his consciousness that, even as he raises the poems of Horace, Ovid, Lomonosov, and Derzhavin to a new level in his "Monument," his own poem becomes part of that "textuality" that awaits a future "miracle of transformation." The cultural history of Pushkin's Monument entails several such transformations.

Also writing in 1999, the 200th anniversary of Pushkin's birth, Stephanie Sandler introduces a special issue of *Slavic Review* devoted to Pushkin. She highlights the approaches of several contributions in the volume that "are all variants on traditional influence studies, but each goes much further toward an intertextual approach, and toward offering new interpretations based on the sources adduced."[36] A few years later, Pushkinist David Bethea argues that "the psychic mechanisms underwriting the works of the mature Pushkin lie somewhere between the Bloomian notion of influence ... and the depersonalized notion of intertextuality."[37] For these scholars, Pushkin's monumental allusions are intensely personal to the poet, but they are not limited to a Freudian sense of needing to overcome.

In his 2008 study of Pushkin's "allusive devices," Andrew Kahn builds on the work of Bethea and Proskurin to triangulate intertextuality, "anxiety of influence," and Pushkin's view of originality and poetic identity, demonstrating the evolution of Pushkin's "mode of echoing" from imitation to the assertion of his own originality.[38] Along the way, Kahn argues that Pushkin embraces imitation of his predecessors and the education of future poets: allusion as a practice by which not only to educate oneself in the aesthetic practices of the past but also to raise them to new levels of perfection.[39] Like Proskurin, Bethea, and the authors whose articles Sandler edited, Kahn searches for a paradigm in which to restore to allusion all of its metatextual complexity that relies on tools like "anxiety of influence" and intertextuality to go beyond the sterile mid-twentieth-century practice of source hunting. These scholars conceptualized allusion as both a formal linguistic fact and a deeply personal, spiritual practice that triggers both belonging and individuality, that embraces both emulation and iconoclasm, and that reflects a collaborative sense of what it might mean to be alluded to in the future.

This trend in the study of Pushkin's allusive practice corresponds to turn-of-the-century developments in other fields as well. In English literature, Christopher Ricks navigates the issue by asserting the importance of intention and the beauty of tact in allusive practice as a corrective to the complete absence of the author in intertextuality, while also admitting the negative aspects of Bloom's theory of influence with its "melodramatic sub-Freudian parricidal scenario, his sentimental discrediting of gratitude, and his explicit repudiation of all interest in allusion as a matter of the very words."[40] Classicist Stephen Hinds, while suggestively *not* making explicit reference to Bloom, discusses a trend of "philological fundamentalism" in "Latin allusive studies" that moves in the opposite direction from the more widespread emphasis on intertextuality and the "implicatedness of *all* literary language in intertextual negotiations."[41] According to Hinds, the problematic trend of philological fundamentalism privileges authorial intent, to the exclusion of a whole host of intertextual dynamics, as the deciding factor in whether or not to evaluate or identify an allusion in the first place. To this extreme Hinds opposes what he calls "intertextualist fundamentalism," the complete (and erroneous) exclusion of the author in order to emphasize the reader as the site of meaning creation.[42] Proskurin, Bethea, Sandler, Kahn, Ricks, and Hinds all looked to the practice of allusion for a way to articulate how author, reader, and textual tradition exist in a multiplicity of interrelations that can itself be a metapoetic source of thought about poetry and its many meanings in the world.

Pushkin's Monument and Allusion follows these scholars by turning to monumental sculpture as a metapoetic mechanism by which to complicate the influence-intertext binary; its materiality and explicit blending of space and time in a visual medium offer a valuable prism through which to refract authorial intent and audience response. The fact that eighteenth- and nineteenth-century monumental sculpture in Russia employs allusion as one of its basic generic devices increases its value as a counterpoint for analysis of literary allusion. Especially from the perspective of semiotician Iurii Lotman's writings about "text in the text," or, in our case, the "monument in the monument," monumental sculpture highlights how allusive practice "generates new meanings" and becomes a site of both collaboration and innovation through multiple generations of textual culture.[43]

Lotman defines "text in the text" as a rhetorical structure by which a text or a part of a text is incorporated into another text. His claim is large in scope, including, but going well beyond, the study of allusion as such. He argues that culture broadly speaking is "a complexly structured text, breaking apart into a hierarchy of 'texts in texts' and creating a complex interweaving of texts."[44] He elaborates on how the mechanism requires a dual structure, the incorporated part of the older text and the framing part of the new text. The transformation of the text that occurs in this scenario ("text in the text") is not so much a misreading or distortion (*iskazhenie*) of an objective structure that should be avoided as it is the "generation of new meanings" (*generirovanie novykh smyslov*).[45] In Lotman's system, moving into the future does not require overcoming the past but rather involves generating new meanings alongside those that already exist and without which new meanings would be impossible.

The relationship between incorporated text and framing text leads into his discussion of monumental sculpture and the relationship between pedestal and statue. Falconet's Monument to Peter the Great serves as the *locus classicus* for Lotman's claim. The pedestal, or frame, is modelled to represent a cliff, becoming a meaning-bearing part of the monument that both emphasizes its representational nature while inviting the viewer to see all of the non-representational elements around the statue (the Neva River, for example) as inherently meaning bearing. Lotman then describes Paolo Trubetskoi's Monument to Alexander III (crafted from 1897 to 1906), which depicts horse and rider also on a cliff, galloping up to the edge of the abyss and then coming to a heavy stop. The meaning of Peter's leap into the future so starkly contrasted with the meaning of Alexander's reactionary refusal to move forward that the sculptor was advised to design a different pedestal.[46]

For Lotman, the pedestal facilitates the allusion; but, as the frame, it has the related function of emphasizing the interplay between the empirical reality of the setting and the artistic reality of the art. His observation accounts for other monuments as well. Montferrand's Alexander Column in St Petersburg reveals a similar design, breaking down into a "text within a text within a text." Framed by a pedestal of its own, the dominant feature of the monument is the polished granite pillar that distinctively references the rough-cut cliff off which Peter's horse leaps. This pillar then serves as the pedestal for the angel with Alexander I's face at the top of the monument. Opekushin's Pushkin Monument features a similar allusive pedestal that exalts the statue's verticality: the pedestal quotes two stanzas of Pushkin's "Monument," which alludes to Montferrand's and Falconet's monuments, and then leads the gaze of the viewer upward to a statue of Pushkin that seems like the fulfilment of the verticality referenced in Pushkin's poem ("higher than the Alexandrian Pillar") (figure I.7).[47] Trubetskoi's monument, begun only a few decades after the dedication of the Pushkin Monument and emphatically *not* vertical, could well be analysed as a reference not only to Falconet's cliff but to the whole trope of monumental verticality that by then had emerged in the works of Falconet, Montferrand, and Opekushin as a sort of nested allusion verging on a commonplace.

Given this theoretical articulation of "text in the text" and its organic connection to nineteenth-century monumental sculpture, it is also helpful to refer to Lotman's authoritative work on Pushkin's biography. When dealing with the issue of Pushkin's conceptualization of his poetic legacy in "Monument," Lotman writes:

> History is conceptualized by Pushkin not as something opposed to personality, but as a living chain of living human lives. History is a generation (*pokolenie*) of simple, "unhistorical" personalities; it is a chain in which the graves of the ancestors, the round-dance (*khorovod*) of living people grasping one another's hands, and the cradles of children compose a single circle of immortality. Progress happens in the accumulation of the memory of humanity, in other words, culture, and in the spiritual growth of the individual person.[48]

According to Lotman, Pushkin's proud claim to immortality in "Monument" rests on the poet's role in this sort of cultural "accumulation" that in his theoretical works he defines as an expanding hierarchy of "texts in texts."[49]

The key intervention in *Pushkin's Monument and Allusion* is to highlight the interpenetration of poem, statue, and performance that evolves from Pushkin's monumental allusions. The materiality of the Pushkin Monument emphasizes the nature of the multiple, collaborative authorship that gives rise to its multifaceted dimensions of allusion. Pushkin must be considered an author of the material monument,

I.7 The Pushkin Monument, the sky, and verticality as monumental trope, 2018.
Anastasiia Makarycheva's 2018 photograph of the Pushkin Monument against
a cloud-covered, dusky sky illustrates how the trope of verticality functions.
The frame cuts out all of the earthly dynamics that might make the statue
appear to move, as well as the pedestal by which the statue is connected to the
earth. Pushkin contemplates no advertisements, no buildings, no pedestrian
passers-by. The only movement is that of the clouds, creating the illusion of
ascent. Reprinted with the permission of the photographer.

even though with good reason he seems to be an author quite against his will. Opekushin authors the monument itself, but Dostoevskii initiates the culture of performance that will steadily grow in significance well into our contemporary moment. The materiality of the Pushkin Monument in urban space also enables the longer historical view of this study. When Pushkin's monumental metaphors are realized in the material world, they attract multiple literary relationships at once. For this reason, the aesthetics of the Pushkin Monument requires a theoretical move beyond the traditional approach of analysing one author's allusions to another author or text. To interpret the Pushkin Monument, one must conceptualize the multigenerational collaboration of many poets interacting with each other around one set of allusions in a single urban space.

In addition to illuminating the idea of allusion as a relationship among many poets, the materiality of the Pushkin Monument highlights allusion as a cognitive event in the mind of the reader.[50] The monument inserts itself into the daily lives of millions of people who pass by; the human, natural, built, and verbal environments surrounding the Pushkin Monument ensure allusion a place in the minds of the general reader, the people, beyond the narrow esoteric confines of high art and its well-educated critics and privileged patrons. It is physically present in Russian culture in a way that a text like Anna Akhmatova's *Poem without a Hero* can never be. This is not to say that it is better known or understood, only that its material presence can raise the question of reader proficiency in a way that the printed text cannot. For generations, many of the people who interact with the Pushkin Monument on a daily basis have remained ignorant of the allusive depths beneath its surface, a dynamic that for authors like Bulgakov, Toporov, and Tolstaia evokes anxiety about the future reader every bit as much as it represents a writer's interest in preceding poets or immortality.

Finally, the materiality of the Pushkin Monument emphasizes its evolution from verbal to visual to performative culture. Its material presence is a key feature of the spatial semiotics of Pushkin Square, while at the same time its material stability in the changing architectural landscape of Moscow emphasizes its temporality as both a past and future object. In the twenty-first century, any allusion to Pushkin, or any other romantic poet for that matter, involves a complex history of concentric spheres of mediation for both authors and readers. This study documents how those spheres develop over time.

It is certainly ironic that the materiality of the Pushkin Monument facilitated the innovations described in this book. Pushkin seems pretty clearly *not* to have envisioned a material monument at all in his 1836 poem.[51] But this irony is counterbalanced in his poem by the kenotic surrender of his poetic work to the future poets who saw in the materiality of the Pushkin Monument – something Pushkin feared and detested – the opportunity to expand the tropic dimensions of allusion itself, one of the most fundamental tropes in literary art. *Pushkin's Monument and Allusion* simply tells the story.

Pushkin's Poem: Monument and Allusion (1811–1836)

Exegi monumentum

I have raised to myself a monument not made by hands,
The people's path to it will not become overgrown,
It raises its unsubmissive head higher than
    The Alexandrian Pillar.

No, I will not die completely – in my sacred lyre,
My soul will outlive my dust and elude decay –
And I will be honoured, as long as in the sublunar world
    At least one poet is alive.

Rumour of me will go throughout all of great Rus',
And all of her many tongues will know my name,
The proud grandson of the Slavs, the Finn, the now wild
    Tungus, and the Kalmyk, friend of the steppes.

And long will I be loved by the people,
Because I evoked kind-hearted feelings with my lyre,
Because in my harsh age I glorified freedom
    And called for mercy to the fallen.

To god's command, O Muse, be obedient,
Fearing no offence, demanding no laurels;
Accept praise and slander indifferently,
    And do not debate with a fool.[1]

Before Pushkin's Monument was either a statue or a performative space, it was a little-known poem distinguished by dense, innovative allusions to both literary and material monuments. That poem, Pushkin's "Monument" (August 1836), and its allusions begin the story of Pushkin's Monument. While the poem preceded the statue and performances, there is always more to a good beginning than mere chronology. In this case, the poem "Monument" is also very much an end – Pushkin died in January 1837 and "Monument" is often seen as his own assessment of his life's work. As both a beginning and an end, "Monument" expresses the ambivalence that drew Pushkin to the motif of statues that come to life in the first place. Even while surveying his past accomplishments, Pushkin's metapoetics of allusion in "Monument" reveals his thinking about a future legacy and metamorphosis, audience and immortality: it is an ending point for his poetry, a starting point for imagining his legacy, and a conceptual foundation that will shape the statue and performances that come later.

To unpack the significance of "Monument," we first must delve into Pushkin's attraction to the motif of the lifelike statue. Pushkin's frequent use of the image of the statue that comes to life in earlier works like his *The Bronze Horseman* and *The Stone Guest* shape interpretations of "Monument," where monumental statuary is a metaphor for his poetic immortality. And yet the image evolves to become something more complex in "Monument" than it can be in earlier works.

Underlying this evolution is the ambivalence of the lifelike statue: is the statue lifelike because it is on the verge of coming to life or is it lifelike because a living being has been reduced to inert stone? Has death reduced Pushkin to inert matter, or has Pushkin, in death, gone from one state of material being to a greater, immortal existence? The metaphor of monumental statuary captures this ambivalence, and yet "Monument" is not primarily preoccupied with metaphysical speculation or materialist pessimism. The ambivalence of the lifelike statue functions more significantly as a metaphor for the future reception of Pushkin's works. Just as the metamorphosis of the lifelike statue can be perceived as either the miracle of new life or the tragedy of life cut short, so Pushkin sees two different modes of immortality for his works based on two different types of reception. The first moves up: aesthetic refinement, new life, new ideas. The second moves down: simplification, reduction, utility. The first direction requires an active creator – a future poet who engages with, alludes to, Pushkin's poetry. The second is the more common – future naive readers, the descendants of the "people" (*narod*), who in Pushkin's lifetime were still illiterate. While these two groups do not have equal stakes in ensuring Pushkin's immortality, they are also not opposed in a simplistic, good/bad binary. Rather, the paradigm of the lifelike statue suggests that Pushkin embraced the kenotic descent of his poetry to lesser forms of reception: naive readers who failed to grasp the heights of its aesthetic riches nonetheless might benefit from its spiritual utility. The ambivalence of the lifelike statue indicates that, if Pushkin's poetry should become less in order that the naive reader might become more, this too can be a worthy fate. Unpacking Pushkin's thinking about his future audience and their differing relationship to his works requires reconstructing the historical cultural connections between immortality, metamorphosis, allusion, and monumental statuary available to Pushkin in 1836.

The first part of the argument explains how the concepts of the lifelike statue in two classical sources, both close to Pushkin in their own ways in 1836, illuminate Pushkin's "Monument." Having established how the metaphor works, the second part of the argument explores how the lifelike statue metaphor facilitates various facets of the relationship between allusion, the future poet, and the naive reader. Pushkin's allusions in "Monument" demonstrate the extent to which he felt himself moving inexorably from the role of future poet, a role he cherished, to that of a past poet. And yet even as Pushkin contemplated his own personal metamorphosis, the relationship between poet and audience was being transformed before his eyes. While poets who preceded Pushkin wrote for patrons or intimate friends, Pushkin acutely sensed that future poets would write for an anonymous reading public. Allusion, as an activity requiring the action of both a writer and a reader, was transformed in the process.

The paradigm of the lifelike statue in "Monument" dominates allusions to the Pushkin Monument in Moscow: it continues to have significance only inasmuch as it continues to be "brought to life" – "read," "transformed," made to engage with new ideas, buildings, images, and generations of readers. Likewise, as in the poem, the future poet and the naive reader play the most crucial roles in allusions to the Pushkin Monument. It all begins with the poem.

Part I

Pushkin's Paradigm for the Future of Allusion

Many well-known ties bind the Russian poet Alexander Pushkin to the Latin poet Ovid (43 BCE–17/18 CE). Pushkin himself emphasized the parallels between his exile to the south under Alexander I and Ovid's exile to the same region under Augustus. Readings of Ovid's works have provided productive insights into many of Pushkin's individual poems as well as his "mythopoetic consciousness."[2] In order to substantiate Pushkin's metaphor of the lifelike statue in his 1836 "Monument," this chapter must reopen one of the less-frequently considered connections between Pushkin and Ovid: their imitations of Horace's *"Exegi monumentum."*[3] With good reason, scholarly consensus has long defined the "Monuments" of Latin poet Horace (23 BCE) and eighteenth-century Russian poet Gavriil Romanovich Derzhavin (1795) as the primary network of referentiality in Pushkin's "Monument" (1836). Other eighteenth-century translations and imitations of Horace in Russia, particularly those of Mikhail Vasil'evich Lomonosov and Alexander Nikolaevich Radishchev, have been shown to be important as well.[4] But Ovid's imitation must also have held a certain allure for Pushkin.[5] Ovid concludes *Metamorphoses* (circa 8 CE) with an imitation of Horace's "Monument" in which he claims immortality "beyond the stars" that at least equals and perhaps surpasses the deifications he describes for Julius and Augustus in the lines immediately preceding this final *envoi*. Ovid's imitation of Horace is indeed more than just an imitation; it is the final monumental reference in a series of works about mythic statues and sculptures. The same could be said of Pushkin's "Monument."

The Cappadocians, perhaps the most important thinkers of the early Eastern church, were steeped in the culture of classical antiquity and relied on the language of antiquity – words like "metamorphosis" and concepts like the ambivalence of the lifelike sculpture – to forge sophisticated theological arguments. Their foundational work on ideas like the Incarnation and *theosis* would become authoritative doctrine in the Eastern church. In their writing, the lifelike sculpture metaphorically represents the tension between flesh and spirit at the heart of Christ's descent into the material form of his creation in order that humans can be transformed back into the image of God in which they are created.

In the early period of his exile, Pushkin explored a personal connection to Ovid and his work: in "Monument" and several other poems written on Stone Island in 1836 (commonly referred to as the "Stone Island Cycle"), Pushkin explored the thematics of Orthodox theology in a serious tone that seems to contradict the blasphemous playfulness of earlier works. Given these interests, the study of both an Ovidian and a Cappadocian aesthetics of the lifelike statue offers new insight into Pushkin's monument metaphor in 1836. The critical idea that binds them all together is that a statue can function as an icon, as an image that stands in for a more complex narrative, or it can function as the inspiration for ekphrasis, the device by which an image is described in narrative form. The mutual interaction of word and image underwrites the power of the lifelike statue to operate in both directions, sometimes simultaneously, as is the case in Pushkin's "Monument": for every lifelike image there is a story as to how it came to be lifelike. The iconic and ekphrastic modes of Pushkin's "Monument" reflect the iconic and ekphrastic modes of the lifelike statue in Ovid's *Metamorphoses* as well as the iconic and ekphrastic modes of the sculptural metaphors foundational to Eastern Orthodox concepts of Incarnation and *theosis*. This additional layer of the creative tension between paganism and Christianity often noted in Pushkin's "Monument" reveals how Pushkin's fascination with Orthodoxy in the "Stone Island Cycle" contributes to the evolution of his earlier interest in the lifelike statue, often referred to as Pushkin's "sculptural myth."[6]

Why Ovid and the Cappadocians?

The tension between imitation and originality lies at the core of the "Monument" poem genre and complicates the relationship between the lifelike statues of Ovid, the Cappadocians, and Pushkin. Pushkin's fascination with Ovid during his earlier exile is well known, but there is no textual proof that Pushkin was actively thinking about or alluding to *Metamorphoses* in 1836. Likewise, Pushkin's interest in Orthodox themes in the "Stone Island Cycle" is well known, but he most certainly was not reading the Cappadocians' writing on Incarnation and *theosis*. On what basis, then, does it make sense to read these diverse writings together?

Ovid has frequently been dismissed as a source for "Monument." In his detailed analysis of the poem, M.P. Alekseev briefly considers Ovid's imitation of Horace as a possible influence on Pushkin alongside more substantive arguments about Horace and Derzhavin.[7] He cites Costello's "Pushkin and Roman Literature" (1964), which speculates that Pushkin could have been working with a reference to Ovid's

"Tristia," if only it were not so obvious that he was directly dealing with Horace. Alekseev observes that Ovid too was influenced by Horace and that he imitated *"Exegi monumentum"* in the last lines of *Metamorphoses*.

Alekseev's treatment of the Ovid connection ends with this note. Furthermore, he ridicules the parallels that Lednicki finds between Pushkin's "To Ovid" (1821) and "Monument," referring to them as "pure fantasy" (*chistaia fantastika*). To substantiate his claim, Alekseev cites four lines from "To Ovid" that seem directly to contradict the claim to immortality and fame in "Monument":

Увы, среди толпы затерянный певец,
Безвестен буду я для новых поколений,
И, жертва темная, умрет мой слабый гений
С печальной жизнию, с минутною молвой …

Alas, among the crowd a misplaced singer,
I will be unknown to new generations,
And, an obscure victim, my weak genius will die
With my sad life, with fleeting fame …[8]

There is room to disagree with Alekseev's dismissal: the inversion could be seen as an indirect reference. The opposite of something is as interesting as its parallel and as strongly connected. When writing "To Ovid" in 1821, the young Pushkin in exile could not directly imitate Ovid's claims to immortal fame, so he imitated them inversely. As an older Pushkin contemplated death, a more permanent type of existential exile from his readership, it would make sense for him to return to his earlier thoughts about Ovid and earthly political exile.[9]

However, the ways in which Pushkin and Ovid engage with the aesthetics of the lifelike statue go beyond direct textual references. While it is difficult to prove direct influence or allusion, the conceptual similarity between the lifelike statues of Pushkin and Ovid suggests a shared conclusion as much as an imitation. A fascination with monumental sculpture brings the poets together in a way that surpasses their imitations of Horace. One might speculate that fascination with sculpture as a motif leads them to imitate Horace's poem more than a fascination with Horace's poem itself.

Pushkin's interest in monuments extends from his earliest days at the Lyceum in Tsarskoe Selo, where he studied the Latin classics intensively, to his works written immediately preceding his death. The neoclassical sculpture and monuments in the glyptotheca of Catherine the Great span from Pushkin's earliest verses in 1814 to the final chapter of *The Captain's Daughter*, dated 19 October 1836. The sculptural motif dominates works in between as well: it resurfaces in the myth of the destructive statue that Roman Jakobson identified in *The Bronze Horseman*, *The Stone Guest*, and *The Golden Cockerel*.[10] In *Metamorphoses*, Ovid too includes a wide array of stories about humans transforming into material images and sculptures coming to life. The motif of the lifelike statue is arguably one of Ovid's most effective: it begins and ends *Metamorphoses* in crucial ways that suggest the poet was particularly drawn to it. The demonstration that follows suggests not so much that Pushkin is alluding to Ovid's lifelike statues or actively reading *Metamorphoses* in 1836 as that both poets relied on the same aesthetic ambivalence of the lifelike statue: is the stone coming to life or is a life being reduced to stone?

While Pushkin objectively studied Ovid and read *Metamorphoses* as well as Ovid's other works, the same certainly cannot be said of the Cappadocians. Most likely Pushkin never read them and may never have heard of them. Here again, however, there is no need to argue that Pushkin was reading Ovid or the Cappadocians in 1836. It is sufficient to claim that his classical education at the Lyceum, combined with his lifelong interest in sculpture and his specific interest in Orthodox themes in the "Stone Island Cycle" of 1836, brought the Russian poet to a similar conclusion about lifelike sculpture. The Cappadocians act as a textual intermediary between the paganism of Ovid and the Russian Orthodoxy of Pushkin's era. Like Pushkin, the Cappadocians conceptualized Christianity through the lens of their classical education. The fact that they come to the same conclusions about the sculpture metaphor speaks to the power of Pushkin's aesthetic insight into Orthodoxy. What is more, it evokes a moment in which paganism and Christianity appear not to be at odds but rather in productive aesthetic dialogue.

The lifelike sculpture stands at the centre of the intersection between Christianity and classical culture in aesthetic ways that transcend iconoclasm, and yet this is not to claim that Pushkin was personally interested in dogmatic theology or its roots in classical antiquity. Questions of personal piety aside, Orthodox Christianity was for Pushkin a well of aesthetic inspiration in both parodic and neutral keys. In this sense, too, the theological aspects of Pushkin's monumental motifs parallel Ovid's celebrated irony, satire, and sarcasm in the myths he retells.[11] To the point, Pushkin's poem *Gavriliada*, a blasphemous portrayal of the Annunciation, can be read as "a New Testament theme transposed into the key of *Metamorphoses*."[12] The transposition belies Pushkin's aesthetic sense that the very moment of the Incarnation, the moment of Jesus' conception, is a great mystery in that it is a story whose details cannot be imagined without some consequential blasphemy. On this note, it is helpful to consider Alyssa Dinega Gillespie's thesis that Pushkin's "Prophet" (1828) is "a mythopoetic narrative of poetic genesis and a successor to *The Shade of Barkov* in Pushkin's personal poetic mythology."[13] Her argument about the parallels between prophecy and inspiration in the obscene *The Shade of Barkov* and the serious poem "Prophet" supports the idea that the Incarnation could be for Pushkin both an object of blasphemous satire in representing the physical conception of Christ as well as an aesthetically interesting paradigm of kenosis.

Both Ovid and the concept of metamorphosis that Pushkin had access to in the Orthodox church emphasize the ambivalence of the lifelike statue: the creation that has the potential to rise to the image of the creator or to return to its unformed material basis. But how does this discovery relate to Pushkin's Orthodoxy? The question is fraught with peril. On the one hand, there are the dangers of "presumptuousness, oversimplification, and moralizing" or rehashing "run-of-the-mill verities that are 'new' only to us" that Olga Sedakova describes in her analysis of the theme of foolishness and intelligence in "Monument."[14] Stephanie Sandler endorses Sedakova's analysis and notices "refreshingly pagan notions deriving from the ancient Latin source and a worldview where monuments incarnate the spiritual power of the dead" alongside the "Christian nuances."[15] In a similar vein, it is hard to disagree with Oleg Proskurin, who writes, "for Pushkin, religious symbols ... were necessary only insofar as they helped to manifest his message about the sacredness of poetry – a sacredness that could not be accommodated in any religious creed."[16] Ovidian irony towards sacred narrative certainly seems to be a viable mode for interpreting Pushkin's "Monument," with regard both to the tradition of writing a "monument" poem and to the religious concepts like Incarnation and *theosis* that he parodied in earlier works (not only in *Gavriliada*). As a counterbalance, however, the serious tone of the poem, its connection to the paschal themes of the "Stone Island Cycle," and its allusions to Pushkin's beloved friend Anton Del'vig (1798–1831) weigh heavily in arguments that "Monument" cannot be satisfactorily read as a parody.[17] On this basis, it makes sense to look to Ovid's *Metamorphoses* and the writings of the Cappadocians to better understand what is at stake in Pushkin's metapoetics of allusion in "Monument." After all, if allusion really is a primary mechanism for the posthumous metamorphosis that Pushkin envisions in 1836, the ambivalence of the lifelike statue in these classical sources has much to teach us about Pushkin's "Monument."

The Lifelike Statues of Ovid

One aesthetic principle stands out in the sculptural motifs of Pushkin and Ovid: they operate in both ekphrastic and iconic modes. In her comparison of ekphrasis in Russian and French poetry, Maria Rubins defines ekphrasis as "intersemiotic translation."[18] If ekphrasis is the translation of the visual into verbal signs, iconism represents the same process, but inverted: the translation of the verbal into visual signs.[19] Ovid's sculptures function in an ekphrastic mode when they move up on the matter/spirit scale. When a sculpture comes to life, it is brought to life by the addition of some spirit, some divine or demonic spark. One of the defining tropes in ekphrasis is verbally to describe the statue as alive.[20] To raise matter to sentience and reason is to endow it with spirit, a miracle celebrated in the genre of ekphrasis. But neither Ovid nor Pushkin limits his interest in sculpture to its ekphrastic potential. Ovid's sculptures sometimes operate in an iconic mode when beings endowed with sentience and reason transform into something less free and rational: the living being becomes a river, a laurel tree, or a stone sculpture that fulfils an iconic function for the story that motivated the transformation. The iconic/ekphrastic symmetry of the lifelike sculpture reveals the ambivalence of sculpture as the liminal point where it can be impossible to determine whether it is matter that was *given* an immortal soul or *deprived* of one.

Many of Ovid's lifelike sculptures correspond to the ekphrastic mode. In one of the first metamorphoses, the Titan Prometheus "molds" earth and rainwater into "the image of the omnipotent gods."[21] Humans as a crude representation of the gods in rough material form reappear in many of the sculptural transformation myths in the work. When the earth is repopulated after the flood, Deucalion and Pyrrha toss stones (the "bones" of mother earth) behind them that begin to take on human form, "not well defined, but like roughed-out statues."[22] Thus, in both the pre- and post-flood worlds that Ovid describes, the statue motif plays a crucial role in establishing the connection of the spiritual and material in human form: humans are earth and stone formed in the image of the gods and brought to life by some divine spark, the very miracle celebrated in ekphrasis.

As the events of Ovid's narrative progress temporally from creation myths to his own historical moment of the transition of the Roman Republic to the Roman Empire, more refined matter transforms into more refined beings. For example, the Pygmalion myth differs from the creation myths in that the artist creates an ideal ivory form that then is brought to life as an image of perfection.[23] The simple clay and crude stones in the early myths are replaced by a different medium (ivory), artistic talent, and forethought: Pygmalion certainly did not toss behind his back the ivory out of which his ideal appeared, brought to life by Venus.[24] His sculpture is not a "roughed-out statue" but feminine beauty incarnate. One step further in the refinement of humans from matter to spirit comes at the end of *Metamorphoses* – the deification of Julius and Augustus Caesar, who become stars. These metamorphoses are the climax of what began when Prometheus moulded clay into human forms and endowed them with *mind*, with *reason*, and "told them to lift their eyes to the stars."[25] The monuments to these emperor-gods that increasingly adorned the public spaces of the early Empire were the earthly reminder of their metamorphosis and deification.

In imitating Horace, Ovid adds his own deification to the mix, prophesying his immortal life "beyond the high stars," higher than Julius and Augustus.[26] However, unlike Horace, who "has raised a monument," Ovid has "completed his work," which cannot be destroyed by the "wrath of Jove or corrosive time." Significantly, he claims not a monument but immortality. Not only does Ovid's divergence comment on Horace's original, it introduces a moment of subtle irony: the deification of Julius and Augustus represented in the many sculptures that depict them as gods could certainly provoke the wrath of the gods as it does in myths like "Niobe and Latona." Niobe turns to a marble statue of herself that weeps eternally after watching her fourteen children die. Her statuesque form is set on a mountain as a reminder of the terror of "divine wrath" and the dangers of human presumption in the company of gods.[27]

Niobe and Latona and other such myths suggest that the vector of transformation from matter to spirit in Ovid is not unidirectional. Pygmalion's ivory statue is marvellous because it is so lifelike and actually comes to life: the statue of Niobe is so terrible because the grief and loss immortalized in her marble form are the grief and loss of a living being.[28] Interspersed throughout the transformations from stone and sculpture to human and/or divine form are transformations of the human and divine into insentient matter. Mercury turns Aglauros into a statue that is darkened by her envy.[29] When some servants of Ino grieve her death, caused by Juno, the cruel goddess turns them into stone in the midst of their lamentations and refers to them as her "cruelty's greatest memorial."[30] The myth of Echo and Narcissus also shows a transformation from sentient being into semi-sentient stone. The nymph Echo, cursed by Juno to utter only "the briefest of speech," wastes away to nothing and her bones turn to stone that can only repeat what someone else says.[31] The lifelike statue in these myths reduces the living word to an inert image that becomes an icon of the verbal narrative.

With regard to a poet's posthumous reception, we will see a similar pattern at work in Pushkin's "Monument." It only takes one living poet to raise Pushkin's works to new life, to endow them with a divine spark that results in a miraculous metamorphosis. But there is another possible direction for Pushkin's works. Readers can also reduce Pushkin's works to quotations, deprive them of their full complexity – reify canonical understandings and clichéd interpretations of works that should be always full of new, life-giving insight. And yet it is not that simple. There is another sense to the iconism of the lifelike statue, one that Ovid's stories do not relate. To understand the potentially positive meanings of the iconic moments in Pushkin's "Monument," we must turn to its seminal formulation in Eastern Christian thought – the Cappadocians.

Incarnation and Theosis as Sculptural Metaphor

The roots of Eastern Christianity's ideas about Incarnation and *theosis* in antiquity clarify the organic connection between what might otherwise seem to be opposed traditions (pagan/Christian, Ovid/the Cappadocians). Metamorphosis and the ambivalence of the lifelike monument that triggers both ekphrastic and iconic transformations played an important role in the thought of the Cappadocian fathers: Basil the Great, Gregory Nazianzus, and Gregory of Nyssa. It was their cultural historical moment that defined the legacy of the pagan past for the emerging Eastern form of Christianity.[32] The synthesis they find between the two has much to say about the frequently cited pagan/Christian balance in Pushkin's "Monument," albeit situated within differently inflected vectors of cultural power.

In *Christianity and Classical Culture*, historian of Christian thought Jaroslav Pelikan analyses the writings of the Cappadocians to demonstrate the connection between Orthodox thought and its roots in classical culture. The continuity that Pelikan identifies between *metamorphosis* and *theosis* in Gregory of Nyssa's writings is particularly revealing:

The first time, [God the *Logos*] took dust from the earth and formed humanity; this time, he took dust from the Virgin and did not merely form humanity, but formed humanity around himself. The first time he created; this time, he was created. The first time, the *Logos* made the flesh; this time, the *Logos* was made flesh, so that he might change our flesh to spirit, by being made partaker with us in flesh and blood.[33]

Pelikan's words reveal that the Incarnation implies not only a lowering of the word to flesh (Incarnation) but also that the goal of such descent was so that "our" flesh might be raised to spirit (*theosis*).[34] In a different passage from Gregory of Nyssa's writings, Pelikan finds another sculptural metaphor: "A related sculptural metaphor for the restoration could refer to it as 'modeling us anew from the evil mould of sin once more to God's own image.'"[35]

The metamorphosis of human nature for the Cappadocians rested on the idea that in Adam all humans were created in the image of God, but the image was lost, destroyed, distorted by the fall into sin. Human nature has two possible vectors: "Human nature, though destined for the heights of participation in the divine nature through *theosis*, had instead proven itself capable of finding innumerable pathways downward."[36] In Ovid there are also two sorts of possibilities for human metamorphosis. On one hand, the flesh, the stone and clay from which humans are created, can be brought to higher forms of rationality and life. On the other hand, humans can also metamorphose into lesser forms of freedom and rationality. For the Cappadocian Fathers, only through the Incarnation could the image of God in man be restored. The idea of man made in the image of God is a sculptural metaphor that in many ways recalls the ambivalence of Ovid's ekphrastic and iconic statues. However, the relationship between the Incarnation and *theosis* adds a new dimension to Ovid's use of the sculptural metaphor: the lowering of the divinity to human form is what makes it possible for humans to regain the image of God.

The Cappadocians added complexity to the ambivalence of the lifelike statue, a complexity that Pushkin also exploits in "Monument." Pushkin relies on a future poet to metamorphose his works in the future – to save them from becoming inert and lifeless. But he also submits them to a broader readership that, while unable to participate in the heights of poetic achievement, benefits from his works all the same, even in their clichéd, canonical, "iconic" form. Having contemplated how the ambivalence of the lifelike statue works in antiquity, we can now begin to see in Pushkin's "Monument" a new perspective on his juxtaposition of the poet (an active figure capable of transforming his works) and the "people" (a passive readership interested more in his fame and the social utility of his works).

The Lifelike Statue and Pushkin's "Monument"

Like Ovid's imitation of Horace's "Monument" ode, Pushkin's "Monument" also celebrates the iconic and ekphrastic modes that monumental sculpture in the literary text can evoke. Particularly in the first stanza of the poem one sees the tension between ekphrasis and iconism. In its ekphrastic mode, the first stanza represents a verbal depiction of an object of visual art, a monument. References to the most significant monuments in the Petersburg of Pushkin's day strengthen the ekphrasis: the Bronze Horseman and the Alexander Column. Jakobson identifies the reference to the Bronze Horseman in the semantically loaded phrase "not made by hands," arguing that Pushkin employs it in parody of V.G. Ruban's 1770 reference to the Thunder Stone as "mountain not made by hands" (*nerukotvornaia gora*).[37] The reference to the Thunder Stone makes even more sense when contrasted with the Alexander Column in Petersburg, one of the possible referents of the enigmatic phrase "Alexandrian Pillar."

The poet Vasilii Andreevich Zhukovskii, Pushkin's mentor and the official who would oversee the publication of Pushkin's works immediately following Pushkin's death, made this connection in a very public way. In his 1834 essay about the dedication of the Alexander Column, Zhukovskii saw in its polished granite an allusion to the rough-hewn Thunder Stone that represents the refinement of Russia under Peter's heirs: if Peter created Petersburg and Russia out of rough stone, his heirs worked it into a thing of great strength and refinement.[38] Pushkin places his own monument in the same allusive progression: the unrefined Thunder Stone transforms into the refined marble of the Alexander Column, which results in yet a greater and more refined substance – the poetic word, the medium that in its ekphrastic mode transforms these material monuments into a verbal monument of greater substance and value. Jakobson sees a conflict here between word and idol.[39] However, in light of Pushkin's interest in the lifelike statue, it makes more sense to see a progression from unrefined matter to refined matter to word (spirit) that exemplifies ekphrasis both as a genre and as a concept of the transformation of image into word.

As ekphrasis, Pushkin's "Monument" lies on the cusp of a broader shift in Russian culture from the image to the word. As Russian culture entered the mid-nineteenth century, "the literary text – narrative or libretto – took precedence over the visual and the aural. The divinization of the Word – logocentrism – displaced the visual dominant."[40] But Pushkin's "Monument" itself reflects the transitional moment: the visual and iconic counterbalance the emerging cultural logocentrism.

Iconic moments in Pushkin's "Monument" emphasize the necessity of image as visual and material to communicate the profundity of the non-visual and spiritual essence of Pushkin's poetic work. In choosing the image of a monument as an icon for the totality of his verbal work, Pushkin chooses one that has profoundly visual and material, as well as verbal, meanings. Allusions to the Bronze Horseman and the Alexander Column reiterate this point. It is not enough to suggest a connection to the monuments of world literature created by the poets who wrote versions of Horace's *"Exegi monumentum"*; Pushkin must also define his own monument by comparison with the two most prominent works of monumental sculpture in the Russia of his day. The choice of "monument not made by hands" triggers both the ekphrastic and iconic concepts of the visual/verbal dichotomy in Russian culture by alluding both to Ruban's ekphrasis of the Bronze Horseman and to the Orthodox paradigm of iconography from which the term originates. The place of "Monument" within the paschal structure of Pushkin's "Stone Island Cycle" reinforces the connection.[41]

Significantly, the iconism of Pushkin's poem is not limited to the phrase "not made by hands" and goes beyond the idea of a visual representation of the word. The theological argument for the use of icons in Orthodox worship claims them as a necessary part of a full doctrine of the Incarnation. If God really became flesh in Jesus Christ, then he could be seen and therefore must be represented visually. To destroy or forbid the image of Christ is tantamount to denying the Incarnation.[42] In the first stanza, the ekphrastic mode seems to dominate, and Pushkin seems to celebrate "the word" (logocentrism); however, if one considers the theological implications of the Incarnation as a kenotic descent from spirit to matter, from word to flesh, the rest of the poem moves in a more iconic direction.

The iconism of "Monument" challenges Jakobson's interpretation of Pushkin's "sculptural myth" as primarily iconoclastic. It also contradicts a second aspect of Jakobson's seminal argument. Jakobson discusses Pushkin's interest in the ambivalence of the statue, but he does so through a semiotic lens, discussing the differing aspects of signifier and signified, united in the material form of the sculpture. He writes, "We have therefore established two types of the poetic metamorphosis of a statue. How then are they realized in *lyrics*? Subjectivity is the basis of all lyric poetry. It is a question, then, of the poet's subjective conception: *the immobile statue of a mobile being is conceived either as a moving statue or as a statue of an immobile being.*"[43] While Jakobson's strictly opposed binaries (either/or), seem well suited to the myth of the destructive statue he identifies in *Bronze Horseman*, *The Stone Guest*, and *The Tale of the Golden Cockerel* (the middle stage of Pushkin's interest in statuary), "Monument" reflects the end of Pushkin's development and calls for a different, non-binary, structure. Jakobson's binaries exclude the concept of transformative progression, whereas Ovid's progression of lifelike statues as a central device in *Metamorphoses* fits Pushkin's interest in the monument metaphor. This is of even more importance in "Monument" as Pushkin contemplates the problems of a poet separated from his audience by death. Furthermore, as the preceding discussion of the Cappadocians shows, Christianity drew on classical paganism in positive ways that counteract the iconoclasm referenced by Jakobson.[44]

Pushkin's "Monument" combines both the Orthodox and the classical paradigms. While his word stands at the apogee of the progression from Falconet's stone monument to Montferrand's granite monument to Pushkin's "monument not made by hands," the height of his achievement is not something that he grasps absolutely: there is also an implied descent as his words go out to the people, sometimes falling into the fertile mind of at least one "poet," sometimes landing in the poor soil of at least one "fool." In contrast to the untouchable immortality of Ovid's transformation "beyond the stars," Pushkin's immortality is conditional, dependent on the "sublunar," earthly, physical existence of an earthly poet capable of transforming Pushkin's works into yet others. In particular, one line stresses the condition for Pushkin's immortality: "as long as in the sublunar world at least one poet is alive." This line is significant for the whole poem not only because it reflects Pushkin's desire to maintain an earthly form of immortality (as opposed to the universal motifs that define the immortality of Horace, Ovid, and Derzhavin) but also because it makes room to oppose writerly reception, the creative transformation of Pushkin's works through the power of a future creative poet, to the static reception of a future reader.[45]

Juxtaposing Pushkin's second stanza to Derzhavin's second stanza reveals evidence that supports such a reading.

Derzhavin:

Так! – весь я не умру, но часть меня большая,
От тлена убежав, по смерти станет жить,
И слава возрастет моя, не увядая,
Доколь славянов род вселенна будет чтить.[46]

So! – all of me will not die, but the larger part of myself,
Having eluded decay, at death will begin to live,
And my glory will grow, unfading,
As long as the universe esteems the Slavic peoples.

Pushkin:

Нет, весь я не умру – душа в заветной лире
Мой прах переживет и тленья убежит –
И славен буду я, доколь в подлунном мире
    Жив будет хоть один пиит.

No, I will not die completely – in my sacred lyre,
My soul will outlive my dust and elude decay –
And I will be honoured, as long as in the sublunar world
    At least one poet is alive.

In line two of this stanza, Pushkin relocates Derzhavin's "to live" (*zhit'*) to the first half of the line ("will outlive my dust"; *moi prakh perezhivet*) and moves Derzhavin's "having eluded" (*ubezhav*) to the end ("elude decay"; *tlen'ia ubezhit*). That reversal allows Pushkin to set up the rhyme "will elude"/"poet" (*ubezhit/piit*), reframing Derzhavin's universal, public imagery with the earthly, private imagery of one poet. As Bethea notes, Pushkin's transformation of Derzhavin's lines reveals Pushkin's preference for the private consciousness in opposition to Derzhavin's preference for public consciousness.[47] But the logic of the life-like statue as a paradigm for Pushkin's future metamorphosis suggests that, in addition to the private/public contrast, Pushkin's reworking of Derzhavin implies a contrasting mechanism of reception. Derzhavin's use of "to esteem, honour" (*chtit'*) does not necessarily imply a creative, transformative act. A poet can honour or esteem another poet, but poets must do more to earn their title. A poet must create and in so doing transform the works of other poets, a point underscored by the *Exegi monumentum* genre. Poets must read, but they also must write. Furthermore, the near rhyme of Pushkin's "poet" (*piit*) with Derzhavin's "to esteem, honour" (*chtit'*) is itself suggestive of how Pushkin transforms Derzhavin. Etymologically "to esteem, honour" (*chtit'*) is connected to "to read" (*chitat'*). By transforming the last word of the second stanza from *chtit'* to *piit*, Pushkin raises Derzhavin's condition for immortality from esteem for a nation to an individual poetic response.

Through emphasis on writerly reception, Pushkin's metamorphosis into an immortal being takes on more of the image of God as understood by the Cappadocians than might be expected. Metamorphosis of human nature for the Cappadocians was the restoration of the image of God, the goal of *theosis*. The image of God emphasized three attributes: reason (*Logos*), freedom, and immortality.[48] The conditions of the immortality Pushkin envisions for himself suggest an image that is very like the reason, freedom, and immortality by which humans are recognized as made in the image of God. By focusing on his words, his poetry, his own freedom and immortality, the image of the monument allows Pushkin to frame his legacy in the terms of Christian *theosis*, of regaining the image of God, in addition to the allusions evoked by the connection of the monument to the pagan deities described in Ovid's *Metamorphoses*.

Pushkin's transformation from mortal to immortal in "Monument" differs from what Horace, Ovid, Lomonosov, and Derzhavin describe, in that, in addition to the immortality of his name, he emphasizes writerly reception, *allusion to his poetry*, as the vehicle of immortality. Ovid claims that his "name will never die," whereas Pushkin claims an immortality that reflects the metamorphosis of *theosis*, not only in himself but in those who recognize reason, freedom, and the immortality of humans, even though they have "fallen."[49]

The precondition of his glory in the second stanza is that there will be one poet alive in the *sub*lunar world. In the context of the lifelike statue, a poet can certainly be read as someone who will do more than just read Pushkin's works. A poet creates: he will read them and transform them into yet other great works of literature.[50] Pushkin's transformation does not end with his death and removal to some cold and distant interstellar space but rather finds new form, a new body, as his words inspire the works of future poets.[51] This is not to say that Pushkin excludes a simpler, utilitarian type of non-poetic reader from his legacy. In the fourth stanza, he long will be loved by flesh-and-blood posterity not for having achieved greatness but for the fact that his poetry elicits "kind-hearted feelings" and glorifies freedom and mercy. While the primary condition of his glory hinges on the future poet of stanza two and the possibility of writerly reception, the notions of readerly reception in stanzas four and five also connote kenotic descent. The abstract deification and fame described by other authors of a "Monument" poem is brought back to earth from the expansive universe, below the stars and moon, to the realm where flesh and spirit still strive with one another in an uneasy symbiosis, where it is still unclear whether people as living sculptures will be raised to the divine image in which they are created or lowered to the matter from which they are formed.

Pushkin's "Monument" draws on the ambivalence of the lifelike statue to complicate the idea of future reception in the whole "Monument" genre. In this light, writerly reception or allusion, the mechanism by which a future poet transforms Pushkin's works, must be seen as central to Pushkin's vision of his poetic immortality. And yet that is not to say that he completely disdains other forms of future reception, most notably readerly reception among the "people" or by the "fool." In part two, we will turn to a more detailed analysis of Pushkin's own allusions in "Monument" and some of Pushkin's other works to see more clearly how the distinction between the future poet and the future naive reader relies on allusion in the years leading up to Pushkin's work on "Monument."

Part II

Allusions, Monuments, and the Future Poet

The combined context of Ovid's lifelike statues and Orthodox concepts of Incarnation and *theosis* reveal Pushkin's motif of monumental sculpture as a paradigm for the future of allusion, the device upon which his future immortality depends in "Monument." However, Pushkin does have a stake in defining just how that future poet might treat his works, because Pushkin himself was at one point a living poet looking back on the poets of the past. In several key works, Pushkin provides a model for the "future poet," a model that indicates his interest in having a future poet do for him what he did for the poets who preceded him. Pushkin's growing sense that he is turning into the ossified past colours his thinking about the future in "Monument," which explains the emphasis of the middle three stanzas on reception (the future poet of the second stanza, the non-Russian imperial subjects in the third stanza, and "the people" of the fourth stanza). While Horace and those who imitated him also emphasized the future of their fame, Pushkin's addition of the future poet diverges from the tradition to emphasize continued metamorphosis instead of static canonicity. Unlike other "Monument" writers, Pushkin leaves his immortality unfinished, incomplete, in the hands of a future poet. Of the three spheres of reception (poet, imperial subjects, and "the people"), only the future poet has the capacity to do for Pushkin what he has done for the poets of antiquity and Russia's eighteenth century. Only a poet has the skill and inspiration to allude to Pushkin's works in ways that ensure that his soul in sacred lyre will outlive his dust and elude decay. Only a future poet can breathe new life into Pushkin's petrified form.

That understanding illuminates the fifth stanza in new ways. The imperatives "be obedient," "accept," and "do not argue" set it apart from the past and future tense verbs in stanzas one to four, and the commands cease to make sense as a personal credo for Pushkin's own future creation. Pushkin's work is complete. Rather, these imperatives can be interpreted as variations on the theme of *waiting* to be brought to life, *waiting* for the creative vision of a future poet whose allusions to Pushkin will add new dimensions of meaning to his poetry. Pushkin is not telling himself to wait for some future deserved recognition or how to create future works, but rather *how to wait* for his future metamorphoses.

Allusions to the Past: Becoming a Past Poet

To understand Pushkin's vision of the future poet, we must first consider two aspects of Pushkin's allusions in "Monument." Pushkin is at once considering the possibility of a future poet engaging with his works through allusion even as he enacts the role of future poet by engaging with a set of poets for whom he is the future. He is at once the poetic master who is bringing the ossified, statuesque Horatian "Monument" genre to life even as he recognizes that his immortal "Monument" will be reduced to cliché, in need of a future poet's attention.

Pushkin's awareness of becoming a past poet stands out in his choice to imitate the Horatian "Monument" tradition. The epigraph and first stanza of "Monument" densely allude to the Russian eighteenth century and the Roman past. The odic genre recalls the Russian eighteenth century and its engagement with the culture of antiquity. Pushkin's epigraph, the first line of Horace's Latin poem, introduces the notion of allusion right away, as well as the monumental genre of inscription: Catherine's dedication on Étienne Maurice Falconet's Monument to Peter the Great is in both Latin and Russian, and by copying its form, Pushkin alludes to Horace while simultaneously placing himself on equal footing with Catherine as the author of the monument as well as with Peter the Great, to whom the monument is dedicated. Catherine raised a monument to Peter; Pushkin has raised a monument to himself.

Derzhavin's allusion to Catherine I as "Felitsa" in his imitation of Horace further implicates the eighteenth-century moment as of particular interest in Pushkin's imitation. It was the age of sculpture, of interest to Pushkin both as the age that produced Falconet's monument as well as the age he wrote about in his first poems dedicated to Catherine's glyptotheca in which he spent considerable time while studying at the Lyceum in Tsarskoe Selo. The fraught relationships of poet and emperor further the connection between Horace's moment under Augustus and Derzhavin's moment under Catherine. Both Horace and Derzhavin experienced the patronage of the sovereign while at the same time claiming some measure of intellectual and aesthetic freedom.

Not all of their contemporaries could walk the same fine line. As a notable representative of the generation after Horace, Ovid was exiled from Rome by Augustus in 8 CE, the same year that he was finishing *Metamorphoses*.[52] The most famous of Horace's Russian eighteenth-century imitators to be exiled was Alexander Radishchev (1749–1802) – exiled to Siberia by Catherine II until after her death. In one of the drafts of "Monument," Pushkin considered "following after Radishchev" (*vsled Radishchevu*) as a possibility for the line that took the final form of "in my harsh age."[53] The Horace-Derzhavin subtext thus also implies a secondary Ovid-Radishchev subtext of great personal interest to Pushkin. In this sense, allusions to the contradictory relations between poet and emperor in Rome and in eighteenth-century Russia create an important interpretive paradigm – they evoke Pushkin's contemporary political moment under Alexander I and Nicholas I.

Allusions to Rome and the eighteenth century in "Monument" are balanced by an invitation to read the poem in light of works by his close contemporaries and by Pushkin himself. The past Russias of Derzhavin and Radishchev merge with the Russia of Pushkin and his contemporaries. Of these contemporaries, the most significant are the Polish poet Adam Mickiewicz (1798–1855), who made a significant impression on Pushkin, and Pushkin's dearest Lyceum friend, Anton Del'vig (1798–1831). Pushkin's engagement with Mickiewicz's interest in the Monument to Peter the Great is well-documented, in particular in relation to Pushkin's poem *The Bronze Horseman*.[54] If "not made by hands" parodies Ruban's panegyric ekphrasis of Falconet's monument, then it must also certainly implicate Mickiewicz, whose parody of Ruban would have been very familiar and whose interest in the Monument to Peter the Great deeply shaped Pushkin's own creative inspiration.[55]

Allusions to Del'vig are perhaps even stronger than those to Mickiewicz in "Monument" and have been extensively treated.[56] Pushkin's return to the monument was also a return to the Lyceum and the beginning of his literary career. Alekseev pulls together evidence from Pushkin's writings about the Lyceum and the meetings of its graduates, his correspondence with Del'vig, and Del'vig's poetry, to suggest that Pushkin had Del'vig in mind as well as Horace-Derzhavin while writing "Monument."[57] With respect to the metapoetic function of allusion in "Monument," the overarching significance of the Mickiewicz-Del'vig layer is the idea that Pushkin saw himself and his times slipping into the past, succumbing to the petrification of the eighteenth century and Rome before it. This sense that Pushkin's own contemporary moment was on the verge of becoming the past clearly affects interpretation of what is perhaps the most controversial allusion in the poem: the meaning of the phrase "Alexandrian Pillar."

Layers of Monumental Allusion in "Alexandrian Pillar"

The multiple layers of allusion in phrases like "not made by hands" and "Alexandrian Pillar" metonymically reiterate the layers of past allusion inherent in the tradition of imitating Horace: the classical context (the

Pharos of Alexandria, the Colossus of Rhodes), the eighteenth-century context (Falconet and the Bronze Horseman), and the contemporary as it becomes the past (Pushkin, Alexander's Column).

Part of the intertextual interest of Pushkin's allusions in "Monument" lies in his ability to juxtapose his allusions to those of Horace and Derzhavin. Much has been made of Pushkin's choice to diverge from the traditional pyramids as the point of comparison for his legacy. But the intertextual nature of his writing in "Monument" cannot escape the classical references inherent in the textual tradition of imitating Horace and the tradition in monumental sculpture to reference the monumental art of the classical world. "Alexandrian Pillar" is an interesting formulation because it stands in for and creates contrast with the signifiers it replaces. As the capital of Egypt, famous for the pyramids, the choice of "Alexandrian" as a modifier for the only literal monument referenced in the poem allows Pushkin to transform the geographical location of the pyramids into a multi-tiered allusion ripe with political clout in his own contemporary world.[58]

Given the time in which Horace composed his ode, many scholars have looked for Alexandrian monuments that might be of interest in interpreting the poem. David Bethea neatly summarizes a widely accepted understanding of the allusion: a column in Alexandria that is dedicated to the emperor Diocletian in the fourth century "is clearly a calque for the massive Alexander Column, unveiled in 1834 on Palace Square in St. Petersburg in a ceremony demonstrably not attended by Pushkin."[59] Alekseev provides a detailed summary of the various strongly opinionated interpretations provoked by this allusion before laying the groundwork that supports Bethea's more concise formula.[60]

As a potential referent, the Pharos of Alexandria, a lighthouse built in the third century BCE by the Ptolemaic kingdom and one of the tallest buildings in the world for centuries, inspired interest among twentieth-century Western scholars for a time. As Michael Wachtel indicates, Ruban's inclusion of references to both the Colossus of Rhodes and the pyramids in his eighteenth-century ekphrasis of the Bronze Horseman lent support to the idea that Pushkin had in mind a literal ancient Alexandrian monument of great height.[61]

Katya Hokanson takes Pushkin's replacement of the Egyptian reference in Horace and Derzhavin with the reference to the Alexander Column in "Monument" as ironic:

> By using a contemporary reference instead of an ancient one, Pushkin evokes the defeat of Napoleon and alludes to a potential comparison of Tsar Alexander to Emperor Augustus, since just as Augustus had defeated

Antony and Cleopatra, Alexander had defeated Napoleon, who had famously conquered Egypt in 1798; his invasion included a battle fought near the pyramids. It was, however, Nicholas who ordered the raising of the monument to his brother, which emphasized his own importance as well, just as Catherine emphasized hers by constructing the statue of Peter the Great. Hence Pushkin evokes Nicholas as well as Alexander by choosing the column as his reference point.[62]

Her tightly constructed paragraph indicates the breadth of the possible allusions evoked by the phrase.

As indicated by Alekseev, Bethea, and Hokanson, the phrase "Alexandrian Pillar," while not opening up its potential meanings too far, creates the dual possibility of referring to the ancient world as well as the contemporary one: Alexandrian Pillar *and* Alexander's Column. Hokanson and Wachtel also indicate the interest that Falconet's Bronze Horseman holds for the first stanza: although not mentioned directly, parody of Ruban's panegyric holds interesting potential for interpreting the phrase and for thinking about Pushkin's "Monument" in general. But it, too, holds its own references to the Roman world: Falconet designed Peter's equestrian form as a reference to the equestrian statue to Marcus Aurelius in Rome.

Allusions to antiquity and the interest it held for Russian culture in the eighteenth century coincide with the network of connotations of "Alexandrian Pillar" during Pushkin's lifetime. Emphasis on Pushkin's personal biographical relationship to the Romanovs and their monuments has inspired its own set of contradictory interpretations of the phrase. Sandler demonstrates the strong draw of the allusion by juxtaposing two competing interpretations.[63] Renate Lachmann observes that "Alexandrian" could lead to an interpretation of Pushkin's self-consciousness of his African heritage as well as the verse form of the Alexandrine in which the poem is composed.[64] In contrast, M.F. Murianov denies any sort of connection to the city of Alexandria, but notes that Nicholas I visited a dacha named Aleksandria, a detail that further implicates both tsars in the phrase.[65]

Within the context of the wide-ranging interpretations of the layers of allusion in "Alexandrian Pillar," the first stanza of "Monument," and the intertextual nature of the Horatian ode itself, these allusions to the past have received considerable attention. As concerns the future poet and allusion in "Monument," they set the stage for a departure from the Horatian-Ovidian-Derzhavinian subtext that is even more provoking than his substitution of "Alexandrian Pillar" for the Egyptian pyramids. In place of a static future fame that is predicated on the glory of an empire, Pushkin turns his attention to the changing relationship between a poet and his future unknown readership.

Pushkin creates his own monument, but he does so within the constraints of the lifelike statue as having the inherent ability to come to life again. In bringing the ode to new life, Pushkin pushes into the future and sets a model for innovation and playful resuscitation of past, ossified genres. The dramatic shift, however, is away from the demonic monument come to life in *The Bronze Horseman* and *The Stone Guest* (Jakobson's myth of the destructive statue), towards an Ovidian/Cappadocian ambivalence about the lifelike statue. It seems inexorable, perhaps to Pushkin and certainly from a historical perspective, that he and his works were turning to stone – seemingly at the command of the aesthetic gods of the age, which denigrated his poetry as light-hearted and lacking in substance.[66] Pushkin was mortal and destined to be deprived of that divine spark which animated his mortal body with intelligence and volition. Both he and his works were entering the same moment of canonization from which he had resuscitated many previous poets and forms. From the first stanza, with its many allusions to a past on the verge of swallowing his own historical "present," Pushkin moves to considering the future of his works, and it is to this that we now turn.

Patronage, Audience, and the Future of Allusion

In Pushkin's poem "Monument," dense allusions to the past set the poem's metapoetic theme in the first stanza. But then Pushkin spends three stanzas reflecting on the future of his works. Allusion is a site of anxiety about future readers as well as a site of poetic innovation and hope for future poetic engagement with one's work. It makes sense that Pushkin would turn to the theme of audience within his metapoetics of allusion given his interest in the patron-poet relationship of eighteenth-century Russian literature. The appearance of the anonymous reading public came to dominate author-reader configurations within Pushkin's lifetime. The question of a lasting poetic legacy automatically raises the issues of patronage and audience. A changing relationship between poet and audience also indicates a development in the device of allusion: what happens to allusion when you start writing for an anonymous reader whose frame of reference may differ significantly from yours?

In the eighteenth-century context, patronage allowed for very specific and detailed allusions to conversations, places, and ideas because the poet knew his audience's frame of reference. Allusions could be tailored to personal interests and private conversations. The device of allusion, when writing for an anonymous readership, is both a more complicated and a more general task. As the motif of the lifelike statue in so many of Pushkin's other works shapes the meaning of "Monument," so the themes of allusion, patronage, and audience in Pushkin's oeuvre must inform the interpretation of stanzas two to four. Three conceptual lenses aid in appreciating the meaning of these middle stanzas of "Monument" as they relate to allusion. The first lens draws on Luba Golbert's analysis of patronage as a thematic concern of Pushkin's retrospective look towards the eighteenth century to frame his ideas about the shifting relationship between poet and audience in the future. The second lens highlights the relevance of Pushkin's idiosyncratic fragment "Egyptian Nights" (1835) as a major clue to understanding the connection between allusion and the future of poet-audience relations in "Monument." The third lens draws on dialectically opposed twentieth-century interpretations of the people and the poet in the middle three stanzas and reveals how, by reading these stanzas through Pushkin's metapoetic vision for the future of allusion, we can learn from both sides of the argument.

Patronage and the Ode

As an eighteenth-century genre, the ode implied a mutually beneficial relationship between poet and patron. However, with the turn of the century and the advent of romanticism, the writers of odes "shifted their position in relation to their patrons and their social function within the nation."[67] As a genre that celebrated the role between patron and artist and assumed common ideological ground, the ode "bound the subjects and the patron/monarch within the same set of putative state aspirations."[68] Pushkin revisits this already old process in his "Monument," but he imbues the old form with new meaning. Although the odes of Horace, Ovid, and Derzhavin speculate on the idea of future immortality, they primarily look backward and conform to the common "set of putative state aspirations" shared by the writers and their patrons. Following Dostoevskii's interpretation of Pushkin as having worldwide significance, Pushkin's expansion of his future fame beyond the bounds of the state to which Horace and Derzhavin limit themselves (Italy/ Rome, Russia) has commonly been interpreted as a move to embrace his worldwide significance. But tearing down the traditional patron/ poet dynamic could also be reinterpreted as a move from an immortality based on the already past glory of the Empire to an unknown future not limited to a political geographical entity. The idea is not so much that Pushkin's words will grow beyond the boundaries of the Russian

Empire but that his works will be immortal independent of the existence of the Russian state as such. Where Derzhavin saw the patron and the state as his primary readers, Pushkin can envision a future poet who recognizes and responds to Pushkin's work, bringing it to life, as a situation independent of empire as the underwriter of aesthetic life.

Having established the ode as the generic site of innovation of the poet/audience relationship, Luba Golburt turns to Pushkin's retrospective assessment of "Derzhavin's moment." Allusion thus becomes a barometer for gauging the decaying bonds between poet and audience. Golburt explains how, when writing for a patron, one rarely needs to question if the patron will understand the poem they sponsored. Throughout Pushkin's career, she elaborates, that trust was eroded by new methods of production and circulation: "reception by individual readers, whether authority figures or friends, is eclipsed by the anonymous reading public."[69] The lack of trust a poet feels for his future audience shapes the contrast between the future poet and the future reading public that orders the inner three stanzas of "Monument." Stanza one represents a complex set of allusions that reinforce the interdependence of verbal and visual culture and the polysemy of the word "monument." Stanza five, on the other hand, really has no direct allusions to monuments beyond the one created at the command of the gods/God. The question it seems to be posing is, what will become of this monument in the future? By changing the conditions of the ode from a primarily historical and imperially focused set of expectations, in which an audience's reception could be predicted and relied upon, to a future set of readers who represent unknown worldviews and reactions, Pushkin brings to life the genre of the ode even as he redirects the components of its genre expectations to encompass the future and an unknown audience.

This theme, like the monument theme itself, is one that captures Pushkin's attention at several stages in his career. Golburt interprets Pushkin's "To Zhukovskii" (1818) as Pushkin's commentary on his fellow poet's relationship to his audience. What at first appears to be laudatory turns out to be problematic. Zhukovskii writes "for the few" (*dlia nemnogikh*), an idea Pushkin seems to embrace. However, Golburt argues that the identity of that few is implicated by Zhukovskii's publication of several instalments of poetry entitled "For the Few," specifically for Aleksandra Fedorovna, the wife of Nicholas Romanov, who would soon become Nicholas I. Golburt argues that in an age when patronage is increasingly questioned, Zhukovskii's audience poses a potential problem for the continuation of the dialogue between Pushkin and Zhukovskii inherent in the poem's title ("To Zhukovskii").[70]

In a similarly insightful reading of "To N. Ia. Pliuskova" (1818), Golburt demonstrates Pushkin's ability to adapt, to modify the ode according to new poet/audience alliances. "The two poems ["To Zhukovskii" and "To N. Ia. Pliuskova"] can be read as early manifestoes of the new poetic possibilities available to a poet who divests himself of a hierarchical relationship to his consumers at court, and believes in the imminence of spiritual kinship and the potential for co-creativity with the reader, while also continuing to contemplate past genres and institutions of reception."[71] In "Monument," Pushkin undertakes a similar stance, but distances himself even further from the audiences of power. His accomplishments, built upon the patronage of monumental art by Catherine and Nicholas in the first stanza, surpass them, even as he recreates the odic form of Horace and its imitations in eighteenth-century Russia. Likewise, his immortality is not based on the reception defined by the imperial Russian powers of the past but looks for a "spiritual kinship" that manifests itself in co-creativity. However, that co-creativity exists not in what may be merely a sympathetic reading audience but in one with the potential to allude to Pushkin, to rework and artistically dialogue with Pushkin's words, bringing them to new life.

In a later poem that addresses Pushkin's historical interest in the age of Catherine, "To the Grandee" ("K vel'mozhe," 1830), Golburt shows how Pushkin's interest in the lifestyles of the eighteenth century continued the poet's interest in reader/poet relations. Although Pushkin was criticized for currying favour with power by the poem's initial readers, Belinskii argues a decade later that the poet's achievement in "To the Grandee" was more about restoring a bygone age than flattering those close to power. Golburt cites Belinskii: "This portrait of a grandee of the old era is a marvelous restoration of a ruin into the original shape of a building" (*divnaia restavratsiia ruiny v pervobytnyi vid zdaniia*).[72] She goes on to critique reception of the poem in the 1830s, Belinskii's in the 1840s, and subsequent scholarship by demonstrating how none of the commentators had analysed the poet's statements on patronage "for their possible *metapoetic* implications."[73] She argues that "To the Grandee" "though never explicitly commenting on poetic craft, reinhabits forms of inspiration that had circulated in the eighteenth century but had since lost their currency."[74]

Golburt's contribution to the interpretive range of these poems also suggests an important context for re-evaluating Pushkin's anxieties about reception as articulated in "Monument." In many works, Pushkin consistently "reinhabits forms of inspiration" that had lapsed into "ruin," to use Belinskii's metaphor, and that required revitalization. As Golburt's analysis of the metapoetic element of patronage demonstrates, Pushkin's anxieties about audience and reception coincided with his concern for respecting, valuing, and resuscitating poetic forms that had become outmoded. Such forms became a sort of code in which Pushkin could inscribe his own problematic relationship to patronage under Alexander I and Nicholas I. Golburt concludes that "patronage was a quintessential eighteenth-century practice against which Pushkin modulated his understanding and critique of a whole range of past and present social relations, historical distinctions, and forms of creative life. The unsettling conclusion was that, for all intents and purposes, the oppressive 'union with the tsars' might in Pushkin's age, too, not have been 'dissolved' just yet."[75]

Golburt's insightful readings of the metapoetic implications of patronage for Pushkin suggest a similar process at work in his metapoetics of allusion. Only the future poet seems free from the bounds of the state as patron. In stanzas three and four, Pushkin's readers are defined in contradictory terms. The peripheries of the Empire (stanza three) seem to indicate that the patron/poet relationship implicit in the eighteenth-century ode are intact: the Tungus and other token ethnicities will know of Pushkin because they will be brought into the realm of the Empire, the mechanism by which Pushkin's fame will grow. But stanza four seems to undo the poet's dependence upon the Empire to reach an audience: the rhyme "to the people"/"freedom" (*narodu/svobodu*) and the utilitarian emphasis of Pushkin's poetry that "evokes kind-hearted feelings" and "proclaims mercy to the fallen" hints at the undermining of the traditional odic confluence of patron/poet aspirations. In any event, by introducing the future poet in stanza two, Pushkin creates the truly revolutionary distinction from the poets (Horace, et al.) whom he imitates. This future poet is bound neither by state nor by political creed but is free to innovate and breathe new life into the ossified forms of Pushkin's past poetry, a pattern that Pushkin's fascination with the eighteenth-century models very effectively.

The patron/poet relationship inherent in the ode is one lens through which to view the emphasis of the middle three stanzas on reception. The shifting ground of the relationship between poet and audience changes the nature of allusion as well. When a poet does not know the name of his reader, how can he know that reader's frame of reference? If the theme of patronage was inherent in the odic genre of "Monument," Pushkin's many works that also treated the theme of the people and the economic constraints placed on poets by a new anonymous reading public further complicate interpretations of the middle three stanzas of "Monument." "Egyptian Nights" is particularly revealing in this regard.

"Egyptian Nights"

"Egyptian Nights" reveals the connection between Pushkin's concerns with patronage, audience, allusion, and genre as they relate to the device of allusion. Written in 1835, unfinished and unpublished, "Egyptian Nights" tells the story of the interactions between a Russian poet, Charskii, and an Italian improviser who asks Charskii to help him gain entrance to the best houses in Petersburg. At first sceptical, Charskii is deeply challenged by the Italian improviser's facility to be inspired by the thoughts of someone else as well as by his willingness to perform his art for material gain. If the first skill makes a positive impression on Charskii, the second disgusts him. Pushkin's fragment consists of three prose chapters that tell the story of Charskii's conversations with the improviser. Interspersed within these prose accounts are two performances by the improviser inspired by a theme supplied by Charskii.

Several factors work together to suggest that "Egyptian Nights" reflects a concern for future reception that parallels Pushkin's metapoetics of allusion in "Monument." First, Pushkin's interest in the ancient world (the Horatian genre as such and the layers of allusion in "Alexandrian Pillar") suggests that Pushkin's mind turned to Egypt and Alexandria more than once in the last years of his life.[76] Second, the distinction that Pushkin draws between Charskii as an audience and the Petersburg elite as audience parallels the distinction he draws between the poet in stanza two of "Monument" and the anonymous reading public that dominates stanzas three and four. Thirdly, sculpture and the sculptor in "Egyptian Nights" provide one of the primary metaphors for the improviser's craft, adding a metapoetic dimension to the autobiographical nuances in Pushkin's sculptural metaphors. Finally, the emphasis on poetic inspiration drawn from someone else (*chuzhoe slovo, chuzhaia mysl'*) as the core conceit of "Egyptian Nights" indicates Pushkin's interest in the metapoetics of allusion and supports the claim that allusion is a central conceit in "Monument."

In one of many telling exchanges between Charskii and the improviser, Charskii is surprised that the improviser needs no audience, no applause, no response from a public audience. The improviser explains: "Where can I find a better audience? You are a poet, you will understand me better than them, and your quiet encouragement means more to me than a whole storm of applause."[77] In this formulation, the improviser's point of view seems to echo the poet/people dichotomy of stanzas two to four in "Monument."

His words might seem to underscore the traditional reading of the "sublunar poet" as one who will understand Pushkin correctly. But that would mean to identify Pushkin's stance as a poet with the improviser's and to relegate Charskii to a passive participant in the poetic process. After dismissing the non-poet audience in favour of Charskii's single-minded attention, the improviser commands him to sit down somewhere and to give him a theme.[78] Here is the real key: Charskii the poet is both audience and participant. He provides the improviser with a very metapoetic idea that at once underscores and undermines the situation of the improviser: *"The poet himself chooses subjects for his songs; the crowd has no right to rule his* [the poet's] *inspiration"* (emphasis in the original).[79] To include Charskii in the crowd here would be to miss an important moment: the improviser is inspired by the idea of a poet, one who stands apart from the crowd and who does not rule the improviser's inspiration but rather gives it new life, even as the improviser brings to life the unformed, unfinished idea of the poet. Their discourse stands apart and above the response of the audience, which is left out of the equation by both Charskii and the improviser. In "Monument," the "poet of the future" ensures Pushkin's immortality in the same way that the improviser brings to life Charskii's personal preoccupation with the high calling of the poet.

In his reading of "Egyptian Nights," David Herman concludes with the idea that Pushkin could not become the future poet that he envisioned and that financial constraints required him to become. He interprets the unfinished fragment as an impasse out of which Pushkin could not imagine a way.[80] One gets the sense from Herman's interpretation that Pushkin felt antagonism towards this other poet, the Italian improviser, who represented the "poet of the future and his brave new world."[81] Herman argues that the "distance between the Pushkin of 1835 and the Pushkin of 1831 can in a sense be measured by the role reversal that distinguishes 'Egyptian Nights' from 'Mozart and Salieri' – the character Pushkin's narrator sympathizes with is now, as far as we can tell, the *less* talented of the pair."[82] While Herman correctly interprets the end that threatens the poet Charskii in "Egyptian Nights," the hopeful tone of "sublunar poet" in "Monument" provides an important corrective. Perhaps, to borrow Herman's formula, the distance between the Pushkin of 1836 and the Pushkin of 1835 can be measured by the extent to which he relinquishes his own word (*svoe slovo*) in "Monument" to the transformative powers of another poet. After all, in contrast to the poet Charskii, who eschews "someone else's word" (*chuzhoe slovo*), the Italian in "Egyptian Nights" is capable of transforming someone else's word into something new, something of his own.[83] After having given the improviser a theme and hearing his extemporaneous poetry, Charskii exclaims, "The thought of another has barely fallen on your ears and already it has become your own property, as if you have been carrying it around, nurturing it, developing it constantly."[84]

The improviser responds with a sculptural metaphor:

> In what way does a sculptor see the hidden Jupiter in a lump of Carrara marble and bring him into the world, with chisel and hammer breaking apart his shell? … In the same way, nobody but the improviser himself can understand the speed of an impression, the close connection between one's own inspiration and someone else's external will.[85]

This conversation between Charskii and the improviser quickly turns to the subject of how much to charge for his performances, a topic that is disgusting to Charskii but that the improviser obviously loves. Yet, the connection here between the "poet of the future" (Herman's phrase) and Charskii reflects Pushkin's interest in what will happen to his poetry and gives important clues for interpreting the "sublunar poet" upon whom Pushkin's legacy depends. To borrow the improviser's sculptural trope, Pushkin's metaphorical monument is both a finished work of sculptural art and a block of exquisite marble from which an inspired future poet will bring to life new sculptures.

The genre of the fragment itself invites readers to interact with, to continue, to give new life to the artistic concept of the author. Herman articulates this thought at the end of his article: "What needs to be read now is not the significance of the text's conclusion, but the symbolic meaning of its incompleteness."[86] But perhaps incompleteness is not so much an invitation to complete Pushkin's text, which Herman does in enlightening ways. Perhaps it is more an invitation to see the fragment as a concept, given over to a future improviser with the same level of talent as the Italian improviser, a desire to have an interlocutor engage with his ideas, not on the level of reading but in a creative, artistic fashion.

Alexandra Smith considers this idea of the fragment as the possible future allusion by focusing on the image of the urn as a central symbolic moment in "Egyptian Nights." The improviser chooses the theme of Cleopatra and her lovers out of an urn. Smith suggests that the urn alludes to Keats's "Ode on a Grecian Urn" (1820), which focuses on a young lover about to kiss his beloved, but whose desire is frozen in perpetuity. Smith sees a parallel to Keats's theme of perpetual desire about to be realized in the ending of the improviser's poem. Just as the improviser chooses his theme out of an urn, Cleopatra chooses the order of the three lovers doomed to die for their love out of the urn: first the soldier Flavius; then the philosopher Chriton; and last the unnamed, inexperienced youth. The fragment ends when Cleopatra looks at the passionate youth, prolonging the moment of desire instead of depicting its consummation, as in Keats's poem. In addition to the allusion to Keats, Smith sees an allusion to Pushkin's "Tsarskoe selo statue" ("Tsarskosel'skaia statuia," 1830), in which the statue of a young woman holds a broken urn out of which flows an eternal stream of water that "symbolizes the immortal flow of poetic speech."[87] Taken together, these allusions convincingly support her thesis that "the urn image also embodies the poet's own self: it contains fragments of texts and images that might be picked up by future readers and performers."[88] Both Smith and Herman indicate the future allusion as a theme in "Egyptian Nights" – in genre (fragment) and imagery (urn). Pushkin's juxtaposition of Charskii to the improviser as "future poet" works together with his thematization of allusion to tie together the frame prose narrative and the improviser's poetry.[89]

"Egyptian Nights" provides a provocative paradigm for interpreting the "future poet"; but it also represents the culmination of many of Pushkin's ideas about the expanding audience of the Russian readership and its implications for art. After all, the improviser performs in Italian, a language that Charskii understands but that the audience does not. A similar linguistic distance animates stanza three of "Monument," in which the peoples indicated as perpetuating the rumour of Pushkin (as opposed to interacting with his poetry) speak Russian only as a second language: "the proud grandson of Slavs" (often interpreted as a reference to the Poles), "the Finn," "the Tungus," and "the Kalmyk" all speak *other* languages. Within the context of "Egyptian Nights," this fact underscores the ambivalence of Pushkin's phrase "Rumour of me will go," especially in the light of Charskii's response to the improviser's concern that no one will attend the event because few in Petersburg understand Italian. Charskii reassures him that they will come – some out of curiosity, some just to spend the evening somehow, others to show off that they do know Italian, but that the most important thing is just to be in style – the language of poetry itself is of no interest to the crowd whatsoever.[90]

The Poet, the People, and the Problem of Audience

As Golburt shows, Pushkin's engagement with the forms of the eighteenth century demonstrates his interest in the metapoetics of allusion with regard to the shifting landscape of patronage and audience as well as his dedication to reinventing the forms of the past. "Egyptian Nights" provides evidence for his vision of the future of allusion and the dynamism of a future poet who can find inspiration in "someone else's word" (*chuzhoe slovo*). These arguments clearly point to Pushkin's future immortality as dependent on the "sublunar poet" of stanza two. However, Pushkin's shift to the thematic of a mass readership in stanzas three and four has divided scholarly interpreters, particularly in the twentieth century. The debate about the interpretation of the people and its relationship to Pushkin's art in "Monument" splits roughly into two camps: either the poet is seen as a good reader in contrast to the people as poor readers, or poet and people are seen as different but ultimately positive segments of a broad readership. The concept of the people has been at the centre of many interpretations of the poem both because it figures prominently in the poem (it is featured in stanzas one, two, and four) and because of its implications for interpreting the political and aesthetic themes of empire, audience, fame, and the purpose of poetry.

Soviet Pushkinist Sergei Mikhailovich Bondi summarizes the first argument, even as he works to argue against it:

> I repeat, that, because of their convictions, several scholars (Vladimir Solov'ev, M. Gershenzon, V. Veresaev) cannot come to terms with the idea that the aspects of his poetry that Pushkin enumerates [in stanza four] are his achievement before humanity. It is not just an over-intellectualization for them to claim that this evaluation is mentioned by Pushkin not as his own, but as the incorrect understanding of his poetry on the part of the people, and that Pushkin calls on his muse to make peace with their inevitable misunderstanding [in stanza five] …[91]

To counteract this seemingly defunct (but nonetheless in need of debunking yet again) argument that disparages the ability of the people to understand Pushkin in all his complexity, Bondi dedicates the rest of his article to laying out the Soviet "correct" interpretation:

> Although it would seem that now no one holds this point of view [that understands the people as incapable of understanding Pushkin's poetry], and more than once correct explanations for the reasons of the acute contradiction between the last stanza of "Monument" and all the ones that come before it have been suggested, all the same it seems to me necessary to once again return to this topic and by doing so remind everyone of the concrete conditions that brought this poem to life.[92]

Bondi assumes that Pushkin envisioned a future readership among the people that could "correctly" understand his works and their utility. Bondi supports this argument in part by many quotations from those closest to Pushkin who suspected a lack of depth and meaning in his work.[93] Misunderstood by even his closest contemporaries, Pushkin was thus forced to speak directly to the future generations of his readers as the only audience that would understand the genius of his poetry.[94]

Bondi's interpretation of the fourth stanza relies on his understanding of the uses of the people in the first and third. He identifies the form ("kind-hearted feelings,") and content ("freedom" and "mercy for the fallen" as direct allusions to the emancipation of the serfs and the Decembrists) as the features of Pushkin's work that the poet himself values and sees as the justification for his lasting and worldwide fame. In particular, Bondi emphasizes Pushkin's repeated requests for Nicholas I to mitigate the sentences of the Decembrists in exile and the many moments in Pushkin's works that can be interpreted as political.[95] His position follows the traditional interpretation of "Monument" by those who see in the people a future readership that evaluates the utility of Pushkin's poetry correctly. The utility of his poetry in its aesthetic, moral, and political senses ensures his fame among future generations.

Based on this reading, Bondi finds no difference between the poet of stanza two and the people mentioned in stanzas one, three, and four: "As long as *poetry exists in the world* (regardless of the political or any other status of Russia or the Russian people), the glory of Pushkin will live ..."[96] In Bondi's interpretation, the existence of poetry is interchangeable with the notion of the future poet. But poetry that is already written and a poet who has the potential to write new poetry differ vastly. Furthermore, in positing identity between the collective people and the individual poet, Bondi misses one of the most striking of Pushkin's departures from the Derzhavinian subtext. Bondi compares the succession of empires with Pushkin's succession of nationalities. As Horace was for the Roman Empire and Derzhavin was for the Russian Empire, so Pushkin is for all humanity. In Bondi's positive reading of the people as audience, he echoes the metamorphosis from the rough-hewn Thunder Stone to the polished granite of the Alexander Column to Pushkin's poetic word in the first stanza: from Roman Empire to Russian Empire (as Third Rome) to all humanity. But the idea of all humanity as Pushkin's target audience in "Monument" is problematic, especially in light of Pushkin's reworking of Derzhavin's version of this line. Derzhavin writes, "As long as the universe esteems the Slavic peoples."[97] Pushkin borrows Derzhavin's form, but transforms it into something quite different: "As long as in the sublunar world at least one poet is alive." Pushkin shrinks Derzhavin's cosmos to "just one poet." Deleting the language of ethnic and linguistic singularity (Derzhavin's "family of Slavs") rejects the concomitant notions of empire but also undermines collectivity: the universe of Derzhavin with its universal connotations and the entire Slavic collectivity differs drastically from the earthly world and individual poet with no collective ethnic or national identity in Pushkin's "Monument."[98]

Likewise, Bondi cites the "sublunar poet" as proof that the fifth stanza of "Monument" is unnecessary since "everything has already been said" about Pushkin's immortality and future world significance in stanzas one through four.[99] Conflating the poet and the people leads to the quandary in which the critic, extolling Pushkin as the greatest of Russian and world poets, also accuses him of wasting words. According to Bondi, Pushkin had to write this last stanza because Derzhavin had a fifth stanza. Pushkin transforms it into a simple explanation, an apology, for why he, who for the most part avoided alluding to his poetic status, has to write about himself in such broadly laudatory tones.

Bondi's conflation of the poet and the people raises the problem of the last stanza, which departs from the triumphant tone of Pushkin's predecessors (including Ovid) and from the generally positive assessments of stanzas one through four.[100] Why end "Monument" on such a dark note? If his poetry is really immortal, why even speak of contemporary slander, offence, stupidity? In the traditional interpretation, Pushkin is saying to himself that he should not pay attention to the popular reception now, either positive or negative, because he knows that his contemporaries will not understand him. But this interpretation ignores the aesthetic element here as well as the praise that he has predicted for himself in the future. It is not the worldwide significance or the praise that justifies Pushkin's greatness at all, just as contemporary poor reception does not disqualify its significance. If we read "Monument" as a metapoetic reflection on allusion, however, the catalogue of imperatives in the last stanza can be read as variations on one command: wait. After all, the author of "Monument" is not a young Pushkin laying out a credo for the future of his own efforts.

For Pushkin's metapoetics of allusion, the contrast between poet and the people in the poem represents the monumental form of his poetry in both the ekphrastic and iconic modes of the statue metaphor he employs: without direct reference to individual works or even to any of his poetry, non-Russian people can know of his name and they can value his petitions to Nicholas I on behalf of the exiled Decembrists. Pushkin the name, Pushkin the statue-monument can stand in for the works and make them unnecessary – simply the icon of a story that is shaped by inherently non-poetic factors. But the unpacking of his works, the ekphrastic miracle that would bring them to life is relegated to the poet capable of creatively engaging with Pushkin's works, finishing his fragments, developing his thoughts, and parodying his idiosyncrasies, even while learning from his achievements. As I argue in the previous section, Pushkin values both of these modes of his future existence: while the inherent contrast between the poet and the people must be recognized and interpreted, the differences do not have to lead to dismissal of one in favour of the other. The Pushkin Monument occupies that liminal state between ekphrasis and iconism that makes it interesting both in its potential to be raised to a higher level of refinement and in its iconic descent that, within the Christian paradigm of Incarnation and *theosis*, has the power to transform an unwashed but perhaps redeemable readership into higher states of existence defined by freedom and mercy. These are the hopes of the "reception" stanzas (stanzas two, three, and four), hopes that emerge out of an understanding of Pushkin's metapoetics of allusion as defined by the metamorphosing lifelike statues of Ovid and the Cappadocians. Stanza five, with its dictate to wait, indicates Pushkin's vision of a still-unknown future for his own lifelike monument full of ekphrastic and iconic potential.

A metapoetic reflection on allusion as a device of transformation, Pushkin's "Monument" breathed new life into the long-dead genre of Horace's "Monument" ode. Pushkin transforms the monuments of Horace and Derzhavin along the lines of Ovid's lifelike statues and their resonance in Cappadocian concepts of Incarnation and *theosis*: his poetry is great not only for what it has been but for what it will become through the transformative allusions of a future poet. The story of Pushkin's innovation does not end here, however. In emphasizing the centrality of allusion in his future reception through the motif of monumental sculpture, Pushkin also left open the door for his poem to become a statue and a performative space. The "descent" of Pushkin's poem "Monument" into the form of Opekushin's statue corresponds in many ways to the sort of kenotic descent of word to image, spirit to matter, that we see in the Ovidian/Cappadocian paradigm of the lifelike statue. The material statue brought Pushkin's poetry into a different cultural dimension, one closely connected to the many naive readers who would walk by it. At the same time, the material form also made possible the performance of a future poet that heralded the advent of a new dimension of allusion. But for that story, we must turn to the next chapter and analysis of the three-dimensional masterpiece of visual art that is Alexander Opekushin's Pushkin Monument in Moscow.

Chapter Two

Opekushin's Pushkin Monument: Statue and Performance (1836–1880)

It took several decades, but eventually Pushkin's 1836 poem "Monument" metamorphosed into a material monument in central Moscow. The process did not flow organically from Pushkin's concept of the lifelike statue in "Monument." On the contrary, instead of alluding to Pushkin's works in innovative ways, Vasilii Zhukovskii, the first poet to respond to Pushkin's poem, censored it. In doing so, he disrupted Pushkin's careful distinction between the reception of a future poet and that of a naive "people." Censorship contributed to interpreting Pushkin's poem visually, which led to a reductive, simplified, literal understanding of the poem that emphasized the reception of a naive people to the exclusion of a future poet. This trend was evident in the first model for a Pushkin Monument, proposed in 1860, and it continued to dominate subsequent proposals, including Alexander Opekushin's final model, the one that would be dedicated in 1880 to become the first Pushkin Monument.

The visual, statuesque dimension of Opekushin's design corresponds to the iconic function of the lifelike statue metaphor that Pushkin developed in his poem "Monument." The statue of Pushkin became an image that stands in for the complexly intertwined narratives of Pushkin's life and his works. The descent is not the end of the story, however. When the Pushkin Monument finally became a material reality, a "future poet" did appear, and he alluded not just to Pushkin's poem "Monument" but also to its unique symbiosis with Opekushin's statue. This performance initiated yet a third, performative dimension of the Pushkin Monument and restored the ekphrastic side of the lifelike statue metaphor. Along with it, the future poet, so important to Pushkin's concept of his future reception in the poem "Monument," assumed a central place in the cultural history of the Pushkin Monument.

Zhukovskii's Censorship of Pushkin's
Allusions in "Monument"

The story of the appearance of the statue to accompany Pushkin's poem "Monument" begins with Vasilii Andreevich Zhukovskii (1783–1852), Pushkin's one-time teacher and mentor. He bears much of the responsibility for the metamorphosis of Pushkin's poem "Monument" into the Pushkin Monument in Moscow. The first poetic response to Pushkin's "Monument" did not come from a future poet but from Zhukovskii, in many ways a past poet who outlived Pushkin. Ironically, Zhukovskii did not creatively transform Pushkin's works by alluding to them but rather censored Pushkin's most creative allusions. Admittedly, he was working under pressure. Pushkin died on 29 January (o.s.) 1837. Already on 6 February the head of the secret police, Alexander Benkendorf, wrote to Zhukovskii that all "papers that might harm the memory of Pushkin" must be delivered and burnt in Zhukovskii's presence.[1] "Monument," with its politically and culturally provocative allusions, would likely have fallen into this category. Zhukovskii transformed Pushkin's "Monument," not so as to bring it to new life through allusion but by censoring the allusions that would almost certainly have condemned Pushkin's "Monument" to the flames of Benkendorf's fire before it could ever reach a wider audience. But even before this censorship, Zhukovskii made two crucial decisions that would shape the future visualization of the "Monument" poem: he ordered Pushkin's death mask and submitted to Nicholas I the first request for a Pushkin monument. Thus in both verbal and visual terms, Zhukovskii set the trends that contribute to the literalization and visualization of Pushkin's "Monument" – the creation of the statue.

In his letter to Pushkin's father, Sergei L'vovich Pushkin, detailing the moments leading up to and immediately after Pushkin's death, Zhukovskii writes,

> I will describe in a few words what happened after his death. Fortunately, I remembered in time that I should get a death mask made. It was made quickly; his features had not yet begun to change. Of course, that first expression given to him by death was not preserved, but all the same we have an attractive image – it is not death, but sleep.[2]

In effect, this death mask represents the first posthumous step towards monumentalization, and it played a role in the ideas of both incarnation and allusion that were to become part and parcel of the aesthetics of the Pushkin Monument. The existence of the death mask as an authoritative source for what Pushkin "really" looked like would eventually become a determining factor in the selection of Opekushin's model. Zhukovskii immediately emphasized the visual and material component of Pushkin's legacy by requesting a monument and monumentalizing the visual image of the poet's face. While the artist failed to capture the expression just after Pushkin's last breath, Zhukovskii claimed that the mask preserved an attractive view of the face, a physical imprint of a sleeping poet, not a dead one. Even in this early stage of immortalizing the poet's image, Zhukovskii anticipated the nuance of how important a lifelike image of the poet's face would be.

Zhukovskii's almost immediate request for a monument to the poet in some ways explains the urgency he saw in making the death mask and in doing so quickly, before the expression of sleep was replaced by one more corpse-like. Although his request for a monument and the death mask were not public affairs, Zhukovskii determined elements of the monument even as he perceptively navigated the tricky political terrain of advocating for the private family concerns of Pushkin as a husband and father as well as for the poet's public legacy. Nicholas I affirmed all of Zhukovskii's requests with the exception of the monument.[3] That fact alone, taken together with Zhukovskii's concern for the visual component of Pushkin's legacy, goes hand in hand with his later censorship of "Monument."

While the precise timeline is somewhat unclear, when Zhukovskii was communicating with Nicholas I about the fate of Pushkin's debts, family, and estate, it seems that he had not yet had the time to become fully acquainted with all of Pushkin's unpublished works. In those first days after the poet's death he did not yet realize the full implications of what requesting a monument to Pushkin would mean in light of all of Pushkin's unpublished poems about monumental statuary – *The Bronze Horseman* and "Monument" foremost on that list. In any event, although the idea of a monument to Pushkin was certainly in the air, the first formal request to the tsar for a monument to the poet belongs to Zhukovskii. Nicholas I's refusal of such a monument foreshadows the long uphill battle that, under Alexander II, would eventually result in the Pushkin Monument's being entirely financed by private donations, with the permission, but without the participation, of the tsar himself.

The details of Zhukovskii's censorship of "Monument" attracted the attention of many scholars, but only after the 1880 Jubilee. For nearly fifty years the changes that Zhukovskii made went unnoticed and were accepted as the authoritative version of what became one of Pushkin's most famous poems.[4] However, what is striking in the development of the Pushkin Monument is that Zhukovskii censored

Pushkin's allusions to the Bronze Horseman and the Alexander Column in Petersburg. In doing so, he disturbed Pushkin's poetics of allusion defined in chapter 1.

It is hard to say exactly how Zhukovskii understood Pushkin's ambiguous line "Alexandrian Pillar," but the fact that he chose to censor it suggests that he knew that neither Nicholas I nor Benkendorf would approve of the association with the Alexander Column in St Petersburg. Furthermore, Zhukovskii himself had a role to play in this allusion. It was Zhukovskii's speech that noted the connection between the Thunder Rock and the Finnish granite of the Alexander Column in 1834: Zhukovskii's own arguments here could have come back to him as he read "Monument" after having taken Pushkin's death mask and requested that Nicholas I give permission for a monument to Pushkin. He was too personally invested in the political implications of these allusions to miss them completely.[5]

When preparing the poem for the 1841 edition of Pushkin's works, Zhukovskii made two major changes to Pushkin's original to avoid problems with censorship.[6] In the first stanza, Zhukovskii removed "Alexandrian" and replaced it with "Napoleon's" (*Napoleonova stolpa*). In the fourth stanza, Zhukovskii rewrote the first and third lines to avoid the blatant rhyme "to the people/freedom" (*narodu/svobodu*). Along the way he was able to replace Pushkin's reference to "extolling freedom in my harsh age" (*Chto v moi zhestokii vek vosslavil ia svobodu*) with the comparatively toothless "I was useful in the lively charm of my poems" (*Chto prelest'iu zhivoi stikhov ia byl polezen*). Zhukovskii's censorship saved this poem from the destruction threatened by Benkendorf at Pushkin's death, but it also ensured that several generations of readers learned Pushkin's poem without access to the allusions that Zhukovskii's censorship elides.

What exactly did those first generations lose as a result of their naiveté? What did it mean for the poem's reception? The answers to these questions are also the key to understanding how Zhukovskii's censorship contributed to the literalization and visualization of the monument in the decades leading up to Opekushin's final design. In "Monument" there is a delicate balance between readerly and writerly reception. By disrupting the progressive allusions to the Bronze Horseman and the Alexander Column in stanza 1, Zhukovskii cut off the implications for what would come after the Pushkin Monument, how the metamorphosis would continue. But Zhukovskii's censorship obscures more than the aesthetic progression of refinement evoked by the association of the Alexander Column with the "Alexandrian Pillar" in Pushkin's stanza 1. The phrase "Napoleon's Pillar" added by Zhukovskii evokes associations of nationalism and the great achievement of the Russian people in their victory over Napoleon. The aesthetics of Zhukovskii's allusion are such that 1) it simplifies the allusion ("Napoleon's Pillar" is much less ambiguous than "Alexandrian Pillar"); 2) it deletes the notion of aesthetic refinement that is an important part of writerly response (the future poet); and 3) it distorts the theme of reception in the poem by emphasizing nationalism and national greatness as an element of Pushkin's legacy through the addition of "Napoleon's Pillar."

This is not to say that the theme of the people was not already present in Pushkin's "Monument." On the contrary, the reception of the people was an important counterpoint to the future poet. Pushkin did not discount the naive readers of the future. He did not disinherit them from the prospect of his greatness. But their passive reception should contrast with the active response, the refinement, of the future poet as reflected in the allusions evoked by "Alexandrian Pillar."

The delicate balance that Pushkin's allusions strike in the poem "Arion" illustrates the fine line that Pushkin could walk in constructing complex allusions. Sergei Davydov interprets "Arion" as a poem in which Pushkin negotiates between his allegiance to his exiled friends and his subordination to their exiler, Nicholas I. By interpreting the mythological subtext of "Arion" as another way of thinking about Pushkin's relationship to the Decembrist movement, Davydov shows how Pushkin manipulated the allusions for both of his audiences while retaining his honour: "Most important, the poet did not wish to resolve the contradiction between tribute and reproach. In a truly protean – and seemingly disingenuous – manner the 'mysterious singer' is both: Orpheus, singing to his rowing comrades [the Decembrists], and Arion, miraculously saved from the murderous crew [Nicholas I]. As far as Pushkin himself is concerned, he remained an honorable man, selflessly appealing for royal 'mercy for the fallen ones.'"[7]

Stanza four of "Monument" suggests a similar duplicity: Pushkin seems eager to be beloved of the people for the utility that they will see in his poetry (*narodu/svobodu*), while at the same time distancing himself from their evaluation in favour of the more aesthetically informed criteria of stanza two (his future glory is predicated not on this adoration of the people but on the future poet). The phrase "Alexandrian Pillar" thus encodes both of these possibilities: as a monument to the victory over Napoleon, the association of the Alexander Column evokes a sort of nationalism, but it is tempered by the aesthetics of allusion that emphasizes not a national victory but a process of aesthetic refinement. Davydov's insightful reading of how Pushkin manipulates the mythological allusions in "Arion" provides a parallel for the balance Pushkin created between readerly and writerly reception in "Monument," a balance that Zhukovskii's censorship of "Alexandrian Pillar" disrupts to emphasize the people and the nation.[8]

In another passage, Davydov's analysis sheds light on Pushkin's sensitivity to the way others used his poetry. Davydov documents all the ways in which the Decembrists modified Pushkin's poetry to make it even more radical: "Pushkin knew how readily his verses fell prey to causes that he no longer endorsed."[9] Both before and after 14 December 1825, Pushkin's verses circulated in apocryphal versions among seditious segments of the population, to the point that Pushkin, in "An Imaginary Conversation with Alexander I" (1824), writes "every illegal work was ascribed to [him], while every witty concoction to Prince Tsitsianov."[10] The ability of Pushkin's audience to distort his works through alluding to them (creating apocryphal versions of them) thus represents another anxiety for Pushkin about the future of his poetry. His posthumous legacy is largely beyond his control, leading to the dictates of stanza five of "Monument" that move beyond utilitarian receptions of his work to contemplate the aesthetic experience itself as the true purpose of his art. Especially in his censorship of the phrase "harsh age" and the "to the people/freedom" rhyme in stanza four, Zhukovskii anticipates how Pushkin's lines might be read as allusions to his own poetry, to his earlier political verses such as "Liberty" ("Vol'nost'"). On the political level, Zhukovskii censors lines that might appear to criticize the regimes of Alexander and Nicholas and to advocate for the abolition of serfdom. But on an aesthetic level Zhukovskii censors allusions to Pushkin's poetry, allusions to his connections to the Decembrists. Here the sweetness and utility of Pushkin's original formulation ("kind-hearted feelings" balanced by "harsh age" and the poignant rhyme "to the people/freedom") is replaced with sweetness and sweetness ("kind-hearted feelings" mixed with "the living charm of poetry"). The utility that Pushkin seems to allude to is his verse that can be read, and was read by the Decembrists, as undermining the authority of autocracy and the institution of serfdom. Whereas Pushkin leaves himself open to this reading in "Monument" by alluding to this part of his oeuvre, the part for which he himself was exiled, Zhukovskii's censorship erases it.

To put it another way, is Pushkin following or departing from the model of Derzhavin's "Monument," which lists the qualities that Derzhavin wanted to guarantee his fame? Or, more in line with the interpretation of early-twentieth-century critic Mikhail Osipovich Gershenzon, does Pushkin predict what the people will see in his work (as opposed to the aesthetic criteria that Pushkin himself is more concerned with)? To answer these questions, Davydov's reading of the allusions in "Arion" once again becomes useful. When Pushkin's version of stanza four is read against Derzhavin, it seems that Pushkin might be lauding the politically subversive nature of his art in Imperial Russia. When it is read against Pushkin's own poetry that denigrates the naive audience in works like "The Poet and the Crowd" and "Egyptian Nights," it seems as if he is suggesting an ironic distance from the utility of his poetry (valued by the people) and its higher, aesthetic essence. Of course a middle-of-the-road interpretation can incorporate both perspectives (*dolce et utile*), but allusion that can be interpreted in multiple ways, like Pushkin's allusions in "Arion," is the critical idea for understanding the relationship between Pushkin's poem "Monument" and the process that resulted in Opekushin's statue. Both interpretations of stanza four require a willingness to posit allusions to one or more literary texts or historical/biographical events.[11] In both cases, the allusions suggest a problematic relationship to the naive reader as well as to the state, both of which seek to restrict the meaning of the poem by censoring its allusions (Zhukovskii's position that hints of Radishchev and/or the Decembrists must be excised) or restricting them too narrowly (Soviet reception that insisted that concrete allusions to Radishchev and the Decembrists defined interpretation of the entire stanza and, in a sense, the poem).

Pushkin's self-censorship of the Radishchev allusion he considered in place of "my harsh age" helps us to understand the effects of Zhukovskii's censorship of this line. The 1836 reference to Radishchev in an early manuscript version of "Monument" must be understood in the context of Pushkin's politically ambivalent mood, indicated by the 1836 article about Alexander Radishchev that Pushkin wrote for *The Contemporary*. Davydov writes, "While the former ["Monument"] mention is a homage to the bard of 'Liberty,' the latter is an ad hominem invective against the founding father of Russian radicalism."[12] Thus the allusions of stanza two lead into stanza five, which returns to the lofty ideals of aesthetic ecstasy and leaves the quotidian prohibitions of political life behind. Davydov cites "From Pindemonte" (13 July 1836) as proof that Pushkin did not seek the right to rule or interpret law and did not care whether power was held by the tsars or the people. This poem too ends in a series of imperatives to Pushkin himself:

Quite other, better rights are dear to me,
I crave another, better freedom:
Be subject to a king or to a people –
   Who cares? So let them be.

> To no one
> Give account; thyself alone
> Oblige and serve; for power, for a livery
> Bend not your conscience, thoughts, or neck;
> At your own whim roam here and there,
> At nature's divine beauties marvel,
> And tremble joyously in tender ecstasies
> Before the works of art and inspiration.
> – That is happiness! Those are rights …[13]

These lines, also part of the "Stone Island Cycle" and written in the month preceding "Monument," indicate the same aesthetic aim as that in stanza five of "Monument." What is more, the poet is exhorted to roam here and there, admiring nature and other works of art. In his article on the "Easter Triptych," Davydov points out the similarities between "From Pindemonte" and "Monument," including "the proud declaration of independence before the secular powers and the rejection of the *vox Caesaris* and *vox populi* in favor of some supreme power."[14] Perhaps these similarities could be extended to include the notion of allusion itself as a key component of their connection. If in "From Pindemonte," which in Davydov's argument begins the "Stone Island Cycle," the poet is exhorted to experience ecstasy when reading or appreciating works of "art and inspiration," then in "Monument" the movement is away from reception towards the creative production of art worthy of its predecessors: the artistic response that heeds neither praise nor slander but rather seeks to renew, to transform, to bring to new life the monuments of the past.

As this analysis demonstrates, Zhukovskii's censorship destroys the delicate aesthetics of allusion in Pushkin's "Monument." To complete the parallel with "Arion" as Davydov interprets it, Zhukovskii did away with the ambivalence of the Orpheus/Arion allusion so that Pushkin's allusions would not so readily be interpreted as being above the wishful reading of either the Decembrists or Nicholas I. The poem survived because Zhukovskii was able to render it politically innocuous: nationalism and the naive reader are privileged over the more complex and nuanced writerly reception of a poet. But by simplifying Pushkin's aesthetics of allusion for this political purpose, Zhukovskii also paved the way for the trend that during the 1860s and 1870s would result in the literalization and visualization of Pushkin's monument metaphor.

Before turning to analysis of that trend, I need to elucidate one other major factor. Alekseev suggests that there may have been a few individuals who were acquainted with Pushkin's original version of

"Monument" before Zhukovskii censored it for publication in Pushkin's collected works.[15] Even this small, privileged circle tended to think about "Monument" in visual terms: they often referred to the poem as Pushkin's "portrait," an unofficial name for the poem that perhaps originated with Pushkin himself.[16] How exactly the idea of "Monument" as a "portrait" would have played out, however, is something that will never be known. All of these contemporaries of Pushkin died before Nicholas I and before the movement to erect a monument to Pushkin began in earnest. A.I. Turgenev died in 1846, Gogol died in 1852, and Zhukovskii himself died the same year. None of them would be alive to comment on the poem's reception in the competitions for the monument's design, and none would have been around to point out, in the politically more relaxed atmosphere of Alexander II's reforms, that Zhukovskii's censorship would be engraved on the monument instead of Pushkin's original.

Among these early readers, Belinskii (died 1848) also played a critical role in the poem's reception. Where Zhukovskii was the first privately to ask Nicholas I for a monument to Pushkin, presumably *before* reading "Monument," Belinskii was the first to call publicly for a monument to Pushkin. Significantly, Belinskii only knew the poem in Zhukovskii's censored version. Alekseev notes that Belinskii writes about the "Monument" poem in a letter to V.P. Botkin in early 1840, and, based on his paraphrase of the poem, that Belinskii knew the poem in its censored form, without the "Alexandrian Pillar" or other politically volatile references.[17] Perhaps the influence that Zhukovskii had on Belinskii's first reading of "Monument" is the single greatest determining factor in the aesthetics of allusion that would eventually become incarnated in Moscow's urban space in 1880.

The way in which Belinskii concluded his eleventh (and final) article on Pushkin (1846) reflects his understanding of the poem and also influenced later visualizations of the monument that emphasized the popular reception of a naive reader over the writerly reception of a future poet. Belinskii writes, "the time will come when he [Pushkin] will be considered a *classic* poet in Russia, and people will be educated and develop not only their aesthetic but also their moral feelings on his creations … Of course, the time will come when posterity will raise unto him an everlasting monument, but what is so peculiar for us contemporaries is that we still lack a proper edition of his works."[18] As the first printed call for a monument, Belinskii's formulation predicted and legitimized the visualization and literalization of the monument metaphor while also putting off for the future the problem of a wider readership for Pushkin among the uneducated masses.

Transforming the Poem into Statue: The Naive Reader
and Visual Allusion to Literary Art

Literalizing and visualizing the monument metaphor posed an aesthetic problem for the designers of the monument. It was clear from the start that the monument needed to make visual allusion to Pushkin's written works, but the form those allusions should take was the subject of intense aesthetic debate. Likewise, it was obvious that the monument would allude to "Monument," but how other works could or should be visualized was controversial. At the core of this debate was the idea of the people, the naive reader of the future, an idea privileged by the conceptualization of the statue as a literal allusion to the poem "Monument."

It is not a coincidence that visual allusion and the naive reader go together in discussions of the emergence of the final design for the monument to Pushkin. On the one hand, Zhukovskii's various interventions determined this trend. On the other hand, the idea of a public monument itself, especially within the larger debate about Pushkin as a "national poet" that accompanied the movement, emphasizes both visual culture and mass reception.

The literalization of the monument metaphor was an international trend. Just as Pushkin was not the only poet to imitate Horace's *"Exegi monumentum,"* so the literalization of Horace's monument metaphor was in no sense a strictly Russian affair. The tradition of writing Horatian odes was closely connected to the early-nineteenth-century European tradition of erecting monuments to poets.[19] And yet Pushkin's specific version of the poem, Zhukovskii's censorship of Pushkin's innovative allusions to the Russian tradition of monumental statuary, and the specific cultural historical context in which the move to erect a monument to Pushkin took place resulted in a uniquely Russian emphasis on literalism and the naive reader, the people.

The Russian tradition of honouring poets with monuments shows how the theme of the naive reader is a new development. A monument to mid-eighteenth-century poet and scholar Mikhail Lomonosov had been erected in Arkhangelsk in 1829; a monument to late-eighteenth-century poet Gavriil Derzhavin in Kazan' was erected in 1847; and a monument to late-eighteenth- and early-nineteenth-century poet Ivan Krylov appeared in the Summer Garden in Petersburg in 1855, among others.[20] In each of these monuments, aspects of inspiration like a winged genius and a Muse, in addition to visualizations of the author's creations, dominated the sculptor's design. Significantly, however, as imitations of Horace's *"Exegi monumentum,"* neither of the monuments to Lomonosov and Derzhavin emphasized the imitations of Horace written by the poets they memorialized. None of these monuments dealt with the same political implications of the people as a naive reader.

As the first three attempts to design a monument to Pushkin would show, literalizing Pushkin's "Monument" was part and parcel of the drive to erect the monument from the very beginning. By the time the first model was proposed in 1860, the connection between Pushkin's "Monument" and his future literal monument was so organic that it went largely unexamined. The first model was proposed in 1860 by two artists, Nikolai Akimovich Laveretskii and Lev Isaakovich Bakhman.[21] Their proposed monument consisted of two parts: the upper part depicted Pushkin's relationship to the writer of the future and the people, while the Muse looks on in grief at Pushkin's tragic death. The lower part of the monument, the pedestal, was a complicated design that visualized aspects of Pushkin's accomplishments in various genres: lyric poetry (the first two lines of the "Monument" poem); folk tale (a scene from *Ruslan and Liudmila*); drama (a scene from *Boris Godunov*); and a literal fountain, recalling Pushkin's epic, *The Fountain of Bakhchisarai*.

This first model constellated the relationship between allusion and the people that would come to dominate discourse about the design of the Pushkin Monument over the next two decades. First, in the upper part of their model, Laveretskii and Bakhman visually alluded to the three figures that dominate Pushkin's "Monument": the future poet, the people, and the Muse. In future models these figures were discarded in favour of visual allusion to Pushkin's works, which was the primary function of the lower part of the monument with its visual allusions to representative works from four different genres. The literalization and visualization of the "Monument" poem was already in full effect at this early stage, including images of the future poet, the people, and the Muse as well as the inscription of the first two lines of Pushkin's "Monument" on a scroll held by a second figure of the Muse, who is inscribing "to Pushkin" on the grotto that recedes into the pedestal in the front quadrant of the monument. In this way, Laveretskii and Bakhman visualize both the figures of the poem as well as the words themselves: "I have raised to myself a monument not made by hands, / The people's path to it will not become overgrown."

Foreshadowing the debates to come, Laveretskii's and Bakhman's proposal stirred a considerable amount of controversy in the press. Two specific criticisms were levelled: the statue of Pushkin himself appeared to portray him as a "lefty" (*levsha*), and the representation of the people appeared condescending – a child with outstretched arms, as if he were catching a piece of candy thrown to him by the poet. Laveretskii and

Bakhman responded in print, claiming that these criticisms misrepresented their design; but what is telling is that the literal *realism* of the depiction of Pushkin and the figure of the people were the most contentious elements. These concerns overshadow the idea of the future poet, who is almost completely ignored over the next few decades of rigorous debate about the monument.[22]

It is understandable why the people were such a problematic figure in the development of the monument. Historically speaking, the emancipation of the serfs ushered in a new period of concern among the intelligentsia as to what form a fair and just society should take, while at the same time the vast majority of Russia's peasantry were illiterate and did not know of or read Pushkin's works at all.[23] In light of such an obvious *disconnection* between Pushkin and the people in the 1860s, 1870s, and 1880s, just exactly how should the relationship between them be depicted visually? This aspect of Pushkin's poem was understandably hard to take literally, and yet that was the focus of the monument itself: it was to be a monument that included the whole people.

Two more proposals quickly followed Laveretskii's and Bakhman's. In 1862, I.N. Shreder responded to critiques that Laveretskii and Bakhman's model was too allegorical by depicting Pushkin alone, with the Muse slightly above and behind him, and with Pushkin poised to record the words inspired by the lyre in the Muse's hands. While Shreder cut out the problem of visually depicting the future poet and the people altogether, he complicated the pedestal by visually alluding to twice the number of Pushkin's works. Where Laveretskii and Bakhman had divided the pedestal into four parts, Shreder's 1862 design included four depictions in low relief on the four sides of the square pedestal, with four high-relief depictions at each corner of the pedestal.[24]

N.S. Pimenov also proposed a model for the monument in 1862. Like Shreder, Pimenov declined to visually reference the future poet of Pushkin's poem. His composition included two winged figures on opposite sides of the pedestal, just beneath Pushkin's feet: one holds a laurel wreath and an unfurled scroll with the printed text of "Monument"; the other represents the Muse. Pimenov overtly refused to visualize any of Pushkin's specific works ("Monument" being the glaring exception), instead including a plaque on the back side of the monument with a list of Pushkin's works. The focal point of the pedestal, however, returned to an allegorical visualization of the people. A strong male peasant (with Pimenov's own facial features), stands poised with hammer drawn back ready to strike the final blow in the dedication of the monument: "To Pushkin – Russia." Only the period is missing, a detail meant to allegorically address the idea that only in the future, when future generations of the people had learnt to read and appreciate Pushkin's works, would the monument have achieved its full meaning.[25]

None of these proposals was accepted, partly because of a lack of funds, and the movement to erect a monument to Pushkin stalled for the remainder of the decade. These first projects did, however, lay out the aesthetic dilemmas that would determine the final selection of Opekushin's design: Pushkin's poem "Monument" must be visualized in such a way as to allude to Pushkin's works and depict Pushkin himself with a great degree of perceived lifelikeness. But perhaps the most difficult dilemma was how to emphasize Pushkin's future reception among the naive readership of the people, which, during the 1860s, 1870s, and beyond, did not know Pushkin's name, much less his works.

Momentum for a Pushkin Monument was renewed in the late 1860s, largely because of the energy of two brothers, Konstantin and Iakov Grot.[26] Under their direction, the trends established by the models of Laveretskii, Bakhman, Shreder, and Pimenov continued. The people continued to be of primary concern as well as the problem of how to visualize the "Monument" poem in a literal monument vis-à-vis visualizations of Pushkin's other works and the implied audience that both erects and visits the monument.

The setting of the monument, in addition to the design of the monument's internal components, became another factor in the renewal of the drive for a Pushkin Monument.[27] Originally, the monument was supposed to be erected in the relatively private location of the Tsarskoe Selo Lyceum from which Pushkin had graduated. However, the organizing committee decided to move the monument to Moscow, the poet's birthplace and a more widely accessible location. The change of venue dovetailed with the idea of renewing the popular subscription to fund the project. The need to increase contributions from various social classes to finance the project justified the need for a more public venue.[28] The dual emphasis on increasing both the visibility of the monument and the number of donations made the focus on the people even more central to the renewed concept of the monument. The committee reasoned that the more people could look forward to seeing the monument themselves, the more likely they would be to contribute to its financing.[29] Ironically, the logic to move the monument to Moscow thus follows the commercial logic of the bookseller in contrast to that of the poet, who prefers the "dark shelter of solitude" (*temnyi krov uedinen'ia*) to the commercial concerns of earning money by selling his art.[30]

The committee seems to have been guided, however, not by Pushkin's poetry on this matter but by the current cultural political atmosphere. In his 1880 biography *Derzhavin's Life*, Iakov Grot discusses the monument to Derzhavin in Kazan'. Grot documents the order by Nicholas I during the erection of the monument that it must be in the university itself, surrounded by buildings and cut off from public view. From its dedication in 1847 to 1870, the monument to Derzhavin stood in this rather private and out of the way location. In early 1867, however, the Kazan' *zemskoe sobranie* requested permission from Alexander II to move the monument to a location where it would reach a larger audience. Alexander II granted permission and the monument was moved. It is significant that Grot also included responses from the illiterate folk to the monument in its new, more publicly accessible, location. The following conversation was overheard and published by Count Sal'ias in 1872:

> the cast-iron general from the *universtitution*, where they teach students, went to the *thee-ater*, and I heard they stood him up here on the square, because for this monument to such a person, a nobleman and a general, to have to stand in the yard of the *universtitution* just isn't fitting.[31]

Grot adds another anecdote of a similar nature: "From a different perspective, however, cabbies standing by the monument and cursing each other say 'Oh, you idol! What a Derzhavin you are!'"[32]

The idea to move the Derzhavin Monument likely influenced the committee's reasoning to change the venue for Pushkin's Monument in 1870. Given the anecdotes about the Derzhavin Monument, the committee quickly could have become disillusioned as to the effect such a move would have on enlightening the people. In any event, Alexander II approved the proposal to change the location of the monument to Moscow, sanctioning the end of Tverskoi Boulevard on 16 June 1872.[33] The fact that Grot emphasizes the popular reception of the Derzhavin Monument in his 1880 biography suggests how tied together these two events are and the ambivalent status of the people as naive readers in the decades-long process of conceptualizing the Pushkin Monument.

The renewed subscription to finance the monument was successful. By the beginning of 1872, fifty thousand rubles had been collected, and by the beginning of January 1873 the total had reached more than seventy thousand rubles, the majority of what was needed.[34] Along with the financial success of the renewed subscription came the first competition for a design in 1872. Many models were proposed and covered the range of possibilities from a simple statue of Pushkin in various poses to more complex models with elaborate secondary sculptures and visualizations of Pushkin's works in low relief. None satisfied the committee or critics who wrote about the exhibit in the press, in large part for the same reasons the models from the early 1860s had failed to satisfy critics.[35]

One model exemplifies the extent to which the emphasis on the people had overtaken the idea of the future poet in Pushkin's "Monument." In his detailed account of the competitions, Librovich describes a project in which Pushkin stands on a pedestal as if declaiming poetry. At the four corners of the pedestal below stand four figures that represent the Russian folk oral tradition: a songwriter, a *gusli* player, a monk, and an actor. The figures fall silent as they hear Pushkin's voice.[36] In this design, the idea of the folk artist has entirely replaced the literary future poet of Pushkin's poem. Furthermore, it is unclear how the silence of the folk artists is to be interpreted: the image implies, but does not depict, their ability to improvise with Pushkin's word (*chuzhoe slovo*) as the improviser in "Egyptian Nights" is able to.[37]

Four projects emerged from this competition as winners, although they, too, were considered not to be suitable for the final design: Opekushin, Zabello, Shreder, and Bok and Ilenka. Of these, Parmen Petrovich Zabello's model featuring Pushkin alone, standing with hat in his hands, and an understated pedestal was the favourite among art critics.[38] This was a key turning point when it became clear that "less is more" – that the idea of an elaborately sculpted pedestal with visual allusion to many of Pushkin's works was less appealing than a realistic image of the poet himself.

A year later, in 1874, the committee organized a second competition. Out of this round of proposals a similar range of criticisms was found, all pointing to the frustration that, as one critic wrote, all of the models were "stitched together according to one and the same, long since exhausted and hackneyed model."[39] Another critic summed up the problem of the relationship between pedestal and statue:

Even in the best of these projects, a sort of fateful lack of correspondence between the statue and its pedestal was shocking: if the figure of Pushkin was at least tolerable, the pedestal was worthless because of its extreme, so to speak, squalor of design. Likewise (and this was true of most of the projects), if the pedestal seemed in some degree worthy of a monument to a poet-titan (*pevets-ispolin*), the statue itself offended the eye with its – *tranchons le mot* – insignificance, if not downright amusing comedy.[40]

As in the first competition, the committee found the projects of Opekushin, Zabello, and Bok worthy but refrained from choosing one because they felt that the public must also endorse the design. Judging by the reactions published in the press, the public had high expectations that were still unmet. Librovich writes that the public wanted a monument "that must at least in part embody in itself 'all of Pushkin,' must convey the idea, a concept of the poet."[41] The end of the second competition clarified, at least in retrospect, that in order to "embody all of Pushkin," less visual allusion could do more. The projects of Opekushin and Zabello (figure 2.1) in particular were successful in de-emphasizing the pedestal (in some cases leaving it out altogether) in favour of a realistic image of Pushkin's face and careful attention to his pose and clothing.[42]

Still, even as late as 1875 and 1876 elaborate projects from notable sculptors continued to attempt to allude visually to "all of Pushkin." The most famous attempt is a sketch by Mark Matveevich Antokol'skii (figure 2.2), which features a large cliff with Pushkin sitting at the top in a throne-like chair: the "tsar'" of his created worlds. A staircase winds round the cliff and statues of characters from Pushkin's works climb up towards the poet.[43] Tolstoy's famous criticism of the project is found in part 7 of *Anna Karenina*. Levin is at the theatre trying to form an opinion of the fantasia he has just heard, *King Lear on the Steppe*,[44] and expresses his disappointment in the music:

> Levin maintained that the mistake of Wagner and of all his followers lay in trying to make music enter the domain of another art, and that poetry commits the same error when it depicts the features of a face, which should be done by painting, and, as an example of this kind of error, he mentioned a sculptor who carved in marble certain poetic phantasms arising around the pedestal of his statue of a poet. "The sculptor's phantasms so little resembled phantasms that they even clung to a ladder," said Levin.[45]

Levin's comments cut to the core dilemma in designing the future Pushkin Monument. Visual allusion to the poet's work was so embedded in the idea of what the monument should be that it made for easy parody – and yet the pervasiveness of visual allusion as the dominant motif of the monument suggests just how tightly connected the concept of monument, works, and national tradition had become.

Furthermore, Levin's remarks indicate the tension that contemporaries felt in terms of the mixing of media: visual and verbal. On the one hand, figures like Zhukovskii, Belinskii, and later Nadezhda Sokhanskaia advocated for a monument to the poet and apparently saw no contradiction between the medium and Pushkin's own poetry about monuments or his disdain for busts.[46] Even Levin's comments do not delve into Pushkin's own thoughts about his legacy but rather focus on the problematic aesthetic moment of 1) trying to depict a literary character in visual art form, and 2) trying to depict a character out of

2.1 Proposed designs for a Pushkin Monument by I.N. Shreder, P.P. Zabello, and A.M. Opekushin, 1875. In O.B. Mai's 1875 sketches of models by Shreder (left), Zabello (centre), and Opekushin (right), one can see the contrasting approaches to the pose of the statue and the design of the pedestal. Whereas the designs of Zabello and Opekushin are realistic and simple in pose and clothing style, Shreder's still exhibits the temptation to allegorize the figure of Pushkin. Contrasting the pedestals reveals the same trend. Opekushin seems to plan for verbal texts alternating with understated images in low relief, while Zabello leaves the pedestal out altogether. Shreder still clings to the idea of visually depicting multiple characters from Pushkin's works. The image is in the public domain and available on Wikipedia: https://ru.wikipedia.org/wiki/Памятник_А._С. _Пушкину_(Москва,_Пушкинская_площадь)#/media/File:Проекты _памятника_А._С._Пушкину,_1875.jpg (last accessed 3 November 2018).

2.2 Proposed design for a Pushkin Monument by M.M. Antokol'skii, 1875.
Lebedev's 1875 drawing of M.M. Antokol'skii's design for the Pushkin
Monument reveals how persistently some sculptors insisted on alluding to
Pushkin's works visually. The image is in the public domain and
available on Wikipedia: https://ru.wikipedia.org/wiki/Памятник
_А._С._Пушкину_(Москва,_Пушкинская_площадь)#/media/
File:Проекты_памятника_А._С._Пушкину,_1875.jpg
(last accessed 3 November 2018).

the same medium that depicts their creator: how can Pushkin and his
"phantasms," fundamentally different in their essence, be cut from the
same cloth?[47]

The solution to these problems was eventually found in a third competition organized in 1875 to give Opekushin and Zabello the chance
to refine their entries that had been awarded prizes in the second competition.[48] In the end, the design that would appease critics and public alike came in the form of the one-to-one correspondence between

Opekushin's well-executed statue of Pushkin and a pedestal with lines from Pushkin's "Monument" on two of its sides in low relief. Visual allusion was restricted within the design of the monument to the visual/verbal play on Pushkin's own metaphor: verbal poem "Monument" and the visual statue of the monument on Tverskoi Boulevard.

In the final contest alone Opekushin presented six different versions of the Pushkin Monument.[49] What made the eventual model stand out to critics at this final exhibition was the visual likeness of the statue's face to his death mask and to Kiprenskii's portrait.[50] Still later, in 1879, when Opekushin had finished the plaster casts of the monument and put them on public display in his workshop, literalism dominated interpretations of the monument. One reporter remarked on the improbability that Pushkin would walk around with a cloak on but his hat in his hands:

> We must assume that Pushkin probably had the habit, during his walks about the city, of taking off his hat and standing with a bared head. If even this suggestion is accurate, then there is no need to convey other particular details in the monument, in which posterity should see only a personification of the personality of the genius, or an allegorical representation of his works. With that in mind, the figure of Pushkin without a cloak and with a bared head would be more natural.[51]

Instead of reflecting on the nature of Pushkin's works, the critic is instead drawn to pondering quandaries of a less literary nature: if Pushkin didn't need his hat, why did he need his cloak?

The interpretation of Pushkin's Monument as a depiction of him literally walking around Strastnaia Square also inspired the idea that somehow the statue alluded to Pushkin's famous lyric about death and solitude: "Whether I stroll along noisy streets" ("*Brozhu li ia vdol' ulits shumnykh*"). This poem seemed to dominate the reception of Opekushin's statue even more than Pushkin's "Monument," especially in the period of the competition, before it was clear what form the architect Bogomolov's pedestal would take.[52] Already in this early stage of the design (without Bogomolov's pedestal), the statue seemed to blend into its frame because Pushkin's left foot sticks out beyond the pedestal, underscoring the perception of its movement and lifelike presence in the public square.[53]

The design of Bogomolov's pedestal goes without much commentary in contemporary or later scholarly sources. All of the emphasis of contemporary critics, both professional and public, is entirely focused on Opekushin's statue – its pose as both realistic for a public square and in some way reflective of Pushkin's lyric poetry. Likewise, later critics like Librovich (writing in 1890) and scholars like Shmidt, Beli-aev, and Chubukov leave questions about the pedestal unasked.[54] In her recent, thoroughly researched volume on Opekushin's Pushkiniana, Ol'ga Anatol'evna Davydova reproduces several archival documents that provide some evidence as to how little attention was given to the engraving in the various budgets and contracts between Opekushin, Bogomolov, and the committee. In Opekushin's 1875 "approximate budget," amid considerable detail about the size, design, and materials of the pedestal, no mention is made of the poem or how or when it will appear on the pedestal or how much the engraving of the poem would cost.[55] Davydova reproduces some sketches from Opekushin's archive from the last four months of 1875 that indicate a stable concept of the pedestal that resembles the one eventually assembled on Strastnaia Square. But these sketches show the pedestal from the front and not the sides: they provide no insight into Opekushin's thoughts on how the poem should be represented on the pedestal.[56] Similarly, the 1879 contract for the casting of the statue and the decorative elements of the pedestal details the laurel wreath with pen, the four garlands, the chain, and the lampposts according to Bogomolov's design. The only mention made of stone in this contract has to do with a problem with the granite pedestal: it cracked and had to be fixed, so the metallic pieces were to be stored at the factory no later than May of 1880.[57] How did Opekushin and Bogomolov come to agree on the design and its execution? Why did it play such a small role in the final choice of Opekushin's model, given that Opekushin had proposed other poses and had designed several pedestals, none of which resembled the one Bogomolov eventually crafted? When the granite cracked in 1879, did it damage the text of the poem? If so, who fixed it? These questions have remained unasked and unanswered.

In part, the lack of curiosity about the pedestal stems from the extent to which a literal understanding of "Monument" determined discourse about the statue. The lines from the poem that emphasized both the people and the idea of a public monument had appeared in the first proposal by Laveretskii and Bakhman and continued to dominate many other proposals, including Opekushin's own. The fact that the decision to quote "Monument" is overlooked in scholarly analysis of Opekushin's final design suggests the extent to which it was something of an assumption. The literalization and visualization of the monument metaphor had been accepted and was more palatable than the visualization of Pushkin's other works (Antokol'skii's being the most famous example). At the same time, elaborate visualizations of Pushkin's other works attracted the focus of critics away from thoughtful critique of what it might mean to visualize "Monument."

Contemporary focus on the people also explains why the literal understanding of "Monument" did not attract much criticism. Designs for this statue correspond to the age of reforms, between the first public proposal for a monument to Pushkin (1861) and the assassination of Alexander II in 1881. Finalized before Alexander III's reactionary reign, the concept of the people in the development of the statue reflects the idealized vision of the people among both the liberal Westernizers and the populists (*narodniki*). At the same time, it glosses over the more problematic understandings of the people in Pushkin's other poetry and in "Monument" itself.[58] All of the models that included lines from "Monument" on the pedestal took them from stanzas that included a reference to the people: stanza one (the people's path), stanza three (the peoples of the empire), and stanza four (the people who love Pushkin's poetry because it is *"dulce et utile"*).[59] Laveretskii and Bakhman employ the reference to the people from stanza one; Pimenov does not include a written version of any part of the poem, but the peasant who is depicted etching the dedication seems to reference either stanza one or stanza four. A later project by S.I. Ivanov presented after the selection of Opekushin's project in May of 1875 includes an inscription of the first two lines of stanza four in addition to other lines from Pushkin's poetry.[60]

Opekushin's design for the monument was so successful because it avoided the difficulty of alluding to verbal art in visual form by focusing on Pushkin's own monument metaphor, itself a play on the polysemantic meaning of "monument" as either a verbal or visual work of art. Igor Shmidt explains how Opekushin's design stood out from the many other models proposed by other accomplished sculptors because of its straightforward simplicity and realism. All allegorical and complex designs were rejected in favour of the straightforward simplicity of Pushkin's facial expression and clothing. The design of Bogomolov's pedestal reflected a similarly severe approach.[61] The parallel realism of the design of the statue and its pedestal, according to Shmidt, is part of the lasting genius of its design.[62]

Shmidt's commentary hints at a deeper truth. None of the other works that were proposed as part of the Pushkin Monument could have the same sort of relationship to the statue as Pushkin's "Monument" poem. A figure of Onegin, Tat'iana, the Undertaker, or Herman on a Pushkin Monument would not seem to foresee the statue of which it is a part. The relationship between pedestal and statue suggests a new and different kind of monumental allusion – the poem seems to foresee the statue of which it is a part, while the statue alludes to the poem on its pedestal.

Discussion of the Pushkin Monument often focuses on the monument's novelty. In addition to being the first monument to Pushkin, it is the first major national monument to a man of letters. It is also the first to be funded by popular contributions and not the coffers of the state.[63] But it is also the first monument whose central conceit is one of the most important devices in both monumental statuary and literary art: allusion. It is the first monument, at least in Russia, to be conceptualized not only as a memorial to the life of a great person but as the realization of a specific literary text to which it alludes.

This is not to say that complex allusions are new with Opekushin's design. In some way every monument has a unique relationship to allusion. Falconet's Bronze Horseman alludes to the equestrian statue of Marcus Aurelius in Rome and to the figure of St George the dragon slayer, not to mention Petersburg itself, the defining frame of the monument. And yet Falconet cannot allude to a verbal text that seems literally to foresee something along the lines of Falconet's monument. While Peter premeditated the existence of Petersburg, no documentation suggests that he foresaw a monument like Falconet's. Likewise, the Alexander Column alludes to Falconet's Bronze Horseman and the Vendôme Column in Paris as it memorializes Alexander's victory over Napoleon. But here again, the objects to which the Alexander Column alludes cannot in any way be seen to predict the Alexander Column itself: the vector of the allusion extends in only one direction.

What is new in Opekushin's design is the verbal and visual simultaneity: Pushkin's verbal art is realized as a permanent fixture in the built environment of Moscow. A literary text has reached into the future to shape the built environment *in its own image*. Whether or not Pushkin actually envisioned a material monument, and all evidence seems to suggest he didn't, the conceit of Opekushin's design is that the statue mirrors the text etched onto its pedestal, the text of Pushkin's poem.

In its final design, Opekushin found a strict sort of literal allusion between the statue and the pedestal, one that incorporated Pushkin into the cityscape and, as it were, the people, while allusions to the future poet and the Muse, which had appeared in earlier proposals, were deleted. This strict coherence of visual and verbal allusion facilitated other associations with Pushkin's poetry, most notably "Whether I stroll along noisy streets." But this too seemed to play into literal association: the statue seemed to depict Pushkin wandering about Strastnoi Square. Over two long decades of debate about what form the monument should take, Opekushin refined a poetics of allusion to balance its visual and verbal elements: cityscape and Pushkin's poetry about it, statue and pedestal, all of which will be surrounded by an ever larger crowd of the people.

The future poet, a central figure in Pushkin's "Monument," seems to have been erased in Opekushin's final design. During and after the Jubilee, many poets wrote poetry about the monument and many imitated Pushkin's imitations of Horace, but the monument leaves out the second stanza and the future poet, seeming rather to emphasize the reception of the reader, and, more specifically, the naive reader.

However, a future poet soon made himself known.

Allusion in the Performances of Turgenev and Dostoevskii

As people gathered in Moscow in early June of 1880 for the Jubilee Celebration, the Pushkin Monument clearly existed as both a poem and a statue. The statue seemed to visually and literally allude to the verbal poem in such a way as to privilege the reception of the naive readers, "the people," who would literally gather around the Pushkin Monument in the present and for generations to come.

However, the Pushkin Monument was still incomplete. The performances of Pushkin's heirs, the future "poets" he foresaw in the poem, would complete the verbal and visual dimensions of the monument. The aesthetics of allusion in Opekushin's monument informs the speeches of Turgenev and Dostoevskii, both of whom address the Pushkin Monument, allusion, originality and imitation, the future poet, and the naive reader. These speeches more than any other event at the Jubilee reflected the aesthetics of allusion in Pushkin's poem and Opekushin's statue: analysis of them reveals the space of the monument as a rich setting for performing the role of future poet in Pushkin's "Monument." Turgenev's speech came first and primarily treats these themes in the even-handed logical manner of a disciplined critic. Dostoevskii, on the other hand, responded in the role of the future poet himself and, in doing so, established an important third, performative, type of allusion to accompany the visual and verbal balance in Opekushin's monument.

To a remarkable extent, Turgenev and Dostoevskii gave the same speech.[64] Both authors focus on allusion as a defining aspect of Pushkin's work by framing their speeches in terms of imitation and originality. Both authors focus on Pushkin's appropriation of Western models. Both perform one of Pushkin's poems that they deem appropriate for the occasion. Both work with understated allusions to Pushkin's poem "Monument," allusions that, even though understated, resonate all the more loudly for the emphasis the Jubilee placed on Opekushin's monument. Both speeches address the theme of allusion in Opekushin's monument, in particular focusing on the problem of the people as a naive readership and looking to the future poet for aesthetic innovation.

Turgenev's speech begins with the problem of imitation and originality by defining Pushkin as a poet "who unites two fundamental principles: the principle of receptivity and the principle of self-sufficiency."[65] Turgenev defined receptivity and self-sufficiency as national characteristics by which Russians appropriate Western forms.[66] He does not limit the idea of receptivity only to imitation of the West, however. He notes that Pushkin was also receptive to "popular life and popular speech" but that he transformed both Western and folk models through his "self-sufficiency." Turgenev writes, "Pushkin's self-sufficient genius – if one does not consider a few, insignificant exceptions – freed him from both the imitation of European images and the seductions of a falsely popular tone."[67] Rather, Turgenev asserts a few paragraphs later, Pushkin had the ability, "to transmit common truths in original fashion, which is the very essence of poetry, of that poetry in which the ideal and the real are reconciled."[68]

The core of Turgenev's concern with allusion is revealed in his discussion of Pushkin's *The Covetous Knight* and has to do with Pushkin's use of foreign models. He writes, "We must ascribe this ability of his to a mighty power to assimilate foreign forms in an original manner, an ability that foreigners themselves actually concede we possess by their somewhat condescending acknowledgment of our capacity for 'accommodation.'"[69] And it is here that Turgenev finds basis for his argument that Pushkin is a great *Russian* artist: not only in creating great original models, but in creating a literary language. Turgenev argues that one can find "all levels of expressivity encompassed within the language formulated by Pushkin; Russian creativity and Russian receptivity have been gracefully combined in this magnificent language."[70] In Pushkin's works as well as the literary language he used to create them, Turgenev defines Pushkin's genius by this ability to transform, to metamorphose the model, be it Russian or foreign, into something original.

Dostoevskii also builds his speech around the concepts of allusion, originality, and imitation. Like Turgenev's speech and Opekushin's monument, Dostoevskii explores the question of what makes both Pushkin and Russia original. Unlike Turgenev, however, Dostoevskii had cause also to publish an "explanatory note" to his speech in August 1880, just a few months after his performance. The furor that his speech had unleashed provoked Dostoevskii to write this second document that clarifies and elucidates many of his points. For the purpose of this argument, I will cite from the text of the speech as well as the text of his "explanatory note" side by side, since they are mutually illuminating texts. As my argument unfolds, the differences between Dostoevskii's and Turgenev's ideas will become clearer: Dostoevskii may have felt the need to explain the complexity of his thought after the fact of his performance because it was more aesthetically complex and fundamentally reconceptualized allusion to the Pushkin Monument.

Just as allusion is central to Turgenev's speech and Opekushin's design, so it is central to Dostoevskii's thinking about Pushkin. In his "explanatory note" Dostoevskii makes four points when trying to make sense of the initial rapturous reception to his speech and the subsequent discord it evoked in the weeks that followed. In his first and second points, Dostoevskii points out that Aleko, Onegin, and Tat'iana are types, types that would inspire many future allusions that eventually come to be known as the superfluous man and the strong woman. His third point addresses Pushkin's special genius as the ability to fully express and incarnate other nationalities in his works – Pushkin's Italians are really Italians, as opposed to Shakespeare's Othello, who could have been a representative of any national culture and still have been Othello. But there is some ambiguity in Dostoevskii's thinking. It's not *just* that Pushkin can create Italian-like Italians. Dostoevskii formulates the idea like this: "The point is not only in his capacity to respond, but in the amazing completeness with which he assumes alien forms."[71] On this point, Dostoevskii's formula, "amazing completeness with which he [Pushkin] assumes alien forms," differs little from Turgenev's concept of Pushkin's "mighty power to assimilate foreign forms in an original manner." This formulation must also be read in its aesthetic sense, which is perhaps even more fundamental to Dostoevskii's thinking than the national argument. If his first two points discuss Pushkin's ability to inspire future artists, this third point singles out Pushkin's ability to rework, to allude to the works of other national poets in such a way as to rise above imitation and create something new and original.

In the fourth point of his "explanatory note," Dostoevskii's approach diverges from Turgenev's. Turgenev recognizes the idea that Russia accommodates the cultural forms of Western Europe as central to his arguments about Pushkin's place in Russian culture. Dostoevskii, however, conflates the language of imitation and originality with the language of national "genius" or "soul"; this is the closest he comes to laying bare his device of building his discussion of national identity on the foundation of allusion. This question of imitation and originality, after all, is the core antinomy of allusion in which the old is imitated in such a way as to make it new again. When Dostoevskii claims this ability as something inherently Russian (as opposed to an aesthetic device or principle as in Turgenev's speech), he conflates the practice of allusion with a sense of national identity. Why, Dostoevskii rhetorically asks, must Russia not develop organically, according to its own national strength, as opposed to "slavishly" copying or "slavishly imitating Europe"?[72] Just as Pushkin's borrowings were never purely imitative or derivative, so the Russian national character has a unique relationship to what it borrows from other cultures. These four points, made by Dostoevskii with a retrospective look back at his speech, demonstrate how fundamental allusion, imitation, and originality are to Dostoevskii's own understanding of his performance.

In the speech itself, Dostoevskii frequently juxtaposes imitation and originality. He introduces his arguments about Aleko with thoughts on the tension in allusion between imitation and originality. "The accepted view is also that during the first period of his work Pushkin imitated the European poets – Parny, André Chenier and others, particularly Byron."[73] Dostoevskii admits that Pushkin was influenced by these authors, but quickly asserts that even these early poems "were no mere imitations."[74] Before moving on to *Onegin*, Dostoevskii asserts again that "No, this is not an imitation, this is a brilliant poem!" – a uniquely Russian answer to a universal question.[75] When introducing his third point, Dostoevskii again addresses imitation and originality: "Pushkin was always a complete, integrated organism, so to say, an organism bearing all its beginnings within itself and not acquiring them from without. The outside world only aroused in him those things already stored in the depths of his soul."[76] Pushkin's genius was innate: works by others only brought out in Pushkin that which he already perceived independently.

The climax of Dostoevskii's speech also hinges on this claim about imitation and originality.

> Pushkin alone, of all the poets of the world, possesses the quality of embodying himself fully within another nationality. Take his "Scenes from Faust," his "Covetous Knight," his ballad "Once There Lived a Poor Knight." Read "Don Juan" once more, and were it not for Pushkin's name on it you would never guess that it had not been written by a Spaniard. What profound, fantastic images there are in the poem "A Feast in Time of Plague!" But in these fantastic images you hear the genius of England …"[77]

Pushkin is prophetic because of his ability to understand the works of world literature and give expression to them in an original, Russian form. This claim is the justification for all of Dostoevskii's thoughts about Pushkin and his capacity for allusion as an ability that aesthetically reflects a defining feature of the Russian national character that still has to make its most profound contribution on the world stage in the future.

Both Turgenev and Dostoevskii focus on the topic of originality and imitation in part because it had been a major aspect of the discourse about national identity since the 1840s. But on the aesthetic level, both authors recognize the way it resonates with Pushkin's poem "Monument" and in Opekushin's monument, the occasion their speeches address. In "Monument," Pushkin reworks Horace and Horace's Latin imitators, as well as the works of Derzhavin and other Russian poets: the relationship between Bogomolov's pedestal and Opekushin's statue only reinforced the power of "Monument" as a subtext for their speeches.

Turgenev addresses the statue and the poem in a comparatively straightforward way. He states as much in the first sentence of his speech: "We have assembled to hail the erection of a monument to Pushkin, a monument to which all of educated Russia has contributed."[78] His choice to declaim Pushkin's 1830 lyric "To the Poet," along with his emphasis on the future poet and the problems associated with the naive readership of the people (themes to which I will return shortly) all build on the text of "Monument" and its unique relationship to Opekushin's statue and the surrounding urban environment.

Dostoevskii alludes to Pushkin's "Monument" in a more oblique manner. Where Turgenev begins with the statement of the obvious ("we have assembled to hail the erection of a monument"), Dostoevskii begins with a claim that Pushkin is a "prophetic" phenomenon. At first glance, this may not seem to relate to "Monument" at all. But Dostoevskii's claim is supported by the monument: Pushkin's poem "Monument" seems to have predicted the material form of Opekushin's monument. Likewise, while Dostoevskii does not make it explicit, Pushkin's sculpture metaphor itself plays a role in Dostoevskii's speech. Dostoevskii describes Pushkin's characters as monumental sculptures: "they stand before us as if carved in stone ... this majestic Russian image Pushkin found in the Russian land, brought forth and sculpted, and whose indisputable, humble, and majestic spiritual beauty has now been placed before us forever ..."[79] Surely this idea of Pushkin's works as sculptures eternally before the gaze of Russia carries the connotations of Opekushin's monument with its allusion to Pushkin's poem.

Turgenev and Dostoevskii also differ over the meaning of "the people" with regard to the Pushkin Monument. Turgenev's more direct critical approach tackles the problem head on. In his first paragraph he emphasizes the fact that "all of *educated* Russia has contributed" to the Pushkin Monument.[80] He spends several paragraphs justifying how Pushkin can be a national poet even though the "common people" do not read him.[81] Finally, he concludes his speech on the relationship of the "children of our common people, who do not now read our poet" to "this noble bronze face erected in the very heart of the ancient capital." Comparing Pushkin to Shakespeare, he writes that "every person who has newly learned to read inevitably becomes his reader" and ends with a comment he overheard from "some youthful, unintentionally lisping lips: 'This is a monument to a teacher!'"[82] For Turgenev, Opekushin's monument thus becomes a sort of educational shrine for the naive reader, the future children of the illiterate people, newly awakened to Pushkin's aesthetic feat. Turgenev conceptualized the relationship between the naive reader and the monument in much the same way as the later Soviet art historian Igor Shmidt: future generations will gather around the Pushkin Monument and "prove" that they are a more educated, freer people.[83] In their minds, the monument not only alludes to Pushkin's great past but becomes a meeting place for the newly initiated aesthetic minds of the future.

Turgenev's emphasis in his speech on Pushkin as the great teacher of future generations of readers among the people reflects his unsuccessful attempt to convince Tolstoy to participate in the Jubilee. Where Turgenev insists on a future readership for Pushkin among the people, Tolstoy distinguished between literature for an educated readership and literature for peasants. Pushkin belonged firmly in the first category, the primary reason Tolstoy refused to attend the 1880 Celebration.[84] On this note, Turgenev gave a balanced and careful response that recognized the current relationship between illiterate Russia and Pushkin but that reasonably looked to a future in which high art would be accessible to an increasingly large segment of the nation.

Dostoevskii's version of the dynamic between Pushkin and the people is less rational and harder to accept. In the speech he writes:

> No, I will say positively that there has not been a poet so able to respond to the whole world as Pushkin; and the point is not only in this ability to respond but in its astounding depth and in his ability to infuse his spirit into the spirit of other nations, something that was almost complete and so was marvelous as well, because nowhere in any other poet anywhere in the world has such a phenomenon been repeated. This we find only in Pushkin, and in this sense, I repeat, he is unprecedented and, in my view, prophetic, for ... it was just here that his national Russian strength

was most fully expressed, that the national spirit of his poetry was expressed, the national spirit as it will develop in the future, the national spirit of our future, already concealed within our present and expressed prophetically.[85]

Dostoevskii repeats this idea in his "explanatory note" that prefaced the publication of the speech in *A Writer's Diary*: "This capacity [to assume the form of the genius of other nations] is an altogether Russian one, a national one, and Pushkin merely shares it with our entire People; and, like a perfect artist, he is also the most perfect expression of this capacity, at least in his work, the work of an artist. Our People do bear in their souls this aptitude for responding to the entire world and for universal reconciliation ..."[86]

In both his later "explanatory note" and his oral performance, Dostoevskii posits Pushkin's capacity for the aesthetic device of allusion, the device by which imitation metamorphoses into originality, as the most national – the most Russian – feature of his work. It is nothing less than a prophecy of the future of the Russian national spirit (*narodnost'*). Whereas Turgenev sees the people as future readers of Pushkin's poetry, Dostoevskii sees Pushkin's aesthetic brilliance as the representation of the collective people – not his future readers, but his co-nationals. Pushkin, whose defining characteristic as a poet is the ability to perfectly balance the antinomy of imitation and originality in allusion, is the most "perfect" aesthetic expression of the defining national character trait of the people. In this, the Russian people have the ability to "save" Europe by taking Western ideas and giving them new, messianic, Russian expression.

The most striking difference in the aesthetics of the two speeches emerges when they are viewed as performances. The future poet on whom Pushkin predicates his future glory in "Monument" is recognized by both to be a significant figure in the Celebration, but they respond to it differently. Turgenev offers hardly more thought on the future poet than many of the sculptors who proposed models during the competitions leading to Opekushin's final victory. Framing his sentence in the debate about whether or not Pushkin was truly Russia's national poet, he writes:

But, having found its natural boundaries, poetry has become forever strong. Under the influence of an old but not yet outmoded teacher – we firmly believe this – the realm of art, the artistic enterprise itself, will stride forth again in all its might, and – who knows? Perhaps a new, still unknown, select individual will surpass his teacher and will completely

deserve the label of national-universal poet that we do not permit our-
selves to bestow upon Pushkin, although we do not dare to deprive him
of it, either.[87]

Turgenev recognizes Pushkin's role in the future of Russian *belles-
lettres*, but sees here little more than perhaps a student who outdoes his
teacher.

Turgenev also hints at the future poet in his choice of poem to recite
during his speech. Reciting Pushkin's poetry during the Celebration was
a consistent item on the agenda, and Turgenev's choice of "To the Poet"
indicates the tone of Turgenev's speech and in general recalls the fifth
stanza of Pushkin's "Monument" with its imperatives to ignore both
praise and slander and the judgment of fools and the ignorant crowd.
Turgenev, like many of his Soviet heirs, is careful to correct Pushkin's
judgment of the people, suggesting that even his consideration of the
role of the future poet is overshadowed by his concern for establishing
the legitimacy of future naive readers. Turgenev writes, "Pushkin was
not altogether correct here, though, especially in relation to the subsequent generation. The causes of this loss of popularity lay neither in 'the
judgment of fools' nor in 'the laughter of the cold crowd.' Those causes
lay deeper. They are sufficiently well known; we need only mention
them to you."[88] Turgenev here is hinting at the age of reforms, in the
transition from a "literary epoch to a political one."[89]

Dostoevskii's approach to this future poet is much more subtle and it
holds the key, not only to why his speech was greeted with such enthusiasm while Turgenev's evoked only a mediocre response, but also to
understanding how the aesthetics of allusion in the Pushkin Monument
develops in the future. Dostoevskii's vision of the future poet firmly
establishes a performative dimension to the visual and verbal aesthetics
of Opekushin's monument, a feat that earns him the role of that future
poet himself.[90]

One way in which Dostoevskii engages with the idea of the future
poet as laid out in "Monument" is by listing all the Pechorins, Chi-
chikovs, Rudins, Lavretskiis, and Bolkonskiis "and a host of others
whose appearance itself testified to the truth of the idea first set forth
by Pushkin."[91] The idea of Pushkin's second stanza is that he will not
wholly die as long as at least one poet, one aesthetic creator who has
the ability to respond to Pushkin's works as only a poet can, is alive. In
Dostoevskii's "explanatory note," these characters exist as proof that
Pushkin has not wholly died, as proof of his glory, which Dostoevskii
is sure to affirm: "We owe him a great tribute."[92] Conspicuously, Dostoevskii leaves out his own characters, who certainly belong in this very

list. Rather than place himself in the list of Pushkin's imitators, he subtly adds his own language of "native soil" (*pochva*) and his Slavophile interpretation. Pushkin, Dostoevskii claims, is great not only for having pointed out the problem of post-Petrine Russia in the likes of Aleko and Onegin, but also for having searched out the comfort (*uteshenie*) "in our native soil" (*v pochve nashei*).[93]

Dostoevskii states this same idea in a different way in the speech itself. He writes:

> Our great poet left all these treasures of art and artistic vision as signposts for the artists who came after him and for those who would toil in the same fields as he. One can positively state that had Pushkin not existed neither would the talented people who came after him.[94]

Pushkin has laid the groundwork for Dostoevskii's contemporaries and future generations of writers, but, as Dostoevskii draws to the end of his speech it is clear that the work Pushkin started is not finished.

Not only is Pushkin the inspiration for future poets, his early death has left a significant task for the nation: "Pushkin died in the full flower of his creative development, and unquestionably he took some great secret with him to his grave. And so now we must puzzle out this secret without him."[95] Dostoevskii inserts himself into this conversation about the future of Pushkin's works, allusions to many of which dominate Dostoevskii's own masterpieces. But this, too, is a "prophecy" that has been fulfilled and to which Dostoevskii, the Pushkin Monument, and the whole Jubilee attest: Pushkin lives because since his death there have been a great many more than just one lone, single "sublunar" poet.[96]

Dostoevskii's Innovation: Allusion, Urban Space, and Performance

The true brilliance of Dostoevskii's speech is not so much that he elaborates on the role of the future poet but that he performs that role himself by making original use of the possible dimensions of allusion at his disposal. One of the underlying allusions that informs Dostoevskii's speech is facilitated by the venue in which he performs it. The speech was given in the Hall of Columns of the Assembly of the Nobility (*Blagorodnoe sobranie*) in Moscow, near the Bol'shoi theatre.[97] It cannot be a coincidence that Dostoevskii gave his "Pushkin Speech" in the same hall in which Pushkin depicts Tat'iana's first meeting with her future husband, the old Russian general, even as she daydreamed wistfully of her beloved countryside, blind to the vulgarity of the ball all around her but mesmerized by the village scenery "where *he* appeared to her."[98] When Dostoevskii reflects on Tat'iana's love for the Westernized Evgenii and her loyalty to the Russian general as a prophetic image of the Russian soul, the prophetic nature of Dostoevskii's argument about Western- izers and Slavophiles is reinforced by the fact that they are pronounced in the same room in which Tat'iana sees her future, torn between a love for the West and her innate Russian originality. At the very moment she pines for her young and dashing Evgenii, the fat general is unable to take his eyes off of her, a fact quickly noticed by her aunts.[99]

Some evidence suggests that such an obscure allusion on Dosto- evskii's part was intentional and not just coincidental. Leaving aside the fact that the author of the "Pushkin Speech" is also the author of *Crime and Punishment* with its deep sensitivity to the allusions facilitated by urban space, Dostoevskii paraphrased a key passage connected to the ball in *Eugene Onegin* held at the Assembly of the Nobility. Earlier in his speech, when discussing Tat'iana, Dostoevskii remarks that perhaps it would have been better if Pushkin had named the poem for Tat'iana instead of Onegin.[100] Pushkin ends the ball scene with a similar refer- ence to the tension between Onegin and Tat'iana as main characters in the poem: "But here we must congratulate my dear Tat'iana with her victory and turn our path in a different direction, so as not to forget about whom I sing ..."[101] When Dostoevskii mimics Pushkin's narrator by suggesting that *Evgenii Onegin* could have been named for Tat'iana, he also hints at the parallel between the setting of his performance and Tat'iana's conquest of the fat general.[102]

Dostoevskii's sensitivity to the cultural history of the venue with regard to *Eugene Onegin* mirrors his sensitivity to the cultural moment in which he performed the speech. The conflict in Tat'iana between her receptivity to Onegin and the West and her loyalty to Russia and the general that Dostoevskii extols in his speech, a conflict that she over- comes, to some observers seemed to have been overcome in a broader sense by Dostoevskii's speech in the very same room. From this per- spective, Dostoevskii's performance of his speech about Tat'iana in the setting of the Jubilee fulfils the prophetic potential with which Pushkin endowed her.

The extent to which Dostoevskii is interested in allusion is also dem- onstrated by his primary claim that Pushkin is a "prophetic manifesta- tion," an assertion that is framed as an allusion to Gogol. Dostoevskii begins his speech with Gogol's claim that "Pushkin is an extraordinary and, perhaps, unique manifestation of the Russian spirit," to which he quickly adds that Pushkin is also a "prophetic one."[103] The aesthetics of Opekushin's monument, its very design lending itself to interpretation as a prophecy fulfilled, underscores Dostoevskii's claim while at the same time laying the groundwork for his spatial allusion to the ballroom in which Tat'iana is presented with her fateful choice. Pushkin's monument metaphor is "fulfilled" in the Pushkin Monument: Tat'iana's meaning is fulfilled (at least temporarily) by the reaction to Dostoevskii's speech in the Hall of Columns at the Assembly of the Nobility when Slavophiles and Westernizers embraced and reconciled their differences.

Later that evening Dostoevskii's repeated performances of Pushkin's poem "The Prophet" cement the connection. "The Prophet," rarely mentioned during the Celebration before Dostoevskii's speech, becomes attached to the Pushkin Monument and serves as the emotional high point of the entire Celebration, reinforcing Opekushin's literal interpretation of Pushkin's poem as a *realized allusion*, however problematic such an interpretation may seem in retrospect. As Marcus Levitt writes,

> The excitement [from Dostoevskii's speech] carried over into the evening's literary-musical presentation, which brought the celebration to a close. Dostoevsky replaced Turgenev as favorite and was called out for several encores, at which he recited Pushkin's poem "The Prophet" twice by heart. The evening again concluded with an "apotheosis" of Pushkin, only this time Turgenev ceded to Dostoevsky the honor of crowning Pushkin's bust.[104]

The laurel wreath that Pushkin refuses to demand in "Monument" is the choice for repeatedly honouring the poet after his death. The 1880 celebration made it clear that Pushkin's works were raised to a new level, one that he did not claim for himself but left in the hands of future poets.

An important aspect of Dostoevskii's vision of Pushkin as prophetic is his understanding of the meaning of Pentecost for the artist-prophet. Defining the meaning of Pentecost in the "Pushkin Speech," Marcus Levitt writes, "The artist-apostle possesses a superior ability to comprehend the beautiful, the miraculous nature of existence, and incorporate it into his art … Such artist-prophets are able to understand and express the 'future Word' latent in the beauty of the world – to envisage, in other words, the Second Coming."[105] Underlying Dostoevskii's sense in which Pushkin is a "prophetic manifestation" is the way he reimagines the poetic transformation of reality in successive generations of poets, the "future word," as an aesthetics of allusion that harks back to the theme of renewal through poetic metamorphosis in "Monument."

Dostoevskii's "Future Word"

Dostoevskii's "Pushkin Speech" complemented Opekushin's monument in a way that Turgenev's speech could not. To contemporary observers of the 1880 Jubilee this was evident. Participants saw a fundamental connection between the unveiling of Opekushin's monument and the ecstatic reception of Dostoevskii's famous speech. Consider the following quotation from the memoirs of N.N. Strakhov, a key participant in the Jubilee:

> The first moment of ecstasy came, as it seems to me, when we went out into the Square [from the church of the Strastnoi Monastery, where the *panakhida* was served], when the canvas was pulled off from the statue and we, to the sounds of the music, set off to lay our wreaths at the base of the monument ... Beginning with this short ceremony, everyone was overcome with a joyful, celebratory mood that didn't cease for three whole days ... The general impression of the event was extremely enthralling and joyful. Many people said to me, that there were minutes, when they could hardly hold back or couldn't hold back their tears. This joy grew and grew ... and only on the third day did it achieve its greatest tension of complete ecstasy.[106]

The laying of wreaths at the monument on the first day and the repeated crowning of Pushkin's bust with laurels after Dostoevskii's emotional performances of "The Prophet" are the beginning and ending points in an arc of events that have become foundational to many different aspects of the study of Russian culture.[107]

Observers of the Jubilee tried to define the reasons why Dostoevskii's speech was such an "event." Why was his performance the climactic conclusion of the opening ceremony? Why was there such a profound reaction to his speech in the moment, a reaction that quickly dissipated in the following months? Strakhov explained the elation as the culmination of a generally ecstatic Jubilee. Marcus Levitt suggests that the success of *The Brothers Karamazov* and *Diary of a Writer* "had done much to bolster [Dostoevskii's] reputation among the general reading public," and contributed to the speech's success.[108] Others consider the speech the beginning of the Pushkin myth.[109] Solov'ev interpreted this unique moment of ecstasy as Dostoevskii's broadcasting of an impossibly utopian vision of Russian universality that resonated with his audience, but only because it ignored the way in which Dostoevskii's deeply offensive thoughts about non-Russian nationalities and religions expressed in other works contradict the essence of the universality he proclaimed in the "Pushkin Speech."[110]

In pointing out the contradictions in Dostoevskii's thought, Solov'ev also makes the insightful observation that Dostoevskii "was more of an artist and a visionary than a strictly logical consistent thinker."[111] Both Kanevskaia and Levitt have also commented on the rhetorical and aesthetic brilliance of Dostoevsvkii's speech as contributing factors to its legendary success.[112] Levitt shows how Dostoevskii's use of paradox disarms and persuades his imagined Westernizer listener to accept contradictory ideas. For example, Russia's economic backwardness actually makes her more acceptable as a bearer of universal truth.[113] A similar use of paradox allows Dostoevskii to assert, according to Levitt, that "Russia's 'imitativeness' and lack of identity, which Russians had bemoaned since the start of the century, itself emerges as the essence of her greatness," a greatness with a particularly Dostoevskian sort of messianism.[114]

The aesthetics of the Pushkin Monument, however, suggest a complementary aesthetic explanation for the unique and unrepeated moment of ecstasy created by Dostoevskii's speech. On the surface Dostoevskii's rhetorical devices were meant to convince, and, for a short time, were remarkably successful. But they were so successful, at least in part, because Dostoevskii's aesthetics of allusion in the "Pushkin Speech" operated independently of his arguments about Russian national identity and the Slavophile/Westernizer debate. Dostoevskii's performance resonated with the interaction of poem and statue in Opekushin's Pushkin Monument, and this performance, more than his thoughts on Russian universality or Pushkin's greatness, is what becomes Dostoevskii's unique "future word."[115]

Gary Saul Morson underscores the aesthetic dimensions of Dostoevskii's inclusion of the Pushkin Speech in Dostoevskii's *Writer's Diary*. He argues that Dostoevskii presented the speech as a plot composed of three incidents: the speech itself, the immediate and overwhelmingly positive reception of the speech, and the inevitable disappointment that came later. For Morson, Dostoevskii's presentation of these events repeated the "drama of utopian hope and disappointment" that characterized Dostoevskii's work in 1877 about the Eastern War.[116] Taken together with Dostoevskii's claims of *not* being a critic, it makes sense to read him as a poet more than a thinker. He created a story with a plot that unfolds in a setting and in conversation with a whole host of literary precedents and antecedents, one of the recurring themes of the speech. In renewing Pushkin's "Monument" through Opekushin's monument and his own performance of the "Pushkin Speech," Dostoevskii achieved a new poetic word, but soon after recognized that his word would also be doomed to petrification and slander at the hands of a hostile crowd.

Dostoevskii intuitively perceived the aesthetics of allusion in Opekushin's design and exploited it in his speech – an aesthetics of allusion that combined the verbal, visual, and performative potential of the monument in a fundamentally new way. As the culmination of the dedication of the Pushkin Monument, Dostoevskii's performance was a profound aesthetic event that cemented the existence of the Pushkin Monument as a poem, a statue, *and* a performative space. In other words, Dostoevskii's attempt at prophecy, if judged by his own standard of the speech as the reconciliation of Westernizers and Slavophiles, cannot be considered an "event" because it did not happen. But that was the rational, logical side of his argument. The form of his performance did prophesy a new kind of allusion, a multidimensional allusion that relies on the verbal, visual, and performative potential of urban space to collect mutually referential texts over time. Dostoevskii's prophetic exploitation of the Pushkin Monument finds future realization in the works of many future poets who develop the aesthetics of allusion in Pushkin Square in fascinating ways, a topic that unfolds in the next chapter.

Chapter Three

Bulgakov's *Master and Margarita*: Crisis of the Future Poet (1880–1937)

The public appearance of Alexander Opekushin's statue and Fedor Dostoevskii's performance at the dedication of the Pushkin Monument in 1880 marked a crucial moment in the cultural history of the Pushkin Monument: poem, statue, and performance coalesced as defining elements of the allusions by which future poets might bring it to new life. Up to this point, our task has been to understand how this happened. First, we explored Pushkin's metapoetics of reception in the poem "Monument" to establish a new interpretation of the poem. The poem "Monument" supplies the concepts that continue to dominate the cultural history of the Pushkin Monument: the metaphor of the lifelike statue, allusion, a future poet, and naive readers. As we have seen, Pushkin's thinking about future reception illuminates both the history of the statue and Dostoevskii's key performance of the role of a future poet.

Telling the story of how the Pushkin Monument came to facilitate this new sort of verbal, visual, and performative allusion required relying heavily on the scholarship of Russian, Soviet, and Western Pushkinists: Librovich, Gershenzon, Alekseev, Bondi, Chubukov, Levitt, Bethea, Proskurin, and Sandler, among others. In turning to the twentieth century, the cultural history of the Pushkin Monument poses a different task and a different set of primary and scholarly sources. The future of the Pushkin Monument is not so much concerned with what Pushkin's thoughts, creative process, and biography mean. These are the narratives that gave form to the Pushkin Monument in Moscow. The future of its story has to do with what "future poets" have done with that form: how the Pushkin Monument as poem, statue, and performance has been transformed in the subjective visions of creative individuals. Interpreting their innovative approaches to the Pushkin Monument tells us not so much how poem, statue, and performance came to be, but rather how allusions to the Pushkin Monument have shaped larger questions of culture, literacy, tradition, and the purposes of art.

One of the first significant transformations of the Pushkin Monument was to conflate the image of the future poet with the image of the future naive reader. Through this conflation, allusions to the Pushkin Monument highlighted the crisis of the future poet in Soviet culture. If a future poet does not know Pushkin's works, how can he allude to them? For that story, we turn to one of the great cult novels of the twentieth century: Mikhail Afanas'evich Bulgakov's "sunset novel," *Master and Margarita* (written 1928–40).

Allusion is a central trope in *Master and Margarita*. From the first scene in Patriarch's Ponds to the closing lines of the novel, sophisticated allusions to world culture, the nineteenth-century literary tradition in Russia, and Soviet culture of the 1920s and 1930s continue to provoke scholarly inquiry. But *Master and Margarita* also in many ways belongs to the "Monument" genre. It is Bulgakov's last and greatest novel, a work that does not stand apart from but rather sums up his whole oeuvre, and in this it has much in common with Pushkin's "Monument."

The parallels do not end there, however. Bulgakov makes specific allusion to the Pushkin Monument as poem, statue, and performative space in writing *Master and Margarita* and in doing so reflects the transformation of the monument at a critical juncture of Russian cultural history. As a synthesis of several cultural trends, Bulgakov's *Master and Margarita* represents a high point in allusions to the interrelated verbal, visual, and performative dimensions of the Pushkin Monument. Through the monument, Bulgakov employs a unique type of spatial allusion that represents a different attitude to allusion as well as a new take on the monument itself. Unlike Dostoevskii, or the poets Vladimir Maiakovskii and Marina Tsvetaeva who were Bulgakov's contemporaries, Bulgakov does not define himself as the future poet in the presence of the Pushkin Monument. Rather, he draws on the Pushkin Monument as a subtext to explore the implications of a future naive poet, conflating the traditional figures of future poet and naive reader.

Bulgakov's innovative allusions to the Pushkin Monument shape interpretation of the entire novel. In posing this new question – what if the future poet *is* a naive reader? – Bulgakov's transformation of the Pushkin Monument develops two major themes in *Master and Margarita*. Firstly, Bulgakov places Pushkin at the centre of the question of how art should be created and consumed in Soviet culture. Secondly, allusions to the monument provide a subtext that casts the poet-turned-professor, Ivan Bezdomnyi/Ivan Ponyrev, as a naive future poet. Interpretations of Bezdomnyi/Ponyrev, the protagonist who unites all of the disparate elements of the novel from beginning to end, continue to clash over his status as disciple and artist. Bulgakov's engagement with the tradition of performing the role of future artist and contemplating the future of the naive reader at the Pushkin Monument sheds new light on the enigma of Bezdomnyi/Ponyrev and the future of the master's novel. The cult of Pushkin in Russia reached a new height at the same time that mass literacy started to be realized – but this did not seem to indicate a positive future for Russian literature. On the contrary, as Bulgakov's novel suggests, the future reception of the Russian literary tradition seemed all the more imperilled.

1880–1937: The Background for Bulgakov's Conflation of Future Poet and Naive Reader

After its dedication in 1880, the Pushkin Monument receded to the background as public celebrations of the poet were shaped more by the 1880 Jubilee than by the aesthetics of the monument itself. Organizers emphasized not the innovation of a future poet but the education of the illiterate masses. Pushkin's immense popularity among an increasingly literate public was evident in the historic sales of his works in 1887, when the fifty-year copyright on his works expired.[1] The state capitalized on this popularity in 1899, organizing a celebration of the 100th anniversary of Pushkin's birth on a truly massive scale. The event reveals a collective notion of Pushkin as a national institution with special meaning for the acculturation of newly literate readers and a convenient banner for national identity, leaving little room for the transformative power of a future poet.[2] The crude manipulation of Pushkin's works and legacy for financial or ideological gain distressed the intelligentsia who observed the 1899 celebration, which would forge the template for Soviet appropriation of Pushkin as a national poet. While the late nineteenth century saw many foundational scholarly studies of Pushkin's life and works, the monument itself ceased to be a focus of aesthetic innovation. Much to the contrary, it entered the domain of cliché as busts of and monuments to Pushkin proliferated.

Only after the Revolution and Civil War did poets re-enter the space of the monument and anniversary commemoration in an innovative capacity. The 1920s saw important commemorations in 1921 and 1924 that emphasized the ambivalence of the monument metaphor as something simultaneously both public and private. Key poets and members of the literati gathered for a low-key, private event in Petrograd in 1921 to commemorate the eighty-fourth anniversary of Pushkin's death and to emphasize their intellectual and aesthetic links to pre-revolutionary attitudes towards Pushkin. Their thoughts turned to Dostoevskii's 1880 "Pushkin Speech," in part because 1921 was also the centennial of Dostoevskii's birth.[3] In significant speeches by the poets Vladislav Khodasevich and Alexander Blok, the monument metaphor is perceived negatively – as a thing belonging to the masses in contrast to their private, poetic relationship to his works.[4]

Khodasevich played a key role, both as an observer and as a participant. In his description of Blok's speech and later in "The Swaying Tripod," Khodasevich articulates the unique role of the future poet in a time of growing gloom. As Sandler writes,

> The similarity [between Blok and Pushkin] recalls the premise of "The Swaying Tripod," that to speak truthfully of Pushkin, one must be like him. Pushkin is not, then, merely a password to be called out in the dark, but also a poet to emulate. For all the pessimism of Khodasevich's speech, he believes that modern poets and critics may yet resemble Pushkin. Subsequent anniversary events may not state this premise so categorically, but they will live out its logic. Khodasevich's passionate, self-referential words forewarn of the inclination of twentieth-century poets to inform their poems and essays about Pushkin with their own autobiographies.[5]

Indeed, throughout the 1920s, the Pushkin Monument became a meeting place for poetic minds as they debated the form revolutionary art should take in Soviet society. The imagists staged a performance in Pushkin Square described by Sergei Esenin in his autobiographies from 1922 and 1923. Claiming a shortage of paper as their inspiration, Esenin and his imagist colleagues wrote blasphemous verses on the walls of Strastnoi Monastery, and the artist Did-Lado hung a sign around Pushkin's neck that read, "I'm with the imagists."[6] Esenin wrote several poems on the theme of a bronze monument of his own. After his suicide in 1925 his body was returned to Moscow for burial. The coffin was carried around the Pushkin Monument in posthumous recognition of his poetic achievements.[7]

The imagists were not alone in exploiting the poetic nuance of Pushkin Square: their ideological opponents, the futurists, also explored what the Pushkin Monument could mean for the art of the future. In 1924, in response to the 125th anniversary of Pushkin's birth, Maiakovskii wrote "Jubilee," a now famous poem in which he invites the bronze statue of Pushkin on a night-time tour of Moscow. The two poets, Maiakovskii and Pushkin, consider their poetic fates as well as the poor quality of Soviet poetry in the 1920s. Again in 1928, Maiakovskii wrote "A Joke Resembling the Truth," a bit of agitational propaganda advocating for the destruction of Strastnoi Monastery so that Pushkin could have a more direct conversation with the *Izvestiia* newspaper. The paper's administrative office was in the Pushkin Monument's line of sight, but was obscured by the bell tower of Strastnoi Monastery.

Other performances at the Pushkin Monument were of a less publicized nature. Bulgakov himself, still something of a newcomer to Moscow in the early 1920s, participated in "The Green Lamp," a literary group that met to read and discuss their writings, frequently continuing their conversations in a more free and expressive manner late at night around the Pushkin Monument.[8] The group loved Pushkin and the classics, representing yet another aesthetic conviction that clashed with those of both the imagists and the futurists, but its members nonetheless found a similar value in performing their roles as writers in the space of the Pushkin Monument.

The 1937 Jubilee was the culmination of a process that in many ways put an end to Pushkin Square as a site of public contestation. The architectural symbol of this development was the destruction of Strastnoi Monastery, seemingly once and for all resolving the dilemma for Soviets caused by the Pushkin Monument's apparent contemplation of Orthodoxy. Official ideology adopted Pushkin as the model revolutionary poet. In official interpretation, the Pushkin Monument was a fitting memorial to the political and social utility of a poet's life and works, a secular icon of a model to be emulated.[9] The idea of the people as naive readers undercut official discourse, which sought to make Pushkin and art accessible to all.[10] The Jubilee was a forum in which the state asserted its authority to define both Pushkin and his readership, an ever-growing percentage of the newly literate "people." Stephanie Sandler notes the emphasis in 1937 on the new readership: "powerful contrasts were drawn between average Russians in 1837, enserfed and illiterate, and those of 1937, described as proud workers able to read Pushkin for themselves."[11] Accordingly, distinctions between a naive reader and a future poet at the foot of the Pushkin Monument disappeared. How could a Soviet citizen reading Pushkin be naive?[12]

Behind the scenes, the situation was much more complex. Marina Tsvetaeva's essay "My Pushkin" was written in 1937 and deserves mention here, not as a source for Bulgakov's allusions, but rather as contextual evidence for Bulgakov's innovation.[13] Like Esenin, Maiakovskii, and many other poets before them, Tsvetaeva recounts her personal interaction with the monument by way of interpreting the interplay between poem, statue, and performative space.[14] In contrast to Maiakovskii, Tsvetaeva plays on the dynamic between the naive reader and the future poet generated by the Pushkin Monument to describe her own poetic biography. She is not the accomplished poet proudly claiming a place next to Pushkin like Maiakovskii but rather the naive child who develops a special love for the Pushkin Monument by playing with her porcelain doll in its presence and by naively swinging on the chains that encircle the monument. As the adult poet and narrator of these memories, Tsvetaeva performs her own evolution from naive girl to future poet. When she was a girl, the Pushkin Monument was a destination for her walks; as an adult, she scorns Zhukovskii's censorship and relishes the original version restored to the monument in the year of her writing.

The underlying trope that brings the Pushkin Monument to life in Tsvetaeva's essay is the juxtaposition of her naive view of it as a child with the mature poetic voice of her narrator. For example, naive childhood fascination with Pushkin's Africanness turns the Pushkin Monument into an icon of anti-racism through complex allusion to "blackness" in poem, statue, and the performative culture of the monument. Through her mature poetic voice, Tsvetaeva's childhood naiveté alludes to a long and controversial history of fascination with Pushkin's heritage.[15] Tellingly, one of Pushkin's first biographers, P.I. Bartenev (who, incidentally, brought Pushkin's original, uncensored version of "Monument" to the public attention in 1880), was also one of the first scholars to connect Pushkin's ethnic and racial hybridity to his success as a national poet. Catherine Theimer Nepomnyashchy and Ludmila A. Trigos observe that Bartenev "makes explicit what Dostoevskii [in his 'Pushkin Speech'] leaves unspoken," that is, that Pushkin's multiracial background is what makes him so responsive to non-Russian cultures.[16] To this performative dimension, the child Tsvetaeva unwittingly juxtaposes the statue of Pushkin as literally black, especially in contrast to her porcelain doll. The chains surrounding the monument reinforce the mature Tsvetaeva's horror at Zhukovskii's censorship of Pushkin's poem "Monument." As Liza Knapp notes, in Tsvetaeva's mind, "Zhukovskii had tried to make a slave out of Pushkin."[17] Tsvetaeva's naive childhood perception of "blackness" merges with the mature poet's powerfully subjective voice, which triangulates race, poetic responsiveness, and rebellion against oppression.

Tsvetaeva's engagement with the motif of the lifelike statue reveals the same pattern of raising her naive vision to sophistication through her mature poetic voice. Tsvetaeva recounts the fateful day Pushkin's Monument came to visit her as a child, turning the trope of the statue-come-to-life into a childhood memory. That memory, in turn, coincides with the function of her essay, which celebrates Pushkin's elemental chaos (*stikhia*, or "chaos," a play on *stikhi*, or "verse") and immortal life as a fundamental component of her poetry. Pushkin's verse and the monument itself are very much alive in this essay. Her childhood self-consciousness of being somehow recognizable to both her tiny porcelain (white) doll and to the gigantic cast-iron (black) statue is framed by the voice of Tsvetaeva the poet: "And soon I will grow up."[18]

The conclusion of her essay again returns to this same concept: "And, I can say even more: the ignorance of my youthful conflation of chaos with verse (*stikhii so stikhami*) turned out to be insightful."[19] Tsvetaeva's innovation is to see in her naive perception as a child a profound truth that she comes to understand as a poet and implements as a trope in her essay. In this way, her essay responds to 1937 both by taking Pushkin back from the official, public sphere ("my Pushkin" as opposed to "our" Pushkin), and also by juxtaposing her childish, naive perceptions of Pushkin with her own narrative voice as a mature poet. There was a certain genius in her naive readings of Pushkin, but it required her future voice as a poet to formulate them in a meaningful way. Tsvetaeva's essay reveals the extent to which the Pushkin Monument and the future of poetry were of concern to many in 1937 and how the Jubilee crystallized the issues for poetic observers of the events. Pushkin was made public property, but that public was in many ways a naive readership. The future poet who could find in Pushkin something beyond the accepted clichés of national genius and the self-serving official mythology became a major point of concern.

Poet and émigré critic Vladislav Khodasevich also reflected on the crisis in his own way in 1937. While he does not interact directly with the Pushkin Monument in Moscow, on 23 January 1937, he wrote a memoir that details his failed attempts, before his emigration, to pass on his knowledge of Pushkin to Soviet audiences through the organization for proletarian culture, Proletkul't. In this memoir, Khodasevich recalls how "future poets," like the already established proletarian poet Mikhail Gerasimov, and "naive" readers (a not-altogether-negative category in Khodasevich's memoir) respond to his lectures.[20] The date of the essay recalls Khodasevich's own "Monument" poem, written near an earlier anniversary of Pushkin's death, 28 January 1928.[21] In 1928 Khodasevich was still hopeful that, even though he sensed the end of his own poetic output, there could be a future for Russian poetry in emigration.[22] Lines from Khodasevich's "Monument" like "In me there is an ending and a beginning" and "But still I am a firm link" indicate hope for poetic succession, more modest than Pushkin's, perhaps, but "firm" nonetheless.[23] However, by 1938, Khodasevich was less optimistic. In emigration, too, the future of Pushkin's reception seemed bleak.[24]

Bulgakov's great innovation, and the reason this chapter focuses on *Master and Margarita* when so many other poets and artists of this time also interacted with the Pushkin Monument in fascinating ways, was to forge the connection between the Pushkin Monument and the device of allusion as a critical site of negotiation between the reader and the poet. In *Master and Margarita*, allusion, as opposed to the "making strange" facilitated by childhood in Tsvetaeva's "My Pushkin," is the underlying trope. Bulgakov takes a different and profoundly new approach to the Pushkin Monument. Instead of depicting the role Pushkin's art played in his own poetic path (a trope employed by Maiakovskii and Tsvetaeva), Bulgakov crafts dense allusions to the Pushkin Monument through a conflation of a naive reader and a future poet. The future poet he depicts interacting with the Pushkin Monument is not a poet for whom Pushkin is a kindred poetic spirit. Riukhin is not a naive reader who has overcome his naiveté to become a good reader and, even more, to respond, through his own creative energies, to Pushkin's genius. Riukhin is not a poet reflecting on his first experiences of the Pushkin Monument as fundamental to his poetic fate. Rather, Bulgakov characterized Riukhin as a naive reader attempting to be a poet and thus constellated the crisis of poetry and poetic tradition in Soviet Russia. Bulgakov alludes to the Pushkin Monument not as an emblem of tradition and poetic succession but rather to frame an apocalypse precipitated when ignorance assumes the office of the poet.

Conflating the Reader and Author in the 1920s and 1930s

Bulgakov's innovation reflects two broader trends in Soviet aesthetics that merged author and reader in various ways. Evgenii Dobrenko theorizes that the rejection of pre-revolutionary high culture did not stem from either the avant-garde or the Proletkul't, but rather, "based on the corresponding aesthetic threshold of the masses' perception of art, [the rejection] *originated from the broadest masses* of city and country."[25] Newly literate masses could not relate to some pre-revolutionary culture because they lacked the frame of reference. Not only did this reflect a naiveté that made interpreting allusion difficult, it also resulted in an impulse to create a different and more accessible type of art – to become an author. As Dobrenko writes,

> The new strategy of reception was born of cultural collapse in a revolutionary culture, when the "old culture"' acquired a new recipient. The new reader, spectator, or listener forms the optics of his perception *during the very process* of "getting accustomed to culture." This is an exceptionally

complex and painful process. In its course a sharp break in the already developed aesthetic experience of the masses occurs as well. It is accompanied by an acute crisis of all traditional forms of receptive activity and, as a result, by total negativism of the masses toward culture in general: both toward "the old culture" and toward the revolutionary culture born in the paroxysms of that culture. The twofold result of this process is the refusal to use preexisting art and the stimulus to create one's own art – in other words, the rejection of co-creation in light of the desire for individual creative activity. This situation *regenerates the recipient as an author*.[26]

In its essence, the naive reader becomes an author because it is too "painful" to engage in co-creation with authors of the past.

The rupture between the newly literate reader and the culture of the past explains one element of how the author/reader dichotomy was shifting; but censorship threatened the relationship from a different side. Censorship preoccupied Bulgakov because in his own experience it erected a significant barrier between his texts and his audience. In *Master and Margarita*, Bulgakov overcomes this isolation through fantastic, supernatural interaction between Ivan and the Master's novel about Pilate. Ivan only perceives the novel through interaction with Voland or in a dream state.

In her analysis of *Master and Margarita*, Carol Avins notes the merging of author and reader in the discourse of the First Congress of Soviet Writers in 1934: "Writers were called upon to regard the reader as a collaborator – even a teacher – in the creative process." Avins then quotes Gor'kii's closing remarks, which further define the writer-reader relationship: "the all-union proletariat, our reader – a reader-friend, who … lovingly surrounds us and teaches us how to work."[27] However, that relationship was frequently disrupted for Bulgakov. As Avins writes, "It is this sort of blockage in the contact between author and audience that Bulgakov creates ways to circumvent in *The Master and Margarita*. Unless it can be circumvented, writer and reader may indeed be 'one' – not in the sense meant by policymakers, but in the sense that the writer constitutes the sole audience."[28] Avins's analysis shows how Soviet ideology sought to reconfigure the writer-reader relationship, but also how censorship threatened to reduce a writer's audience to the writer alone.

As Dobrenko and Avins suggest, collapsing the dialogic roles of reader and author poses threats from multiple sides. In *Master and Margarita*, both the notion of censorship (the Master's novel was censored) and the newly literate reader/poet who knows nothing of pre-revolutionary culture (Ivan Bezdomnyi) threaten the future of true art in

Soviet Moscow. Without an audience to read it or a poet to respond to it, what can the future hold for the Master's novel?

By conflating the future poet with the naive reader, Bulgakov reformulated a broader cultural concern with erasing the meaning-creating distance between author and reader.[29] While Ivan Bezdomnyi is the central character who expresses this theme, he is doubled by several other future "poets" who are also naive "readers": Levi Matvei and Sasha Riukhin.[30] Levi Matvei's distortions of Ieshua's words are plainly problematic to Ieshua himself. When Pilate questions him about inciting the people to destroy the temple, Ieshua responds by evoking the people's lack of education. They twist his words, Ieshua continues, because Levi Matvei writes them down all wrong.[31] By insisting on this problematic relationship between Ieshua and his "disciple," the Master brilliantly complicates the relationship between his account of the Passion and the Gospel narrative from which it diverges. The Master alludes to the Gospels here, inviting his readers to enjoy his novel as a revitalized account of one of the most well-known dramas in Russian culture, the Passion of Christ. The Master is able to give new meaning to the Gospel narrative in the context of militant Soviet atheism, not by insisting that atheism is wrong or that Christ really was the Son of God, but rather by proving that the Gospel narrative, even though it be deprived of its supernatural claims of Christ's divinity, can lay bare the subversion of truth by political ideology.

The Master's novel operates according to Pushkin's paradigm of reception in "Monument." The Master is a future poet whose allusions to the Gospels create new layers of depth and insight. He brings the Gospels, one of the most monumentalized narratives in European culture, back to life as only a true artist can.[32] Pushkin's paradigm of reception in "Monument" also explains the crisis of who will respond to the Master's novel at the end of the novel: what if there is no sublunar poet? To understand that side of the equation, we must take an extended look at Sasha Riukhin, the naive future poet who doubles Ivan Bezdomnyi, and his engagement with the Pushkin Monument as a poem, statue, and performative space.

Riukhin, Allusion, and the Pushkin Monument
(Anatomy of a Scene)

Riukhin appears for the first time in the manuscripts of *Master and Margarita* in 1931, and even at this early stage is connected to Pushkin; however, there is no mention of the Pushkin Monument. In its place the narrator describes a mouldering plaster statue of the recently deceased Soviet poet Alexander Ivanovich Zhitomirskii holding a book in one hand and the hilt of a sword in the other in the garden in front of Griboedov House.[33] The image appears in a chapter entitled, "There Were Doings at Griboedov's," and resembles what will in later manuscripts break into two chapters: "There Were Doings at Griboedov's" and "Schizophrenia, as Was Said." The fragment ends when Riukhin returns to Griboedov House from escorting Ivan to the clinic. He has a terrible time finding a tram back to Moscow after taking leave of the doctor, but eventually manages to find one. His nerves are shot. He drinks vodka at the restaurant at Griboedov House, becoming more sober the more he drinks. A dark malice directed towards Pushkin and fate begins to grow in his soul.[34] At that point, the manuscript breaks off in mid-sentence.

A second partially completed "Griboedov House" scene breaks off well before Riukhin makes it back to Griboedov House in a second manuscript from 1931.[35] Again, in a version dating from approximately 1933, the "Griboedov House" chapter breaks off with a note in Bulgakov's handwriting: "Further: Ivan the apparition and the scene in the hospital."[36] Effectively, the ending of the scene remained consistent with its first version in 1931. A similar scenario takes place in Bulgakov's next revision of the scene in late 1936 or early 1937.[37] The narrative leads up to the place where Ivan appears at Griboedov House and breaks off. Thirteen blank pages remain in the notebook, a quantity that the editor of the manuscripts, E.A. Kolysheva, suggests would be just enough for the scene with Ivan at the clinic as it appeared in previous manuscripts.[38] The ending of the Griboedov House scene remains stable from its first appearance in the manuscripts in 1931 through 1936 and perhaps into the first months of 1937, the time of the 1937 Pushkin Jubilee. Bulgakov seems content not to tinker with the ending of the chapter at all, focusing his revisions on the first part of the chapter.

In 1937, during the months after the centennial of Pushkin's death in January, Bulgakov drafts a new version of the ending that enhances the Pushkin theme by adding the Pushkin Monument (fourth redaction).[39] In this 1937 version, Bulgakov splits the events at Griboedov House and Ivan's trip to Stravinskii's clinic into two chapters for the first time. As in the 1931 version, Riukhin returns to Moscow in a tram, but he gets out at the foot of the Pushkin Monument and addresses it directly, saying, "It's all fine for you!"[40] The Pushkin Monument replaces the Zhitomirskii Monument from 1931, but does not feature allusions to Pushkin's poetry or the statue or poetic performances. Riukhin simply seems to envy Pushkin and moves on. From this point on until his death in 1940, however, Bulgakov revised Riukhin's words and actions and descriptions of the Pushkin Monument to create an increasingly dense poetics of allusion.

During the remainder of 1937 and perhaps into 1938 (fifth redaction), Bulgakov drafted yet another scene between Riukhin and the Pushkin Monument.[41] Bulgakov significantly revised the scene again in the penultimate draft of the novel, composed between 1938 and 1940 (sixth redaction).[42] Each draft reveals an increasing awareness of the importance of the scene for the novel and a heightened sensitivity to allusive power in the verbal, visual, and performative dimensions of the Pushkin Monument. In each draft, Bulgakov tweaked the narration to highlight the device of allusion until it dominates the scene.

Evidence from Bulgakov's revisions illuminates several moments in the following analysis. For example, in the 1937–8 draft, Bulgakov changes Riukhin's name to Ponyrev, Ivan Bezdomnyi's surname at the end of the novel. At one point, he mistakenly started to write Riukhin, but stopped in mid-word ("Riukhi"), crossed it out, and proceeded with Ponyrev.[43] Then again at the end of this same draft, he mistakenly wrote Ponyrev when referring to Ivan, which he crossed out and replaced with "Bezdomnyi."[44] These mistakes and autocorrections reveal the extent to which Riukhin was emerging as a significant double for Ivan in the context of the Pushkin Monument.

Another example reveals Bulgakov's attention to allusion during the revision process. In the 1937 draft, the chapter ends with an image of daylight that ignores Riukhin's presence: "The day warmed up above the city; the edge of the sky started to turn gold."[45] In the 1937–8 draft, Bulgakov revises this concluding sentence to emphasize the poet rather than the city: "Day heaved itself irresistibly on the poet."[46] This revision does two things. First, it incorporates Riukhin into the sun and moon imagery that is so prevalent in the rest of the novel. Second, it works as an allusion to Pushkin's poem "Monument," which features a poet alive in the sublunar world as the key component of Pushkin's future glory. As Riukhin relinquishes his claim to the status of poet and regrets the moonlit night he wasted trying to help another poet, "day heaves itself" upon him.

Many revisions like these two examples result in the final version of the end of chapter 6 ("Schizophrenia, as Was Said").[47] The hack poet Sasha Riukhin returns to Griboedov House after a long night at Stravinskii's clinic. Riukhin has accompanied a younger version of himself, Ivan Bezdomnyi, to the clinic, after Ivan disrupts a routine evening at Griboedov House with his odd behaviour and insistence that the devil was there, among his "brethren in literature." As he returns to Moscow in the back of a truck, Riukhin's thoughts turn from Ivan's fate in

Stravinskii's clinic to that of his own fate as a poet. The Pushkin Monument interrupts these thoughts at a key moment, and Riukhin "attacks" the statue, his last significant act before disappearing from the novel. However, Riukhin's interaction with the verbal, visual, and performative dimensions of the Pushkin Monument explains much about Ivan Bezdomnyi's evolution as a character and one of the novel's most persistent themes: the future of art in Soviet society.

Explanation of these meanings requires dissection of Bulgakov's innovative interaction with Pushkin's poetry, Opekushin's statue, and several significant performances related to the Pushkin Monument. In the Riukhin scene, Bulgakov transforms the verbal, visual, and performative dimensions of the Pushkin Monument into a generator of multidimensional allusion. As a way of dissecting the scene to explain its intricacy, I have identified the most important allusions in the scene and analysed them separately.[48] Artificially isolating the allusions in this way clarifies their overlapping functions. As a result, we can see Bulgakov's innovation more clearly: each allusion in some way reveals Riukhin to be a conflation of the figures of the naive reader and the future poet traditionally evoked in the presence of the Pushkin Monument. Riukhin is both, and his character succinctly poses one of the most important questions in the novel: what happens when the future poet *is* a naive reader?

The Meaning of Riukhin's Name

Riukhin's name, when interpreted in connection with the Pushkin Monument, illustrates his status as a future poet who fails because he is a naive reader. His name alludes to the folk game of *gorodki* in which players attempt to knock down a set of five wooden pins, called *riukhi*, by throwing a bat at them from a set distance. The word has other meanings, however, that also confirm Riukhin's status as a hack poet. In his etymological dictionary, Max Fasmer explains how the word is also used to call pigs, making its etymological connection to *ryt'* ('to rummage') and *rushit'* ('to ruin') more clear. Riukhin is much more likely to make a mess of Pushkin's poetry by rummaging through it like a pig or knocking apart its rationally composed parts, as in *gorodki*, than to bring it to life.

Taken alone, these meanings impart a less-than-favourable impression of Riukhin as a poet, but the "speaking name" also satirically juxtaposes Riukhin to Pushkin. After all, Sasha, or as Ivan deridingly calls him, Sashka, Riukhin's first name, is a diminutive form of Alexander, Pushkin's first name. Their last names support this connection – Riukhin is an imperfect rhyme for Pushkin, contrasting folk culture like *gorodki* and swine-calling with the father of Russian *belles-lettres*. In the game *gorodki*, the *riukhi* are set up in a predetermined series of fifteen images that players then attempt to knock down.[49] Thus the game itself and the wooden *riukhi* evoked by Riukhin's name and poetic fate are contrasted with the bronze monument – the small and light-weight *riukhi* are meant to be knocked down, destroyed, while Pushkin's Monument signifies immortality and indestructibility. The irony is deepened by the description of Riukhin trying to keep his seat on a wooden stump in the back of the recklessly driven truck. The wooden pin (*riukha*) is sitting on a wooden stump (*obrubok*) and barely managing to stay on its unsteady pedestal. The tumultuous image of an inferior, "wooden" poet about to topple contrasts with the cast-iron statue of Pushkin on the firm foundation of his poetry symbolized by the "Monument" poem on the pedestal.

Pushkin's Monument: Poem, Statue, Performance

The verbal dimension of Pushkin's Monument, the poem "Monument," is the most prominent subtext with which Riukhin's thoughts, words, and actions interact. Riukhin contemplates his own poetic fate by unwittingly distorting Pushkin's poem "Monument" even as he rides past the pedestal on which it is immortalized.

The imagery of sunrise in this scene, especially when read against Pushkin's "Monument," threatens Riukhin's status as a poet.[50] Sunlight and moonlight motifs consistently shape the meaning of many scenes in *Master and Margarita*, and Pushkin's moon imagery in "Monument" strengthens the motif in the Riukhin scene. Riukhin returns to Moscow at the earliest point of sunrise, when the street lamps still burn but no longer offer any meaningful light. The future poet of Pushkin's "Monument," however, lives in a "sublunar" world – a world that has much more in common with the private, aesthetic world of the Master and Margarita than sun-drenched Yershalaim or the infernal heat of daytime Moscow. In this regard, it is a fitting coincidence that Riukhin rejects his future as a poet and disappears from the novel just as "day heaved itself irresistibly on the poet."

Riukhin's thoughts and actions further erode his status as a poet. Without even realizing that he is in the presence of a concrete reflection of Pushkin's glory, Riukhin considers the poor prospects of his own poetic "glory" (*slava*). Riukhin's thoughts lack the nuance of Pushkin's poem, which, if he were a good poet, he would be able to respond to in a creative way. Pushkin predicates his immortal glory not on the quality of his poetry (something that in Pushkin's poem stands quite apart from its popular reception) but rather on the life of a future poet. On the one hand, it would seem that Riukhin correctly evaluates the quality of his poetry, but he could resolve to ignore contemporary reception and ideological pressure to focus on more aesthetic and personal goals. He could resolve to read more and learn more and continue to strive for aesthetic truth more than popularity or ideological correctness. But to do that, he would have to transcend the offence that he feels at Ivan's insults (even though, and this is the key moment, he agrees with him). In contrast to the statue's lack of response – it indifferently (*bezrazlichno*) looks down on Riukhin's anger and refuses to enter into debate with a fool – Ivan's criticism cuts Riukhin to the quick and thwarts whatever latent poetic potential he may have had. Just before his disappearance, he drinks himself into oblivion, having understood that there is nothing left for him but to forget.[51] Forgetting as Riukhin's only option is even more ironic for having been triggered by the *memorial* to Pushkin's immortality.

Riukhin is far from living up to Pushkin's image of a future poet in "Monument"; rather, his ignorance of the details of Pushkin's death and poetry characterize him as a naive reader. His most obvious mistake is anachronistically to refer to D'Anthès as a white guard who shot Pushkin in the thigh. This mistake is just the first clue, however, to how Riukhin misunderstands Pushkin's "Monument." Seemingly ignorant of the many poets who have innovatively responded to Pushkin's poetry and, by extension, seemingly ignorant of his own potential as a future poet to engage with Pushkin's poetry in innovative ways, Riukhin credits D'Anthès with ensuring Pushkin's immortality.[52]

Riukhin distorts Pushkin's "Monument" in still other ways. For example, his diatribe against Pushkin, sneering at his sheer luck, and his dismissal of Pushkin's "Winter Evening" ("*Buria mgloiu*") reveal ignorance of Pushkin's assessment of his poetry in "Monument." In stanza four, the stanza that Riukhin could have read from his vantage point on the truck as it turned down Tverskoi Boulevard, Pushkin claims that he will be loved for evoking "kind feelings," for "extolling freedom," and for "calling for mercy to the fallen." Riukhin's malice towards and envy of Pushkin's fame are not informed at all by Pushkin's thoughts. The "kind-hearted feelings" of Pushkin's poetry contrast with Riukhin's malice, and Riukhin's adoption of Archibal'd Archibal'dovich's indifference to the detainment of Bezdomnyi contrasts with Pushkin's claims to have "praised freedom" and to have "called for mercy to the fallen" even as it coincides with dawn, the moment in which Riukhin ceases to be a poet.

While unpacking the verbal dimensions of allusion in the Riukhin scene requires the active knowledge of Bulgakov's reader, since Riukhin seems utterly unaware of it, Riukhin *is* fully aware of the statue. When he sees it, he stands to his full height (a parody of Pushkin's "higher than the Alexandrian Pillar"?) in order to challenge the monument and arrives at the conclusion that Pushkin achieved success merely because he was lucky. This response to the statue suggests a significant misunderstanding of Pushkin's poetics of reception. Pushkin loathed the idea of a sculpted image of himself and expressly did not want one.[53] The visualization and literalization of Pushkin's monument metaphor was the result of a process of privileging the naive reader over the poet, and Riukhin is certainly a product of that trend. Riukhin sees the statue not as an aesthetic object but as concrete proof of Pushkin's popularity and success as a poet. What he misses, however, is Pushkin's poetry. He has accepted the official line of Stalinist rhetoric about Pushkin and is foolishly envious of it. The fact that Riukhin envies Pushkin's reception among the masses and yet can see no value in Pushkin's verse foreshadows his demise. He says to himself that he writes bad poetry because he does not believe in what he writes, but we should take his self-assessment with a grain of salt. Perhaps this is partly true, but there are other elements at stake here. At least one reason he writes bad poetry, based on his words and actions at the Pushkin Monument, is because he is *ignorant* of the tradition in which he writes.

Pushkin the statue is an image of immobility, a state that Riukhin seems to envy even as other poets like Pushkin, who did not want to be immortalized in a graven image, and Maiakovskii, who saw immobility as unnatural, sought to avoid or overcome it. Riukhin's envy of the statue's immobility is a surer sign of how bad Riukhin's poetry is than his own self-assessment, however honest it may be. Riukhin lacks a poet's thirst for aesthetic truth. He is primarily interested in fame and glory, which he will never achieve. In this regard, Riukhin embodies the contradiction of a poet who is also a naive reader. He has the office of a poet, but he interprets the Pushkin Monument as a naive reader, seeing in it proof of a nation's adoration and assuming that everything that Pushkin endured as a poet contributed to his status as a national poet. He sees the monument as proof of the type of reception that he wants for himself, but that very attitude towards the monument lacks poetic intuition and knowledge of the monument's history.

In regard to both poem and statue, it is Riukhin's performance that reveals his ignorance. The three dimensions of the Pushkin Monument operate seamlessly in this scene to depict what the end of poetry could look like, what it could mean if the only poet left were a hopelessly naive reader. Riukhin's thoughts about Stravinskii's clinic continue this theme.

"The thought that there is no worse fate in this world than losing one's mind? … But that is, after all, a common thought."[54]

As he considers his experience at Stravinskii's clinic and his own future as a poet, Riukhin distorts more than just Pushkin's Monument. Riukhin's thought that "there is no worse fate in this world than losing one's mind" distorts several of Pushkin's poems at once, poems that have a direct bearing on the thematics Riukhin is contemplating. But Riukhin is unable to recognize the poetry he is distorting, much less interpret it in a meaningful way. Rather, he dismisses the sentence as a "common thought" (*obshchaia mysl'*), a cliché. Far from being a common thought, the sentence deserves to be parsed for its complex meshing of the ideas of three of Pushkin's poems, "God forbid I should lose my mind," "To Chaadaev," and "'Tis time, my friend, 'tis time."

The first variants of this line appear in the fifth redaction (1937–8). In this version, Bulgakov revises Riukhin's thoughts to have him do more than just envy Pushkin at the foot of the Pushkin Monument. As Riukhin attempts to sort out what is bothering him so much after his trip to Stravinskii's clinic, he thinks to himself, "The thought that it is terrible to lose one's mind? Yes, that …"[55] In this sentence, Riukhin's thoughts echo the sentiments of Pushkin's poem "God forbid I should lose my mind," which seems an appropriate response to have after witnessing Ivan's apparent mental collapse. And yet Riukhin fails to penetrate the depths of Pushkin's thoughts on freedom, poetry, and insanity in the poem. Rather, he dismisses the troubling thought of a perfectly sane poet restrained for having lost his mind in order to contemplate his own wounded vanity.

In this same passage (fifth redaction), Riukhin does not address the Pushkin Monument at all, but rather expresses his envy for the material success of a contemporary Soviet poet, Dvubratskii. While Bulgakov removes any direct mention of the Pushkin Monument in the narration, Riukhin's thoughts still distort Pushkin's poetry as it was associated with Pushkin Square during 1937. Many famous photographs of the centennial celebration of Pushkin's death show a poster of Pushkin hanging on the bell tower of Strastnoi Monastery. The last five lines of Pushkin's "To Chaadaev" are printed at the bottom of his image with an obviously ideological, Soviet interpretation attributed to them: "Comrade, believe! / Our star of captivating happiness will arise, / Russia will awake from her slumber, / And on the wreckage of autocracy, /

Our names will be inscribed!"[56] Far from contemplating the ideological or political history of this poem, Riukhin envies the material success of this Dvubratskii who has somehow managed to be famous and get a car despite his awful poetry. Riukhin's next thoughts distort the words of "To Chaadaev" when he thinks, "But I am unlucky, there is no happiness for me, I got the wrong star."[57] Pushkin's "star of captivating happiness" has been reduced to the image of one bad poet grumbling about another bad poet's talent for getting the Soviet writing establishment to pay for a car.

In the fifth redaction, the *absence* of reference to the Pushkin Monument reinforces the irony of Riukhin's thoughts. He fails to recognize or reflect on Pushkin's poem about losing one's mind, on the one hand, and, on the other, distorts the concept of poetic glory in "Monument" and "To Chaadaev" represented in Pushkin Square by envying Dvubratskii's material success.

In the sixth redaction (1938–49), Bulgakov's revisions of these lines show him searching for the right balance of describing the Pushkin Monument and alluding to Pushkin's poetry through Riukhin's distortions of it. After writing several different versions, Bulgakov settles on the formula for this line that combines the earlier allusions to "God forbid I should lose my mind" and "To Chaadaev" into one line. In this new version (the final form it will take), when Riukhin is trying to sort out why he is so troubled after leaving Stravinskii's clinic, he wonders, "The thought that there is no worse unhappiness in the world than the loss of reason? Yes, yes, of course, that too. But that is such a common thought."[58] The idea of having "the wrong star," not Pushkin's "star of captivating happiness" but rather a star of unhappiness, has been combined with the idea of how awful it would be to be deprived of reason. But Bulgakov's last revision adds a key phrase that relates to this constellation of freedom, happiness, and poetic fate: "there is no worse unhappiness in the world" (*khudshego neschast'ia … net na svete*). Also one of the key allusions at the end of *Master and Margarita*, the fifth line from Pushkin's "'Tis time, my friend, 'tis time" reads like this: "There is no happiness in this world, but there is peace and freedom."[59] Riukhin's thought that "there is no worse unhappiness in the world than the loss of reason" thus reveals a complete muddle of three of Pushkin's poems that relate directly to the ideas of freedom (*volia*), happiness (*schast'e*), and poetic fate. These same themes are also addressed in Pushkin's poem "Monument," underscoring Riukhin's confusion and ignorance as he contemplates his future as a poet.

Bulgakov's final version makes it clear that Riukhin is ignorant of Pushkin's poetry by making him think that this very complex sentence is a "common thought." This is the key phrase that prevents Bulgakov's readers from attributing these complex allusions to Riukhin's poetic talent. The fact that Riukhin has this thought but dismisses it as a cliché reveals not only his ignorance of Pushkin's poetry but also the poverty of Riukhin's ability to contemplate the issues Pushkin's poetry raises.

The evolution of the allusions in this one line is instructive for several reasons. Bulgakov's editorial choices increase the density of allusion to Pushkin's poetry through the agency of the Pushkin Monument. This one line would not have the same power to distort Pushkin's poetry were Riukhin not to think it in the same narrative space in which he contemplates the monument. The evolution reveals Bulgakov's process of discovering the way the Pushkin Monument can facilitate these complex allusions. But it also reinforces Riukhin's characterization as the future poet who is also a naive reader. Theoretically, as a poet he should be able to interact with Pushkin's poetry in productive ways. As shown in this analysis, his ignorance precludes him from recognizing Pushkin's poetry, much less finding in it new depths of meaning or insight. Finally, it is also significant that "God forbid I should lose my mind," "Monument," "'Tis time, my friend, 'tis time," and "To Chaadaev" were either politically problematic for Pushkin, unpublished during his lifetime, or both. Riukhin's ignorance of these poems, and by extension, their textual history, clashes with his claim that whatever misfortune befell Pushkin inevitably led to his glory because of luck.

"Whether I stroll along noisy streets" and "Winter Evening"

The nineteenth-century association of "Whether I stroll along noisy streets" with the monument highlights the pettiness of Riukhin's envy. Perhaps if he had read the poem and understood it, Riukhin's vision of his own poetic future would not have been so bleak. The first two stanzas of Pushkin's poem set up the same constellation of issues that Riukhin contemplates as he enters Pushkin Square but address them with more composure and a deeper sense of what life is really about.

> Whether I stroll along noisy streets,
> Or enter into a crowded cathedral,
> Or sit among senseless youths,
> I devote myself to my dreams.
> I say, "The years will rush by,
> And though many of us are not seen here,
> We all will go down beneath the eternal arch –
> And someone's hour is already at hand."[60]

Pushkin's poem became a clichéd association with the monument in the nineteenth century for several reasons. His statue appeared to be wandering about the noisy streets (Tverskaia Street); the statue could be interpreted as walking towards the Strastnoi Monastery; and it was often surrounded by Moscow's youths. In this same space, both Pushkin and Riukhin are absorbed by their thoughts of the future and death. The difference is that Riukhin's envy contrasts sharply with Pushkin's resignation. Pushkin was not so much concerned with his future as a poet in this poem; rather, he recognized his mortality and was perfectly content not to have fame and glory but instead to have young life near his eternal resting place and to have the natural world, even though it is indifferent to his poetry, display its glory by his grave. Riukhin does not seem so much to reject Pushkin's concept as to be ignorant of it. In contrast to Pushkin's concern in his poem, Riukhin's focus on the material needs of his future and, in earlier drafts, his envy of Dvubratskii's material success, reveal him to be both a shallow poet and an ignorant one.

The only one of Pushkin's poems that Riukhin *does* seem to know is "Winter Evening." But here, too, the fact that *this* poem comes to his mind in the presence of the Pushkin Monument says more about his ignorance than his poetic recall. Many other poems would have elaborated on the topic of Riukhin's thoughts while also engaging with the thematics of the Pushkin Monument more directly than "Winter Evening": "Monument," the poem represented on the statue's pedestal, "To Chaadaev," the poem hanging across from the monument in 1937, or even "Whether I stroll along noisy streets," the poem most closely associated with the Pushkin Monument in the nineteenth century.

Riukhin not only has a poor sense of the way that allusion works in Pushkin Square; he also disparages one of Bulgakov's favourite Pushkin poems. His naive recollection of "Winter Evening" at the Pushkin Monument functions as an allusion to Stepan Il'ich Bitkov, the state informer who doggedly follows Pushkin throughout *Alexander Pushkin*, Bulgakov's play about Pushkin's last days.[61] Critics have disagreed over whether Bitkov is a threatening or sympathetic figure, but perhaps the nature of these disagreements would change were the emphasis to shift to contextualizing Bitkov's naiveté.[62] Bitkov repeatedly reads "Winter Evening" in naive ways, with special emphasis on his naiveté in the first scene and the last scene of the play, where the context highlights his inability to grasp anything in the poem beyond the fact that the wind he hears outside in the storm literally sounds like a child crying. What strikes him when he first hears it is how aptly the simile "starts crying like a child" describes the sound of wind during a storm. Bitkov is in Pushkin's apartment, observing the scene of Pushkin's death as an informer, when he hears Aleksandra Nikolaevna Goncharova (Pushkin's sister in-law) say the first stanza aloud, and yet at this point Bitkov does not yet know that Pushkin authored these lines. They stick with him throughout the play, although his reading of them does not progress in sophistication or understanding.[63] On the contrary, the more poems he learns the more muddled his understanding becomes. At the end of the play, Bitkov has a conversation in a remote post station in the middle of the night with the station master's wife in which he reveals how naively he reads both "'Tis time, my friend, 'tis time" and "A Winter Evening."

Weary of the burden that Pushkin's death has put on him as an informer, Bitkov confesses to the station master's wife:

> As soon as they bury him, well, then my own soul can at last find repentance. On vacation. He is going off to a distant abode, but I'm going on vacation. Oh, how many poems I had to learn all over again, no matter how clumsy they were … Yes, he composed poetry … And because of those poems no one has any peace, neither him, nor the authorities, nor me, the servant of God Stepan Il'ich … I've been going after him all over the place … but he had no fortune … no matter how he wrote he missed the target, went in the wrong direction, wrote the wrong thing …[64]

In these lines Bitkov ironically cites one of Pushkin's unpublished poems to contrast his own suffering to the "distant abode" with which Pushkin closes "'Tis time, my friend, 'tis time." Likewise, he complains of how Pushkin has deprived him, an informer, of the "peace" (*pokoi*) that Pushkin yearns for in the poem. Completely focused on his own comfort, Bitkov also refers to Pushkin's verses as clumsy. As if that were not enough, Bitkov misquotes the poem by saying that Pushkin had no fortune (*fortuna*) instead of happiness (*schast'e*) and then ignorantly concludes his condemnation of Pushkin by insisting that everything the poet wrote was in some way "wrong."[65] Context renders such a poor reading of "'Tis time, my friend, 'tis time" even more ironic – Bitkov is accompanying Pushkin on that last journey to his eternal resting place.

In the final allusion to Pushkin's poetry in the play, Bitkov recalls "Winter Evening" because of the storm that is raging outside the post station. Once again the context renders his reading ironic, reinforcing Bitkov's status as a naive reader as well as a pernicious informer. Bitkov focuses completely on the sound imagery of the poem, referring to the wind that is literally whistling outside (*"Slyshish', verno, kak ditia?"*). He continues to perform the rest of the first stanza for the station master's wife but is cut off by the sound of the station master knocking on the door just as he reaches the last word of the stanza, which, coincidentally, is "knocking" (*"kak putnik zapozdalyi, k nam v okoshko zastuchit"*). Completely absorbed in making the sound imagery literal, Bitkov misses the rest of the poem, which is much more than a literal depiction of a snow storm. "Winter Evening" reveals Pushkin's inner turmoil, personal and poetic, and the comfort he found in the warmth of drink, his peasant nanny's company, and her folk narratives. Bitkov's situation is similar – he is cold and tired and is drinking with an elderly peasant woman on a stormy winter evening. However, Bitkov calls her a fool (*"Nu chto s baboi razgovarivat'! Okh, dura!"*), unlike the persona in Pushkin's poem who finds comfort and refuge in her presence. Far from being an understanding and sympathetic reader, Bitkov represents the naive and misguided newly literate reader, capable of persecuting poets without any understanding of what they are doing.

Bulgakov completed most of the work on *Alexander Pushkin* in 1935, but the play was cancelled in the fall of 1936 (it had been intended for 1937 in connection with the Jubilee), in part because of a vicious attack on Bulgakov's play about Molière in the previous spring (1936).[66] As Bulgakov began expanding the allusions to Pushkin in the manuscripts of *Master and Margarita* over 1937 and 1938, it seemed that *Alexander Pushkin* had been irreversibly repressed. However, in the spring of 1939 new discussions began about staging the play. Within six months it was approved for production and, since by late January 1940 Bulgakov was too ill to sign for himself, Elena Sergeevna signed a contract with the Moscow Art Theater in his stead on 22 January 1940.

Bulgakov intensively worked on the Riukhin scene several times beginning in the spring of 1939, returning to it several times in the fall, and finalized it in December of 1939, a timeframe that corresponds to renewed hopes about the staging of *Alexander Pushkin*.[67] In light of this textual history, the parallel images of Bitkov and Riukhin as naive readers of "Winter Evening" and "'Tis time, my friend, 'tis time" reveal Bulgakov's heightened sensitivity to naive readers and allusion in general, but especially with regard to Pushkin's poetry.

Bulgakov created the final Riukhin scene knowing that interest in *Alexander Pushkin* had been renewed and the play would likely be staged. Both the play and the sunset novel feature allusions to "Winter Evening." In this sense, Riukhin's fixation on "Winter Evening" alludes to several things at once. The biographical allusion recalls Bulgakov's defence of Pushkin in the 1920s and the attacks on Alexei Turbin in the same decade, and is sort of a vindication of Bulgakov and his collaborator on the play, the Pushkinist Vikentii Vikent'evich Veresaev, both of whom were publicly accused of using Pushkin for personal gain. But the intertextual literary reference juxtaposes Bitkov to Riukhin in the sense that, while Bitkov likes one line of the poem, his understanding of it is obscured by ignorance and self-pity. Riukhin doesn't understand what is so great about it, which is a commentary both on his attitude to Pushkin's success and, conceivably, his attitude to Bulgakov's play, *Alexander Pushkin*. Bulgakov's biography and play become targets for allusion in equal measure with Pushkin's biography and texts, suggesting that *Master and Margarita* can be read as Bulgakov's own version of the "Monument" poem. It is Bulgakov's "sunset" novel, his great and cherished masterpiece in which his death and the future of his works figure prominently. Riukhin's dismissal of "Winter Evening" gives both Bulgakov and Pushkin the opportunity to assert their indifference to such ignorance and to rise above it. Neither Pushkin (the monument) nor Bulgakov deigns to respond to Riukhin's attack on "Winter Evening," the unifying allusion in Bulgakov's play *Alexander Pushkin*, because both works speak for themselves and, to paraphrase Pushkin's "Monument," it is useless to argue with a fool.

Riukhin's Mistakes: D'Anthès's the "White Guard," Pushkin's
"Thigh," and the Problem of Maiakovskii

In addition to grumbling about "Winter Evening," Riukhin misstates two facts about Pushkin's death that characterize him as a naive reader while also alluding to Bulgakov's novel *White Guard* and the play adapted from it, *Days of the Turbins*, as well as other Soviet poems about Pushkin's duel with D'Anthès and subsequent death and martyrdom. Firstly, Riukhin anachronistically refers to D'Anthès as a member of the pro-tsarist military force, called the "whites" during the Civil War. Secondly, he misstates the facts of Pushkin's wound: Pushkin was wounded in the stomach, not the thigh.

Some scholars have seen in the term "white guard" an allusion to Bezymenskii's play *The Shot* (*Vystrel*), in which Bulgakov's lead character in *Days of the Turbins*, Aleksei Turbin, is denounced as a "son of a bitch," an oppressive anti-revolutionary figure who deserves to be shot on sight. Bezymenskii also personally denounced Bulgakov publicly in an open letter published on 14 April 1926.[68] This allusion adds weight to the theme of envy in the novel as a reflection of Bulgakov's personal experience of public denunciations and personal attacks because of his art. Riukhin, like Bezymenskii, is capable of naive readings and vicious personal attacks. More generally, the term "white guard" could also recall denunciations of Bulgakov's *Days of the Turbins*, and the related denunciations of Bulgakov himself that referred to him as a "white guard," in part because of the title of the novel *White Guard*, in part because Bulgakov did serve with the whites during the Civil War.[69]

This biographical note aside, Riukhin's mistakes also sound ironic in the context of "Monument" because Riukhin attributes Pushkin's glory to D'Anthès, ignoring or disagreeing with Pushkin's idea that he will have glory as long as one poet is alive in the sublunar world. Riukhin either misses or purposefully distorts the essence of Pushkin's poem. In the first case he is a naive reader, in the second a malicious one.

The most detailed interpretations of Riukhin's loaded phrase "white guard," however, relate to Bulgakov's complicated relationship with Maiakovskii. Aesthetically they stood at opposite ends of the spectrum – Maiakovskii the consummate futurist and icon of the avant-garde; Bulgakov the traditionalist. Without a doubt, Riukhin's interaction with the Pushkin Monument recalls several of Maiakovskii's declarations about both Pushkin and Bulgakov. Some scholars see in Riukhin's anachronistic use of the term "white guard" a reference to Maiakovskii's anachronistic description of D'Anthès in "Jubilee" as a class enemy ("And who were your parents? What were you doing before 1917?").[70] In a similar vein, Maiakovskii's parody of naive readers of Pushkin in "Jubilee" parallels Bulgakov's depiction of Riukhin. Maiakovskii first attributes to Olga, not Tat'iana, the famous letter to Onegin. Likewise, he conflates the dream scene in which Onegin says "Mine" with Onegin's letter to Tat'iana. As Stephanie Sandler writes, "The lines ridicule newly literate readers of Pushkin, whose garbled accounts of *Onegin* and other texts would have mixed genuine uncertainty with a confusion of details."[71]

The connection to Maiakovskii is supported by several other moments in the scene, although how that connection should be interpreted is open to question. Lesskis and Atarova note that Riukhin's admission that he does not believe in anything that he writes reflects Maiakovskii's own aesthetic path. Maiakovskii's close friend, Iu. P. Annenkov, tells a story of his last meeting with Maiakovskii in 1929. Maiakovskii confessed that, "I have already ceased to be a poet." He began to sob and whispered, "Now I am a ... bureaucrat ..."[72] This admission does bear a surface resemblance to Riukhin's recognition that he writes bad poetry, but there is a major difference. Riukhin admits that all of his poetry is bad, whereas Maiakovskii claimed to have once been a poet but to have lost faith and subverted poetic truth for the purposes of the state. Where Maiakovskii profoundly grieved having ceased to be a poet, Riukhin can take no pride in any of his poetic accomplishments.

The interpretation of Lesskis and Atarova echoes Gasparov's interpretation of the Riukhin scene as a parody of Maiakovskii. Gasparov begins by seeing in Riukhin's attack on the Pushkin Monument an allusion to Evgenii's protest against the Bronze Horseman.[73] While Evgenii's act of shaking his fist at Peter bears a surface resemblance to Riukhin's similar gesture towards Pushkin, there are also significant differences. Riukhin and Pushkin are both poets: Evgenii is a bureaucrat and Peter an emperor. Furthermore, Riukhin doesn't go mad. Yes, he has a difficult psychological experience, but it has to do with coming to terms with the fact that he is a bad poet, not with going mad from grief over the loss of his beloved. Gasparov also notes the connection between Bulgakov's epithet for the monument, "metal man" (*metalicheskii chelovek*), as a reference to Pushkin's formulae that Jakobson first noted: "Bronze Horseman" and "Stone Guest." These details, in connection with the broader trope of having a conversation with the Pushkin Monument in Maiakovskii's "Jubilee," provide a basis for Gasparov's argument that Riukhin is a parody of Maiakovskii.

Seeing Riukhin as a parody of Maiakovskii, however, is problematic. Certainly, Riukhin is characterized negatively and perhaps parodies the collective image of envious and naive Soviet poets among whom Maiakovskii may have been included in the 1920s. However, by 1937, 1938, and 1939, when Bulgakov intensively developed the scene to include the Pushkin Monument, Riukhin takes on a very different function in the novel. Maiakovskii's negative allusions to Bulgakov in various poems and plays reflect their antithetical aesthetic convictions, but it would be unfair to Bulgakov to assume that he held a grudge against Maiakovskii until his death in 1940. On the contrary, Bulgakov was shaken by Maiakovskii's suicide in 1930, attended his funeral, and drafted a poem reflecting on it with direct allusion to Maiakovskii's suicide note. Bulgakov makes no attempt at revenge in this poem, but rather asks why Maiakovskii's ship was "abandoned at the wharf before its time."[74] Such an attitude hardly seems to be reflected in Riukhin the naive future poet. In fact, in January 1940, Bulgakov added the phrase, "Give Maiakovskii a proper reading," to a list of topics that he would like to study and address.[75] In this context, it is hard to imagine Bulgakov attributing Riukhin's ignorance to Maiakovskii. Despite their disagreements, Bulgakov came to respect Maiakovskii in the period during which he drafted and revised the Riukhin scene. Parody of Maiakovskii seems out of the question.

What is more, Riukhin does not experience anything like the psychological trauma that Evgenii experiences as a flood victim. Riukhin has visited Stravinskii's clinic and is disturbed by what has happened, but he is more concerned about his role as a poet. Contemplating his future is difficult but can hardly be compared to losing Parasha in the flood. Furthermore, as Gasparov points out, Maiakovskii does not attack Pushkin or the monument in "Jubilee" or, for that matter, the later propagandistic poem "A Joke Resembling the Truth." The difference in their approaches to the Pushkin Monument is significant and reflects negatively on Riukhin more than it parodies Maiakovskii. Maiakovskii makes Pushkin's Monument come to life and recognizes Pushkin's poetic accomplishments even as Maiakovskii attempts to update Pushkin, to teach him about contemporary life and the concerns of the proletariat. Riukhin's failure to bring the monument to life contrasts with, rather than parodies, Maiakovskii's poem.[76] Maiakovskii interacts with Pushkin's verse and Pushkin's concerns in "Monument," whereas Riukhin's ignorance of Pushkin's verse makes it impossible for him to renew its life for a future generation.

Another problematic aspect of the Maiakovskii allusion is that Riukhin envies the statue as an emblem of Pushkin's fate. Maiakovskii and Pushkin both disliked the idea of their own monument.[77] "Jubilee" ends with Maiakovskii exploding his own monument. The allusion to Maiakovskii and "Jubilee" underscores Riukhin's naiveté. Riukhin in this regard should not be interpreted as a parody of Maiakovskii's "Jubilee," which after all expresses frustration at the mummification of Pushkin that Bulgakov may have recognized as quite justified in 1937 (if not in 1924). Rather, the statue itself now has Maiakovskii's "Jubilee" on its side: the Pushkin Monument got down and walked around with Maiakovskii, but Riukhin could not make it move. The statue's immobility says more about Riukhin's imminent demise as a poet than it does about Pushkin's immortality.

The point of the Pushkin Monument is that it intrudes into Riukhin's conscience because of its literal materiality and visuality, which in turn only highlight his ruinous readings of Pushkin's poem "Monument" and his unfortunate reading of the public celebrations (like the 1937 Jubilee) and the poetic performances (like those of Dostoevskii, Maiakovskii, and others) that contrast so sharply with his own. The statue's materiality and visuality are what make a whole new verbal dimension beyond "Monument" possible, but it is a dimension that is inaccessible to Riukhin. Many poems exist in this material space. Some literally occupied the space (like the last five lines of "To Chaadaev," printed on a poster that hung from the Strastnoi Monastery bell tower in 1937). Some are figuratively present through intertextual association (like Maiakovskii's "Jubilee" and "A Joke Resembling the Truth"). Because this space is so steeped in allusion, Riukhin's thoughts read like a diary of misquotation, characterize him as a helplessly naive reader, and lead inexorably to his ephemerality as a poet.

The coincidence that both Riukhin and Maiakovskii in "Jubilee" end their conversations with the Pushkin Monument at dawn is sometimes interpreted as evidence for parody. This framing of the allusion, however, is problematic because it ignores the first layer of allusion in both scenarios: the sublunar poet of Pushkin's "Monument." In "Jubilee," Maiakovskii alludes to this moon imagery by bringing the Pushkin statue to life at night and returning it to monument form before dawn.[78] Bulgakov also alludes to the image of Pushkin's sublunar poet, but in a negative way: "Day irresistibly heaved itself upon the poet." Riukhin seems to have embraced the clichéd Soviet enthusiasm for Pushkin's "Bacchic Song," one of Pushkin's most widely reprinted poems in 1937.[79] The last line of the poem, "Long live the sun, let darkness vanish," stands in sharp contrast to the "Winter Evening" that Riukhin references at the Pushkin Monument.[80] As Stephanie Sandler writes, "Praise for the light of day and denunciation of excess when reason should flourish were themes that resonated well with public discourse in the mid-1930s."[81] Through the juxtaposition of Pushkin's poetry, the monument, and dawn, Bulgakov alludes not to Maiakovskii, but – together with Maiakovskii – to the sublunar poet Pushkin wrote of in "Monument" as the final condemnation of the naive future poet Riukhin.

Riukhin, Ivan, and the Significance of their Naiveté

In the Riukhin scene, Bulgakov sets a new trend in alluding to the Pushkin Monument. Riukhin's interaction with the Pushkin Monument deserves analysis because of the dense allusions inspired by its verbal, visual, and performative dimensions, all of which point to the conflation of the traditional figures of the future poet and the naive reader. Bulgakov's move reflects a larger sociological pattern: the more literacy rates grew, the more the moral and spiritual state of Russia's reading public disappointed the hopes of the intelligentsia that the ability to read would translate into cultural literacy and moral progress. But why would Bulgakov incorporate such an intricately constructed scene through such a minor character as Riukhin? The answer here lies not in the character of Riukhin himself but in Riukhin as a double for Ivan Bezdomnyi. Through Riukhin, Bulgakov most clearly engages with the subtext that features Ivan Bezdomnyi as a central character in the development of two major themes: 1) Soviet appropriation of pre-revolutionary culture and 2) the crisis of poetic succession that it implies.

Considerable evidence supports reading Ivan and Riukhin as doubles. They have mirrored ages: Ivan is twenty-three and Riukhin is thirty-two. In earlier drafts of the scene, Ponyrev (Ivan Bezdomnyi's last name at the end of the novel) is one of the variants of Riukhin's last name.[82] They are both Soviet hack poets with "speaking" names: "Bezdomnyi" means "homeless" and connotes a popular trend in the 1920s and early 1930s of adopting pseudonyms as typified by poets like Bezymenskii ("nameless"), Bednyi ("poor"), Gor'kii ("bitter"), Golodnyi ("hungry"), and Pribludnyi ("stray").[83] Both Riukhin and Bezdomnyi are described as "fools" (*durak*): Ivan by a voice very much like Voland's and Riukhin by his own inner narrative. Riukhin and Bezdomnyi both experience crises in which they recognize just how bad their poetry is and that they have no future as poets: Ivan in Stravinskii's clinic under the influence of the Master, and Sasha in the presence of the Pushkin Monument.

The crowning parallel is that neither Riukhin nor Bezdomnyi has the cultural literacy required to understand allusion. Documenting Riukhin's cultural illiteracy reveals the significance of Bezdomnyi's illiteracy as a key component of his characterization. Just as Riukhin is ignorant of the Pushkin Monument, Ivan Bezdomnyi is ignorant of both the Gospels and Faust, the two cultural myths with which he becomes most deeply engaged in the novel.

Ivan's ignorance of the Christ myth provides one of the reader's first impressions of his character. Berlioz explains to Ivan why the poem he has written about Jesus has to be completely rewritten. The narrator interjects, trying to explain Ivan's mistake: "It's hard to say exactly what tripped up Ivan Nikolaevich – the descriptive power of his talent or his complete unfamiliarity with the question he was writing about."[84] The second explanation, Ivan's ignorance, seems to be what is on Berlioz's mind as the editor gives a brief lecture to Ivan on the ancient historical accounts of first-century Rome with a brief foray into comparative religion. For Ivan, all of this was "news."

Ivan's naiveté also sets the tone for his first conversation with the Master. Having admitted that his poems are "monstrous" and having sworn never to write poetry again, Ivan recounts the events that led him to Stravinskii's clinic. The Master immediately recognizes Voland, which provokes Ivan to ask, "Well, who is he, anyway?"[85] Ivan is stunned by the answer, but the Master's erudition helps him identify Voland as Satan. He describes Ivan as "innocent" (*devstvennyi*) and "ignorant" (*nevezhestvennyi*), and immediately guesses that, if the physical appearance of Voland didn't tip him off ("different eyes, the eyebrows!"), then Ivan must never have heard the opera *Faust*. From Ivan's question (an allusion to *Faust* that is also the epigraph of *Master and Margarita*) to his mumbled excuse for not recognizing the visual allusion to Mephistopheles, Ivan's conversation with the Master reveals his status as a naive reader.[86]

By underscoring Ivan Bezdomnyi's naiveté with regard to the Christ and Faust myths, Bulgakov emphasizes Ivan's naiveté as a reader of yet another work: the Master's novel. In fact, Ivan never reads any of the Master's novel. He listens to the first episode in Voland's narration, he dreams the second episode, and there is no direct evidence that he ever reads the third and fourth episodes that Margarita rereads after Voland restores the Master and the manuscript. From this perspective, the Pushkin Monument is a subtext that shapes the ending of the novel in significant ways. At the end of the novel, Professor Ponyrev entertains the idea of continuing the Master's novel, but he has been shown to be a profoundly naive reader. The fact that he has become a historian in some ways mitigates his naiveté, but Bulgakov provides no concrete evidence that Professor Ponyrev ever addressed his complete ignorance of the Gospels, *Faust*, or even the Master's novel.

Professor Ponyrev's status as the Master's disciple, the future "poet" who has the potential to continue the Master's work, has been interpreted in many ways. Some see in Professor Ponyrev an incredibly successful "poet" – the narrator of *Master and Margarita* who overcomes his ignorance to become a brilliant author in his own right. Some see him as a failed disciple, incapable of continuing the Master's work.[87] In treating Bezdomnyi/Ponyrev as a guide for the uncouth Soviet reader, Maria Kisel takes a more ambivalent approach: "But is Bulgakov's message that a literary text is a relic, meant to be preserved without alteration? The example of his own novel points to the contrary as *The Master and Margarita* itself represents a transposition, whereby a valuable historical text [i.e., the Passion of Christ] is introduced via the literary code of a new culture – the Soviet feuilleton [i.e., the entertaining Moscow chapters with their many similarities to the low-brow feuilleton]."[88] Her question and answer frame the problem of reception along the lines of the aesthetics of the Pushkin Monument. Kisel's study presents a compelling case that Bulgakov came to the conclusion that the naive reader has the potential to become a future poet.[89] *Master and Margarita* transforms pre-revolutionary culture in such a way as to educate other newly literate readers, to teach them the value of allusion and acquiring a broader frame of reference.

And yet the scene with Riukhin and the Pushkin Monument demonstrates that a different outcome is altogether too possible. Not all future naive poets metamorphose into the sublunar poet capable of bringing Pushkin back to life. Naiveté also has the potential of degeneration into stubborn ignorance and cliché, reducing Pushkin to propaganda (as in the use of *The Covetous Knight* to extort a false confession from the ignorant Bosoi) and inanimate stone. In conflating the naive reader and future poet in *Master and Margarita*, Bulgakov discovers in the verbal, visual, and performative dimensions of the Pushkin Monument a new form of complex allusion. At the same time, he captures his generation's crisis of preserving pre-revolutionary Russian culture for future readers far removed from its most fundamental narratives.

Chapter Four

Toporov's Petersburg Text:
Rejecting the Statue (1937–2003)

Mikhail Bulgakov's *Master and Margarita* represents the culmination of an iconic tradition that interprets the poem, the statue, and performances in the space around it as separate but indivisible dimensions of Pushkin's Monument. His innovative allusions are new in part because of their verbal, visual, and performative complexity. However, as the poems of Vladimir Maiakovskii and Marina Tsvetaeva's essay "My Pushkin" show, other poets also overcame the challenge of brilliantly alluding to the increasingly long history of the Pushkin Monument. Bulgakov's approach is remarkable because it refashions the relationship between the two traditional actors with which the Pushkin Monument is primarily concerned: the naive reader and the future poet. He conserved the unity of poem, statue, and performance in the Pushkin Monument to address one of the urgent aesthetic questions of his historical moment: cultural continuity after the Revolution. If the future poet is so naive as to lack the basic capacity to understand Pushkin's poetry, who will continue Pushkin's legacy? Through the unity of its verbal, visual, and performative dimensions, the Pushkin Monument stands in for an extensive catalogue of related texts and performances. In this regard, the monument itself acts as an icon, an incarnation of Pushkin's poetry in urban space that leaves at least some hope for a future.

Not surprisingly, there is also an iconoclastic tradition of alluding to the Pushkin Monument that rejects or disfigures one or more of its three elements and thereby opens up new interpretations of the relationship between the future poet, the naive reader, and allusion to a shared tradition. It is also significant that the most notable developments in this iconoclastic tradition emerge decades after the 1937 Jubilee: a different sort of approach is necessary to bring the Pushkin Monument to life after an experience like 1937. These iconoclastic engagements with Pushkin's Monument are as vital to its future as their iconic counterparts.

Vladimir Toporov's *Petersburg Text*, a semiotic theory of literature and urban space, represents one such iconoclastic approach to the Pushkin Monument. After the Pushkin Jubilee in 1937, official cliché silenced poetic innovation in the space of the Pushkin Monument for decades. As he worked to finish his *Petersburg Text* in the 1990s, Toporov responded to this oppressive cliché by developing Pushkin's thoughts about the future poet and the future reader in the poem "Monument" to create a theory of the dynamic context of monumental sculpture. In two scholarly articles, one about Falconet's monument to Peter I (1994) and the other about Montferrand's Alexander Column (researched in 2003, but unpublished), Toporov theorized the performances of a creative viewer (like Pushkin's future poet) and a naive viewer (like Pushkin's naive reader) around the same St Petersburg monuments that Pushkin alluded to in his poem "Monument." In doing so, Toporov created a different sort of monument to Pushkin – not a visual statue in Moscow but his theory of the "Petersburg Text," the verbal tradition of writing about Petersburg urban space that Pushkin initiated.

Before the discussion turns to an analysis of Toporov's theory, however, one urgent question needs to be addressed. If the Pushkin Monument is in Moscow, why does its cultural history include what may seem like an extended digression on St Petersburg? On the surface, it may seem as though Petersburg has nothing to do with Opekushin's Pushkin Monument in Moscow. However, Petersburg and the Petersburg Text are encoded in the monument in significant ways. The monument was originally intended for Petersburg, not Moscow.[1] Pushkin's allusions to Falconet's Bronze Horseman and Montferrand's Alexander Column place it in the tradition of writing about Petersburg that is most frequently referred to using Toporov's felicitous phrase "Petersburg Text." Monumentalism lies at the core of Petersburg Text, as is evident in its often-cited "source" (*istok*), Pushkin's *The Bronze Horseman*.[2] The future poet and the naive reader also play a crucial role in Petersburg writing. Anna Lisa Crone and Jennifer Day explore how Toporov's writings on the Petersburg Text reveal the identification of the author with urban space and architectural monuments as a dominant trope in Petersburg writing.[3] But just as there is a special place for the true poet in Petersburg, Julie Buckler reminds us that there has been plenty of naive and clichéd Petersburg writing.[4] All of these reasons support reading Toporov's *Petersburg Text* as a significant engagement with Pushkin's poem "Monument." But still questions remain: what about the other "Moscow" dimensions of the Pushkin Monument? What about Opekushin's statue and the long history of performances around it?

As the following arguments should make clear, there are several reasons why Toporov's work is integral to the cultural history of the Pushkin Monument, even though Toporov does not address it directly. Toporov's engagement with Pushkin's poem "Monument" not only falls into the purview of the history of the poem's reception – it also provides supporting evidence to substantiate Pushkin's paradigm of the lifelike statue as a metaphor for his future reception. Toporov transposes the key components of allusion in Pushkin's "Monument" (allusions to the Bronze Horseman and Alexander Column, concern with the future poet and the naive reader, and the aesthetics of the lifelike statue) into a theory of three-dimensional art. While this theory does not directly address the Pushkin Monument in Moscow, it actually does work well as a theoretical explanation of its verbal, visual, and performative dimensions. That his theory works so well to explain the parts of the Pushkin Monument indicates its organic, albeit iconoclastic, relationship to it.

There is more, however. During the first century of the cultural history of the Pushkin Monument, little attention was paid to one of its central internal contradictions. Pushkin's "Monument" is a Petersburg poem, and, as the arguments in this chapter suggest, a very significant one, since it "ends" the Petersburg Text of Russian literature. But the statue is in Moscow. Consequently, the performances around it are in Moscow. Toporov's engagement with Pushkin's poem and the idea of performance in St Petersburg is a natural outgrowth of the Moscow/ Petersburg tension within the monument. In addressing this tension, Toporov's work rescues the monument from the cliché into which it had degenerated after 1937. In proposing a compelling alternative to the Pushkin Monument, Toporov simultaneously assures its place in the progressive, allusive triumvirate of Russia's sculptural "firsts": the Bronze Horseman, the Alexander Column, and Opekushin's Pushkin Monument.

After 1937

The 1937 Pushkin Jubilee was a watershed in the tradition of layering verbal, visual, and performative allusion in the space of the Pushkin Monument: it had broad implications for the future development of allusion. Bulgakov began incorporating the interplay between poem, statue, and performance into the manuscripts of *Master and Margarita*, employing the Pushkin Monument as a major subtext for the crisis of cultural continuity that characterizes the relationships between the "masters" and the "disciples" in the novel. The year 1937 also saw the publication of Jakobson's landmark analysis of Pushkin's sculptural myth. In the same year that Bulgakov exploited the verbal, visual, and performative dimensions of the monument to activate a dense network of allusions, Jakobson made a first theoretical attempt to explain the statue as central to Pushkin's poetic mythology based on allusions to many of the same texts that inform Bulgakov's allusions. Walking a thin line between "vulgar *biographism*" and "vulgar *antibiographism*," Jakobson elaborates the themes of immobility and the relationship between a "work" and the "situation" in which it was created and to which "the work is never indifferent."[5] In the same way that Bulgakov makes literary allusions to many other poets' verses about the Pushkin Monument, Jakobson highlights the role of Pushkin's symbolism of the statue in Blok, Khlebnikov, and Maiakovskii: "Pushkin's symbolism of the statue continues to affect Russian poetry to the present day, and it constantly points to its creator."[6] Bulgakov in novel and Jakobson in theory mark the significance of 1937 as a tipping point in the use and study of allusion to the Pushkin Monument.

Ironically, the same Jubilee that provoked Bulgakov's aesthetic and Jakobson's theoretical advances would also muffle them in the following decades.[7] For reasons not directly related to the Pushkin Jubilee, their reception histories reveal a remarkably similar delay. Bulgakov's work, still incomplete at his death in 1940, did not reach a broad readership until its much later publication in 1966 and 1967. Likewise, Jakobson's article was published in Czech in 1937 and, as its translator claims in 1975, "this brilliant study was still relatively unknown outside of Czechoslovakia some three decades after its publication."[8] Scholarship on Pushkin's poem "Monument" also reflects this pattern: the first major scholarly publication to address the poem, M.P. Alekseev's authoritative work on the sources and criticism of Pushkin's poem "Monument," was published in 1967. These dates may at first seem like unrelated phenomena with different explanations: censorship, in the case of *Master and Margarita*; language (Czech), in the case of Jakobson's theoretical essay; and the 125th celebration of Pushkin's death in 1962, in the case of Alekseev's scholarly monograph.[9]

The coincidence of these publications, however, points to a larger legacy of the 1937 celebration: Pushkin and the Pushkin Monument had entered the realm of official cliché and, for many, represented not a locus of innovative allusion but rather alluded all too clearly to the realities of Stalinist terror that made the Pushkin Jubilee seem more like a feast in time of plague than anything else. As Sandler writes, "The 1937 jubilee required a hardening of soul and spirit to its violence, distortions, and genuine dishonesties. One cannot overestimate the irony that a commemoration, which is after all a public experience that has the potential to *heal* trauma and to be a positive moment of national self-definition, itself became the occasion for further injury and pain."[10] The trauma that Sandler describes is one explanation for the time lag between the allusions of Bulgakov and the theory of Jakobson in 1937 and the next development of the future of allusion in the theories of Moscow-Tartu Semiotics. Angela Brintlinger, in her book on finding a "usable past" for writers in the first decade of the Soviet Union, suggests another. The "cacophony of voices" that writers of Pushkin's stature felt the need to allude to in 1937 effectively shut down their ability to write anything at all. By contrast, lesser talents, more comfortable with perpetuating cliché because they do not or cannot attend to the "cacophony of voices" at all, were the ones to celebrate Pushkin in 1937.[11] After a year like that, the Pushkin Monument became too marked as propaganda and cliché to be the source of poetic innovation.[12] It could only be rejected.[13]

Well before 1937 there was a strong tradition of rejecting the monument and the performances enacted in its space. Tolstoy boycotted the 1880 Celebration; in the 1920s Maiakovskii wrote his famously iconoclastic poems about the monument; and in 1937 Tsvetaeva problematized "our Pushkin" in favour of "my Pushkin." All were pushing back against the potential appropriation of the poet's works for ideological propaganda that the public nature of the monument made possible. In 1975, the same year that John Burbank published his translation of Jakobson's article, Abram Tertz's iconoclastic *Strolls with Pushkin*, published abroad, attempted to revive Pushkin from the "wreaths and busts"of the official Pushkin cult.[14] The metaphor of strolling itself is reminiscent of Maiakovskii's desire for Pushkin to come down off his pedestal on Tverskoi Boulevard and walk about contemporary Moscow. Upon its publication, and again in 1989 when *Strolls with Pushkin* was finally published in the Soviet Union, it caused an uproar and was perceived as an attack on Pushkin himself, not on the official cult of Pushkin. These responses represent the extent to which the Pushkin Monument, at least to many readers, was dead to innovation.

Consider the following example of how Tertz engages with the Pushkin myth in *Strolls with Pushkin*. The narrator dismisses the claim that Pushkin worked hard over his manuscripts as an attempt by Soviet critics to curry favour with Soviet authority. Even if he did work hard, the narrator claims, Pushkin needed the image of the lazy, non-serious poet to create his greatest works. He writes,

> He didn't play, but lived, joking and playing, and when he died, having
> pushed the game too far, Baratynsky, they say, together with the other

commissars who sorted through the papers of the deceased, among which, for example, intruded *The Bronze Horseman*, exclaimed, "Can you imagine what astonishes me about these poems more than anything else? The abundance of thought! Pushkin was a profound thinker! Who would have expected it?" (I am citing from Ivan Turgenev's speech at the unveiling of the monument to Pushkin in Moscow.)[15]

Tertz then satirizes the Soviet cliché that causes Soviet school children to wonder at how Baratynsky could have missed the depth of thought in Pushkin's works.[16]

The connection here between Baratynsky's discovery of Pushkin's *The Bronze Horseman* and Turgenev's allusion to it in the Pushkin Jubilee of 1880, which Tertz summarily dismisses, has to a certain extent as its target the results of the 1937 Jubilee and the Soviet industry of Pushkinolatry that it generated. Stephanie Sandler ends her study of the twentieth-century myth of Pushkin with Tertz (the pseudonym of Andrei Siniavskii): "Sinyavsky was one of the last writers in the twentieth century to contribute to and debunk Russia's myth of Pushkin, and he thus offers a fine endpoint for this study. He also points the way to the future."[17]

Another legacy of 1937 is that innovation met with resistance among theoreticians of allusion. The extent to which Soviet ideology stifled the study of Pushkin's allusive practice provides important context for the degenerative metamorphosis of allusion into cliché. Oleg Proskurin describes how the study of the influence of and interaction with other texts had dropped off by the 1930s.[18] The emphasis of socialist realism as a reflection of reality discouraged the exploration of source studies or allusion studies in favour of connections to lived reality. Official ideology pushed theorists to look for the "reflection of reality" and dismissed the study of allusion broadly speaking. Pushkin's complicated relationship to literary tradition, past and future, in official theory became the study of his path from romanticism to realism.[19] Pushkinists who did choose to explore allusive practice, like V.V. Vinogradov, framed their work to conform to the official cliché that these allusive practices helped Pushkin to seek a "deeper reflection of reality" (*bolee glubokogo otrazheniia deistvitel'nosti*).[20]

If scholars had to conform to this ideological pressure around the study of allusion, the type of popular interest that the Pushkin Monument attracted inevitably resulted in more and increasingly simplistic distortions, misreadings, and clichés.[21] Complexly sophisticated approaches to the study of allusion in Pushkiniana emerged only decades after the Pushkin Jubilee.

Vladimir Nikolaevich Toporov's work on Petersburg Text grows out of the Moscow-Tartu School of Semiotics, a group of scholars who managed to address and transcend many of these deficits in Soviet literary scholarship beginning in the 1960s and 1970s.[22] Petersburg Text situates the problem of literary tradition within the confines of a real city that develops a life of its own in literature. Given the tension between privileging the study of "reality" over allusion in Soviet scholarship, the Petersburg Text strikes a clever bargain: the "reality" of St Petersburg takes on a literary life through intensive allusive practice resulting in the Petersburg Text. Writing about the Petersburg Text in Russian Symbolism, Mints, Danilevskii, and Bezrodnyi provide a succinct formulation of the process as "the combination of a poetics of *realia* and a poetics of citation."[23] The complexly intertextual idea of the Petersburg Text, in addition to the theoretical tools that emerge out of its scholarly contemplation, confront the problems for official Soviet aesthetic theory that were posed by the ambivalence of Pushkin's allusions. In order for the Petersburg Text to appear, authors had to respond to their predecessors in recognizable but innovative ways. The clichés, or dead allusions, of socialist realism foreclosed the possibility of complex innovation as a sort of cultural elitism on the one hand and the fear of making a mistake on the other.

The cultural historian Il'ia Kalinin clarifies how, within the hyperideological context of Soviet literary scholarship, the Petersburg Text pushed back against Soviet clichés by calling for "spiritual renewal." For Kalinin, Toporov's theory had an "unmediated relation" to Toporov's own historical moment in the early Brezhnev years, a moment defined by the, in Kalinin's words, "new 'Moscow period.'"[24] The ideological context out of which Toporov's Petersburg Text emerged in the 1970s gives way in the 1990s to a context in which many monuments were torn down and new ones raised, a culturological fact that nearly always accompanies significant shifts in political ideology. In this new ideological context, Toporov turned his attention from literature to monumental sculpture and developed a theoretical approach to St Petersburg's signature monuments, the Bronze Horseman and the Alexander Column. Even in this post-Soviet period, Toporov is still concerned with allusion as a theoretical and ideological device. In the following sections, Toporov's archival notes and scholarly articles reveal a profound resemblance to Pushkin's ideas about allusion and future reception in the poem "Monument" and to the performative dimension of monuments in general. With regard to the statue, however, Toporov takes an innovative turn – he replaces it with a verbal construct based on allusions to Pushkin's works about Petersburg, the Petersburg Text.

Poem: Toporov's Archival Notes and
Pushkin's Poem "Monument"

In the last decade of Toporov's life (1994–2005), his work on St Petersburg's monuments reflects many of the themes and ideas in Pushkin's poem "Monument." However, because Toporov never finalized his work, reconstructing the direction of his thoughts requires supplementing what he did publish, the article on the Bronze Horseman and the dynamic context of three-dimensional art, with several significant archival notes from the period that point towards his thoughts on a second article about the Alexander Column.

The first note reveals the connections between Toporov's thoughts about the future of the Petersburg Text and Pushkin's idea of a future poet in the poem "Monument."[25] At first, Toporov hesitates to embark on elaborating the future of the Petersburg Text. Toporov considers how, at the end of his work on Petersburg Text, so much attention has been paid to the past and so much material gathered that the question of the future "naturally arises," and yet he struggles with the right way to frame questions about the future and whether or not we need to ask them in the first place.[26]

Later in this note, however, he overcomes his hesitation and convinces himself that some things are inevitable and then lays out a list of cryptic theses about the future of Petersburg.[27] To a remarkable extent, Toporov's thinking in this note parallels that in Pushkin's "Monument." Toporov mitigates the dangers of prediction by putting it on a spectrum with the possible, something that Pushkin also does in "Monument." Instead of predicting a specific future for any one work, Pushkin leaves it open to the very real possibility, even from the perspective of August 1836, that a future poet will allude to his work in an unpredictable way. In retrospect, Dostoevskii could allude to Opekushin's Pushkin Monument as the realization of a prophecy. However, without the perspective of history, both Pushkin and Toporov tend to downgrade their visions of the future to an exploration of what is possible or even probable as opposed to what will surely come to pass.

Another aspect that Toporov's notes share with Pushkin's "Monument" is the vision of future metamorphosis motivated by the mobility, or, to use Toporov's term, the "dynamic context," of Petersburg monuments. Pushkin relied on the refinement implied by the allusion of the Alexander Column to the Bronze Horseman as a metaphor for the metamorphosis of his works through the allusions of a future poet. As my later discussion of Toporov's published work on the "dynamic context" of sculpture will show, Toporov was interested in the ways in which the Bronze Horseman and the Alexander Column moved as a result of a co-creator, a viewer in motion around them, a thesis he develops in other notes and articles. These notes clarify the importance of Pushkin's poem in Toporov's thinking about sculpture, monuments, and the end of the Petersburg Text. For both men, dynamism, motion, and metamorphosis are opposed to stagnation and decline; aesthetic for Pushkin, moral-ethical for Toporov.

The futures of both poet and semiotician also address the problematical practices of empire. Pushkin predicts that rumour of him will spread in all directions: north (Finn), west ("proud grandson of the Slavs," often interpreted as a euphemism for the Poles), east (Tungus), and south (Kalmyk). Toporov restricts his focus more narrowly to the Petersburg province (Finns, Karelians, Estonians, Votes, Izhorians, Vepsians), but both are concerned with the harshness of empire: Pushkin's claim to utility is that he "glorified freedom" "in [his] harsh age" and "called for mercy for the fallen," while Toporov wonders why Russia has become so "soulless, short-sighted, merciless." Pushkin ends his poem with the command to listen to "god's command," while the linguist in Toporov muses on the etymologies of *chudo* and *chutkii* in the proto-Slavic **chuti*, which also has the general meaning of being attuned to all sensory perception, an important source of inspiration for a poet.

Toporov reflects on the metaphysics of Petersburg as a spatial paradox (or "the space of the paradoxical"), a somewhat cryptic reference to the underlying paradox that, in Toporov's often-cited definition of the concept, animates the Petersburg Text of Russian literature: "the path to moral salvation, to spiritual rebirth (*vozrozhdenie*) in conditions where life is perishing in the kingdom of death while falsehood and evil prevail over truth and goodness."[28] As I argue in chapter 1, Pushkin's metapoetics of allusion in "Monument" posits a similar concept of a lifelike, moving immortality that pits rebirth through the genius of a future poet against the violence and clichés of empire and utilitarian aesthetics. Pushkin's "Monument" expresses the Cappadocians' paradoxical theology of the kenotic descent of Christ, who became flesh and suffered death in order to make *theosis*, the process of being restored in the image of God, possible.

Like Pushkin, Toporov was interested in both the ascent and the descent from divinity that underlies the monumental trope. A viewer can make Peter ascend into the heavens by approaching the monument, but descent is inevitable as the viewer backs away. Similarly, Pushkin may ascend higher than the Alexander Column in the first stanza of

"Monument," but descent is implied in the rest of the poem with its emphasis on the sublunar poet and an ambivalent reception in the future. An archival note from his "Grey Notebook" demonstrates Toporov's dedication to this idea. On 7 September 2003, Toporov spent a whole day observing and recording the motion of the sun and clouds as the dynamic (meaning "in motion") backdrop for the Alexander Column.[29] His observations climax in what he describes as the "apotheosis" of the angel around 11:30 a.m. as the Petersburg autumnal sun strikes the back of the angel in a stunning display of gold and azure; however, the angel descends back into darkness at around 9:10 p.m. Toporov ends his note with a simple statement: "This is the catatheosis."[30] Readers of Pushkin's "Monument" have often noticed a similar dynamic: the Pushkin Monument rises higher than the Alexander Column, but it also descends back down into rumour, the pragmatics of utilitarian views of art, offence, slander, and an ignorant readership.

Positing these parallels is not to claim that Toporov consciously engaged with Pushkin's "Monument." On the contrary, Toporov may or may not be thinking of Pushkin's "Monument," but his deep engagement with Petersburg in Russian literature, the Petersburg Text, which coalesced around Pushkin's seminal texts, led Toporov to define the future of his most monumental contribution to scholarship along the same lines as Pushkin.[31] Whether or not the parallels are intentional, they speak powerfully to the "monolithic" nature of the Petersburg Text and the central role that the tropes of monumental sculpture have to play in it – both at its beginning with Pushkin and in Toporov's Petersburg Text.[32]

A second note from Toporov's archive demonstrates that Toporov's ideas about the Petersburg Text and the future resonate with Pushkin's concept of the future poet as the precondition of immortality.[33] Tsiv'ian interprets the note to mean that the "Petersburg Text becomes self-sufficient and dictates to the city its future."[34] The Petersburg Text as a "supertext (*sverkhtekst*)" ambiguates the distinction between subject and object in a similar way that Pushkin's metapoetics of allusion ambiguates the relationship between past and future poet. Toporov saw in the Petersburg Text an agent, a subject that determines the future (fate) of Petersburg. Pushkin's metapoetics of allusion relied on the ambivalent concept of monumental sculpture as the poet-subject's metamorphosis into the object that must be granted new life, new agency, in the poetry of future poets. Just as the Petersburg Text discovers things in Petersburg that do not yet exist in the city, so Pushkin's fate hinges on the work of a future poet who can find in Pushkin's works as yet unknown or undiscovered meanings.[35]

A third archival note suggests yet another profound relationship between Toporov's final efforts on the Petersburg Text and Pushkin's "Monument."[36] Two tiny shreds of paper, preserved in Toporov's archive and published by Tsiv'ian in 2011, reveal his focus on the relationship between Falconet's Bronze Horseman and Montferrand's Alexander Column. For example, the "gazes" of the two monuments look in different directions. The Bronze Horseman points out horizontally, the angel looks downward. Peter looks to the west and upward, the angel looks to the earth. Peter seems to look out to an undetermined future, while the angel focuses on the earth. Peter is leaping away from the earth, while the angel is humbly lowering its head. Peter's hand is commanding, pointing to the horizon, while the angel's hand reaches upward towards the cross it holds.

Tsiv'ian published the note as archival augmentation for an exhibition the previous year dedicated to "V.N. Toporov's *Petersburg Text*: A History of Creation." The organizer of the exhibition, T.M. Dviniatina, conceptualized its contents along the lines of the duality Toporov posited between the Bronze Horseman and the Alexander Column. Her concept for the exhibition eloquently expresses the focus of Toporov's later work on monuments, but it also self-consciously recognizes the imprint of Pushkin on Toporov's ideas.[37] For example, Dviniatina describes the Alexander Column as bowing a "submissive head," alluding to the text of Pushkin's description of his own monument with its "unsubmissive head." The concept of the exhibition itself seeks to look into the history of the creation of the Petersburg Text through the thematic axes of these two monuments, both of which play a critical role in Pushkin's metapoetics of allusion in "Monument." The answer to her question "Why did we [meaning the organizers of the exhibition] choose these two monuments?" must implicitly acknowledge that Pushkin and Zhukovskii, well before Toporov, also recognized a genetic relationship between the Alexander Column and the Bronze Horseman.

The design of the exhibition raises the point that both Pushkin and Toporov claimed a place for textual culture higher than the empirical reality emphasized by Petersburg's monumental sculptures. As these notes and Dviniatina's exhibition indicate, Toporov insisted on the metaphysical dimensions of Petersburg Text as something opposed to empirical matter, and Pushkin conceptualized his monument as belonging to a higher reality than the Alexander Column and, by implication, the Bronze Horseman. In seeking a way to end his work on the Petersburg Text, Toporov's thinking followed Pushkin's thinking in "Monument."

Performance: Toporov's Theory of the Dynamic Context
of Three-Dimensional Art

As the preceding discussion has shown, archival notes from Toporov's last decade reveal parallels between Pushkin's thoughts about his future reception in the poem "Monument" and Toporov's thoughts about the future of the Petersburg Text. The culture of performance that Dostoevskii initiated in reference to Opekushin's statue also illuminates Toporov's thinking. In his article on the dynamic context of Falconet's Monument to Peter the Great, Toporov approaches the concepts of monument and performance in much the same way that Pushkin and subsequent generations of poets conceptualized the monument metaphor.[38] Toporov describes the necessity of considering the monument while in motion as a viewer, since that is how the monument creates meaning within its internal spaces (the relationship of the parts of the monument itself) as well as its external environment (the built and natural environment that surrounds it). As the viewer approaches the monument from one angle, the statue interacts with the architectural and natural environment in "dynamic" ways: the perspective changes with each step. Similarly, if the viewer approaches the monument from the front, head-on, the horse eventually completely obscures Peter, to the point that only two seemingly dismembered legs protrude from the horse's sides. Toporov then contrasts this dynamism with clichéd approaches to the monument in which a "canonical perspective," one deemed most appropriate or correct, is chosen from which to perceive the monument.[39]

The concept of dynamism animates the approaches of both Pushkin and Toporov to monumental sculpture.[40] Drawing on evidence from *The Bronze Horseman*, Toporov insists that part of the aesthetic design of the monument is that it grows as you move towards it. Evgenii's mental state changes as he draws near to the monument. When he sat motionless and observed Peter from afar, Evgenii was emotionally stable and rational. However, Toporov writes, "when he approached the monument directly, he was overcome with fear for his very self, and his distraught mind was unable to withstand the trial."[41] Toporov also turns to *The Bronze Horseman* for evidence that even a naive viewer tends to move around the monument in a circular motion (in addition to the direct linear approach), arguing that both types of motion are fundamental to the monument's design: "the same effect also worked on Pushkin's Evgenii – 'Around the pedestal of the idol / the poor madman went round.'"[42]

Evgenii's motion around the monument, as described by Toporov, is what makes it *appear* to move. While Toporov does not explicitly claim a connection between his thoughts on the "dynamic context" of the Bronze Horseman and the trope of bringing the monument to life that Jakobson described in 1937, the implicit connection must be understood.[43] Whereas Jakobson deals in binaries like mobile and immobile, word and image, to explain Pushkin's fascination with monuments that come to life as a sort of biographical myth, Toporov looks to the material/visual reality of the sculpture itself as brought to mobility not through some supernatural or mythical life but by the motion of the living, mobile viewer. Toporov is interested in Evgenii's motion towards and around the sculpture, not in the movement of the sculpture itself.

Toporov's interpretation of Evgenii's motion around the Bronze Horseman contrasts with the poetic tradition that alludes to Pushkin's *The Bronze Horseman* in such a way as to imply that the horseman literally comes to life. For example, Maiakovskii's poem "The Last Petersburg Magic Tale" sets Peter, horse, and snake in motion to have lunch at the nearby Astoria. Maiakovskii displaces the dynamism of the human viewer onto the bronze figures from which the monument is composed: they get down, walk around, and perceive the city in a new way before assuming their old and tired (clichéd) postures. Toporov inverts Maiakovskii's use of the lifelike statue: the monument's dynamism and movement, its life, depend on the movement of the viewer in studied motion around the aesthetic object. Only the viewer can realize the sculpture's poetic potential, set it in motion, and give birth to new meaning.

Toporov goes to considerable lengths to justify this definition of "life" as the type of life that results not from supernatural breath or animation but from knowledge as a form of procreation.[44] That knowledge is the product of motion. In Toporov's thinking, dynamism is the difference between death and the rebirth of meaning in the soul of the "viewer": it differentiates the naive viewer from the co-creator. The naive viewer whom Toporov describes approaches the monument looking for a place to stop and observe it from the "right" place, one of the factors that gives rise to the viewer's satisfaction with clichéd interpretations of the art object. In contrast to this, the viewer who "enacts," who *performs*, the space of the monument through motion brings it to life in a new way, finding in the monumental form hitherto unknown meanings.

While the performative element of Toporov's concept of dynamism reflects the distinction performances at the Pushkin Monument frequently make between future poets and naive readers, it also reflects Pushkin's metapoetics of allusion in "Monument." In chapter 1, I argue that Pushkin's monumental allusions operate on the internal contradiction of the lifelike statue. On the one hand, it can be perceived as inert matter that is on the verge of coming to life, of obtaining a soul. On the other hand, the lifelike statue can be perceived as a once-living being that has been deprived of life, frozen in inert matter with no soul. By claiming his monument as higher than the "Alexandrian Pillar," Pushkin activated both scenarios. He recognized that he would die and transform into inert, lifeless matter, but he also claimed that he would continue to live. Pushkin's "monument not made by hands" has superseded the Alexander Column, which itself was a refinement of the rough-hewn Thunder Stone. By rising higher than these two monuments, he posits for himself a continued ascension in the works of future poets. Pushkin sets the precondition for his "dynamic" immortality as the process of co-creation that relies on a future poet in much the same way that Toporov conceptualizes the performances of naive viewers and co-creators around monumental statuary.

Genre expectations of the ode limited Pushkin's ability to comment more fully on the function of the future poet in 1836. Working within the genre expectations of the scholarly article, however, Toporov takes considerably more latitude in choosing to define exactly how that future poet transforms the work of a past poet. Toporov's notion of co-creator relies on the physical motion of the viewer as "the basis of knowing" (*vedenie*) and the "dynamic" process of cognition (*putipoznanie*) as integral to bringing the monumental object to life.[45] Although Toporov goes into much more detail than Pushkin, his naive viewer and co-creator depict the same duality of the lifelike statue that Pushkin develops in "Monument": canonical cliché leads to static, received interpretations that deprive the art of life and render it immobile, inert, dead. Toporov's definition of cliché as a "necrosis of meaning" works well with the lifelike sculpture that has been deprived of life, brought to a lower form of being on the matter-spirit continuum. Likewise, his model for the viewer as co-creator envisions a future for the monument in which "dynamic" performance, motion around the Bronze Horseman, creates new, unique, and unpredetermined meanings.

Toporov begins his article with this very idea. In the first paragraph, he outlines the "form-generating elements" of the statue that transcend Falconet's original concept. In large part, these meanings rely on the participation of a sympathetic viewer who takes Falconet's aesthetic product into its "future": "the act of the 'viewer' is in the process of its development, and while the monument exists, it will continue, discovering in it new and deeper meanings, in as much as now, namely such a 'viewer' determines the future life of the monument in the space of its conceptual growth and deepening."[46] Pushkin, too, articulates a similar idea of the future "poet" who alludes to his texts to create ever "new and deeper meanings," the mechanism that ensures a dynamic immortality as opposed to a monumentally static one. In this regard, Toporov and Pushkin both identified an idea about monumental sculpture that originated with Falconet. In his cultural history of the Bronze Horseman, Schenker writes, "Falconet designed his monument as a riddle, challenging the viewer to solve it and become thereby an active participant in the creative process. The discovered interpretations, whether intended or not, amplify and enrich the monument's symbolism."[47] Both Pushkin and Toporov penetrate and develop further this aspect of Falconet's design.

For Toporov and Pushkin there is also a sense of *vertical* motion: the monuments rise from earth to sky. In "Monument," Pushkin captures this idea by the verticality implied in the development of the Bronze Horseman to the Alexander Column (which is built to be higher than the Vendôme Column in Paris) and then claims that his monument grows yet higher, into the sky. As demonstrated in Toporov's archival notes, the verticality emphasized in the allusive connection between the Bronze Horseman and the Alexander Column also interested him. But in his article, Toporov demonstrates how the Bronze Horseman has a sort of verticality of its own, one only perceived by the mobile viewer. As the viewer moves towards the Bronze Horseman, Peter rises above the surrounding architectural backdrop and ascends into the sky. While the trope of verticality is inherent in the genre of monumental sculpture, Pushkin and Toporov both employ the trope as a metaphor for metamorphosis and co-creation – a dynamic future in which the work of art is brought back to life through the generation of new meanings.[48]

The parallel is strengthened by Toporov's own allusion to Pushkin's famous "monument not-made-by-hands." Describing the dynamic ascension of Peter, Toporov writes,

From the side of the Senate building (on the level of the earth) it is likewise impossible to find a point from which the statue is seen in its entirety against the background of the "Admiralty" wing (*kulis*), but at the same time, this angle facilitates the view of the dynamic growth of the figure of the horseman, who seems to overcome that "material-fleshliness" that has up until this point, even if only partially, restrained it [the statue] in contact with the earth and with things made by human hands (*s tvoreniiami ruk chelovecheskikh*).[49]

Not only does the phrase reinforce Toporov's more transcendental interests in monumental sculpture, it also alludes to the eighteenth-century use of the phrase by V.G. Ruban and its transformation in Pushkin's "Monument."

Perhaps in a less direct way it is possible to see in Toporov's point about the ascension of Peter a parallel to another oft-quoted and clichéd line from "Monument." The phrase "the people's path to it will not become overgrown" belongs to Pushkin's first stanza, the one that alludes to both Falconet's and Montferrand's monuments and implies motion to and from Pushkin's own metaphorical monument. This same sort of linear motion is what makes the ascension of the Bronze Horseman possible.[50] First, Toporov conceptualizes the "naive" viewer's first experience of the monument along similar lines: Pushkin's "people" approach along well-worn, "institutionalized" or clichéd paths. But likewise, the whole idea of the statue of Peter taking off into the sky as you come closer mirrors the primary dynamic quality that Pushkin attributes to his own monument as having ascended higher than the highest monument in his contemporary world (and higher still in the work of future poets).

Another element of Toporov's thinking in this article reveals a significant relationship to Pushkin's poetics of reception in the poem "Monument" and a dynamic future through the performances of future co-creators. The dynamism of the Bronze Horseman includes more than the motion of its viewers. Its meanings grow and deepen as the architectural "wings" (*kulisy*) that surround it and the sky above it change. When St Isaac's was rebuilt, it generated new meanings in relationship to Falconet's statue, a dynamic that in turn adds nuance to the relationship between the Bronze Horseman and Montferrand's Alexander Column. For example, Toporov documents in detail how the horseman's right hand slips along and points to the cross on the top of the central dome of St Isaac's as the viewer moves around the monument.[51] Then, in a footnote, Toporov documents how Peter I's hand pointing to the cross of St Isaac's Cathedral doubles the Alexander Column: the angel's hand points to a cross as well. In Toporov's view, this coincidence reflects Petersburg's "historiosophical mythology."[52] Peter I is in some ways responsible for the death of his son and Alexander I for the death of his father. At the turn of two different centuries, both men oversaw major shifts in Russian society with regard to European culture and history. The way in which the Bronze Horseman interacts with its surroundings, which include, in Toporov's analysis, the Alexander Column, exemplifies the creation of meaning that happens when texts, in this case, monuments, are placed in the context of new texts in an allusive relationship. The Alexander Column and St Isaac's Cathedral, both of which post-date the Bronze Horseman by decades, reveal new meanings in Falconet's monument. When realized through the performance of a co-creator, they expand and deepen the meaning of Falconet's original monument in ways that he invited but could not have predicted.

St Isaac's also figures into Toporov's analysis of the dynamic context in another equally important parallel between Toporov's theory of three-dimensional art and Pushkin's poetics of reception in "Monument." Falconet's Bronze Horseman is open to the addition of new texts and requires the thoughtful performance of a co-creator to come to life, but such openness comes at a cost. Just as Pushkin is concerned with the naive reader, Toporov interprets the details of the architectural history of St Isaac's as a way to demonstrate another sort of future reception. To be open to the future poet, one must also entertain the possibility of a naive reader.

Toporov prefaces his discussion of the Bronze Horseman with a lengthy digression into one historical detail in the architectural background of Falconet's monument to Peter the Great. As an example of how difficult it is to establish the architectural changes that occur in a space (part of the "dynamic context" that changes the meaning of the monument itself), Toporov turns to the work of a well-known painter of Petersburg landscapes, Benjamin Paterssen (1750–1815). In a 1794 painting, Paterssen depicted the space surrounding Falconet's monument from the perspective of Vasil'ievskii Island. Toporov is drawn to the painting because Paterssen painted a version of St Isaac's that never existed in actual fact. The Italian architect of St Isaac's, Antonio Rinaldi, was forced to leave Russia in 1784. Ten years later, Paterssen depicted the still incomplete St Isaac's according to Rinaldi's original design, not according to what Paterssen the painter literally observed with his own eyes in his personal present. At the time of the painting, the cathedral had been completed up to the level of the cupolas, and Paterssen painted the top of the cathedral as depicted in Rinaldi's documents, to which he had access. However, when Catherine II died (1796, after Paterssen's painting), her heir, Paul I, diverted the marble intended for the completion of St Isaac's to the construction of St Michael's Castle (*Mikhailovskii Zamok*). As a result, the new architect, Vincenzo Brenna, changed Rinaldi's design in 1797, and completed the cathedral in 1802 with brick cupolas instead of the marble intended by Rinaldi.

Brenna's completion of the cathedral was considered to be so awful that almost immediately a competition was begun to design a new St Isaac's, a project that would eventually be awarded to Montferrand in

1818. Toporov writes that, "Rinaldi's St Isaac's should not be judged by the structure that was eventually completed by the architect Brenna in 1802, but by *this model* [i.e., Rinaldi's] and *this painting* [i.e., Paterssen's 1794 painting]. Both are excellent and give a sense of what the cathedral was supposed to have been, but they also allow one to perceive the bitterness of an incompletely embodied, or in even stronger language, a distorted (*izvrashchennyi*) design."[53] In the first part of the essay, Toporov articulated the collaboration that must take place between artist and viewer in three-dimensional art; but here in his analysis of Paterssen's 1794 painting he also articulates the grief and bitterness of a project *misconstrued – distorted* by later artists. The cost of opening up one's artistic creation to this sort of collaboration is the anxiety of having your design, your creation, distorted by another. Rinaldi created a design of great beauty; Paterssen alluded to it and raised it to a new level of being in his painting. Brenna, on the other hand, did not recognize it and distorted it to the point that it was eventually destroyed and then replaced by a new one (Montferrand's design). As with the contrast between the Master's allusions to the Gospels and Riukhin's allusions to Pushkin, Paterssen and Brenna are judged by their ability to engage with Rinaldi's "text."

Toporov may not have knowingly sought to develop or interact with Pushkin's metapoetics of allusion in "Monument." But as a "poet" of his own sort, Toporov intuited and channelled Pushkin's concept into yet another dimension of complexity and innovation. He "raised" Pushkin's metapoetic conception to the level of theory. Through his intensive meditation on the Petersburg Text and the role of the Bronze Horseman within it, Toporov engaged with Pushkin as only a poet can, entering into co-creation with Pushkin and discovering in Pushkin's "Monument" yet another dimension of aesthetic brilliance. On the one hand, Toporov's writing contains "nothing new under the sun." But in St Petersburg, where sun and moon are sometimes difficult to distinguish one from another, Toporov is just the sort of "sublunar poet" whom Pushkin envisioned in "Monument." He spent his scholarly career walking in, performing, the footsteps of Pushkin's characters and the characters inspired by Pushkin's characters to document the Petersburg Text, a scholarly and theoretically innovative approach to the aesthetics of urban space. His work certainly deserves attention as one of the foremost examples of how Pushkin's vision for the future of allusion grew beyond something he could accomplish himself and was renewed, brought to new life once again, in the corpus of Toporov's writings about the Petersburg Text.

Replacing the Statue: The End of the Petersburg Text

Toporov's archival notes and scholarly articles on monumental statuary directly engage with Pushkin's poem "Monument" and the concept of performance as motion and co-creation – two dimensions of the Pushkin Monument. The same cannot be said of his response to Opekushin's statue, however. Instead of triggering a dense network of allusions through Opekushin's statue in Moscow, Toporov's engagement with Pushkin's allusions to the Bronze Horseman and the Alexander Column in "Monument" and his theory of performance as co-creation give a nuanced theoretical articulation to Pushkin's poetics of reception.[54] His iconoclastic exclusion of the statue alludes to the many critics of Opekushin's design, in both the nineteenth and the twentieth centuries, who rejected the literalization and visualization of Pushkin's monument metaphor. And yet the unity of the Pushkin Monument's verbal, visual, and performative elements is such that even in rejecting the statue, Toporov's theory illuminates it in two different ways. First, Toporov's theory explains the Pushkin Monument in all of its dimensions, including the statue. His theory is itself a fascinating metamorphosis of Pushkin's work that refines it by providing a coherent and enlightening theoretical tool by which to explore the cultural history of the Pushkin Monument. Second, Toporov's theory ends the Petersburg Text, framing it as an alternative monument to Pushkin, one that challenges the cultural history of the Pushkin Monument for pride of place even as it explains its aesthetics.

As a theory, Toporov's approach to the study of monumental statuary works well with the Pushkin Monument – it too has a dynamic context that must be "enacted" by a viewer in motion. For example, Toporov interprets the empty spaces within the structure of the Bronze Horseman itself from a dynamic perspective. The gaps between the horse's legs and the coils of the writhing snake change as you move towards and around the statue. The Pushkin Monument too has "gaps" or "spaces" that the sympathetic viewer can put in motion to create meaning. As the viewer approaches the Pushkin Monument in a linear motion, the monument ascends into the sky. By doing so, the viewer fills in one of the "gaps" in the internal spaces of the monument – the first stanza: "The people's path to it will not become overgrown. / It raises its unsubmissive head higher than the Alexandrian Pillar." Likewise, the viewer must walk around the monument from left to right (that is, if she starts facing Pushkin's face), filling in the "gaps" of the poem as she does (only the third and fourth stanzas are represented on the pedestal). The motion of the viewer, a co-creator who understands

Pushkin's poetry, puts the statue itself in motion as the poem is re-created through the viewer's performance. In contrast, naive viewers who stop to contemplate the statue or photograph themselves with it in the background render both themselves and the statue immobile.

The "gaps" in the poem as it is represented on the pedestal require motion and memorization on the part of the viewer, but the architectural "wings" (*kulisy*) of the monument also require a viewer in motion: like the Bronze Horseman and the Alexander Column, the Pushkin Monument interacts with the surrounding built, natural, verbal, and human environments in dynamic ways. The Pushkin Monument's historical point of view looking towards the Strastnoi Monastery and the *Izvestiia* building has changed, but that perspective played significant roles in the interpretation of the monument (as in the nineteenth-century association of "Whether I stroll along noisy streets" or Maiakovskii's poetry in the 1920s). The last five lines of "To Chaadav" hung from the bell tower of the Strastnoi Monastery in 1937 and many other performances and poems have come and gone through Pushkin Square. This "dynamic context," in addition to the motion of the viewer, operates according to the principles Toporov discovered in his article on the Bronze Horseman.

For example, consider Toporov's focus on how the appearance of the Bronze Horseman changes with regard to St Isaac's Cathedral. Toporov goes to great lengths to interpret not only its current visual dynamics but the historical changes to St Isaac's as well. A similar dynamic exists between Opekushin's statue and its historical relationship to the Strastnoi Monastery. In pre-revolutionary iconography Pushkin's head is rarely shown reaching higher than the Strastnoi bell tower. It is certainly possible to photograph statue and bell tower so as to depict Pushkin's head higher than the cross, but typically such photographs antedate the Revolution. By then, as Maiakovskii's poetry, Bulgakov's *Master and Margarita*, and the agitprop posters that covered the facade of the bell tower indicate, it had become something of an ideological cliché to depict literature as greater than the church, as the tool by which spiritual culture continued to develop in a materialist society. If the church had saved souls before the Revolution, writers engineered them after it.

Even more bluntly, the destruction of the Strastnoi Monastery and the relocation of the Pushkin Monument to stand over its ruin indicate a different sort of dynamism, more violent and ideologically motivated than what Toporov describes in his analysis of the Bronze Horseman. By developing the metapoetics of allusion in Pushkin's textual "Monument," Toporov follows in the long line of iconoclasts who destroy or ignore Pushkin's statue in an effort to save him from a very different fate – becoming the tool of state propaganda. Reconstructing these changes in Pushkin Square requires a knowledge of historical detail similar to what Toporov brings to bear on the history of St Isaac's Cathedral as part of the dynamic context with which the Bronze Horseman interacts. Perhaps because Toporov engaged so closely with a poetics of reception that parallels Pushkin's in "Monument," his theory explains the Pushkin Monument, too – the device of ekphrasis transposed into the genre of aesthetic theory.

While his theory functions well as an interpretive paradigm for the Pushkin Monument, Toporov specifically did *not* address Opekushin's statue. Furthermore, he made no overt allusion to performances at the Pushkin Monument or the literature that it inspired and only a few indirect allusions to the poem itself. On the one hand, this could be explained by the fact that Toporov was ending the Petersburg Text – he was focused on Petersburg monuments and Petersburg spaces, but the Pushkin Monument is in Moscow. Why would he address it? However, there is more at stake. Not only does Toporov's theory explain the Pushkin Monument; as the end of the Petersburg Text, it also provides an alternative to it.

Unpacking that conclusion requires a brief detour into the intricacies of Toporov's Petersburg Text. Toporov's student and the keeper of his archive for many years, Tat'iana Vladimirovna Tsiv'ian, insists that "Petersburg Text" is a homonym: two different ideas are bound together in a phrase that is spelled and pronounced the same. First, she cites S.G. Bocharov:

> Vladimir Nikolaevich discovered in our culture the super-phenomenon of the *Petersburg Text*. But it is possible to say with confidence that he *created* it for us, this conceptual reality, that he created and organized his own Petersburg Text in a large cycle of works, which captured what, in one of his works, he referred to as his half-century-long Petersburg *"roman"* – both a research project and a project of the heart.[55]

The two are related but separate phenomena. Toporov created both a theoretical construct, the Petersburg Text, that has entered into the toolbox of many scholars and thinkers, and he also laid out a huge body of work that can be considered (and is considered by his closest students and colleagues) a work of its own, his *Petersburg Text*. Tsiv'ian takes Bocharov's dual understanding of "Petersburg Text" as a "motto" and unpacks it as both a "super-phenomenon" and the creation of Toporov himself. She explains that according to Toporov's design, his Petersburg Text operates according to a strict set of rules that cannot be applied to other cities, especially Moscow. At the same time, she recognizes that the theory of the urban text, which in many ways has grown out of Toporov's writings, has been applied productively to different cities in the works of many different scholars. However, this theoretical construct, she insists, is a "homonym" of Toporov's Petersburg Text, operating under a different set of rules.[56] Bocharov's distinction and Tsiv'ian's insistence on and elaboration of it demonstrate the dual nature of the Petersburg Text and necessitate a dual understanding of how it ends. In the narrow, strict, sense of the term "Petersburg Text," the one that refers to Toporov's collected writings on the subject, the question is why Toporov's turn to Petersburg monuments reflects Pushkin's poetics of reception in "Monument." Why might Toporov as a scholar and thinker, and a bit of a future poet in his own right, have engaged with Pushkin's tropes as a way to end his Petersburg *roman*?

As the outline in Toporov's preface to *Petersburg Text* indicates, his work was unfinished.[57] However, that does not mean that he did not have a sense of what its end should be.[58] By engaging in co-creation with Pushkin's allusions to Petersburg monuments and the poetics of reception in "Monument," Toporov ends his own *Petersburg Text* in the same way that Pushkin and other Petersburg poets have. Reading Toporov's formulation about the *siuzhet* of the Petersburg Text (life, overcoming death through cathartic suffering) in light of Pushkin's "Monument" reveals a striking commonality between Pushkin's interpretation of the ambivalence of the lifelike statue and the Petersburg Text. Pushkin's poetics relies on a progression from matter to word – and Toporov sees something similar when he writes, "Petersburg came to know itself not so much from the depiction of the realities of life, of the daily grind, of its ever deepening history, as much as from Russian literature."[59] In Toporov's formulation, the word ascends higher than the material realities of Petersburg itself and reflects back to Petersburg its true meanings. These parallels between Toporov's theory of monumental sculpture and Pushkin's poetics in "Monument" cast all of his writings on Petersburg Text as a verbal monument to Pushkin – an alternative to Opekushin's statue that acknowledges Pushkin's well-documented aversion to visual depictions of himself and situates Toporov's corpus in the tradition of many other future poets who brought Pushkin's works to life through allusions facilitated by the city of St Petersburg and its monuments. In this sense, Toporov's Petersburg Text rejects Opekushin's statue so as to highlight a more true, more lifelike, or, to use Toporov's terminology, more "dynamic" monument to Pushkin.

With regard to the end of the Petersburg Text in its second meaning, as a "supertext" (one "story" written by many authors), Pushkin's

"Monument" also makes sense as a productive end. The fact that Petersburg Text begins with Pushkin and specifically with *The Bronze Horseman* is almost universally acknowledged; but where it ends is a more volatile question.[60] Did it end with the renaming of the city at the beginning of the twentieth century? Or with the Petersburg poets who lived through the end of Imperial Russia – poets such as Anna Akhmatova and Osip Mandel'shtam? Or in the mid-twentieth century with Soviet Petersburg authors such as Brodsky or Andrei Bitov? Which Petersburg author is the last to contribute? Within the framework of Toporov's theoretical apparatus, is it possible to predict future contributions to the Petersburg Text, or is it a largely static, defined, and closed supertextual system? Other scholars in Moscow-Tartu Semiotics have grappled with this question for a long time: one example is Tsiv'ian's careful attention to how it is possible to make Toporov's writings productive and applicable to many different cities while also respecting his adamant refusal to recognize any urban text but the Petersburg Text.[61]

Andrew Reynolds also poses the question of the end of the Petersburg Text in his provocative analysis of the poet Joseph Brodsky's failure to return to Petersburg. Reynolds reads Brodsky's "last" poem, "August," in light of its allusions to Pushkin's "Monument."[62] According to Reynolds's interpretation, "August" represents a poetic return to the Petersburg Text in lieu of a physical return to Petersburg, while at the same time recognizing in Pushkin the model for the deaths of all Russian poets. He writes, "If Brodsky's Baratynskian definition of himself as the 'last poet' is valid, is this partly because the 'Petersburg Text' has lost its power, or might Brodsky's passing cause its further decline or complete demise?"[63] While, on the one hand, Brodsky seems to welcome a younger generation of poets, he also expresses some anxiety at being bypassed. As Reynolds writes, "Strong poets need poetic progeny, of course, as this is the main way in which their immortality is guaranteed, but there is always a danger that they will in turn establish a new line of succession, one that bypasses the anxious precursor poet. Thus Brodsky has ulterior motives both in wishing that a strong line of kenotic poets continue *and* in being the last in that line."[64] As I argue in chapter 3 and chapter 5 of this book, Bulgakov's *Master and Margarita* and Tolstaia's many allusions to the Pushkin Monument deal with this same ambivalence about poetic succession.

In all of these scenarios, the apocalypticism of the city (the "end" of Petersburg) parallels the apocalyptic crisis of poetic succession: when will the Petersburg Text cease to accept new "contributions"? When will the last Petersburg poet contribute to the tradition of writing about Petersburg? Pushkin's "Monument" plays a key role in this "end."

Reynolds's arguments about Brodsky's return to Pushkin's "Monument" when writing his own "last" poem make a suggestive parallel for Toporov's engagement with Pushkin's "Monument" at the end of his Petersburg Text. For many contributors to the Petersburg Text in its meaning as a "supertext," allusions to "Monument" and the idea of performance as co-creation provide a paradigm for conceptualizing poetic immortality, life overcoming death, along the lines of the Petersburg Text. In this sense, the "end" of the Petersburg Text is threatened by the same conditions as the "end" of Pushkin's immortality – when a future Petersburg poet ceases to exist. When poets like Brodsky face death and the end of their work, the theme of poetic immortality is brought to new life through allusions not to Opekushin's statue but to Pushkin's Petersburg writing, which, mythopoetically if not chronologically, begins with *The Bronze Horseman* and ends with his "Monument."

Contemplation of the "end" as a theme in both the Petersburg Text and Pushkin's "Monument" also sheds light on one of the compositional tensions of the Pushkin Monument: a Petersburg poem on a Moscow statue. In the storied rivalry between Russia's capitals, Petersburg ends where Moscow begins. When we have understood the ways in which Toporov's archival notes and theoretical ideas about monuments interact with the Pushkin Monument as poem, statue, and performative space, it becomes clear that the end of the Petersburg Text, Pushkin's poem "Monument," is also the beginning of another sort of urban monumental aesthetics, one that belongs in Moscow – allusions to the Pushkin Monument.

The opposition of Petersburg and Moscow in the Pushkin Monument leads to different "ends," and yet both the Pushkin Monument and the Petersburg Text evoke the general structure of Russia's myths of "the End." In the conclusion to his study of the apocalypse in modern Russian fiction, David Bethea puts his analysis into a larger perspective, arguing that "the constituent elements of the myth [of the End], what Lèvi-Strauss has called 'mythemes,' remain essentially intact."[65] The "end" in Pushkin's "Monument" and Toporov's Petersburg Text does not engage the end of time or history, the *Parousia*, Russian history, or the horsemen of the apocalypse, which are the subjects of Bethea's analysis. Rather, a different end is at stake: the end of poetry, the cessation of a poetic tradition and poetic immortality, the death of the poetic "gods." However, Bethea's structural observation still holds.[66] When viewed as an "end," the constituent elements that give life to the verbal, visual, and performative dimensions of the Pushkin Monument (the interaction of the lifelike statue, future poet, naive reader, and allusion) present a fascinating set of "enduring combinatory possibilities."[67] In the next chapter we turn our attention to another combination of the elements of the Pushkin Monument. In Tatiana Tol'staia's *Slynx*, the iconoclastic "shattering" of the Pushkin Monument in Moscow frames questions about the end of poetry, and, even more broadly, the end of culture as we know it.

Tolstaia's *Slynx*: Disfiguring the Monument (1986–2000)

As chapter 4 has shown, Vladimir Toporov's disruption of the verbal, visual, and performative dimensions of the Pushkin Monument frames at least two ends: Toporov's own writing about Petersburg as well as the more abstract meaning of the Petersburg Text, the tradition of writing about Peter's city that begins with Pushkin's *The Bronze Horseman*. Toporov's iconoclastic rejection of Opekushin's statue confronts clichés that had deprived the Pushkin Monument of aesthetic life, while at the same time dealing with the larger questions of "the end" that the monument poses: the end of a poet's life and work and the end of the tradition of alluding to his poetry. A naive viewer and a co-creator (the function of the future poet) play key roles in Toporov's theory about the dynamic context of three-dimensional art. The literal and figurative "motion" of these two kinds of viewers can bring a sculpture to life or reduce it to immobility, canonical interpretation, and cliché. If Toporov's iconoclasm disrupted the visual, verbal, and performative unity of the Pushkin Monument to propose a more lifelike monument to Pushkin, another significant iconoclastic approach to the Pushkin Monument suggests a different end altogether. Like the end of Toporov's Petersburg Text, it too emerged in the 1990s, a time when the search for what comes after the end was particularly intense in Russia.

Contemporary author and essayist Tat'iana Tolstaia (b. 1951) has repeatedly returned to the Pushkin Monument in her late-Soviet and post-Soviet fiction to address the crisis of cultural continuity faced by her generation. Her last major fiction to date, the novel *Slynx* (*Kys'*, 2000), relies on an iconoclastic approach to the Pushkin Monument as a central plot device and unifying image.[1] Tolstaia's iconoclasm, however, differs from Toporov's. Toporov rejects the statue and disrupts the unity of the verbal, visual, and performative elements of the Pushkin Monument. In contrast, Tolstaia disfigures each element in equal measure. This means engaging not only with the end of the Petersburg Text but also with a post-apocalyptic Moscow, the setting of the novel. If the extent of her iconoclasm is more sweeping, so are the consequences. What is at stake is not an aesthetic descent into cliché but the regression of humanity as a species. In a sense, the moral and spiritual themes of *Slynx* resemble an extreme negation of the Cappadocian metaphor of the lifelike statue. The degradation in the world of *Slynx* reflects such a complete loss of the divine image that there seems little chance, short of a second Incarnation, of ever finding a way towards some sort of *theosis*. The real tragedy is not so much that Pushkin and his poetry have been irretrievably lost. It is worse: they have become the pretext for cruelty and baseness of the most banal and clichéd variety.

The structure of the novel reveals how Tolstaia, relying on the tropes of Soviet science fiction, destroys the Pushkin Monument multiple times in a dystopian future Moscow.[2] The first destruction sets the premise for the novel: a nuclear apocalypse has destroyed all of Moscow (including the Pushkin Monument) and perhaps the world, which is now inhabited by ignorant mutants. The second and most complete destruction occurs when a member of the old intelligentsia tries to mentor a member of the new, post-apocalyptic society (a future poet) to recreate the lost Pushkin Monument. Their attempts disfigure the verbal, visual, and performative dimensions of the Pushkin Monument more thoroughly than any nuclear blast ever could. The grotesque wooden idol that results from their efforts is once again destroyed in another explosion at the end of the novel. Tolstaia's apocalyptic scenario transforms Pushkin's formula for poetic immortality: in *Slynx*, Tolstaia has created a "sublunar world" inhabited only by naive readers completely cut off from the aesthetic forms of the past. Not even one poet can emerge to interpret Pushkin in productive ways. If *Master and Margarita* poses the question of what would happen if the future poet *is* a naive reader, *Slynx* presents a world in which Pushkin's basic condition for immortality, at least one living poet, cannot be met.

To unpack the meanings of Tolstaia's iconoclasm, this chapter explores how her innovation in *Slynx* engages with several layers of her own oeuvre, the writerly tradition of bringing the Pushkin Monument to life (most notably in the work of Soviet-era authors like Vladimir Maiakovskii, Marina Tsvetaeva, and Abram Tertz), and her own cultural moment – the last decade of the Soviet Union and the first decade of the Russian Federation. Significantly, Tolstaia's allusions also engage with some of the ambivalent aspects of the reception of Toporov's Petersburg Text in scholarly circles. Her approach to urban space in the novel underscores the same tension in the Pushkin Monument between

Moscow and Petersburg that Toporov's engagement with Pushkin's poem and the concept of performance illuminate.[3] In this regard, her novel reads as a sort of end of the Petersburg Text just as much as the end of culture as such, and, together with Toporov's work, underscores the apocalyptic energy that iconoclastic allusions to the Pushkin Monument can unleash.

Bringing the Monument to Life and Other Iconoclasms

Understanding the devastating future of the Pushkin Monument in *Slynx* requires a deeper look into how iconoclasm towards the Pushkin Monument has evolved in the twentieth century. Poems like Maiakovskii's "Jubilee" and Tsvetaeva's "Poems to Pushkin," and Abram Tertz's prose *Strolls with Pushkin* rely on the trope of bringing the monument to life as an iconoclastic strategy to free Pushkin from official "Pushkinolatry."[4] Tertz's *Strolls with Pushkin* created a scandal when it was published in Russia for the first time in 1991 because it was perceived as an attack on Pushkin himself instead of on the official cliché.[5] Many other authors writing in the 1990s also sought to problematize Pushkin's Soviet reception at the end of the Soviet period with the goal of revitalizing Pushkin, frequently with – but sometimes without – recourse to the monument metaphor.[6] As these works show, there is a deep connection between the Pushkin myth and the Pushkin Monument in Moscow.

Tolstaia's works that feature the Pushkin Monument belong in this list. There is, however, something else going on that makes Tolstaia's work unique. Tolstaia engages not only in debunking the Pushkin myth but also in innovative play with the Pushkin Monument as poem, statue, and performance. On the one hand, "bringing the monument to life" was a crucial form of combating the Soviet Pushkin cliché.[7] On the other, while still powerful enough to provoke a scandal, the trope of "bringing the Pushkin Monument to life" had been repeated to the point that it too risked becoming a cliché. Understanding that process is critical for interpreting several of Tolstaia's early iconoclastic depictions of the Pushkin Monument, which were published just before the scandal caused by *Strolls with Pushkin* in 1991. "Night" (1987), "Limpopo" (1990), and "Siuzhet" (1991) reflect ambivalence towards the Pushkin Monument and its cultural history. The intervening years between "Siuzhet" and *Slynx* (2000) produced a much darker vision of the Pushkin Monument, perhaps in part due to the response to *Strolls with Pushkin*.

Generally speaking, Tolstaia's prose is rich with brilliant allusions to Pushkin's poetry.[8] Analysis of her early allusions to the Pushkin

Monument suggests a creative search for alternative iconoclasms as a way to contribute to Pushkin's immortality. They lay the groundwork for understanding the extreme iconoclasm of *Slynx*, which draws on developments in post-Soviet aesthetics and the official cult of Pushkin that culminated in the 1999 celebration of the 200th anniversary of the poet's birth.

Tolstaia's short story "Night" relates the inception and pursuit of the intellectually disabled hero's ambition to become a writer like Pushkin. Forty-year-old Aleksei Petrovich relies on his eighty-year-old mother, *mamochka*, for everything, including his knowledge of Pushkin. Aleksei Petrovich is especially keen on Pushkin's "Winter Evening," which he understands very poorly but can perform perfectly from memory. The idea of becoming a writer occurs to Alexei Petrovich on a walk with his mother when they pass through Pushkin Square. In an otherwise non-specific Soviet cityscape (an ice cream stand, a communal apartment, the sunset reflecting in the windows of high-rise apartment buildings, pigeons), Pushkin Square is the one landmark that kindles cultural recall in Alexei Petrovich's diminished understanding: Pushkin is a writer.[9] Of course there are many landmarks around Pushkin Square that might trigger a greater depth of cultural recall in an educated Muscovite's mind: Tverskoi Boulevard with its rich literary and theatrical tradition, the *Izvestiia* building and its ambivalent legacy in the world of Soviet news, and the Strastnoi Monastery, which, until it was destroyed in 1937, occupied the current location of Pushkin's Monument. What is excusable, even impressive, for Alexei Petrovich, however, provides an opportunity for the reader to wonder just how many people with normal to high intellectual functioning have much cultural recall in Pushkin Square beyond the fact that Pushkin was a "writer."

In the Soviet context, Tolstaia's Aleksei Petrovich seems to tread the same thin line that Soviet guitarist and poet Bulat Okudzhava immortalized in his song about a provincial family having their picture taken at the foot of the Pushkin Monument ("Na fone Pushkina," 1970). Svetlana Boym shows how Okudzhava's song navigates between reflecting "an innocent and spontaneous popular admiration for the great poet" and re-enacting "a stereotypical Soviet cultural gesture."[10] Okudzhava's song is a common poetic response that perpetuates the problematically ideological meanings of the monument while simultaneously seeking to disrupt those meanings.

Boym connects the Pushkin Monument to the practice of memorization by which every Soviet school child, like the forty-year old Aleksei Petrovich, learned poems and passages of Pushkin's works by rote. In her analysis, this is not a positive sort of reading strategy. On the contrary, such an approach to Pushkin's poetry yields knowledge that remains "static" and "dogmatic," so that for many readers, Pushkin is "half memorized" and "half unknown."[11] Like Okudzhava's song and Boym's observations, Tolstaia problematizes the reception of a naive reader through Alexei Petrovich's rote memorization and interaction with Pushkin Square. Rote memorization is a textual strategy that cuts off interpretation of the text memorized; it is also an allusive strategy in that it can lead to recognizing, interpreting, or creating allusions.

Alexei Petrovich declaims Pushkin's "Winter Evening" from memory in mostly nonsensical, but perfectly trochaic, syllables: *"Buriam, gloiu, nebak, roet."*[12] As it turns out, *voet*, "howls," is one of the few words that Alexei Petrovich actually understands in the poem, and he responsively howls, only to be shushed by *mamochka*. In this first reading, Alexei Petrovich demonstrates his limited access to the signifiers themselves and complete incomprehension of the signifieds to which they are attached. His memorization preserves the syllables in crystalline, almost formalist, precision, but the semantic layers of meaning that would allow Alexei Petrovich to interpret the meaning of the poem aside from its form are absent. The irony of this situation is heightened by the similarity between Pushkin's "Winter Evening," in which he spends the evening sitting with Arina Radionovna, and Alexei Petrovich's own evening spent with *mamochka*.

While Alexei Petrovich's memorization leaves little room for the hope that he might engage in meaningful interpretation of the poem, it also facilitates his ability to recognize allusions to the memorized work in another text. The "poem" that he composes at the end of Tolstaia's story can be read as an oversimplified allusion to the dominant metaphor in "Winter Evening": night. Alexei Petrovich's poem is simple: he repeats the signifier "night" (*noch'*) ten times. Helena Goscilo describes its effect: "By story's end the word 'night' is so freighted with conceptual accretions that it can legitimately pass for the poem that Aleksei believes he has composed in merely iterating the word ten times."[13] These "conceptual accretions" come from both Alexei Petrovich's night-time adventures and Pushkin's poem, and the repeated words do eloquently sum up the story. However, they also function in a similar way to Alexei Petrovich's first performance of the poem. All of the mythological and metaphorical contours of night that Pushkin evokes – winter, depression, old age, death, darkness, intoxication, fatigue, sorrow, and fear – are reduced to one lone signifier and left entirely up to the reader to recall. Based on Alexei Petrovich's limited ability to reconstruct meaning from some word or cultural object and his literal interpretation of Pushkin's "begins howling," one must suspect that Alexei Petrovich can articulate very few of the metaphorical connotations of night, whether they originate in his personal experience or in Pushkin's poem.

Alexei Petrovich's naive reading and naive writing do not fail completely: his poem is in its own way a brilliant reading of Pushkin's poem. While they certainly lack variety, his rhyme and rhythm – "night, night, night, night …" – have the poetic effect of counting sheep or mind-emptying meditation. Formally, his poem highlights Pushkin's device of repetition: semantically, it reveals his device of layering the tenors of "night" as a vehicle. Read alone, it might seem like the poetic failure of a weak-minded, imitative poet, but as criticism, the poem stands as an interesting interpretation of Pushkin's verse. As author, Tolstaia asserts her own power to turn Alexei Petrovich, a naive reader of Pushkin, into a future poet. It takes an astute artist to create a story that accomplishes as much as "Night" does: it begins with one word and ends with the repetition of the same word; it satirizes criticism of Pushkin and his reception in the Soviet Union; it depicts a hero's growth; and it rereads one of Pushkin's most famous poems in an interesting way. Even though Alexei Petrovich's reading of "Winter Evening" and his poetic adaptation of it in his poem "Night" are interesting, they mutilate and destroy the richness of Pushkin's original. Only Tolstaia's reader, as opposed to Alexei Petrovich, can understand the beauty of Alexei Petrovich's creation: Tolstaia, not Alexei Petrovich, is the future "poet" who orchestrates the reader's vision.

Tolstaia returns to the Pushkin Monument a few years later in a more complicated narrative, "Limpopo" (published in 1990). "Limpopo" is a short story that chronicles the fates of four characters, a group of friends who came together in Moscow in the mid-seventies. The narrator, the only member of the group still alive, recounts her fifteen-year-old memories of how the idealistic revolutionary poet Lyonechka falls in love with a refugee named Judy. Judy was driven to Moscow by the twin causes of violent civil war in her native African land and her desire to study to become a veterinarian. The title of the story, "Limpopo," alludes to a similar constellation of themes in Kornei Chukovskii's children's tale about Dr Aibolit, who visits Africa to treat sick animals.[14] Playing on the motif of Pushkin's African heritage, Lyonechka immediately conceives a plan to impregnate Judy with his child, who, in inheriting Lyonechka's intelligentsia culture and Judy's Africanness, will be the next Pushkin. The plan has as little connection to reality as the Limpopo River has to Judy's culture or heritage or as Chukovskii's play has to Pushkin's blackness. Before conception occurs, however, at a Soviet reception for members of a sister region made up of minorities, Judy catches cold and, two weeks later, dies. Lyonechka goes insane

from grief. Fifteen years after Judy's death, only the narrator and Lyonechka's Aunt Zina remain to mourn her death. To make matters worse,
the narrator is deprived of her annual visit to Judy's grave because it
has, with no warning, been removed to an unknown location to make
way for a new thoroughfare. The story ends when the narrator visits
Moscow's Pushkin Monument with Aunt Zina to remember the young
lovers' tragic tale, mostly forgotten by everyone else in the turmoil that
characterized Russia in 1990.[15]

As they stand and look up at the face of Pushkin, green from the
weathering of the metal and covered in white pigeon droppings, Aunt
Zina wistfully mutters, "If they'd just made a little more effort – he
would have been born."[16] Her romantic nostalgia reflects considerable
ignorance of the narrator's account of Lyonechka's ill-starred plan to
breed this new Pushkin and the likelihood that the plan could ever suc-
ceed or have anything to do with "a little more effort." The narrator's
recognition that Judy was a completely alienated person in the Soviet
Union, barely understanding the language or much of anything else
and completely cut off from her home and family in Africa, underscores
the tragedy of the Pushkin Monument as the only memorial to her life.[17]
Only Lyonechka's plan to father a new Pushkin with Judy connects her
to the monument. The narrator does not even remember Judy's real
name: she never knew it because when Judy first arrived her name was
so unusual and difficult to pronounce that everyone gave up and just
called her Judy.

On the one hand, the narrator and Zina are naive readers like Alexei
Petrovich in their superficial knowledge of Pushkin's life, art, and monument; however, given that they are educated and supposedly com-
petent members of society, a comparison to Alexei Petrovich cannot
work in their favour.[18] Just how little they perceive in the monument
concludes the story. Zina misquotes the third stanza of Pushkin's poem
"Monument," saying, "The proud grandson of the Slavs and the now
wild ..."[19] Pushkin actually wrote, "The proud grandson of the Slavs,
the Finn, the now wild Tungus."[20] Zina cannot recall how the line ends,
probably in part because she does not correctly remember the part she
quotes. Zina asks the narrator, who also claims ignorance, and the two
walk away before they draw the attention of the police, either unaware
that the answer is written just on the other side of the monument or too
lazy to take the four steps to read it for themselves.

The fact that these two characters cannot remember the ethnonyms
Finn and Tungus highlights their willful ignorance of Judy's African culture and language. By alluding to the fourth stanza of Pushkin's "Monument," with its overt theme of "empire," Tolstaia reveals the cultural

ignorance of her late Soviet characters (they do not know Pushkin) as well as the colonizing ethnocentrism that the fourth stanza seems to perpetuate. The historical context of the story (the impending break-up of the Soviet Union and, by implication, the loss of the nationally defined nation states, "minorities" within the paradigm of Great Russian chauvinism) accentuates the themes of cultural condescension and isolation that motivate the racism Judy encounters before her death. But the context also contributes to the sense that Lyonechka, the narrator, and their friends are alienated from what it means to be Russian even as they are on the verge of no longer being Soviet. The amnesia and apathy of the narrator and Aunt Zina highlight the problematic condescension of an empire's majority towards its minorities while poignantly satirizing the whole idea of giving birth to a new future Pushkin when they cannot be bothered to read the poetry of the Pushkin who really existed even when it is right in front of their eyes.

However, just as Alexei Petrovich's poem "Night" is brilliant even as it is reductive, ambivalence flavours the narrator's final words in "Limpopo": "It's true, I already don't remember even a single word of the rest of the poem."[21] While she cannot recall Judy's name or country or the references to Finn and Tungus, she demonstrates an admirable dedication to preserving Judy's memory. Furthermore, the title of the story, "Limpopo," is just one of those strange foreign words that only someone dedicated to understanding places that are far removed from their reality, like the famous Dr Aibolit of Chukovskii's children's poem "Limpopo," would know. Perhaps the empire of the Romanovs and the Soviets, at least in 1990, seemed to be giving way to an interest in people motivated by shared experiences and fond memories instead of the geopolitical definitions imposed by imperialistic ideologies.

In both of these late Soviet stories, Tolstaia's iconoclasm differs from the iconoclastic tradition that sought to bring the monument to life through informality and alienation. Tolstaia's naive readers do not attempt to make the Pushkin Monument move through their narrative power. On the contrary, by walking past the monument, Alexei is inspired to create a naive poem that points to Tolstaia's narrative power as a future poet. Likewise, the narrator of "Limpopo" and Aunt Zina annually memorialize a plan to conceive and give birth to a new Pushkin by visiting the monument. Through their naiveté, Tolstaia brings Pushkin's fourth stanza of "Monument" to life as a poignant commentary on the living legacy of imperial ethnocentrism.

The iconoclasm in these stories blends the trope of bringing the Pushkin Monument to life with Bulgakov's allusions to it in *Master and Margarita*. Riukhin's ignorance fails to bring the monument to life just as Pushkin Square in "Night" is little more than a backdrop for Alexei Petrovich's desire to become a writer. Likewise, in "Limpopo," the impassive Pushkin Monument at the end of the story is the greatest commentary on Lyonechka's naive idea of bringing Pushkin to life again by having a child with Judy. Tolstaia's short story "Siuzhet" (1991) reveals yet a third strategy in the search for a new iconoclasm: an alternative future in which there can be no Pushkin Monument because Pushkin dies in 1880, not 1837.

Narrated from the perspective of 1937, "Siuzhet" recounts the duel between D'Anthès and Pushkin but with a different outcome: D'Anthès, the foreign villain, dies and Pushkin lives to become a crotchety old man. Pushkin, soon to be eighty, travels to collect material for his history of Pugachev and tries to recall the name of the jerk with whom he fought a duel. A certain little boy named Volodya (the reader later learns that this is none other than the child Vladimir Lenin) hits him in the back of the head with a snowball and taunts him by calling him a monkey (a racial slur on Pushkin's African ancestry). Pain jogs Pushkin's fuzzy memory to recall the name D'Anthès. Pushkin proceeds to beat the child Lenin so severely that Volodya lies in a hospital for a week. While the exertion leads to Pushkin's death, the beating seems to do Lenin some good. The boy Lenin grows up to become the minister of the interior to Nicholas II and the hope and support of his aging mother. These events lead to yet others: the Russians beat the Germans in the First World War, there is no Revolution, and in 1937, on the day that Nicholas II dies, Lenin suffers a stroke and dies from complications soon thereafter. Ironically, 1937 is not the year in which the official cult of Pushkin is raised to new heights, even as unprecedented numbers of poets die premature deaths, but the year in which oppressive rulers die of natural causes. To heighten this irony, the narrator reports rumours that Lenin will be replaced as minister of the interior by a certain Lord Dzhugashvili (i.e., an alternative Iosif Stalin). The narrative breaks off here, leaving the reader to wonder what form the Stalinist Terror of 1937 would take in a Russia where poets live to a ripe old age instead of dying at the age of thirty-seven and later attaining immortality in monumental statuary.

In this alternative Russian future, the Pushkin Monument as poem, statue, and performance is a crucial subtext. The first epigraph for the story comes from Pushkin's poem "And long will I be loved by the people." However, the second epigraph is from Alexander Blok's "To the Pushkin House" (1921): "That is why, at sunset / departing into the nighttime darkness, / from the white square of the Senate / I quietly bow to him."[22] Building on Blok's plea to Pushkin for help in the dark days of February 1921, the implication in "Siuzhet" is that Push-kin is beloved not for his poetry (Pushkin contemplates the bitter truth that no one reads his poetry or his prose) but for having given Lenin a "proper" beating as a child and consequently having saved Russia from well-known griefs and heartaches (admittedly, the monarchist Lenin creates a different set of griefs and heartaches). In this scenario, the political utility of Pushkin's life trumps any sort of future poetic reception. Pushkin's verse did little to change the course of history in comparison with his bad temper and violent nature, which led him to strike a child in the head with a cane.

Even though Opekushin never creates a statue in "Siuzhet," Tolstaia alludes to one of the monument's prominent clichés – pigeon droppings – to preserve Pushkin from death (a different take on bringing him back to life) in the fateful duel with D'Anthès. Instead of dying from the duel, Pushkin lives until 1880 because D'Anthès fires his pistol early when a frightened bird takes flight from a branch overhead, relaxes its cloaca, and drops milky-white pus on D'Anthès's hand. The irony is that the historical Pushkin, immortalized in the tragedy of his death and mar-tyrdom as much as in his romantic life, is forced to endure eternity as a monument that pigeons, rapturously oblivious to the poet's greatness, continuously streak with white as they eliminate the pale, runny stain of their waste.

Finally, Tolstaia replaces the performative dimension of the Pushkin Monument with a clever play on Pushkin's African heritage and age. Had Pushkin not died of his wound, he would have turned eighty at the Jubilee. As is clear from "Limpopo," published just a year before "Siu-zhet," Tolstaia engaged with Tsvetaeva's connection between Pushkin's African heritage and the black colour of the Pushkin Monument, a con-nection that evokes Marina Tsvetaeva's essay "My Pushkin," in which she identifies Pushkin's blackness as an identity shared by all poets.[23] In the same allusive cluster, Tolstaia evokes the 1880 Jubilee, where elite members of the intelligentsia grew ecstatic over Pushkin the dead poet at the foot of his "black" monument, but inversely. The Pushkin of "Siu-zhet" in 1880 is not venerated as a hero but insulted with a racial slur by a child from the intelligentsia class. In "Siuzhet," no future poet makes innovative allusion to Pushkin's poetry; instead, the future Lenin learns a life-changing lesson at his hands.

In "Night" and "Limpopo," Tolstaia depicted the Pushkin Monument in a recognizable present or near past in which naive readers and poets try to bring Pushkin to life with ambivalent results. "Siuzhet" reflects another innovation: a future in which Pushkin is saved from death by bird poop, where there is no Pushkin Monument, where Pushkin is not read, and where the rest of Pushkin's story is devoted not to future poets and their creations inspired by Pushkin but to Vladimir Ul'ianov and Nicholas II.

A pregnant silence separates "Siuzhet" and *Slynx*. Between 1987 and 1991, Tolstaia published three stories that significantly engaged with the Pushkin Monument as poem, statue, and performative space. Filled with political and aesthetic developments, the decade between these stories and *Slynx* contributes to a fourth iconoclasm, darker and more complete. Begun in 1986 and published in 2000, *Slynx* builds on these first iconoclastic interpretations of the Pushkin Monument by incorporating the genre expectations of dystopian science fiction. The central plot device in *Slynx* is the negative vision of a culturally and genetically degraded future in which there is no Pushkin Monument. The question is not what it would mean to bring Opekushin's Pushkin Monument to life but rather what it would mean to face the task of recreating its verbal, visual, and performative dimensions anew after having been cut off from the tradition for centuries. Remaking the monument in the cultural and ecological conditions of *Slynx* turns out to be an extreme form of destruction – a way not to bring the monument to life, but to foreclose its future forever.

The Pushkin Monument, *Slynx*, and Science Fiction

If it is clear that disfiguring the Pushkin Monument plays a central role in the themes and plot of *Slynx*, precisely which genre expectations provide the best frame for interpreting the novel have been harder to define. As the following analysis will show, this is in part because the two go together: in order to destroy the future of the Pushkin Monument, Tolstaia bends the genre expectations of science fiction. The extent to which the connection between genre and the Pushkin Monument is central to the novel can be gleaned from reviews, frequently negative, which often exclude the significance of the Pushkin Monument even as they detail the ways the novel fails to function within (or as a hybrid of) any genre.[24]

Similarly, negative appraisals of *Slynx* that do address Tolstaia's thematic treatment of the Pushkin Monument tie its failure to a specific genre. Scholar of Russian postmodernism Nonna Petrovna Benevolenskaia summarizes scholarly interpretations of *Slynx* as an ideological novel that presents in aesthetic form all the dangers of "literature-centrism."[25] According to Benevolenskaia, Tolstaia's main thesis is that reading books does not enlighten or improve every reader. This thesis, in Benevolenskaia's analysis, is neither original nor substantiated and, moreover, finds imperfect expression in the characters and themes of the novel.[26] Reading Tolstaia's iconoclastic approach to the Pushkin Monument within the context of its cultural history and with a different set of genre expectations, however, suggests that Tolstaia might not be warning of the harms of "literature-centrism," but rather, through the tropes of science fiction, be exploring a possible future in which allusion to a forgotten cultural tradition becomes an inherently degenerative technology. In this formula, Tolstaia is not arguing that "literature-centrism" is harmful but is depicting the aesthetic consequences of trying to restore a cultural tradition that has been completely lost.

While *Slynx* ultimately fails to fit neatly into the traditional opposition of utopian and dystopian genres, positive readings of the novel tend to see this as one of its strengths.[27] As has been repeatedly shown, attempting to squeeze *Slynx* into a known generic category is problematic. The answer is both simpler and more complex than genre labelling: to understand Tolstaia's allusions to the Pushkin Monument we must look at how she engages with the long tradition of Russian and Soviet science fiction.

For example, *Slynx* is rooted in the spatial and temporal categories of Russian modernist science fiction. As Edith Clowes points out, Tolstaia sets her vision of an isolated Moscow two hundred years in the future to echo Evgenii Zamiatin's dystopian portrayal in the novel *We*. Zamiatin's One State also existed for two hundred years inside its walls, cut off from the outside. Where Tolstaia's depiction differs from Zamiatin's, however, is in the vector of technological advancement. Technological advances characterize Zamiatin's city, while Tolstaia's city regresses into a violently primitive society.[28] Along similar lines, Tolstaia engages with Bulgakov's science fiction masterpiece, *Heart of a Dog*. But Benedikt is not a dog who has transformed into a problematic, albeit rational, human; rather, he represents a human who has regressed (through techno-nuclear apocalypse) and begins to show the moral and physical characteristics of a dog, complete with small, wagging tail.

In her post-Soviet science fiction world, Tolstaia does not merely allude to the forms and themes of modernist texts: she engages deeply with their poetics and legacy of cultural transformation. Banerjee's analysis of modernist science fiction maps out important aspects of what Tolstaia also grapples with in *Slynx*. For example, Banerjee writes that, while one late-nineteenth-century publication about science fiction "stressed that it required a modern, techno-scientific sensibility on the part of both writers and readers, Zamiatin celebrated its unprecedented potentials of defamiliarization."[29] In her postmodern novel, Tolstaia redirects this emphasis on technology and defamiliarization from a "techno-scientific sensibility" to the word as a technology, defamiliarizing many famous quotations from Russian poetry as well as the word itself, a strategy evident in the neologism of her title, *Slynx*, as well as in the central plot device of recreating the Pushkin Monument.[30] Allusion is the technology that allows writers to create something new out of the old, but it requires a certain technological sensibility on the part of the reader – a technology of both production and consumption that harks back to the long tradition begun by Pushkin's innovative metapoetics of allusion in "Monument."

Soviet science fiction, and in particular the work of the Strugatskii brothers, animates the future of the Pushkin Monument in *Slynx* in significant ways. Throughout the 1960s, 1970s, and 1980s, co-authors Arkadii and Boris Strugatskii penned numerous classics of Soviet and Russian science fiction, defining significant tropes of the genre. In her analysis of their work, Yvonne Howell writes, "One of the truisms of science fiction genre studies is that in science fiction, reality is 'made strange' in light of a single fantastic premise."[31] This premise also defines Tolstaia's *Slynx*: the one fantastic premise that Tolstaia extrapolates in *Slynx* is the idea that the word is the most basic of scientific technologies and that the loss of the ability to use words precludes any notion of future technological or cultural progress.[32] Like the Strugatskiis, Tolstaia also imagines a future that reverts to a violent and despotic past. Howell writes of the Strugatskiis' play in two acts, *Yids of the City of Peter, or Gloomy Discussions by Candlelight*: "The play's fantastic premise, which casts a shadow of the supernatural over everyday scenes, is that in the year of 1990, at the height of Gorbachev's glasnost reforms, the country could suddenly revert to the dark ages of terror, pogroms, and totalitarianism."[33] Tolstaia picks up many of their themes and develops them in her own way to reflect a similar crisis ten years after the end of the glasnost and perestroika reforms.

Tolstaia's *Slynx* draws on the modernist (Zamiatin, Bulgakov) and Soviet (Strugatskiis) tropes of science fiction, but it also belongs to the post-Soviet fascination with an ever-darkening vision of the science fiction future. Tolstaia herself belongs to that category of Russian post-Soviet authors who embrace science fiction as a genre without tying themselves narrowly to it. Writing about the legacy of the Strugatskiis, Sofya Khagi writes, "Like the earlier era of Mikhail Bulgakov and Evgenii Zamiatin, Russian literature today has writers who are not science fiction authors per se producing serious works in the genre."[34]

Like those of Tolstaia's peers whom Khagi analyses, Tolstaia reshapes the aesthetics of the Strugatskii brothers, whose "uncanny feel for 'the future surer than a pledge'" turns into a post-Soviet "conceptualization of this future as no longer 'around the bend.'"[35] In the 1990s, these authors drew on the Strugatskiis to "dramatize their own increasingly dark visions of modernization, progress, and morality."[36] Tolstaia's depiction of the Pushkin Monument places the fate of Russia's literary future in this post-Soviet science fiction context.

The society in *Slynx* is composed of *golubchiks* (genetically and culturally compromised inhabitants of post-Blast Moscow) and oldeners (members of late Soviet society who do not age as a result of their exposure to extreme levels of radiation). They are isolated not only from their own cultural and architectural past but from the rest of the world. The whole premise of aliens and other planets in the Strugatskiis' oeuvre is subverted by a regression from space travel to complete, earthly isolation: even the oldeners in *Slynx* do not know what has become of the West or the Egyptian pyramids or neighbouring nations. The Strugatskiis' notion of "progressorism" plays a role in *Slynx*, too. As Khagi writes, "The Strugatskiis' oeuvre, for all its skepticism, still holds something of a nostalgic humanistic value for these authors and is employed to offset their own darker stories."[37] In Tolstaia, "progressorism" arguably takes the form of the attempt of oldeners to enlighten the *golubchiks*, in particular in Nikolai Ivanovich's mentorship of Benedikt in order to craft a new Pushkin Monument. But here again, the oldeners (who are, after all, people of the Strugatskiis' generation) prove to be faulty carriers of the tradition. Benedikt absorbs Nikita Ivanych's interest in art, but uses that same interest to justify executing his mentor.

Post-Soviet engagement with the Strugatskiis also reflects a growing sense of the "homeostatic universe," which, as Khagi suggests, "provides a convenient way to read stagnation, not just in post-Soviet Russia, but in global, postmodern, commodified reality." This sort of stagnation reflects the state of allusion in *Slynx*, where a positive reimagining of any work of art is inconceivable. The future poet that Pushkin envisioned has no place in the future depicted in *Slynx*. The Pushkin Monument must be destroyed on every level to motivate an apocalypse where the future of poetry is cut off forever and inhabitants are locked in an eternal present, effectively maintained through repeated destruction (the novel begins with the "blast" and ends with another "blast"). Pushkin's metapoetic concept of the future poet who can find new layers of meaning in his works is left irrecoverably in the past.

Pelevin, Postmodernism, and the Post-Soviet
Pushkin Monument

Within the context of post-Soviet literature and science fiction in the 1990s, post-Soviet novelist Viktor Pelevin's depiction of the Pushkin Monument in *Chapaev and the Void* is an important development for Tolstaia's destruction of the Pushkin Monument in *Slynx*. Critiques of influence and intertextuality and the way they relate to device and cliché were common as Tolstaia was writing at the turn of the twenty-first century.[38] They define her post-Soviet moment, and *Slynx* must be read in the context of earlier postmodern works such as Pelevin's *Chapaev and the Void*, which reflects trends in critical theory at the end of the twentieth century that challenged the interrelation of texts and meanings. On the one hand, authors like Pelevin engaged in the sort of postmodern play that characterizes their generation's approach to language and tradition. But as Angela Brintlinger notes, they also engaged their predecessors "with an almost manic gusto," celebrating the chance to allude in ways that Soviet censorship would not have allowed just a decade or so earlier.[39]

Pelevin begins and ends *Chapaev and the Void* (1996) with images of the Pushkin Monument. When the narrator gets to the end of the book – a future version (1991) of the Moscow in which the novel begins (1919) – the Pushkin Monument and Strastnoi Monastery have disappeared. The poem, statue, and performative space of the Pushkin Monument collapse into an empty urban space: a void. In this last chapter, Pelevin repeats many of the basic plot motifs of the "Musical Snuffbox" scene that opens the novel, although, based on the spatial void left by monument and monastery, the reader recognizes the temporal disjuncture (a mirroring of "19," two years after the revolution, and "91," two years after the fall of the Berlin Wall).[40]

The repetition of the beginning and ending of the novel develops the theme of eternal non-return, insisting on a sort of disconnection between the literary device of allusion and the texts alluded to. In the preface, the editor makes it clear that the book has nothing to do with Furmanov's novel *Chapaev*, and yet the reader cannot help but relate *Chapaev and the Void* to that novel, as well as to its adaptation for film and all of the Chapaev and Petia jokes that abound in Soviet culture. The device of allusion becomes a conceptual and structural vehicle for the thematics of the novel. But in *Chapaev and the Void*, there is no real need to identify the many mis-allusions: rather, they are presented as an alternative reality to be accepted at face value. Metaphorically, the dual images of the Pushkin Monument that begin and end the novel make this clear. The Pushkin Monument is there at the beginning and it is not there at the end, although Petia refers to it as the invisible Pushkin Monument, suggesting that even though it is not there, it is still there.[41]

By bookending *Chapaev and the Void* with the disappearance of the Pushkin Monument and Strastnoi Monastery, Pelevin begins to hint at the monument's metapoetic dimensions. Not only does the monument disappear, along with the most significant architectural ensemble, to use Toporov's term, in its "wings" (*kulisy*), the void (*pustota*) that it leaves seems to Petr to be the "best of all possible monuments": "The bronze Pushkin had disappeared, but the gaping void that had appeared where he used to stand somehow seemed like the best of all possible monuments. Where the Strastnoi Monastery had been, there was now an empty space."[42] This image and Petr's assessment of it function on a metapoetic level: in a work where every allusion is a misquotation, the void left by the Pushkin Monument symbolizes the device of allusion in the work. What is there to allude to but a gaping void, filled with whatever you care to imagine?

Tolstaia picks up on Pelevin's use of the Pushkin Monument but develops it into the sustained conceit of the whole novel. For Pelevin, the Pushkin Monument makes only a cameo appearance: it is a brief but powerful symbol that frames his novel. Tolstaia develops the theme in a more sustained way to address the whole range of meanings that have accrued to the Pushkin Monument from its inception in Pushkin's poetry through the appearance of Opekushin's statue and its unique life in Soviet art and theory. Like *Chapaev and the Void*, *Slynx* is deeply concerned with the future; with allusion as distortion; and with all the textual, sculptural, and performative dimensions of the Pushkin Monument. But *Slynx* goes one step further than *Chapaev and the Void*: the most complete destruction of the Pushkin Monument in *Slynx* occurs not when it is absent but when Benedikt attempts to recreate it.

When Benedikt attempts to recreate the Pushkin Monument, Tolstaia challenges Pelevin's concept of allusion as a void. To counteract the void that Petia sees as the greatest possible memorial to Pushkin, *Slynx* presents what it would be like to recreate the Pushkin Monument in just such a cultural void. Tolstaia's iconoclasm, far from suggesting a void as the ultimate reality, spurs readers to reconnect with the original texts, to rediscover in them a spiritual dimension if for no other reason than to reject the petty cruelty and violence of Benedikt. In *Slynx*, the void left by destroying the Pushkin Monument cannot be the best possible monument to Pushkin because it generates Benedikt's awful caricature. *Slynx* demonstrates that any replacement for the Pushkin Monument, even if only a void, contains as many dangerous threats to civilization as the monument's unfortunate role in propagandistic ideology and oversimplification of the literary word.

"the pushkin": Distorting Poem, Statue, and Performance

Distortions of the poem, statue, and performance culture of the Pushkin Monument epitomize the bleak cultural future depicted in *Slynx*. In recreating the Pushkin Monument (referred to as "the pushkin"), Benedikt effects a more complete form of iconoclasm than destruction ever could.

Tolstaia repeatedly emphasizes Benedikt's ignorance of Pushkin's poem "Monument." While the reader is invited to bring all five of the poem's stanzas to bear on the plot and characters of *Slynx*, Benedikt only hears lines from the first stanza. Deprived as he is of any knowledge of the classical tradition of Horace or Ovid, not to mention the eighteenth-century imitations of Lomonosov, Derzhavin, and Radishchev, Benedikt can only interpret phrases like "higher than Alexander's Column" and "the people's path" literally. When Nikita Ivanych suggests excavating one of the hills to find remnants of Greek and Roman sculpture, Benedikt can only wonder why he would be interested in "stone men, humongous white Rowmans and Creeks." The idea is particularly strange to Benedikt since there are "plenty of our own rowmen, and only one river anyway."[43]

Allusions to Pushkin's first stanza make this even clearer. Benedikt is confused about how high to make "the pushkin" because he does not know how tall the Alexander Column was.[44] His literal reading of "higher" characterizes his approach to reading more generally. His ignorance is reinforced by the fact that he knows nothing of the Alexander Column or the allusion of its refined marble column to the rough-hewn Thunder Stone, the base of Falconet's Monument to Peter the Great. By disrupting Pushkin's allusions to Petersburg monuments and the tradition of the Horatian ode in the first stanza of "Monument," Tolstaia completely seals off the meanings of progress, or of originality and innovation, that they create. Regress can be the only explanation of the movement from Opekushin's original monumental sculpture to Benedikt's caricature of it.

The glaring omission in Benedikt's imitation of Opekushin's statue, which he carves out of a log, is the pedestal engraved with the third and fourth stanzas of Pushkin's poem. Under Nikita Ivanych's mentorship, Benedikt excludes the verbal part of Opekushin's design of the Pushkin Monument, severing the productive aesthetic symbiosis of poem and statue. Alyssa Dinega Gillespie reads the smooth bottom half of the log as a reference to Pushkin's *Tsar Nikita and his Forty Daughters* and a parody of the taboo against talking about Pushkin as a sexual being in post-Soviet society.[45] Her interpretation works well alongside other themes of censorship motivated by the interaction of poem and statue. As shown in chapter 2, Vasilii Zhukovskii's censorship of Pushkin's allusions led to the sort of literal interpretation that Benedikt embraces and takes to an extreme. Zhukovskii's censored version of stanza four of "Monument" appeared on the monument's pedestal until the Soviets restored Pushkin's original in 1937, drawing attention to imperial censorship even as they instituted their own equally harsh version. Leaving the bottom of "the pushkin" completely bare evokes the even more extreme censorship of the poem in post-Blast Moscow: Nikita Ivanych neither recites the stanzas that appear on Opekushin's original Pushkin Monument nor directs his mentee to carve them into the wood. No mention of them is made whatsoever.

"The pushkin" also visually distorts the image of Pushkin to the extent that even Benedikt, accustomed to seeing horrible deformities on a daily basis, feels sorry for him:

> The pushkin stands there like a bush at night, a rebellious and angry spirit; his head bent, two meat patties on the sides of his face – old fashioned sideburns – his nose down, his fingers tearing at his caftan. A shitbird had settled on his head, of course, but that's just what they do, shamelessly: whatever they see they shit on ...[46]

Nikita Ivanych laments the fact that he has no image of Pushkin to show Benedikt, but it hardly seems to matter. Benedikt carves Pushkin with six fingers, and his own description of the sideburns reflects the crudeness of his craft. Even if he were capable of carving a lifelike image of Pushkin, the shitbirds would hardly fail to miss their opportunity for messing it up. While the reader of *Slynx* is invited to notice these gaps and interpret them, for Benedikt there are no meaningful allusions that "the pushkin" can make, neither to Opekushin's monument nor to Pushkin's poem – nor even to a reliable image of Pushkin's facial features.

"The pushkin" destroys the connection between Pushkin's poem and the statue, but it also distorts the relationship between Opekushin's statue and the surrounding urban environment. A scene near the end of *Slynx* reiterates this point. Benedikt is on the verge of participating in the successful coup to oust Fyodor Kuzmich. From the central watchtower, "higher than the trees, higher than the Alexander column," he considers the panorama of the town over which he now enjoys considerable power as a Saniturion.[47] Out of its original context, Pushkin's idea that his works exceed the glory of the oppressive autocracy represented by the Romanovs has been subjugated to a crude version of Jeremy Bentham's panopticon from which to control the *golubchiks* through fear of Saniturions and the mythical, predatory slynx. From this despotic height, Benedikt looks down on "the pushkin," far in the distance, sticking out "like a small black stick in the confusion of streets, and from [the watchtower] the rope looped around the poet's neck and hung with laundry looked like a fine thread."[48] Pushkin's proud claim for a future legacy higher than the Alexander Column has been dwarfed by the future of the watchtower.

The image of "the pushkin" as a small black stick in the confusion of the streets with a noose around its neck clashes with Pushkin's rhetoric in the poem, but it also disrupts the site-specificity of Opekushin's statue with its meaningful posture towards the Strastnoi Monastery, the *Izvestiia* building, and the literary culture of Tverskoi Boulevard. The setting for "the pushkin" is chosen by Nikita Ivanych because, according to his problematic memory, it is where Strastnoi Square used to exist, but in post-Blast Moscow this ancient past has no meaning. Benedikt's "the pushkin" is completely deprived of a meaningful sense of site-specificity. No monastery or *Izvestiia* building, no Tverskoi Boulevard or green space can motivate additional meaning. Art lies prostrate before the utilitarian demands of laundry, the confusion of an ignorant populace, and the political despotism of the watchtower.

In addition to shattering the verbal and visual dimensions of the Pushkin Monument, the story of the inception, erection, and destruction of Benedikt's "pushkin" frequently makes ironic allusion to the performative dimension of the Pushkin Monument.

The idea of having Benedikt erect a material monument to Pushkin occurs to Nikita Ivanych at the funeral of the oldener Anna Petrovna, a cantankerous elderly lady at the time of the "Blast." Since the "Blast," the only remarkable thing to comment on at her funeral is that she managed to preserve the instructions from a meat grinder, instructions which, in the conditions of post-Blast society, are an important relic.[49] Despite her meagre existence and contribution, Anna Petrovna's name triggers Nikita Ivanych's idea about recreating the Pushkin Monument. As he describes the plan to Benedikt, he mixes up two of Pushkin's most famous love lyrics, "I remember the miraculous moment" and "If life deceives you."[50] The first poem is famously dedicated to one of the most consistent of Pushkin's youthful infatuations, Anna Petrovna Kern, who just happens to share the name Anna Petrovna with the woman being buried. Thus for Nikita Ivanych, the Anna Petrovna of whom one oldener says "Who needs her, that little old mean-spirited, communal apartment crone, she just gets underfoot like a poisonous mushroom" recalls one of the most famous visions of poetic beauty in Russian literature. Nikita Ivanych ironically compares her to the Anna Petrovna to whom Pushkin dedicated many of his most famous lyrics.[51] As a leading representative of the Monument Preservation Society, Nikita Ivanych performs an impassioned speech at her grave on the great accomplishment of preserving the instruction booklet for a meat grinder. Although the meat grinder itself has not been preserved, the instructions represent the spiritual value of the meat grinder, and, based on this spiritual culture, the material culture will surely, according to Nikita Ivanych, come into being. Just as with the meat grinder, Nikita Ivanych believes that Pushkin's verbal "Monument" can somehow bring about the material reality of the Pushkin Monument once again.

Accordingly, the language of Pushkin's "Monument" poem serves as an interpretive subtext of Nikita Ivanych's performance. As the leading member of the Monument Preservation Society, he speaks in a capacity that highlights the contradictions inherent in the "Monument" intertext: the whole trope turns on the idea that the poet's literary word is more lasting, more permanent and eternal, than materiality. However, the preservation of monuments only emphasizes just how ephemeral both the poetic word and the material world are. Nikita Ivanych brings up the aqueducts built by the slaves of Rome and the pyramids built by the slaves of Egypt, suggesting that they still may be standing out there in the world. However, he seems not to recognize the contradiction in the need to preserve these symbols of eternity. Furthermore, he praises the instructions for the meat grinder in the words Horace, Derzhavin, and Pushkin used for their collected works: "a monument not made by hands," "harder than copper, older than the pyramids." In his excitement about the spiritual culture of the meat grinder, he equates its instruction booklet with the collected works of many of the pre-"Blast" world's greatest poets. For Nikita Ivanych, the instruction booklet is to the meat grinder as Pushkin's poem "Monument" is to Opekushin's statue.

As this summary suggests, Nikita Ivanych, even as an educated Soviet citizen who has miraculously survived the "Blast," is a problematic "progressor." His performance at Anna Petrovna's funeral reveals his imperfect knowledge of Pushkin's art and suggests that the effects of nearly two hundred years of living among the culturally ignorant *golubchiks* has taken a toll. His association of the Pushkin Monument with Anna Petrovna Kern seems to parody the urban legend about how Anna Petrovna Kern's corpse made its way out of Moscow to her final burial site and met the statue of Pushkin as it was being transported to Strastnaia Square in preparation for the 1880 Jubilee. Modzalevskii records historical documentation that, just before her death, Kern enthusiastically responded to news of the arrival of part of the pedestal for the monument on Strastnaia Square, but Nikita Ivanych's association of the corpse of Anna Petrovna with the meat grinder instruction booklet and the Pushkin Monument suggests the degradation of his own cultural memory in the stark environment of post-Blast Moscow.[52]

Other speeches at Anna Petrovna's funeral deepen allusions to the 1880 Jubilee. The dedication of the Pushkin Monument was a sort of replacement for the funeral Pushkin never had: in 1837 his body was whisked away to his Mikhailovskoe estate and laid to rest away from the eyes of the public. Situated across from the monument, the Strastnoi Monastery served as a tombstone for the poet; the 1880 Jubilee provided a public opportunity to mourn his untimely death. This performative element of public funeral, combined with Dostoevskii's inspired speech and performance of Pushkin's poem "Prophet" as a moment of reconciliation between Westernizers and Slavophiles, is the subtext for the speech that follows Nikita Ivanych's.

Lev L'vovich stands up to represent the dissidents, and his performance undercuts Nikita Ivanych's ecstasy. Instead of seeing in the meat grinder instruction booklet a relic of an idealized past characterized by cultural accomplishments, Lev L'vovich sees in the instruction booklet "monument" not a parallel to the pyramids made by the slaves of ancient Egypt but a product made by slaves of the Third Rome in which he lived before the Blast. The meat grinder for Lev L'vovich symbolizes not culture but the deaths of countless innocent people who suffered at the hands of an unjust and cruel system. He quotes neither Pushkin nor Dostoevskii's "Pushkin Speech" but rather Dostoevskii's underground man: "I say, let the world go to hell as long as I can have my tea."[53] The meat grinder for him is the meat grinder of history – not a cultural achievement but an eternal reminder that, as soon as history finishes grinding the flesh of one generation, the flesh of another will fill its voracious maw. The metaphor Lev L'vovich finds appropriate for the meat grinder is not the immortality of the Pushkin Monument (*pushkinskii pamiatnik*) but cannon fodder (*pushechnoe miaso*), an ironic play on the root of Pushkin's name, *pushka*, or cannon.

The final speech is given by one Liliia Pavlovna, the representative of the Women's Community. The reader is, however, deprived of the content of her speech because Benedikt cannot be bothered to listen to a woman. Instead, Benedikt sits down and gives himself over to imagining his bride-to-be, Olenka, and how she will cook for him and how pretty she is.

Taken together, these performances in *Slynx* parody the intelligentsia's ecstatic reception of the Pushkin Monument as a major achievement in the age of Alexander II's great reforms: the conservative enthusiast Nikita Ivanych, echoing Dostoevskii's enthusiastic speech, equates Pushkin's works with an instruction booklet for a meat grinder; the liberal dissident responds by cynically associating Nikita Ivanych's reference to the Pushkin Monument with Anna Petrovna's meat grinder instruction booklet to discuss people as the cannon fodder for the meat grinder of history; and Lilia Pavlovna, because of her sex, is completely silenced.

If the inception of the idea to recreate the Pushkin Monument is problematic, its erection is even worse. As at Anna Petrovna's funeral, Lev L'vovich participates in the raising but gives a speech that parodies Dostoevskii's enthusiastic performance of Pushkin's "Prophet": "He looks like a pure retard. A six-phalanged seraphim. A slap in the face of public taste."[54] Lev L'vovich inverts Dostoevskii's speech about Pushkin as a genius, replacing it with the vulgar and offensive phrase "pure retard,"[55] while "six-phalanged seraphim" is a misquotation of the "six-winged seraphim" of Pushkin's poem and draws attention to the fact that Benedikt carved six fingers on "the pushkin." His disruption is not limited to the 1880 celebration: Lev L'vovich alludes to Maiakovskii's 1912 futurist manifesto "to throw Pushkin, Dostoevskii, Tolstoy, etc. etc. off the Steamship of Modernity." In the space of Benedikt's "the pushkin," these allusions parody Maiakovskii's attempts to bring Pushkin back to life in poems like "Jubilee" and "A Joke Resembling the Truth."

Benedikt pays six serfs to drag "the pushkin" to the site where it is to be raised. Nikita Ivanych had decided that it should be raised exactly on the spot where it used to be located, which ends up being in the middle of a *golubchik*'s garden. When the *golubchik* understandably protests the destruction of his garden, Nikita Ivanych unsuccessfully tries to bribe him, and then appeals "to the serfs to raise a ruckus so that the people's voice could be heard." The serfs have no interest in protesting, but Nikita Ivanych's idea that they would protest parodies the late Soviet tradition (begun in 1965 in connection with the trials of Siniavskii and Daniel') of protesting around the Pushkin Monument.[56] Finally, Nikita Ivanych gives up, and Benedikt describes how "the chunk of beriawood had to be lugged across the street," which ironically alludes to the moving of the Pushkin Monument across Tverskaia Street in 1950 to the position where it stands today.

Perhaps the most troubling way in which Tolstaia distorts the performative dimension of the Pushkin Monument is at the end of the novel: the public spectacle of the 1880 celebration and the subsequent Jubilees is conflated with the Siniavskii-Daniel' show trial that the late Soviet demonstrators protested in 1965. Benedikt buckles under pressure from his father-in-law, who has replaced the Greatest Murza as the newest dictator, to arrest and execute Nikita Ivanych by burning him on "the pushkin." Benedikt is reluctant to kill his mentor and to destroy his work of art, but his aspiration to "be higher than the Alexander column" and to save art, a nonsensical motivation, drives him on. While the public had largely ignored "the pushkin" up to this point, the titillation of spectacle and execution draws a large crowd. Bound to "the pushkin," Nikita Ivanych deliberately ignites the explosion that ends the novel, destroying himself and "the pushkin" and the whole dystopian future world of *Slynx*.

When read from the perspective of its performative dimension, the end of "the pushkin" creates an odd amalgam of the Pushkin Jubilee, the show trial, a witch hunt, and the apotheosis associated with the mythic cult of Pushkin in Russian culture. Nikita Ivanych the conservative and Lev L'vovich "of the Dissidents" rise into the air as immortals, forever leaving behind Benedikt and the charred remains of "the pushkin." Their only response to Benedikt's questions is the command "Figure it out as best you can!"[57] It is not art or Pushkin that is raised in this apotheosis but rather the cultural figures who reduce Pushkin to an icon (Nikita Ivanych) and the iconoclasts whom that image inspires (Lev L'vovich). Their final words read like a challenge to the reader as well, who must constantly compare her own cultural recall to the twisted misreadings that make up Benedikt's textual universe and the ways "the pushkin" disfigures the verbal, visual, and performative dimensions of the Pushkin Monument.

The novel features many misreadings of the Pushkin Monument, but they all build to this final scene. Such harshness strongly contradicts the words of Pushkin's poem, especially the fourth stanza engraved on the monument in Moscow that features concepts of love, mercy, kind-hearted feelings, and freedom. The statue itself is destroyed both symbolically, when it is transformed from a work of art into an executioner's bonfire, and physically, when it is destroyed in Nikita Ivanych's fire. Similarly, the performance of a future poet at the Pushkin Monument degenerates into the mob violence of a medieval witch hunt.

In "Night" and "Limpopo" there was a sense that some remarkable insight or personal dedication mitigates the ignorance of future poets and readers like Alexei Petrovich, Lyonechka, the narrator, and Aunt

Zina. In *Slynx* it is hard to find such ambivalence. The awful incarnation of the Pushkin Monument ends in a much worse form than it began; cowardice and violence are committed in the name of some ill-defined concept of abstract goodness and cultural erudition. After all, Benedikt is the new Opekushin. Unfortunately, he is cut off from any sort of cultural recall, the very principle that animated Opekushin's monument to Pushkin, because of the cultural apocalypse precipitated by the "Blast." The very culture that could perhaps enlighten him becomes the pretext for his violent and insatiable appetite for books and "art."

Petersburg Text and Iconoclasm

Tolstaia prefigures her disruptive allusions to the verbal, visual, and performative dimensions of the Pushkin Monument by invoking naive interpretations of urban allusions, one of the problems addressed by Vladimir Nikolaevich Toporov's Petersburg Text. This is Tolstaia at her best: one brief exchange between Benedikt and Varvara Lukinishna at the beginning of the novel sets up a dialogue with the Petersburg Text that foreshadows the iconoclasm of Benedikt's ill-fated "pushkin." Laying the groundwork for her complete destruction of the Pushkin Monument in Moscow, Tolstaia parodies some applications of its late-twentieth-century alternative, the Petersburg Text, depicting its descent from fascinating theory to pedantic insistence on a one-to-one correspondence between a literary setting and its urban referent.

Perhaps it seems strange to address a theoretical concept like the Petersburg Text in a Moscow novel like *Slynx*, but in order to completely destroy the Pushkin Monument and any sort of future it might have, Tolstaia must do more than destroy its Moscow context. Mark Griffiths has convincingly shown that Tolstaia's *Slynx* turns Moscow's traditionally invoked concentricity into a symbol of an eternal "cycle of destruction and degradation."[58] In his analysis, the concentric circles that define Moscow spatially are made to define it temporally as well. If Moscow the Third Rome has fallen, a fourth can never be because there can be no forward progress in a cyclical eternity of degradation. With regard to the Pushkin Monument and allusion, however, Tolstaia goes further. Given the organic connection between Pushkin's poem "Monument" and the Petersburg Text, Tolstaia must also address elements of Toporov's theory in order to fully deconstruct the unity of performance, statue, and poem in the Pushkin Monument.

Tolstaia sets up her parody of naive impulses to literalize urban allusions in a conversation between Varvara Lukinishna and Benedikt. Brought together through their common vocation as scribes and a mutual interest in the poetry of the Greatest Murza, they discuss his work during a lunch break. Varvara Lukinishna asks Benedikt about the meaning of the word "steed," since it shows up so often in the poetry of the Greatest Murza (poetry that readers of *Slynx* recognize as Pushkin and Blok or as anonymous folkloric texts such as riddles and folk tales). In post-apocalyptic Moscow, horses are unknown to the *golubchiks*. Varvara and Benedikt are hard-pressed to connect the Greatest Murza's usage of "steed" to reality. They discuss two specific texts in which the word "steed" appears and try to reconcile the differences. The first text is actually a song translated by Pushkin into Russian and included in his "Songs of the Western Slavs" (*Pesni zapadnykh slav'ian*). Benedikt cites this text in support of his hypothesis that a "steed" must be a mouse: "Don't I take care of you, don't I fill your trough with oats?"[59] Based on Tolstaia's description of the diet of the *golubchiks* and the fauna that populates their city, it is evident that only one of a few types of mutant animals could possibly provide the frame of reference for Benedikt. The mouse is, arguably, Benedikt's best guess.

Varvara Lukinishna, however, quotes another text back to him that complicates Benedikt's "mouse" theory. The reader recognizes a common riddle, the answer to which is thunder: "The steed races, the earth trembles."[60] But for Varvara and Benedikt, both of these texts were composed by the Greatest Murza. To Varvara's counter-evidence, Benedikt replies that it must be a very large mouse and cites one of Pushkin's lyric poems about insomnia, since the mice in Benedikt's house keep him awake at night: "Life, you're but a mouse's scurry, why do you trouble me?"[61]

The conversation about the possible meanings of "steed" leads into Varvara Lukinishna's keenest observation in the novel. She remains unconvinced by Benedikt's ridiculous "steed is mouse" theory, and posits in embryonic form the dangerous idea that perhaps the reason the Greatest Murza can speak in such different voices is because he actually did not write all of the poems that he claims to have written. Her implication, which seems annoyingly pedantic to Benedikt, but which Tolstaia's reader must recognize as brilliant given Varvara's limited knowledge, is that 1) "steed" can mean different things in different contexts, and 2) that riddle, song, and poem have drastically different authorial voices. To illustrate her point, Varvara cites the first lines of the first poem of Blok's "Harps and Violins" (*Arfy i skripki*): "The reed pipe sings upon the bridge, and apple trees do bloom. The angel lifts a single star on high, of greenish hue. And on that bridge it is divine to gaze into those depths, those heights ...").[62]

In response, Benedikt displays his arrogant ignorance and frank inability to understand the nature of Varvara's question. Varvara is building her case for the multi-voicedness of the Greatest Murza's poetry, while Benedikt interprets the bridge in the poem literally, with complete disregard to its symbolic function as a platform from which to view the heavens above reflected in the water below. He claims that the bridge must be an allusion to "Foul Bridge" (*Pogannyi mostok*) for the irrelevant reasons that he has caught "worrums" there and that the water is very deep and dangerous. Not only is Benedikt missing Varvara's point about authorial voice, he is completely out of his depth. If before he was wrong about the meaning of "steed," now he is doubly wrong. First of all, it is obvious to the reader that the author of these lines (Alexander Blok) could not possibly have been referring to "Foul Bridge," since the lines were written long before the Blast that destroyed Moscow and all of its bridges along with the Pushkin Monument. Blok's pastoral setting, mythic in its feel, provides another layer of irony: Benedikt relocates the bridge to an urban environment that has been reduced to a polluted village.

Resolute in her inspired line of inquiry, Varvara brushes aside Benedikt's misreading and makes one last attempt to explain her question about the multi-voicedness of the Greatest Murza's writings by citing a different poem that the reader recognizes as Pasternak's "Storm" ("*Metel'*"). Benedikt responds to her claim that this is a completely different voice by once again identifying the area described in the poem with a certain neighbourhood in post-Blast Moscow known for its crime.

In each case, Tolstaia constructs Benedikt's ignorance as a parody of the logic of urban allusion in some applications of the idea of a Petersburg Text. By literalizing the relationship between the bridge of the poem and his urban surroundings, between the "neighborhood" of Pasternak's poem and a neighbourhood in post-Blast Moscow, Benedikt unwittingly parodies the attempt to relate literary setting to urban space. Benedikt's naively literal readings of these poems play into a sense of postmodern intellectualism: it is impressive to recognize the quotations from Blok and Pasternak, but it would require considerable specialization to bring the literature about Petersburg Text to bear on this passage. Consistent with Benedikt's misquotation and misinterpretation of literary texts, his misinformed associations of pre-Blast literature with "Foul Bridge" and "the neighborhood where Pakhom cracked his skull open" reflect one situation described in a scholarly account of the Petersburg Text and Russian symbolism.[63]

In their definition of the poetics of the Petersburg Text in Russian Symbolism, Toporov's fellow semioticians Z.G. Mints, M.V. Bezrodnyi, and A.A. Danilevskii consider the problematic tendency to identify concrete, specific loci as the prototypes for urban settings that remain unnamed within the text itself. They take Blok's play *The Stranger* as an example, and show how various memoirists posit different prototypes for the pub in act one with mutually exclusive certainty.[64] One scholar, V.N. Orlov, in his book on Blok and St Petersburg, writes that a native of Leningrad will "unmistakably recognize this place" as the bridge over the Malaia Nevka leading from the Bol'shaia Zelenina Street to the Krestovskii Island. Mints and her co-authors then cite the author of *The Soul of Petersburg*, N.P. Antsiferov, who made major contributions to the study of his city. Also a native of Leningrad with no less a claim to expertise on literary Petersburg, Antsiferov found this same bridge as Blok's prototype, but reversed the perspective, from the Krestovskii Island towards Bol'shaia Zelenina Street. To further complicate the approach of concretizing literary settings in the physical landscape of Petersburg, the authors cite yet more scholarship. P.P. Gromov theorized that the bridge in the second act of *The Stranger* depicts a bridge over the Karpovka, a smaller river connecting the Malaia Nevka to the Bol'shaia Nevka. Their argument culminates in a footnote about Gromov's conclusion: "The scholar [Gromov] also includes these very remarks in his commentary to the most authoritative current edition of Blok's plays (see Blok, A. *Teatr*, Leningrad, 1981, p. 486), and in both cases [the bridge and the pub] he cites the memoirs of [M.A.] Beketova, who, however, writes not a single word about the setting of the second act."[65]

Having problematized the approach of these well-known scholars who seek a one-to-one correspondence between literary text and urban landscape, Mints, Danilevskii, and Bezrodnyi turn to describing a different "mechanism" by which Blok's *The Stranger* relates to the Petersburg Text. Instead of searching for a one-to-one correspondence between real bridge and literary setting, they define a "poetics of citation" (*tsitatnaia poetika*) that has no single text or referent but functions as a sort of commonplace of the Petersburg Text, invoking all of its various manifestations at once. They conclude their discussion of the bridge in Blok's *The Stranger* with the following claim: "therefore the landscape, which opens act 2 and is also, in fact, filled with the *realia* of Petersburg, is perceived specifically as Petersburg, but not concretely, not 'this one,' but a sort of generalized 'image' of the Petersburg landscape."[66] In other words, an urban bridge does not have to allude specifically to one of Petersburg's many bridges for it to evoke many stories and poems about Petersburg in which bridges play an important role.

The semiotic analysis of the bridge in Blok's *The Stranger* from the perspective of the Petersburg Text highlights multiple layers of problematic reading in Benedikt's response to Varvara's question. Benedikt lacks basic knowledge of Blok and Pasternak as authors: he does not even know their names. Furthermore, he completely misunderstands Varvara's question, reflecting his inability to grasp the ideas of others and the aesthetic functions of voice and allusion. He also misses the complex irony in how the Blok and Pasternak poems that Varvara Lukinishna cites actually interact with each other through the theme of a bridge and urban space.[67] In other words, he has no access to critical thought on the problems of interpreting the connection (or, metaphorically, a bridge) between a literary setting and its prototypes, be they other literary texts, material *realia*, or some combination of the two. It is not a coincidence that scholarship on the Petersburg Text could have provided exactly that sort of nuanced understanding. By presenting the reader with this little intertextual puzzle, Tolstaia reveals the urban text phenomenon inspired by Toporov's Petersburg Text as both the target of and inspiration for her conceit of a sci-fi future in which Russia's cultural heritage has been utterly destroyed, exemplified by the failed attempt to recreate the Pushkin Monument. Nikita Ivanych's passion for setting up posts with street names from pre-Blast Moscow and his attempt to set up the Pushkin Monument in the middle of someone's garden reflect the same trend: he tries to create a one-to-one correspondence between pre- and post-Blast Moscow, two realities that differ as much as Moscow, Petersburg, and their incarnations in a literary tradition.

As this analysis shows, the iconoclasms of both Tolstaia and Toporov function by connecting various aspects of the Pushkin Monument and the Petersburg Text in the 1990s and early 2000s. While the 200th anniversary of Pushkin's birth in 1999 in some ways explains their attention to the complicated cultural history of the Pushkin Monument, it cannot explain why their separate iconoclasms look to the Petersburg Text. For Toporov, the Pushkin Monument provided a way to end his Petersburg Text and frame it as an alternative to a material and visual Pushkin Monument. For Tolstaia, the naive identification of literal, one-to-one correspondences between an allusion and its referent is the opposite of a more complex type of allusion that gives rise to the Pushkin Monument in Moscow and that is celebrated in Toporov's Petersburg Text. After all, the Petersburg Text and the Pushkin Monument in Moscow both operate as complexly nested allusions, as the "combination of a poetics of *realia* and citation," through the interactions of monuments, urban spaces, and the allusions that continue to accrue in the space between.

Tolstaia wrote an essay on the Petersburg Text, "Other Dreams" ("Chuzhie sny," 2002), published two years after *Slynx* (2000), that suggests her own positive relationship to the Petersburg Text with its complicated poetics of allusion. Tolstaia writes that literature and dreams spring from the same source and generate each other and that the works of all those who wrote about Petersburg hung their dreams over the whole city like a thin, wet, spiderweb. She cites Pushkin's *The Bronze Horseman* and Blok's yellow sunrises as well as *realia* that remind readers that Petersburg is not conducive to "simple human life." Her response to this typical complaint against Peter the Great's dream city, that it is not comfortable for humans to live in, is telling: "I don't want a simple human life. I want complicated dreams ..."[68] Tolstaia's desire to allude, to participate in and further the aesthetic visions of other poets and find in them new layers of meaning and beauty, is a fitting way to close this study of the Pushkin Monument. As a poem, a statue, and a performative space, Pushkin's Monument continues to invite such complex and nuanced co-creation.

Allusion and the Naive Reader

Pushkin's Monument has inspired many different kinds of allusion over the course of its history. Allusion is one of the most marked devices in Pushkin's poem; how best to allude visually to Pushkin's works determines the search for the ideal design for the statue; Dostoevskii makes allusion one of the dominant tropes in his "Pushkin Speech," setting the stage for many poetic performances to follow. The image of a future poet, a creative individual who has the capacity to transform a tradition through the power of aesthetic vision, is a critical agent of metamorphosis in the development of each dimension.

While the future poet consistently has been the agent of metamorphosis in this story of the Pushkin Monument and allusion, the naive reader has played a different and more ambiguous role. Over the course of the twentieth century, the naive reader has come to interact with allusion in ways that the nineteenth century could not foresee. The naive reader is a shifting, unstable, image – part of the changing human environment that is a central component of the monument's "dynamic context." To the point, allusion is not a concern of "the people" (*narod*) in Pushkin's poem "Monument." The most complex allusions in Pushkin's poem develop themes of metamorphosis and immortality, and, while Pushkin addresses the idea of a naive reader in other works such as "Egyptian Nights," "the people" in "Monument" are not missing or misunderstanding his allusions. The people are an ambivalent audience for other reasons: they are more interested in rumours, kind-hearted feelings, and political utility than in art itself. Like Pushkin's poem, Opekushin's statue does not explicitly depict the people as engaged in any sort of allusive practice. During the many phases of the competition to design the Pushkin Monument, the still illiterate "people" play a rather different role. They are not the ignorant masses who have no motivation for gaining a broad frame of reference but grateful future readers who recognize and venerate Pushkin's genius. How the sculptor will allude to the people in Pushkin's poem is an aesthetic problem but not one that the people face as a group of naive readers. With the advent of the performative dimension, Dostoevskii forges a connection between naive readers and allusion to Pushkin's Monument. In his "Pushkin Speech," Dostoevskii suggests that the ability to imitate others in an original way connects Pushkin's art to the Russian national character as embodied by the people. Dostoevskii's connection anticipates future developments.

In 1880, with mass literacy still an ideal that would not be fully realized for several decades, thinking about Russia's national uniqueness and originality through such an aestheticized lens provoked a rapturous response. Experiences with peasant readers over the next fifty years proved to be something of a reality check. By the 1920s and 1930s, scholars, theorists, and writers experienced newly literate readers not as a future abstraction but as a confounding reality.[1] Practical experience had led to the recognition that literacy, the ability to read, was a first step on the way to becoming a good reader but by no means a guarantee of how far one would make it on the journey. *Master and Margarita* depicts this reality through a naive reader's experience of allusion. When Riukhin confronts the Pushkin Monument, he shatters the nineteenth-century image of the naive reader as a future good reader. Riukhin is a naive reader who attempts to be a poet but fails. Complex allusions in the scene prove to be his undoing.

Riukhin's demise, however, is not without some redeeming aesthetic quality. The point is not to poke fun at his ignorance. Even though he is ignorant of the allusions he motivates, the function of his ignorance is aesthetically productive. Riukhin's character exemplifies how difficult it is to control allusion in proximity to the Pushkin Monument. Recognizing and interpreting allusion is not a problem only for Bulgakov's character or his reader but also for Bulgakov as author. Is Riukhin simply a parody of Maiakovskii or something more? Is Bulgakov getting revenge on Maiakovskii or pointing to a larger, nobler concept of writerly reception? Does Riukhin's inability to imagine the statue as coming to life reflect negatively on Riukhin *because* Maiakovskii brought the Pushkin Monument to life in sublunar Moscow, or does Riukhin reflect negatively on Maiakovskii for having imagined it? In this regard, Bulgakov's innovative employment of allusion to the Pushkin Monument constellates a larger question about how author and future readers share the burden of interpreting an allusion: as a cultural tradition includes more and more texts that could be alluded to, to what extent can allusion be controlled? The monument's material existence gives it an agency to facilitate allusions to many other poems that are associated with its thematics and specific location in Moscow, but as a naive future poet, Riukhin has no agency in this matter: it is obvious that he cannot control all of these allusions. Yet it is through his thoughts and actions that the reader can reconstruct them.

Just as Riukhin's thoughts give the Pushkin Monument the agency to facilitate allusion, his naiveté transfers some of the agency from the author, Bulgakov, to the Pushkin Monument. The material existence of the statue makes it possible to contrast Riukhin's naive thoughts with many other texts, images, and performances associated with the space, whether or not Bulgakov *intended* the allusions. This is not to say that intertextuality in its pure form is the best paradigm for understanding what happens between the naive reader and the Pushkin Monument. Rather, the Pushkin Monument in *Master and Margarita* plays an agentive, perhaps even authorial, role in supporting multiple and sometimes contradictory interpretations of Riukhin, Pushkin's works, and their significance for the novel. Because Riukhin is naive, the Pushkin Monument has more agency (a form of life?) to evoke allusions that influence the interpretation of the scene.

In Toporov's article on the dynamic context of three-dimensional art, the naive viewer does not motivate complex allusion but rather perpetuates clichés, allusions that have grown stale with overuse and lack of genuine understanding. The naive viewer seeks official perspectives instead of undertaking the hard work of personal, genuine interaction with a work of art. Alluding to Evgenii's circular and linear motion to and around the Bronze Horseman in Pushkin's poem, Toporov describes how the naive viewer seeks the appropriate place to stop and contemplate Falconet's statue from the "correct" perspective. This stasis deprives the statue of life and meaning: when the viewer ceases moving, the statue also ceases to move. But there is an additional layer of "necrosis" here: a static viewer also deprives Pushkin's poem of meaning: to understand Evgenii, one must move around the monument in the same way that he did. To understand Pushkin's allusion to the Bronze Horseman, one must move as his characters move. To understand Petersburg, one must perceive it in motion, dynamically.[2] To understand the Petersburg Text, you have to see Pushkin's "Monument" as the summation of a dynamic context that progresses from the Bronze Horseman to the Alexander Column. Naiveté begets cliché, which leads to nothing less than the death of meaning. Perhaps that process is Toporov's answer to his own question: "Why has Russia become so soulless, short-sighted, merciless?"[3]

The world of Tolstaia's *Slynx* poses a similar question. The re-creation of the Pushkin Monument in Tolstaia's *Slynx* renders grotesque distortions of Pushkin's poem, Opekushin's statue, and the surrounding performative space. Cruelty replaces mercy, slavery replaces freedom, vulgarity replaces inspiration. Those distortions, however, have an unexpected aesthetic function: the future poets and naive readers in *Slynx* who disfigure the Pushkin Monument also highlight its aesthetic complexity and unique agency in preserving cultural memory for the future. Benedikt and other characters like him compel the reader of *Slynx* to reread Pushkin and many other poets in productive ways. As a central element of the novel's plot, the Pushkin Monument is one of the most important texts that must be reread. Benedikt's naive carving and morally corrupt burning of his "pushkin" reveal a new role for the figure of the naive reader in motivating complex allusion: far from destroying an icon that many authors have symbolically shattered in their texts, Benedikt's "pushkin" exemplifies how observing someone else's misreading can be one of the most instructive forms of reading.

Why might the naive reader have come to play such a creative role in allusions to the Pushkin Monument? After all, good readers, who are conspicuously absent from the cultural history of the Pushkin Monument, have the capacity to recognize, hunt down, and interpret complex allusions. Why has the good reader not played a larger role in the cultural history of the Pushkin Monument?

The history of literacy provides one answer. Up to this point, the character of the naive reader in a literary text has been the focus of my discussion, but experiences with real naive readers also play a role in literary depiction. As Russia's readership grew, the author's frame of reference increasingly differed from parts of the contemporary audience, not to mention a future audience that would be more diverse still. In the nineteenth century, the reading public was still a relatively small and homogeneous group. Literary tradition, even though it was rapidly expanding, was still relatively small.[4] As Tolstaia's "Siuzhet" reminds us, Pushkin really could have lived to hear Dostoevskii's speech in 1880. Pushkin's future reader in 1880 might have known Pushkin had the poet lived a natural lifespan, and the future reader definitely did know of Pushkin's children. In 1880, an educated reader realistically could assimilate the most important works of the tradition and navigate complex allusions within the canon. By 1937, that had changed considerably, and even more so in the 1990s. The readership had become larger and more diverse with correspondingly diverse frames of reference, in part due to a relaxation of censorship. Literary tradition, artificially constricted in the Soviet era, had also grown rapidly with the publication of several generations of writings within the few short years of glasnost and perestroika. No longer could an average reader control so many texts; in the difficult years of the 1990s, few readers had the time or the inclination to try.[5]

The contemporary case studies of approaches to the Pushkin Monument that I described in the Introduction continue this trend. The history of cultural literacy also explains the concern for educating the naive reader in Melikhova and Tsekhanskii's plans for restoring Strastnaia Square to its pre-revolutionary appearance. Anxiety about losing a shared cultural frame of reference has grown. Globalization and the Internet have contributed to an even more diverse range of cultural and textual experiences among readers in our current cultural moment. Likewise, Medvedev's performance at the Pushkin Monument, with its rich allusions to Pushkin's poetry and the tradition of protest in Pushkin Square, seems to disregard any notion of a "reader" at all, naive or otherwise. His performance seems personal and private, an aesthetic moment for himself as a poet that requires no audience and precludes any anxiety about a future reception.

The lack of an audience for Medvedev's performance leads into a second answer to the question of why the naive reader facilitates so many allusions to the Pushkin Monument: anxiety about a future reception. The juxtaposition of the future poet and the naive reader is interesting because of their differences, but also because of their similarities: they both create anxiety in the author. The future poet can evoke anxiety in an older poet who recognizes that it is just as likely that his texts will be bypassed as that they will be selected as the referent of a profound allusion.[6] This is especially true as a tradition grows and there are an increasingly large number of "classics" to allude to. To judge from the works of Bulgakov, Toporov, and Tolstaia, a naive reader also can evoke anxiety in the author: without a shared frame of reference, allusion can be completely missed or horribly misinterpreted.

The image of a good reader, on the contrary, generally appears as a comfort, support, and guide. Margarita enters into this role with the Master completely.[7] Toporov verges on conflating the good reader with the future poet in his discussion of the co-creator as having the power "to know" in its procreative meaning. In the context of these works, Benedikt's murder of the best reader in *Slynx*, Varvara Lukinishna, who early in the novel could have been his lover and a valuable guide, seals the fate of his "pushkin."

While good readers like Margarita, Toporov's co-creator, and Varvara Lukinishna play a productive role in shaping and creating the texts of their "lovers," naive readers too have a creative role to play in aesthetic reception. The anxiety they provoke is productive in that it allows authors to bring the full force of tradition to bear on their ignorance.

Riukhin is utterly destroyed, not because he lacks talent, but because, when we read his scene, the allusive history of the Pushkin Monument speaks back to him so forcefully that he stands no chance of surviving as a poet in the future. Benedikt is an anti-hero not because he has not read enough or because he is a bad wood carver; on the contrary, the more he reads and interacts with his "pushkin," the more the cultural history of the Pushkin Monument, Pushkin's poetry, world literature, and folklore condemn his arbitrary, cruel, and shallow aesthetic capacity.

But what of the future of the Pushkin Monument itself? As this analysis has shown, part of its aesthetic composition looks to the future for metamorphosis and renewal. During the anti-corruption protests of spring 2017, the Pushkin Monument once again appeared in newspapers around the world as the unnoticed and unexplained *mise-en-scène* for Russian protesters.[8] Like that of Medvedev, their choice to meet at the Pushkin Monument alludes to a rich cultural history. Whether or not these allusions are intentional, or if they reach an audience (Medevev's readers or the readers of the coverage of the protest in the *New York Times*), the Pushkin Monument itself has the agency to project meaning into their actions. Melikhova and Tsekhanskii foresee a rather different political future in their argument for returning the monument to its original, humble posture across from a rebuilt Strastnoi Monastery. In this future, naiveté must be vanquished through preservation and education. It is hard to say which future will prevail, bringing the Pushkin Monument to life through performative motion (ekphrasis) or hardening its historical architectural context into a restored material and visual reality (iconism). Will future Russian authors continue to bring it to life through innovative forms of ekphrastic or iconic allusion? Will provincial families like the one described in Okudzhava's song "A Visiting Family Takes a Picture Near the Pushkin Monument" ("Na fone Pushkina," 1970) continue to to tread their canonical path?

Toporov's cryptic phrase "the gradation of prediction and the possible" seems particularly relevant when pondering what transformations the future may hold for the Pushkin Monument.[9] I have no intention of making a prediction, but the cultural history laid out in this book indicates two possible sites of innovation: 1) the interrelation of the poem, statue, and performative space can be altered through ekphrastic allusions to "bring the monument to life" or through iconoclastic allusions to shatter its image; 2) the agent of this metamorphosis will be a future poet, a naive reader, or some combination of the two.

Appendix

Pushkin's Poem in the Original

Exegi monumentum

Я памятник себе воздвиг нерукотворный,
К нему не зарастет народная тропа,
Вознесся выше он главою непокорной
    Александрийского столпа.

Нет, весь я не умру – душа в заветной лире
Мой прах переживет и тленья убежит –
И славен буду я, доколь в подлунном мире
    Жив будет хоть один пиит.

Слух обо мне пройдет по всей Руси великой,
И назовет меня всяк сущий в ней язык,
И гордый внук славян, и финн, и ныне дикой
    Тунгус, и друг степей калмык.

И долго буду тем любезен я народу,
Что чувства добрые я лирой пробуждал,
Что в мой жестокий век восславил я свободу
    И милость к падшим призывал.

Веленью божию, о муза, будь послушна,
Обиды не страшась, не требуя венца;
Хвалу и клевету приемли равнодушно,
    И не оспоривай глупца.[1]

Given the incomplete nature of Toporov's work on the "end" of the Petersburg Text, in this appendix I have reproduced the archival notes (in the original and in my translation) that I refer to in the body of the argument. Likewise, since Dviniatina's explanation of the Petersburg exhibit and Toporov's article on the dynamic context of three-dimensional art are unavailable in English, I have included them in this appendix. Authoritative translations of Pushkin's poetry, the speeches at the Jubilee, *Master and Margarita*, and *Slynx* are readily available, but Toporov's work has yet to reach a broader English-language audience.

Archival Note 1[2]

Up until this point this text has been reconstructed based on the materials of the past, and it has had its full force with relationship to the past. Now I have the impression that there is so much gathered and already partially interpreted material that a problem-question naturally arises: what can Petersburg Text offer for a consideration of the *future* of Petersburg? And do we even need to know this future? By the same token, are we not entering into the tenuous region of prediction?

But there are predictions and then there are predictions. A rolling ball. A prediction is fulfilled if no means of preventing its achievement are undertaken. Thus far there are two actors of the fulfilled prediction, in particular, the person capable of making a contribution to that which seems unavoidable.

> The gradation of prediction and the possible.
> Fate. Subject – object.
> Dynamic perception of Petersburg.
> (The Kazan Cathedral, the Bronze Horseman, the Alexandrian
>   Pillar).
> Petersburg and the future = Petersburg and the West.
> Petersburg and the multiethnic, multicultural, polylingual: the
>   West, the Baltics, Scandinavia.
> Why has Russia become so soulless, short-sighted, merciless?
> What has she (Russia) done with the Finns, the Karelians, the
>   Estonians, the Votes (*vod'*), the Izhorians, the Vepsians in
>   the Petersburg Province?
> The more open and kind that Russia becomes, the better it will be
>   for her. As she cares for others, she will learn to be a
>   judicious master (*rachitel'naia khoziaka*) in her own home.
> Miracle (*chudo*) – sensitive (*chut-kii*): **chuti.*[3]
> /4/ The metaphysics of Petersburg is the level of the super-
>   empirical, inseparable from the space of the paradoxical.

До сих пор этот текст восстан<авливал>ся по материалам прошлого и имел свою полную силу в отн<ошении> прошлого. Теперь склад<ивает>ся впеч<атление>, что накопл<енно>го и уже отчасти интерпритир<ованно>го материала столько, что естеств<ен>но возникает проблема-вопрос: что м<ожет> дать П<етербургский> т<екст> для суждения о <u>будущем</u> П<етербурга>? И нужно ли нам вообще знать это будущее? Не входим ли /мы/ тем самым в зыбкую область <u>предсказаний</u> /?/

Но есть предсказ<ания> и предсказ<ания>. Катящ<ий>ся шар. Предсказ<ание> осущ<ествляет>ся, если не будет предпринято нечто предотвращающее его совершение. Уже здесь выступ<ают> 2 участника соверш<ающегося>, в частн<о>сти, ч<елове>ка, способного внести свой вклад в то, что предст<авляет>ся неотвратимым.

Градации предсказ<ан>ия и "возм<ожно>го".

Судьба. Субъект – объект.

Динамич<еское> восприят<ие> Петерб<урга>.

(Каз<анский> собор, Медн<ый> Всадн<ик>, Александр<рийский> столп).

Петерб<ург> и будущее = Петерб<ург> и Запад.

Петерб<ург> и полиэтничн<ость>, поликультурн<ость>, многоязыч<ие>: Запад, Прибалт<ика>, Сканд<инавия>.

Почему Р<оссия> стала такой бездуш<ной>, недально-видн<ой>, немилосердн<ой> /?/.

Что сделала она с финнами, карел<ами>, эстонцами, во-дью, ижорой, вепсами в Петерб<ургской> губ<ернии>?

Чем более открытой и добр<ой> станет Р<оссия>, тем лучше будет ей самой. Заботясь о других, она научится быть рачит<ельной> хозяйкой и у себя дома.

Чудо – чуткий: чути.

/4/ Метафиз<ический/ика> Петерб<ург/(а)> – есть уровень сверх-эмпирич<еский>, неотделим<ый> от пр<остранст>-ва парадокс<ально>го.

Archival Note 2[4]

It [Petersburg Text] claimed knowledge, or more strongly, claimed to discover in the city that which the city did not know about itself, that which could not yet even exist in the city. The text went even farther in its claims, assuming to understand those profound meanings that were unknown to the city. In other words, in exchange for the "cheaply" empirical, the text claimed to be a *self-conscious* organ of the city, not only its voice, but also its centre of reflexivity about the city (about itself, as judge, as guide) [italics in the original] …

Он претендовал на знание, более того, на открытие в городе того, чего сам город о себе не знал, и чего в нем даже могло пока и не быть. И еще далее шел текст в своих претензиях – на понимание тех глубинн<ых> смыслов, к<отор>ые городу были неизвестны. Иначе говоря, в обмен на "дешевую" эмпирию текст претендовал быть <u>самосознающим</u> органом города, не только его голосом, но и центром рефлексии о городе (о самом себе, судьей, ведущим) …

Archival Note 3[5]

T.V. Tsiv'ian published the following notes as archival evidence in support of an exhibition about the Petersburg Text and cited a lengthy quotation from the organizer of the exhibit, T.M. Dviniatina. I reproduce both Toporov's note and Dviniatina's lengthy quotation here in full.

I

1 June 2000

Sp<ace> from the <u>Bro<nze> Horse<man>to the Angel</u> with the cross

B<ronze>   † Angel
H<orseman>

W<est>   <u><affinity for the> double</u>   E<ast>

Peter's gaze to the w., and up, the sky	gaze down onto <illegible>
into the indefinite	onto the earth
captivat., tearing away	specif<ic> /?/, humb<le>
from the ground, <illegible>	
commanding-point.	cross and hand
hand	extended to it

<Affinity for the> double in SPb. Begins with his name, referring both to Saint Peter and, of course, to Peter I.

The city-double: real and artificial, holy and <illegible> "antichrist." Compare in *The Raw Youth*: you close your eyes, and the city disappears, Dost<oevskii's> *The Double*, Mirage And<rei> Bely's *Petersburg* etc.

II

The face of the Angel on Pal<ace> Sq<uare>, 6 June, 10:30, the sunset illumin<ates> the face with its gaze low<ered> to the earth (more accurately, into the earth). The face is ro<und>, like that of Alex<and>er

I, features of resignation on the face and partic<ularly> in its figure, in the l<eft> hand, wings prepared to open, to fly, but as if they know that it won't happen. The serpent, the earth are stronger.

I

1 VI 2000

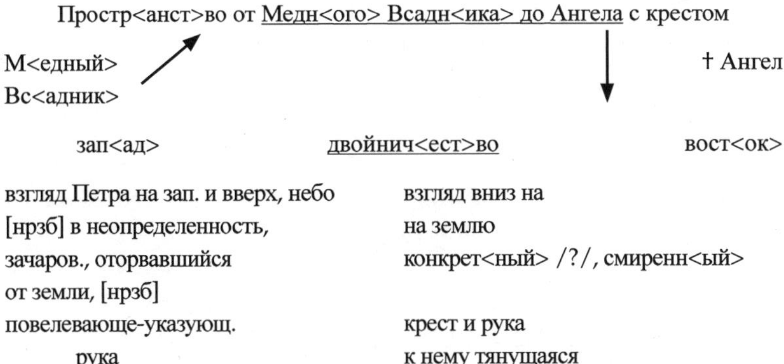

взгляд Петра на зап. и вверх, небо
[нрзб] в неопределенность,
зачаров., оторвавшийся
от земли, [нрзб]
повелевающе-указующ.
рука

взгляд вниз на
на землю
конкрет<ный> /?/, смиренн<ый>

крест и рука
к нему тянущаяся

Двойнич<ест>во в СПб. Начинается с его имени, отсылающего и к Св. Петру и, конечно, к Петру I.

Город-двойник: реальн<ый> и мнимый, святой и [нрзб] «антихрист». Ср. в «Подростке»: закроешь глаза, и города нет, «Двойник» Дост<оевского>, Марево "Петерб<ург> Андр<ея> Белого и т. п.

II

Лицо Ангела на Дворц<овой> площ<ади> – 6 июня 10:30, закат освещ<ает> лицо с опущ<енным> взглядом на землю (точнее, в землю). Лицо кругл<ое>, как у Ал<лексан>дра I, черты обреченности в лице и особ<енно> в фигуре, в лев<ой> руке, крылья готовы к раскрытию, взмаху, но как бы знают, что его не будет. Змея – земля сильнее.

T.M. Dviniatina explains why her exibit relied on juxtaposing the Bronze Horseman and the Alexander Column:[6]

Why did we choose these two monuments? V.N. Toporov attached another, spatial-geographical meaning to the well-known idea of Petersburg's affinity for the double by naming the Bronze Horseman and the Alexandrian Pillar the architectural and conceptual dominants of Petersburg space. Breadth, expanse, and human will animate the first; verticality and an appeal to God animate the second. If the gaze of Peter is fixed on the West, his outstretched hand proudly pointing us upwards and outwards into the distance, calling us into the unknown, then the Angel, equally concerned with earth and heaven, bowing *with a submissive head* [emphasis in the original], looks to the north, but his hand humbly points directly upwards. The juxtaposition of vectors expressed by these monuments gives the coordinates and communicates a dramatic tension to the whole Petersburg space. In the last years of his life, V.N. Toporov was captivated by the idea of the dynamic "self-expansion" of monuments in the natural and cultural environment and developed it on the model of the Bronze Horseman and the Alexander Column. V.N. Toporov managed to write about the Bronze Horseman, but not about the Angel.

Почему мы выбрали именно эти памятники? Дело в том, что известной идее о двойничестве Петербурга В.Н. Топоров придал еще одно, пространственно-географическое значение, назвав Медный всадник и Александрийский столп архитектурными и смысловыми доминантами петербургского пространства. За первым – ширь, простор и человеческая воля, за вторым – вертикаль и обращение к Богу. Если взгляд Петра устремлен на запад, указующая рука гордо показывает вверх и вдаль, зовет в неопределенность, то Ангел, одинаково причастный земле и небу, склоняясь *главою покорной*, смотрит на север, а рукой смиренно указывает наверх. Сочетание выраженных этими памятниками векторов задает координаты и сообщает драматическую напряженность всему петербургскому пространству. В последние годы жизни В.Н. Топоров был увлечен идеей динамического "саморазвертывания" памятников в природном и культурном окружении и разрабатывал ее как раз на примере Медного всадника и Александровской колонны. О Медном всаднике В.Н. Топоров успел написать, об Ангеле – нет.

Toporov on the lifelike statue, the naive viewer, and the co-creator:[7]

It stands to reason that the situation described here, which presupposes an act of "seeing for the first time" and the "natural" viewer, is a little artificial and abstract, but in a certain sense it can be considered a satisfactory model of the reaction of a viewer to an interaction with an "object" of art because also in more complex and differentiated cases (as long as we are not talking about experienced and sophisticated viewers and even more so professionals) one frequently observes elements of a similar clichéd reaction, and the choice of the "canonical" place of surveillance (*mesto obzora*) is only one of the component parts of the cliché. In the same way, another model of perception, which might be described approximately according to the following sequence of actions and their psychological motivations, can be considered satisfactory: it is possible *to see* (*videt'*) (the existence of opportunities) and it is necessary *to see* (*videt'*) (the purposeful positioning that realizes the opportunity), and – in the words of the book of Genesis – it is *good*, but at the same time more is necessary – and this is better – *to know* (*vedat'*) (this corresponds to the Indo-European *u̯eid-: *u̯īd- and *u̯oid-); the basis of knowing (*vedenie*) is the path travelled by the viewer, the dynamics of the change in the stages of path-cognition (*putipoznanie*); but the very best is not only to see and to know (*vedat'*), but also to *know* (*znat'*), for knowledge (*znanie*), the attainment of it, is least of all conducive to the development of clichés as a form of necrosis of meaning; knowledge is always a generation (Indo-European *g'en- "to know," but it is also "to give birth"), and like every act of generation it is always one of a kind and unique, which also constitutes the intrinsic features of the act of creating art (*tvorchestva*); therefore, when "the viewer" becomes a *creator* (*tvorets*) or, more accurately, co-creator with the artist and the space that he "enacts" (*razyigryvaet*), it is possible to say that he *has known* (compare the biblical language *to know one's wife*), *has understood* (to take to oneself a wife) (*poiati zhenu sebe*) the meaning of the "object" of art, in the same way that a wife-bearer-of-children (*zhena-poroditel'nitsa*) is "understood" and "known," and this also constitutes a *second* (the first is the affair of the artist) birth of the created object, but this time in the soul of the "viewer," in the ideal of the one who is able to become congenial to the act of creation.

Разумеется, описанная ситуация, предполагающая акт "первоувидения" и "естественного" зрителя, несколько искусственна и абстрактна, но в известном отношении она может считаться удовлетворительной моделью реакции зрителя на встречу с "предметом" искусства, потому что и в более сложных и дифференцированных случаях (если только речь не идет об опытных и искушенных зрителях и тем более профессионалах) нередко наблюдается элементы подобной клишированной реакции, и выбор "канонического" места обзора (точка зрения) лишь одна из составляющих этого клише. Точно так же можно считать удовлетворительной и модель восприятия, которая может быть описана примерно следующей последовательностью действий и психологических мотивировок их. можно в и д е т ь (наличие возможностей) и нужно в и д е т ь (целевая установка, реализирующая возможность), и – по слову книги Бытия – это х о р о ш о, но вместе с тем и далее нужно – и это лучше – в е д а т ь (соотв. и евр. *u̯eid-: *u̯īd- and *u̯oid-); в основе ве́дения – пройденный зрителем путь, динамика смены этапов пути-познания; но самое лучшее – не только видеть и ведать, но и з н а т ь, ибо знание, обретение его менее всего доступны клишированию как форме омертвения смысла; знание – всегда порождение (и.-евр. *g'en- "знать", но и "рождать"), и как всякое порождение оно всегда единственно в своем роде и неповторимо, что и составляет неотъемлемые особенности творчества; поэтому, когда "зритель" становится т в о р ц о м или, точнее, сотворцом вместе с художником и пространством, которое он "разыгрывает", можно говорить, что он п о з н а л (ср. библейское же познать жену свою), п о-н я л (пояти жену себѣ) смысл "предмета" искусства, как "понимают" и "познают" жену-породительницу, а это и составляет в т о р о е (первое – дело художника) рождение сотворенного, на этот раз в душе "зрителя", в идеале способного стать конгениальным творению.

Notes

Introduction: Dimensions of the Pushkin Monument

1 Personal correspondence with the author, 11 October 2018.
2 My rendering of the poem in prose approximates the meaning of the original: "Я думал, сердце позабыло / Способность легкую страдать, / Я говорил: тому, что было, / Уж не бывать! уж не бывать! / Прошли восторги, и печали! И легковерные мечты … / Но вот опять затрепетали / Пред мощной властью красоты." "Ia dumal, serdtse pozabylo," in Pushkin, *PSS*, t. 3, 315: http://feb-web.ru/feb/pushkin/texts/push10/v03/d03-315.htm. For full information about quotations from Pushkin's works see note 22 below and the Pushkin citation in the bibliography.
3 For a nuanced discussion of this aspect of Pushkin's sculptural myth, see Bethea, *Realizing Metaphors*, 10–13.
4 "Господи, отелись!" For the whole poem with comprehensive annotation, see S.A. Esenin, "Preobrazhenie ('Oblaki laiut …')," in *Polnoe sobranie sochinenii v 7 t., book 2, Stikhotvoreniia (Malen'kie poemy)* (Moscow: Nauka, 1997), 52–6 and 325–36.
5 Melikhova and Tsekhanskii, *Strasti i nadezhdy*, 138.
   "Возрождение Страстного монастыря могло бы явиться тем самым актом покаяния и началом действительного возрождения общества. Уместно вспомнить, что последними крупными духовными объектами, уничтоженными богоборческой властью, были Храм Христа Спасителя в 1931 году и Страстной монастырь в 1937 году.
   "Оба 'мешали': один стоял вблизи Кремля, другой – на главной улице города, на ее возвышенной части, откуда обозревались кремлевские башни. Один восстановлен, дело за другим. Возможно, тогда-то и утихомирятся страсти людские и стихнут раздоры в обществе."

6 "На самом деле, на Пушкинской площади предлагается возродить не памятники, не ансамбль, а историческую память." Melikhova and Tsekhanskii, *Strasti i nadezhdy*, 162.

7 "площадь не должна оставаться пустым пространством в центре города – соблазном для интересов крупного бизнеса." Melikhova and Tsekhanskii, *Strasti i nadezhdy*, 6.

8 "С целью оградить градостроительную ценность от исторически чуждых новаторских строительных перемен и оставить нашим потомкам возможность восстановить исторически ансамбль Пушкинской площади, Комиссия 'Старая Москва' разработала публикуемые здесь предложения." Melikhova and Tsekhanskii, *Strasti i nadezhdy*, 7.

9 Melikhova and Tsekhanskii, *Strasti i nadezhdy*, 145.

10 Ibid., 70.

11 Ibid., 71.

12 "Возродится атмосфера сквера как прогулочного, притягательного места, а не многолюдных протестных митингов и пикетов." Melikhova and Tsekhanskii, *Strasti i nadezhdy*, 148.

13 "Восстановленная колокольня Страстного монастыря с надвратной церковью прп. Алексия, человека Божьего, будет служить молитвенным местом о многих казненных на Страстной площади в 1812 году патриотах-москвичах; монахинях Страстного монастыря, много претерпевших от наполеоновских захватчиков; насельниках этой обители, расстрелянных на Бутовском полигоне в годы лихолетья; погибших от террористического акта в подземном переходе под площадью в 2000 году." Melikhova and Tsekhanskii, *Strasti i nadezhdy*, 148.

14 Melikhova and Tsekhanskii, *Strasti i nadezhdy*, 32–3.

15 Ibid., 37.

16 "Лишенная исторической опоры, став пустым ландшафтным пространством, площадь почти полностью утратила свою целостность …" Melikhova and Tsekhanskii, *Strasti i nadezhdy*, 6.

17 "С возведением в 1880 году на площади памятника А.С. Пушкину скульптора А.М. Опекушина перекресток Бульварного кольца и Тверской улицы превращается в интереснейший, 'многоголосый' (как его назовут потом историки) ансамбль Москвы, сложившийся веками из разнохарактерных объектов." Melikhova and Tsekhanskii, *Strasti i nadezhdy*, 31.

18 Medvedev, *It's No Good*, 19.

19 Ibid., 269.

20 See Maiakovsvkii's poem, "A Joke Resembling the Truth," 1928.

21 Gessen, "Kirill Medvedev: Introduction," in Medvedev, *It's No Good*, 15.

22 Pushkin, "Razgovor knigoprodavtsa s poetom," in Pushkin, *Polnoe sobranie sochinenii v 10-i tomakh*, vol. 2, 174–9. Pushkin's poetry, unless

otherwise noted, is cited according to Aleksander S. Pushkin, *Polnoe sobranie sochinenii v 10-i tomakh* (Leningrad: Izd-vo "Nauka," 1977–9) (hereafter *PSS*). Unless otherwise noted, translationsfrom Russion are my own.

23 Sandler, *Commemorating Pushkin*, 1.

24 Ibid., 2.

25 Ibid., 5.

26 Levitt, *Russian Literary Politics*, 6–10.

27 For the purposes of this book, I am operating with the generally accepted and broad definition of allusion in *The Princeton Encyclopedia of Poetry and Poetics* (2012), 42–3.

28 Ibid., 42–3.

29 See *The Princeton Encyclopedia of Poetry and Poetics* on metaphor and metonymy.

30 Rosenshield, *Challenging the Bard*, 6.

31 Pellicer, "Pushkin's 'To Ovid' and Virgil's Georgics," 147.

32 Rosenshield, *Challenging the Bard*, 21.

33 Pellicer, "Pushkin's 'To Ovid' and Vergil's Georgics," 148.

34 Ibid., 152–3.

35 "Там, где постструктуралисты видят мрачную (или, напротив, карнавализованную) драму поглощения субъекта языком, автор склонен видеть чудо превращения «структурного» в индивидуальное, «текстуальности» – в тексты." Proskurin, *Poeziia Pushkina*, 11.

36 Sandler, "Introduction," 287.

37 Bethea, "Whose Mind Is This Anyway?," 3 and 13.

38 Kahn, *Pushkin's Lyric Intelligence*, 19.

39 Ibid., 31.

40 Ricks, *Allusion to the Poets*, 1–6.

41 Hinds, *Allusion and Intertext*, 18.

42 Ibid., 48–9.

43 Lotman's, "Text in the Text" is itself a "text in the text." Originally published in 1981 as the introductory article to the fourteenth volume of *Trudy po znakovym sistemam* (a volume that carried the title "Text in the Text," Lotman reworked the piece and later included it in *Kul'tura i vzryv* (1992) as an "inserted chapter" (*vstavnaia glava*): by definition a "text in the text." In this introduction I cite the original piece by its publication date (1981) and the "inserted chapter" according to its publication in *Semiosfera* (2000). Lotman, *Semiosfera*.

44 Lotman, *Semiosfera*, 72. "сложно устроенный текст, распадающийся на иерархию 'текстов в текстах' и образующий сложные переплетения текстов."

45 Lotman, "Tekst v tekste," 8–9. "В действительности же прагматический аспект – это аспект работы текста, поскольку механизм работы текста

подразумевает какое-то введение в него чего-либо извне. Будет ли это
'извне' – другой текст или читатель (который тоже 'другой текст'), или
культурный контекст, он необходим для того, чтобы потенциальная
возможность генерирования новых смыслов, заключенная в имманентной
структуре текста, превратилась в реальность. Поэтому процесс
трансформации текста в читательском (или исследовательском) сознании,
равно как и трансформации читательского сознания, введенного в текст
(по сути, мы имеем два текста в отношении инкорпорированные –
обрамляющие, см. ниже), – не искажение объективной структуры, от
которого следует устраниться, а раскрытие сущности механизма в процессе
его работы."

46 Lotman, *Semiosfera*, 66.

47 See chapter 1 for a more detailed analysis of this relationship. For
now I am only arguing for the special role that allusion plays in the
monumental sculpture of Russia's nineteenth century.

48 Lotman, *Aleksandr Sergeevich Pushkin: Biografiia*, 227. "история мыслится
Пушкиным не как нечто противоположное личности, а как живая
цепь живых человеческих жизней. История – это поколение простых,
'неисторических' личностей, это цепочка, в которой могилы предков,
хоровод взявшихся за руки живых и колыбели детей составляют единый
круг бессмертия. Прогресс заключается в накоплении памяти человечества,
то есть культуры, и в духовном росте отдельного человека."

49 Lotman, *Aleksandr Sergeevich Pushkin: Biografiia*, 227. "Гордое сознание
того, что не власть и сила, а дух и культура дают бессмертие, продиктовало
Пушкину стихотворение 'Я памятник себе воздвиг нерукотворный ...'
ставшее его поэтическим завещанием." "The proud awareness that it
is not power and force that grant immortality, but spirit and culture,
dictated to Pushkin the poem 'I have built a monument to myself not
made by hands ...' which has become his poetic will and testament."

50 Lotman, writing about the "text in the text," also specifies this
relationship between the framed text and the framing text as the
mechanism of reflecting the interplay of "real" and "conditional"
on the part of author and reader. Consider the following quotation:
"Вторая функция текста – порождение новых смыслов. В этом аспекте
текст перестает быть пассивным звеном передачи некоторой константной
информации между входом (отправитель) и выходом (получатель)."
Lotman, "Tekst v tekste," 7. "A second function of the text is the
generation of new meanings. In this aspect the text ceases to be a passive
link in the transmission of some sort of constant information between an
entrance (the sender) and the exit (the receiver)."

51 One well-known quotation to this effect comes in a letter from
Pushkin to his wife (14–16 May 1836), just a few months before he

wrote "Monument." "Здесь хотят лепить мой бюст. Но я не хочу. Тут арапское мое безобразие предано будет бессмертию во всей своей мертвой неподвижности." Pushkin, "Pis'mo Pushkinoi N.N., 14 i 16 maia 1836 g. Iz Moskvy v Peterburg," in *PSS*, t. 10, 452. http://feb-web.ru/feb/pushkin/texts/push10/v10/d10-4522.htm. "They want to fashion my bust. But I don't want them to. My Moorish ugliness will be committed to immortality in all of its dead immobility." All quotations of Pushkin's works are taken from this collected edition and translated by myself unless otherwise specified.

1 Pushkin's Poem: Monument and Allusion (1811–1836)

1 Pushkin, "Monument," *PSS*, vol. 3, 340. See the Appendix, p. 203, to read Pushkin's poem in Russian. For other translations of Pushkin's "Monument," see Levitt, *Russian Literary Politics and the Pushkin Celebration of 1880*, 24; Sandler, *Commemorating Pushkin*, 21–2; and Robert Chandler, Boris Dralyuk, and Irina Mashinski, eds, *The Penguin Book of Russian Poetry* (101–2), for Antony Wood's translation. My translation of "*slukh*" as "rumour" instead of the more common "fame" will perhaps seem to some readers idiosyncratic. I chose to emphasize the ambivalence of the word because of my conclusions about Pushkin's ambivalent feelings towards the "people" (*narod*). I am not alone in understanding "*slukh*" in this way. David Bethea writes, "Derzhavin's *slukh* of 'fame' becomes on Pushkin's lips the *slukh* of mere 'rumor' or 'gossip.'" Bethea, *Realizing Metaphors*, 231.

2 For background scholarship on Ovid and Pushkin, see Malein, "Pushkin i Ovidii (otryvochnye zamechaniia)"; Pokrovskii, "Pushkin i antichnost'"; Iakubovich, "Antichnost'"; Lednicki, *Bits of Table Talk*, 95; Costello, "Pushkin and Roman Literature"; Iieste, "Zametki k teme Pushkin i Ovidii"; Sandler, *Distant Pleasures*, 39–56; and Vulikh, "Ovidii." David M. Bethea's discussion of Pushkin's "mythopoetic consciousness" in particular is relevant for my analysis of Ovid's lifelike statues: see Bethea, *Realizing Metaphors*, 10–17 and 89–117; and his "Pushkin's Mythopoetic Consciousness," 15–16. Katya Hokanson's article on Pushkin and Ovid provides analysis of Ovid's significance for Pushkin during exile. Hokanson, "'*Barbarus hic ego sum.*'"

3 See also Gribanov, "Zametki k stat'e Iakobsona 'Statuia v poeticheskoi mifologii Pushkina.'" Gribanov critiques Jakobson's formulation of Pushkin's "sculptural myth." He identifies Jakobson's failure to note the significance of Ovid and the lifelike statues of *Metamorphoses* for Pushkin, although he does not focus on Ovid's imitation of Horace.

4 Proskurin, "Imperia i svoboda: Pamiatnik," in *Poeziia Pushkina*, 275–300.

5 Modzalevskii, "Katalog biblioteki A.S. Pushkina," 9/10: 304. Ovid's *Metamorphoses* was available to Pushkin in several different formats

during his lifetime. He owned two French translations and one edition in the original Latin. The cut pages in the French volumes suggest that they were the primary source of his knowledge of the text.

6 For a seminal definition of Pushkin's "sculptural myth," see Jakobson, *Puškin and His Sculptural Myth*, 1–44.

7 Alekseev, *Stikhotvorenie Pushkina*, 78n38.

8 Ibid., 76 and 76n33. The Russian text is cited as in Alekseev.

9 Stephanie Sandler concludes her work on Pushkin in exile by suggesting that the problem of how to reach a readership is fundamental to the works of this early period. "What makes the writings from Pushkin's exile a distinct, if not uniquely unified group of texts is the way that they enable a new articulation of the problems of reading Pushkin … Far from his audiences in Petersburg and Moscow, Pushkin in exile took up the fantasies of reaching – and, in some texts, vainly reaching toward – his readers." Sandler, *Distant Pleasures*, 212. The preoccupation with reception in Pushkin's "Monument" reveals a similar concern as the poet contemplates the future of his works in 1836. In a similar vein, Andrew Kahn's arguments about Pushkin and Ovid in exile also support the idea that in "Monument" Pushkin returned to his earlier thinking about Ovid: "Above all, 'To Ovid' is meaningful because it structures poetic relationships as a ratio between successor poets and key predecessors." Kahn, "Ovid and Russia's Poets of Exile," 405. A similar dynamic is apparent in "Monument": Pushkin engages with past poets who have written in the "Monument" genre while also predicating his poetic immortality on a future poet.

10 Jakobson, *Puškin and His Sculptural Myth*, 15–17.

11 Marcus Levitt's essay on Russian reception of Ovid's *Metamorphoses* in the eighteenth century analyses the dynamics between pagan mythology and Orthodox Christianity in the seventeenth and eighteenth centuries (143–4) as well as examples of both "high" and "low" eighteenth-century receptions of *Metamorphoses* (145–7). His analysis provides the historical context for the Ovid Pushkin encountered in Russian culture of the early nineteenth century. Levitt, "'Metamorfozy' Ovidiia v russkoi literature XVIII veka."

12 Costello, "Pushkin and Roman Literature," 49.

13 Gillespie, "Bawdy and Soul," 196.

14 Sedakova, "'Non-Mortal and Mysterious Feelings,'" 34.

15 Sandler, *Commemorating Pushkin*, 24.

16 Proskurin, "Pushkin and Metropolitan Philaret," 144.

17 In *Stikhotvorenie Pushkina*, see Alekseev's lengthy discussion on allusions to Del'vig in "Monument" (164–225, especially 220–1), and in *Realizing Metaphors* see Bethea's discussion of the issue of parody and the presence

of Del'vig in "Monument" that significantly refines Alekseev's arguments (218 and 226–31).

18 "The ecphrastic procedure can therefore be seen as an intersemiotic translation, which transforms plastic signs into verbal." Rubins, *Crossroads of Arts, Crossroads of Cultures*, 7.

19 The juxtaposition of iconism to ekphrasis is my own formulation, inspired by Rubins's juxtaposition of "iconographic" to "iconoclastic" literary narratives about the visual arts in Rubins, *Crossroads of Arts, Crossroads of Cultures*, 109 and 262n1.

20 Smoliarova, "How the Bronze Horseman Was Made," 108 and 112.

21 Ovid, *Metamorphoses*, 7.

22 Ibid., 17.

23 David Bethea convincingly argues in *Realizing Metaphors* that, when courting his future wife, Pushkin drew on Ovid's version of the Pygmalion myth. The Paphian artist prays to Venus for the image to come to life and is ecstatic when the ivory turns to flesh under his embrace. Pushkin conceptualized his love for the statuesque Natalie along similar lines: he longed to have her come to life under his embrace. In both personal letters and poetry, Pushkin realized "this double-sided sculptural metaphor in the year of his courtship [1830]" (106–9). In"Pushkin's Mythopoetic Consciousness," Bethea describes how Pushkin turned to the myths in the *Metamorphoses* of both Ovid and Apuleius for multiple examples of the capriciousness of love and its transformations as he looked forward to marriage (17). Bethea's observations about Pushkin's mythopoetic concept of marriage have resonance with the poet's mythopoetic conception of death and legacy. Transformations are inherent to the liminal times of marriage and death, and so it makes sense that Pushkin would find in Ovid's myths a fitting paradigm for thinking about his life in art.

24 Ovid, *Metamorphoses*, 275–6.

25 Ibid., 7.

26 Ibid., 445.

27 Ibid., 153 and 157.

28 In all of these transformations Ovid seems to play with one of the central notions of ekphrasis and iconism as intersemiotic translation, or, in the words of Smoliarova's description of the Bronze Horseman, that "the barrier between life and its representation in the statue should be completely obliterated." Smoliarova, "How the Bronze Horseman Was Made," 108.

29 Ovid, *Metamorphoses*, 59.

30 Ibid., 108.

31 Ibid., 76–8. Narcissus is also described as "like a statue carved from Parian marble." His obsession with his visual reflection (statue-like) is

the visual complement of Echo's curse to aurally reflect what is said by others. While Echo can say nothing original, Narcissus can see no one else. For a relevant discussion of Pushkin's interest in the Echo myth and the nature of allusion, see Cavendish, "Poetry as Metamorphosis."

32 Pelikan, *Christianity and Classical Culture*, 170–1.

33 Ibid., 284–5.

34 Elsewhere Pelikan writes, "The term [theosis], therefore, was an expression both of retrospection and of anticipation. It described the human condition before the fall as one of participation in God through 'the most exact likeness to the image of its prototype [*tei akribestatei homoiosei kata ten eikona tou prototypou*],' and it looked forward to the metamorphosis of human nature after the apocatastasis [restoration] as the recovery, through 'partaking of the divine nature,' of that participation, and thus to the fulfilment of the image of God." Pelikan, *Christianity and Classical Culture*, 135.

35 Pelikan, *Christianity and Classical Culture*, 285.

36 Ibid., 281.

37 Jakobson, *Sculptural Myth*, 29.

38 Zhukovskii, "Vospominanie o torzhestve 30 avgusta 1834," 31. Katya Hokanson points out that Zhukovskii's article states that poetry loses its voice to describe the event of the monument's unveiling, whereas Pushkin reasserts the voice of poetry in "Monument," claiming it to be higher than the Alexander Column and with a wider audience. Hokanson, "Politics and Poetry," 308. Where Zhukovskii sees the end of ekphrasis, Pushkin sees its renewed vigour.

39 "Thus logos (the word) overcomes eidolon (the idol) and idolatry." Jakobson, *Sculptural Myth*, 29.

40 Levitt, *The Visual Dominant in Eighteenth-Century Russia*, 266.

41 Bethea, *Realizing Metaphors*, 225. Bethea points out a different allusion inherent in the word *nerukotvornyi* and related to the paschal theme of the "Stone Island Cycle": the temple (*khram, rukotvornyi i nerukotvornyi*) which the Christ of the Gospels claims he will destroy and rebuild in three days.

42 Ware, *The Orthodox Church*, 41–2.

43 Jakobson, *Sculptural Myth*, 45.

44 Ibid., 37.

45 Pushkin's choice of *piit* is a marked word in the Russian context, set apart from the more common word *poet*. Oleg Proskurin describes the significance of the difference. A *piit* is a sort of apostle who spreads divine truth. He points to Renate Lachmann's argument that *piit* is a substitute for the Horatian pontifex, or "high priest," and to G.G. Krasukhin's work on the corresponding Orthodox context to support his claim. Proskurin,

Podvizhnyi palimpsest, 298 and 444n116. As Proskurin argues, there is also an eschatological component to the office of *piit*, which is of considerable significance with regard to the apocalyptic themes unleashed in Vladimir Toporov's and Tat'iana Tolstaia's iconoclastic approaches to the Pushkin Monument. See chapter 4, 159–65, and chapter 5, 189–90, for a more in-depth discussion of Pushkin's Monument and "the End."

46 As cited in Alekseev, *Stikhotvorenie*, 253.

47 Bethea, *Realizing Metaphors*, 231.

48 Pelikan, *Christianity and Classical Culture*, 129–32.

49 "The fallen" can include the traditional reading of these lines as an allusion to the Decembrists. But, as with nearly all of the words in this poem, a specific allusion does not preclude a more general one.

50 Philip Cavendish identifies a similar concern in Pushkin's "Echo" (1831): "[Pushkin's 'Echo'] anticipates a reversal of Bloomian 'anxiety of influence': the poet betrays anxiety, not about the fact of precursors with whose originality he must compete, and whose influence he must overcome, but about the absence of successors who will imitate and adapt his work, and thus secure his posthumous reputation." Cavendish, "Poetry as Metamorphosis," 441. However, Cavendish does not find a similar interpretation for the "sublunar poet" of "Monument." Cavendish, "Poetry as Metamorphosis," 452.

51 Consider these early lines from the poem "In an album, to Illichevskii" ("В альбом Илличевскому," 31 May 1817): "Oh my kind genius knows, / That I would sooner prefer / To the immortality of my soul / The immortality of my creations." "Ах ведает мой добрый гений, / Что предпочел бы я скорей / Бессмертию души моей / Бессмертие своих творений." A little later in the same poem Pushkin voices the idea that his poems most likely will die: "Let my poems die." "Мои стихи пускай умрут." Pushkin, *PSS*, vol. 1, 227.

52 The reason for his exile is unclear and the subject of much debate, but it did not have to do with the publication of *Metamorphoses*.

53 Alekseev, *Stikhotvorenie*, 235. Alekseev provides the best description of the textual history of the poem (232–44).

54 Lednicki, *The Bronze Horseman*. Chapter 2 ("Genesis, Reminiscences, and Auto-Reminiscences") and chapter 3 ("Pushkin, Mickiewicz, Falconet") are of particular relevance to the Mickiewicz theme.

55 Lednicki, *The Bronze Horseman*, 24.

56 Alekseev, *Stikhotvorenie*, 164–231; Bethea, *Realizing Metaphors*, 227–32.

57 Alekseev, *Stikhotvorenie*, 173.

58 The literal meaning of "*aleksandriiskii*" in Russian indicates a connection to Alexandria, the ancient city named for Alexander the Great. "*Aleksandrovskii*" is the adjectival form for a person by the name of

Alexander, whereas "*aleksandriiskii*" indicates a city named for an Alexander.

59 Bethea, *Realizing Metaphors*, 226.

60 Alekseev, *Stikhotvorenie*, 60–5.

61 Wachtel, *Commentary*, 355.

62 Hokanson, "Politics and Poetry," 308.

63 Sandler, *Commemorating Pushkin*, 23 and 318n55.

64 Lachmann, *Memory and Literature*, 209.

65 Mur'ianov, "Iz nabliudenii nad tekstami Pushkina."

66 Bondi, "Pamiatnik."

67 Golburt, *The First Epoch*, 115.

68 Ibid.

69 Ibid., 118.

70 Ibid., 137. Andrew Kahn's analysis of Pushkin's lyric to Zhukovskii from 1816 reiterates the importance of this dialogue between poets as crucial to the poetic act. Kahn argues that Pushkin asserts "the role of poets in teaching and inspiring one another." Kahn, *Pushkin's Lyric Intelligence*, 30. Even at this early stage in Pushkin's career, as Golburt and Kahn show, Pushkin envisions the future poet as a crucial, perhaps the most crucial, audience.

71 Golburt, *First Epoch*, 139.

72 As cited in ibid., 143.

73 Ibid.

74 Ibid., 144.

75 Ibid., 152.

76 In his critique of Gregoire's hypothesis that "*Aleksandriiskii stolp*" should be translated as "Pharos of Alexandria," Alekseev states that Pushkin also uses the word "*aleksandriiskii*" in "Egyptian Nights" to support the reading of "*aleksandriiskii*" as related to Alexandria. He dismisses the idea of the ancient lighthouse, however, in favour of the Pompeii column dedicated to Diocletian's victory over a revolt in Alexandria. Alekseev, *Stikhotvorenie*, 59 and 62.

77 Pushkin, *PSS*, vol. 6, 249. "Где найти мне лучшую публику? Вы поэт, вы поймете меня лучше их, и ваше тихое ободрение дороже мне целой бури рукоплесканий."

78 Ibid. "Садитесь где-нибудь и задайте мне тему."

79 Ibid. "поэт сам избирает предметы для своих песен; толпа не имеет права управлять его вдохновением" (emphasis in the original).

80 Herman, "A Requiem for Aristocratic Art," 680.

81 Ibid., 676.

82 Ibid., 680n38.

83 Herman interprets this appropriation along the lines of property and the "border between self and other" (668).

84 Pushkin, *PSS*, vol. 6, 251. "Чужая мысль чуть коснулась вашего слуха, и уже стала вашею собственностию, как будто вы с нею носились, лелеяли, развивали ее беспрестанно."

85 Ibid. "Каким образом ваятель в куске каррарского мрамора видит сокрытого Юпитера и выводит его на свет, резцом и молотом раздробляя его оболочку? … Так никто, кроме самого импровизатора, не может понять эту быстроту впечатлений, эту тесную связь между собственным вдохновением и чуждой внешнею волею."

86 Herman, "A Requiem for Aristocratic Art," 677.

87 Alexandra Smith, "Fictionality, Theatricality, and Staging of Self," 414.

88 Ibid.

89 Although Smith builds on Herman's previous work, she also problematizes Herman's interpretation of "Egyptian Nights" as an expression of Pushkin's "anxiety about the future of poetry, and about poets who might emerge from society's lower classes due to the advance of technology and the spread of culture," instead focusing on Pushkin's "realization of the responsible aesthetic attitude to life that relies on dialogic conscience." Alexandra Smith, "Fictionality, Theatricality, and Staging of Self," 393–4.

90 Pushkin, *PSS*, vol. 6, 248.

91 Bondi, "Pamiatnik," 453. "И не мудрено, повторяю, что некоторые исследователи (Владимир Соловьев, М. Гершензон, В. Вересаев), которые по своим убеждениям не могут согласиться с тем, что перечисленные Пушкиным стороны его поэзии являются его 'заслугой' перед человечеством, считают, что именно эти оценки Пушкин приводит не как свои, а как ложное понимание его поэзии, свойственное 'народу,' и что Пушкин призывает музу смириться с этим как с неизбежностью…" Bondi's essay serves well as a summary of the Soviet interpretation of "Monument." The fact that he repeatedly employs the word "I repeat" (*povtoriaiu*) indicates the well-worn path that he finds it necessary to tread once again. Many of his arguments can be found in the volume published by Alekseev a decade earlier. For example, specifically with regard to the polemic around the people, see Alekseev's earlier discussion of the response to Gershenzon's observation that stanza four represents the people's values and not Pushkin's. Alekseev, *Stikhotvorenie*, 48–52. For a salient discussion of Gershenzon's controversial interpretation of Pushkin's poem "Monument," see Horowitz, *The Myth of A.S. Pushkin in Russia's Silver Age*, 70–5.

92 Bondi, "Pamiatnik," 453. "Хотя этой точки зрения сейчас, кажется, никто не придерживается, и не раз были предложены в общем правильные объяснения причин этого резкого противоречия между последней строфой 'Памятника' и всеми предыдущими, все же мне представляется

необходимым еще раз вернуться к этой теме и тем самым напомнить те конкретные обстоятельства, которые вызвали к жизни это стихотворение."

93 Ibid., 455–60.

94 Ibid., 462. "Это стихотворение, повторяю, написано было для потомков, с которыми он мог свободно говорить и откровенно высказывать свое понимание поистине великого значения своего творчества ..."

95 Ibid., 465–75.

96 Ibid., 464. "Пока будет *существовать в мире поэзия* (независимо от положения политического и всякого иного России, русского народа), – слава Пушкина будет жить ..." (emphasis in the original).

97 Alekseev, *Stikhotvorenie*, 253. "Доколь славянов род вселенна будет чтить." See Alekseev's second appendix for the text of Derzhavin's "Monument," as well as many other relevant "Monuments" (244–71).

98 David Bethea also notes a shift from Derzhavin's emphasis on "public consciousness" to Pushkin's emphasis on one poet and "private consciousness." Bethea, *Realizing Metaphors*, 231.

99 Bondi, "Pamiatnik," 475.

100 Ibid., 452–3.

2 Opekushin's Pushkin Monument: Statue and Performance (1836–1880)

1 "Бумаги, могущие повредить памяти Пушкина ..." Letter from Benkendorf to Zhukovskii, as cited in Shchegolev, *Duel' i smert' Pushkina*, 198.

2 As cited in ibid., 170. "Опишу в немногих словах то, что было после. К счастью, я вспомнил вовремя, что надобно с него снять маску. Это было исполнено немедленно; черты его еще не успели измениться. Конечно, того первого выражения, которое дала им смерть, в них не сохранилось; но все мы имеем отпечаток привлекательный; это не смерть, а сон."

3 Levitt, *Russian Literary Politics and the Pushkin Celebration*, 18–19.

4 For a full account of the textual history of the poem see Alekseev, *Stikhotvorenie Pushkina*.

5 Furthermore, Zhukovskii had long been aware of Pushkin's wickedly nuanced art. For more on Zhukovskii's relationship to Pushkin and, in particular, his familiarity with the multiple layers of the poem's meaning, see Proskurin, "'Pobediteliu ucheniku ot pobezhdennogo uchitelia,'" in *Poeziia Pushkina*, 52–5.

6 Alekseev, *Stikhotvorenie Pushkina*, 12–18 and 232.

7 Davydov, "Evolution of Pushkin's Political Thought," 306.

8 It might also be possible to read the progression from Falconet's Bronze Horseman to Montferrand's Alexander Column to Pushkin's

Monument as one that is inherently complimentary to Nicholas I, while at the same time claiming superiority to him. Just as in "Arion," both of Pushkin's audiences can read the poem in the way most favourable to themselves: Nicholas I potentially could have read the relationship between the Alexander Column and Pushkin's poetry as a sort of organic connection. He could see himself as the patron who facilitated the accomplishments of the poet. It seems clear that Zhukovskii did not want to take that risk.

9 Davydov, "Evolution of Pushkin's Political Thought," 303.
10 As cited in ibid., 302.
11 Beyond the place of "Monument" in the "Stone Island Cycle" that lends its Christian imagery particular significance, it is important to note that the device of allusion was central to the concept of every poem in the cycle. As Sergei Davydov writes, "'Hermit fathers …,' 'Imitation of the Italian,' and 'Secular Power' form a micro-cycle of their own, sharing a number of common features. None of the three poems is Puškin's original creation; they are based either entirely or partially on some text of foreign origin." Davydov, "Puškin's Easter Triptych," 39.
12 Davydov, "Evolution of Pushkin's Political Thought," 310.
13 As cited in ibid., 310–11.

> Иные лучшие мне дороги права;
> Иная, лучшая потребна мне свобода:
> Зависеть от властей, зависеть от народа –
> Не всё ли нам равно? Бог с ними.
>   Никому
> Отчета не давать, себе лишь самому
> Служить и угождать; для власти, для ливреи
> не гнуть ни совести, ни помыслов, ни шеи;
> По прихоти своей скитаться здесь и там,
> Дивясь божественным природы красотам,
> И пред созданьями искусства и вдохновенья
> Трепеща радостно в восторгах умиленья.
>   – Вот счастье! вот права …

14 Ibid., 57.
15 Alekseev, *Stikhotvorenie*, 18–31.
16 Ibid., 23–5.
17 Ibid., 28.
18 Belinskii, *Polnoe sobranie sochinenii v 13 tomakh*, tom 7, 579. Translation as cited in Levitt, *Russian Literary Politics and the Pushkin Celebration*, 24.

19 Levitt, "Pushkin's Readers, 1855–1887," unpublished essay (manuscript page 7). Personal correspondence, 4 April 2017.

20 Shmidt, *Russkaia skul'ptura*, 109. See also Levitt, *Russian Literary Politics and the Pushkin Celebration*, 34–5.

21 For a full description of Laveretskii's and Bakhman's project, an image, and the debate about its meanings in the press see Librovich, *Pushkin v portretakh*, 167–70.

22 The extent to which the future poet is forgotten is demonstrated by later descriptions of the project and the debate that it inspired. As late as 1983 Suslov writes, "Multiple allegorical figures – of the Russian people, of the muse of poetry, etc. – dominated the monument to such an extent that the figure of the poet himself, the crowning image of the whole complex composition, was insufficiently expressed." "Многочисленные аллегорические фигуры – русского народа, музы поэзии и т. д. – настолько преобладали в памятнике, что фигура самого поэта, увенчивающая всю эту сложную композицию, не получила достойного выражения." Suslov, *Pamiatnik Pushkinu*, 16. The fact that Suslov names the people and the muse here but relegates the future poet to the category of "etc." reflects the extent to which the figure of the future poet receded to the background because of the intense focus on the people.

23 See Levitt, "Pushkin's Readers," 8–9.

24 The eight works Shreder chose to include were: *The Gypsies, The Prisoner of the Caucuses, Eugene Onegin, The Stone Guest, Boris Godunov, Rusalka,* and *The Covetous Knight.* For a full description of the project, see Librovich, *Pushkin v portretakh*, 171–2.

25 Librovich, *Pushkin v portretakh*, 172–5.

26 Levitt, *Russian Literary Politics and the Pushkin Celebration*, 43.

27 Martin, "The Pushkin Celebrations of 1880," 505–6.

28 Krein, *Rukotvornyi pamiatnik*, 8.

29 Levitt, *Russian Literary Politics and the Pushkin Celebration*, 46–7; Librovich, *Pushkin v portretakh*, 177; Krein, *Rukotvornyi pamiatnik*, 8.

30 "The Conversation between a Bookseller and a Poet," written in 1824. Of course, in the end, the poet agrees with the bookseller that "One can't sell inspiration, / But you can sell a manuscript." "Разговор книгопродавца с поэтом." "Не продается вдохновение, / Но можно рукопись продать." Pushkin, *PSS*, vol. 2, 174–9.

31 Grot, *Zhizn' Derzhavina*, 1021–2. "чугунный генарал из *наверститута,* где студентов обучают, поехал к тиатру, и поставили его тут на площади потому-де, что монументу эдакого человека, вельможнаго и генерала, стоять на дворе наверститута не пригоже."

32 Grot, *Zhizn' Derzhavina*, 1021–2.

33 Levitt, *Russian Literary Politics and the Pushkin Celebration*, 46–7.

34　Ibid., 49–50.

35　Librovich, *Pushkin v portretakh*, 179–80.

36　Ibid., 182.

37　See my discussion of "Egyptian Nights" in chapter 1, 66–9.

38　Librovich, *Pushkin v portretakh*, 182–3.

39　"сшиты по одному и тому-же, давно исчерпанному и давно затасканному образцу." Librovich, *Pushkin v portretakh*, 189.

40　This critic was published in *Krugozor*, vol. 12 (1876), several years after the second competiton. As cited in Librovich, *Pushkin v portretakh*, 186. "Даже в лучших из этих проектов поражало какое-то роковое несоответствие статуи с ее подножием: если фигура Пушкина еще могла быть терпима – пьедестал никуда не годился по крайней, так-сказать, убогости замысла; наоборот (и это в большинстве случаев), когда подножие являлось в некоторой степени достойным памятника певцу-исполину, самая статуя резала глаз своим – tranchons le mot – ничтожеством, если еще не потешным комизмом."

41　Librovich, *Pushkin v portretakh*, 190. "памятник должен хотя немного воплощать в себе «всего Пушкина», давать идею, понятие о поэте."

42　Beliaev and Shmidt, *Aleksander Mikhailovich Opekushin*, 29.

43　Librovich, *Pushkin v portretakh*, 192–203.

44　Milii Alekseevich Balakirev, composer.

45　Tolstoy, *Anna Karenina*, part 7, chapter 5, as cited in the Maude translation. Marcus C. Levitt also discusses this episode in *Anna Karenina* as indicative of the struggle against the "neoclassical" school in sculpture. Levitt, *Russian Literary Politics and the Pushkin Celebration*, 50.

46　Levitt, *Russian Literary Politics and the Pushkin Celebration*, 32.

47　In their analysis of Antokol'skii's project, Beliaev and Shmidt come to a similar conclusion, citing a letter from painter and art critic Ivan Nikolaevich Kramskoi to artist Il'ia Efimovich Repin: "To put bronze sculptures of characters from Pushkin's works as nearly equal to living people meant to endow the monument with a highly undesirable impression. I.N. Kramskoi understood this well in his letter to I.E. Repin, dated 16 May 1875. Kramskoi wrote about the project, '…it is decidedly impossible to put [a monument like this] on the street, in the square, where thousands of people throng, sun in their eyes, dust, noise … and then suddenly – a vision … Mysticism and spiritism in Moscow, in the daytime, on Strastnoi Square?!'" "Ставить же изваянные из бронзы персонажи произведений Пушкина почти вровень с живыми людьми значило придать памятнику весьма нежелательное впечатление. Это прекрасно понимал И. Н. Крамской, который в письме к И. Е. Репину, датированном 16 мая 1875 года, писал об этом проекте: «… решительно невозможно на улице, на площади, где снуют тысячи народа, солнце во все глаза, пыль, шум … и вдруг – видение … Мистицизм и спиритизм в Москве, днем, на Страстной площади?!»." Beliaev and Shmidt, *Opekushin*, 28–9.

48 Levitt, *Russian Literary Politics and the Pushkin Celebration*, 50.

49 Chubukov, *Vsenarodnyi pamiatnik Pushkinu*, 38.

50 Ibid., 39 and 63.

51 Ibid., 63. "Надо полагать, что Пушкин имел, вероятно, привычку во время прогулок своих снимать шляпу и стоять с обнаженной головою. Если даже это предположение и справедливо, то и тогда не следует отдельных особенностей передавать в памятнике, в которых потомство должно видеть только олицетворение личности гения, или аллегорическое представление его творчества. А потому фигура Пушкина без плаща с открытой головою была бы более естественна."

52 Librovich, *Pushkin v portretakh*, 208. For a detailed description of the relationship between Opekushin and Beliaev and the details about how the pedestal was erected, see Chubukov, *Vsenarodnyi pamiatnik Pushkinu*, 50–65. Chubukov does not address the question of how Opekushin settled on which lines from "Monument" he should include, or where to place them.

53 Shmidt, *Russkaia skul'ptura*, 124.

54 Rather, critics tend to focus on the dimensions of the statue and pedestal as reinforcing the perception of Pushkin's figure as life-size, not the relationship between the poem and the statue. Krein writes that, "Art historians have emphasized that the sculptor and architect found a particularly successful scale: from different points of perception the monument appears to correspond in size to a living human figure." "Искусствоведы подчеркивали, что скульптор и архитектор нашли особенно удачный масштаб: с разных точек обозрения памятник смотрится соразмерно живой человеческой фигуре." Krein, *Rukotvornyi pamiatnik*, 18.

55 Davydova, *Uvekovechennyi v bronze*, 69–71.

56 Ibid., 80.

57 Ibid., 84–6 and 91.

58 See my argument about the poem's Soviet reception and the "positive" reading of the people in Pushkin's poetry in chapter 1, 70–3.

59 The theme of *"dulce et utile"* in stanza four seems to allude to Horace's *Ars poetica*.

60 Librovich, *Pushkin v portretakh*, 210–15.

61 Shmidt, *Russkaia skul'ptura*, 122. "All allegorical and many-figured designs were decidedly rejected. The image of Pushkin was considered rich because of its internal organization, in a posture of deep reflection and poetic aloofness. But externally he was represented by Opekushin as one might have seen him in life, dressed in typical clothes of his

era, without substantial formality. For its time, the resolution of the
monument's pedestal, developed by the architect I.S. Bogomolov, was
comparatively austere." "Все аллегорические и многофигурные замыслы
были решительно отвергнуты. Образ Пушкина мыслился богатым
по внутреннему содержанию, в состоянии глубокой задумчивости и
поэтической отрешенности. Но внешне он представлен у Опекушина
таким, каким его могли видеть в жизни, одетым в обычные одежды
своего времени, без существенных условностей. Было выбрано также
сравнительно строгое для того времени решение постамента будущего
памятника, разработанное архитектором И.С. Богомоловым."

62 Shmidt, *Russkaia skul'ptura*, 124. "The poet-citizen, the poet-thinker –
that is how Opekushin conceived and executed the image of Pushkin.
The image of the poet communicates a deeply human, unpretentious
simplicity and sincerity. His inner state, according to the design of the
sculptor, corresponds to the words of the famous poem 'Monument,'
carved in relief on the pedestal." "Поэт-гражданин, поэт-мыслитель – так
задуман и решен Опекушиным образ Пушкина. Глубоко человеческая,
непритязательная простота и задушевность переданы в образе поэта. Его
внутреннее состояние по замыслу скульптора отвечает высеченным на
постаменте словам знаменитого стихотворения 'Памятник.'"

63 Shmidt, *Russkaia skul'ptura*, 109. The Pushkin Monument is not the
first of its type in all respects. In 1847 a monument to Derzhavin was
erected in Kazan', and in 1855 the monument to Krylov was placed in
St Petersburg's Summer Garden. And yet it was the first of its type in
many important respects – for example, its central location in Moscow
and the cultural context of the events of the 1880 Jubilee.

64 Susanne Fusso has recently clarified one underlying reason for these
similarities – Varnhagen von Ense's essay on Pushkin published in
German in 1838 and translated by Mikhail Katkov in 1839. Her arguments
make an important contribution to the study of the Jubilee speeches by
analysing this common source and the role of Katkov at the Jubilee more
broadly speaking. Fusso, *Editing Turgenev, Dostoevsky, and Tolstoy*, 204–41.

65 Turgenev, "Speech," 840.

66 While Turgenev carefully distinguishes between *narodnyi* (folk) and
natsional'nyi (national) in his speech, Dostoevskii does not. With regard
to allusion, the significance of Dostoevskii's conflation of these ideas
becomes apparent in the following analysis. For the context of what these
two words meant with regard to the Pushkin Jubilee, see Fusso, *Editing
Turgenev, Dostoevsky, and Tolstoy*, 222, 225, and 230.

67 Turgenev, "Speech," 841.

68 Ibid., 843.

69 Ibid.

70 Ibid., 842.

71 Dostoevsky, *A Writer's Diary*, 2: 1273.

72 Ibid., 2: 1275.

73 Ibid., 2: 1281.

74 Ibid., 2: 1282.

75 Ibid., 2: 1284.

76 Ibid., 2: 1291.

77 Ibid., 2: 1292.

78 Turgenev, "Speech," 839.

79 Dostoevsky, *A Writer's Diary*, 2: 1290.

80 Turgenev, "Speech," 839. Emphasis mine.

81 Ibid., 841–2.

82 Ibid., 848–9.

83 Shmidt, *Russkaia skul'ptura*, 124.

84 For a summary of Tolstoy's position and Turgenev's reaction to it, see Levitt, *Russian Literary Politics and the Pushkin Celebration*, 96–103.

85 Dostoevsky, *A Writer's Diary*, 2: 1293.

86 Ibid., 2: 1273.

87 Turgenev, "Speech," 848.

88 Ibid., 845.

89 Ibid., 846.

90 Many poets wrote ekphrastic poetry addressed to the monument for the Jubilee. For examples and commentary, see Librovich, *Pushkin v portretakh*, 222–3. Consider, for example, A.A. Fet's 1880 poem about the Pushkin Monument: "Your prophetic word has been fulfilled; Our old shame has looked upon your bronze face …" Fet, *Polnoe sobranie sochinenii*, 364. "Исполнилось твое пророческое слово; Наш старый стыд взглянул на бронзовый твой лик." Even though Fet's poem contributes to the interpretation of the monument as a prophecy fulfilled, I do not consider this type of poetry here because it differs in essence from the aesthetics of allusion in Dostoevskii's speech. Fet and poets like him who wrote verses about the monument are also "future poets" in their own right, but their ekphrases tend not to move beyond the genre boundaries or expand allusion in the way that Dostoevskii's speech does. To put it into the language of metamorphosis, these poems do not raise Pushkin's poetic devices in a new way. On the reader's end of allusion, these poems seem to have little future life. Dostoevskii's speech engenders a stormy debate and shapes the future of the Opekushin monument in ways that their poetry does not.

91 Dostoevsky, *A Writer's Diary*, 2: 1272.

92 Ibid.

93 Ibid., 2: 1271–2.

94 Ibid., 2: 1291.

95 Ibid., 2: 1295.

96 Dostoevskii's memory of the crowd's reaction suggests he was attuned to this role. Dostoevskii writes to his wife on the night after the speech, "suddenly, for example, two elderly gentlemen with whom I was unacquainted stopped me: 'We have been enemies for twenty years, we haven't spoken to each other, but now we have embraced, we have been reconciled. It is you who have reconciled us, you are our saint, you are our prophet.' The crowd shouted, 'Prophet, prophet!'" Dostoevskii, *Polnoe sobranie sochinenii v tridtsati tomakh*, 184. "вдруг, например, останавливают меня два незнакомые старика: 'Мы были врагами друг друга 20 лет, не говорили друг с другом, а теперь мы обнялись и помирились. Это вы нас помирили, Вы наш святой, вы наш пророк.' 'Пророк, пророк!' – кричали в толпе."

97 Kanevskaia, "F.M. Dostoevsky's Pushkin Speech in a Cultural Context," 26.

98 The ball scene takes place at the end of chapter 7, stanzas LI to LV. "где *он являлся ей*."

99 *Eugene Onegin*, chapter 8, stanza LIV.

100 Dostoevsky, *A Writer's Diary*, 2: 1285.

101 *Eugene Onegin*, chapter 8, stanza LV. "Но здесь с победою поздравим / Татьяну милую мою / И в сторону свой путь направим, / Чтоб не забыть, о ком пою …"

102 Dostoevskii revised other allusions to make urban space do the work for him. In an early draft of *Crime and Punishment*, Dostoevskii has Raskol'nikov look at Falconet's Bronze Horseman as he stands on a bridge over the Neva. Later, the significance of the meaning of the Bronze Horseman for Raskol'nikov remains, but Dostoevskii cuts out specific mention of the monument, leaving the allusion to be recreated by the sophisticated reader's knowledge of the urban/literary environment. Scollins, "Pronouncing the 'New Word.'" It seems as though Dostoevskii might be doing something similar when he paraphrases Pushkin's narrator in *Evgenii Onegin* in the Assembly of the Nobility.

103 Dostoevsky, *A Writer's Diary*, 2: 1281.

104 Levitt, *Russian Literary Politics and the Pushkin Celebration*, 127.

105 Ibid., 135.

106 As cited in Kanevskaia, "Dostoevsky's 'Pushkin Speech,'" 38–9.

107 The performance of Meyerbeer's "Prophet" (*Prorok*), inspired by Pushkin's eponymous poem, at the first "apotheosis" of the monument underscores the interpretation of the monument as a prophetic fulfilment of Pushkin's poem while also thematically doubling Dostoevskii's performance of the poem "Prophet" at the end of the Celebration. Levitt, *Russian Literary Politics and the Pushkin Celebration*, 85.

108 Levitt, *Russian Literary Politics and the Pushkin Celebration*, 124 and 139.

109 Bem, "Dostoevskii – genial'nyi chitatel,'" 19; Alexandra Smith, "Pushkin as a Cultural Myth," 123.

110 Solovyov, "The Russian National Ideal," 56.

111 Ibid., 55.

112 Levitt, *Russian Literary Politics and the Pushkin Celebration*, 127–38; Kanevskaia, "Dostoevsky's 'Pushkin Speech,'" 32–44.

113 Levitt, *Russian Literary Politics and the Pushkin Celebration*, 130.

114 Ibid.

115 Susanne Fusso argues that Mikhail Katkov, in his essay on Dostoevskii's death, sees Dostoevskii as having achieved the very status of universal poet that Dostoevskii declared for Pushkin in his Pushkin Speech. She writes, "More broadly, if one thinks back to Katkov's assessment that Pushkin, for all his poetic gifts and skill, did not quite achieve the stature of a world figure in literature, then effectively Katkov sees Dostoevsky as having reached that level of distinction as a universal writer." Fusso, *Editing Turgenev, Dostoevsky, and Tolstoy*, 237.

116 Morson, "Introductory Study," 38–40.

3 Bulgakov's *Master and Margarita*: Crisis of the Future Poet (1880–1937)

1 Levitt, *Russian Literary Politics and the Pushkin Celebration*, 154–8.

2 Ibid., 158–60.

3 Ibid., 160–2.

4 Khodasevich represents the ambivalence poetically: "National pride in him will flow into indestructible bronze forms," an image he contrasts to the "heart-felt tenderness" with which he and those gathered loved Pushkin. Likewise, in his last public speech, Blok denigrated monumental sculpture as irrelevant to the mission of the poet, whose freedom is distinctively not a public affair. See Levitt, *Russian Literary Politics and the Pushkin Celebration*, 161, 213n42, and 213n43.

5 Sandler, *Commemorating Pushkin*, 95–6.

6 For Esenin's description of the performance, see Esenin, *Polnoe sobranie sochinenii v 7 tomakh*, 8–10, 11–13, and the commentary on 391–3. For a description of the sign hung on the Pushkin Monument, see Samodelova, *Antropologicheskaia poetika*, 630. "Художник Дид-Ладо, который расписывал с имажинистами Страстной монастырь, переименовал улицы Москвы в честь имажинистов и вешал на шею Пушкину-памятнику плакат 'Я с имажинистами.'" "The artist Did-Lado, who painted the Strastnoi Monastery with the imagists, renamed the streets of Moscow in honour of

the imagists and hung a sign that read 'I'm with the imagists' on the neck of the Pushkin Monument."

7 Samodelova, *Antropologicheskaia poetika*, 601. Samodelova writes, "Есенина, утратившего жизнь в Ленинграде, 'вернули' в Москву (вопреки его 'родовым корням' из с. Константиново), торжественно обнесли гроб вокруг памятника Пушкину на Тверском бульваре в знак признания поэтических заслуг (что было негативно отмечено рядом эмигрантских критиков) и похоронили на Ваганьковском кладбище." "Esenin, who lost his life in Leningrad, was returned to Moscow (in spite of his 'native roots' in the village of Konstantinovo), his coffin was solemnly carried around the Pushkin Monument on Tverskoi Boulevard as a sign of recognition for his poetic achievements (which provoked negative commentary by several critics in emigration), and he was buried at the Vagan'kovskii cemetery."

8 Chudakova, *Zhizneopisanie Mikhaila Bulgakova*, 172–3. These pilgrimages to the Pushkin Monument suggest that their "Green Lamp" society alludes to the "Green Lamp" society of Pushkin's day. For more on the intensely private allusions and subversive aesthetics of Pushkin's involvement in the "Green Lamp" society of his day, see Peschio, *The Poetics of Impudence and Intimacy.*

9 The complexity of the design of the Pushkin Monument itself was not realized by some observers of the 1937 Jubilee. Consider the following arguments of a Soviet sculptor about pre-revolutionary monuments to Pushkin and their role in interacting with Pushkin's new Soviet readers.

"Monuments to Pushkin in Moscow and Leningrad cannot be called successful in any way. These are monuments in the narrow sense of the word, that is, they are figures of the poet that only remind us that such a poet as Pushkin existed and that his external appearance somewhat resembled what the sculptor has created. There is no thought or idea in these monuments that correctly reveals Pushkin. And yet these monuments are passed by every day by thousands and hundreds of thousands of Pushkin's readers, his friends! The thoughts and feelings of the poet are close and transparent to them; they are moved by the glorious lines of his works. Only now, in our remarkable contemporary moment, has the time come to create for Pushkin a worthy monument; to incarnate in bronze and granite an image of the great Russian genius that is dear to every Soviet citizen."

"Памятники Пушкину в Москве и Ленинграде назвать удачными никак нельзя. Это памятники в узком значении этого слова, то есть фигуры поэта, лишь напоминающие о том, что был такой поэт Пушкин и выглядел он внешне примерно так, как изобразил его скульптор. Мысли, идеи, правильно раскрывающей Пушкина, в этих памятниках нет. А ведь мимо памятников проходят тысячи и сотни тысяч читателей Пушкина, его друзей! Им близки и понятны мысли и чувства поэта, их волнуют великолепные строки его произведений. Лишь сейчас, в наши замечательные дни, настала пора создать Пушкину подобающий памятник, воплотить в бронзе и граните дорогой каждому советскому гражданину образ великого русского гения."

V.V. Lishev, "Voplotit' obraz poeta v monumental'noi skul'pture," *Zvezda* 1 (1937). Reprinted in Molok, *Pushkin v 1937*, 59.

10 As Carol Any writes, "The Stalinized Pushkin became a ubiquitous cliché rendering all other interpretations of Pushkin taboo; yet we should not imagine that it was simply handed down from above in ready-made form at a certain point in time and immediately internalized by the public." Any, "The Red Pushkin," 378. As her analysis shows, in the Writers' Union there were many competing taboo interpretations of Pushkin in 1937. The official image of Pushkin that emerged made him not only socially and politically progressive but accessible. However, underlying this official stance of Pushkin's aesthetic accessibility there still remained the taboo question of whether the mass reader could even understand Pushkin at all. Any, "The Red Pushkin," 382–6.

11 Sandler, *Commemorating Pushkin*, 87. Consider also that "Stakhanovite workers were encouraged to 'master Pushkin and transmit their knowledge to other workers,' thus proving that the masses could attain 'culture,' a major goal of the 1930s." Swift, "Pushkin's 'Skazka o pope i rabotnike ego Balde,'" 137.

12 Evgenii Dobrenko's essay on Pushkin in Soviet culture provides an overview of the Pushkin myth in the twentieth century and sets an important stage for reading the Pushkin motifs in *Master and Margarita*. He summarizes the Soviet reinterpretation of Pushkin's theme of the people as audience:

"It was not enough just to cite the ode 'Liberty' ('Vol'nost''), the poems 'To Chaadaev' ('K Chaadaevu'), 'To the Slanderers of Russia' ('Klevetnikam Rossii'). Something had to be done about the Pushkin who, as the author of 'The Poet and the Crowd' ('Poet i tolpa'), had written contemptuously about 'the rabble.' The theory of 'art for art's sake' was no longer invoked; rather, his contempt was interpreted as merely an idiosyncratic means of self-defense against 'the rabble' to be seen in the context of the post-Napoleonic restoration of Europe and the reaction of the reign of Nicholas I. This 'rabble,' it transpired, was not the people as a whole, whom great art always serves, and who always revere their poets, 'hanging on their every word'; on the contrary, the faults of the mob were redefined in Soviet criticism to mean what Pushkin disliked in 'high-society' or equated with the 'repulsive egotism' of western democracy." Dobrenko, "Pushkin in Soviet and Post-Soviet Culture," 207.

13 Several patterns found in both Tsvetaeva's and Bulgakov's vision of the Pushkin Monument in 1937 invite commentary. For example, Tsvetaeva elaborates on how Pushkin's stomach wound was one of the first things she learned about Pushkin and about poets in general. At three years of age she knew that poets had stomachs. In her naive understanding, D'Anthès killed Pushkin because "he himself couldn't write poetry" (*sam ne mog pisat' stikhi*). Tsvetaeva, "Moi Pushkin," 498. Her understanding of the situation as a child is similar to Riukhin's misconstrual of the scenario as a mature poet, except that he does not even know what the three-year-old Tsvetaeva knew: that Pushkin was wounded in the stomach.

14 For another look at Tsvetaeva and Pushkin, see Sandler, "Embodied Words." See also Shevelenko, "'Byvaiut strannye sblizhen'ia.'" Liza Knapp's arguments about Tsvetaeva and Pushkin's "blackness" are also essential reading: Knapp, "Tsvetaeva's 'Blackest of Black' (*Naicherneishii*) Pushkin."

15 As with so many other allusions to the Pushkin Monument, Tsvetaeva's evocation of Pushkin's blackness opens up potential dialogue with the performances of other poets in this space. For example, in a 1926 sketch, a naive poet by the name of Gavrila, Mikhail Zoshchenko's pseudonym in the satirical magazine *Buzoter*, emphasizes Pushkin's blackness as if it were the only thing that makes them different. "Do I not resemble him?" the caricature of Gavrila asks, pointing to the Pushkin Monument. He continues, "I'm also standing on Tverskoi. I also write rhymes from time to time. It's just that I'm not a Moor!" "Гаврила: Я-ль не похож? Тож на Тверском стою. Тоже стишки пописываю. Вот только-что не арап!" Zoshchenko, "Gavrila I Pushkin," 6. Thanks to Carlotta Chenoweth for drawing this sketch to my attention.

16 Nepomnyashchy and Trigos, "Introduction," 21. Tsvetaeva's entrance into the dialogue of Pushkin's heritage looks forward to Abram Tertz's *Strolls with Pushkin* and Tatiana Tolstaia's short story "Limpopo," which also connects the themes of Pushkin's Africanness, empire, the future poet, and the Pushkin Monument. For more on that tradition, see Nepomnyashchy and Trigos, "Introduction," 29–30.

17 Knapp, "Tsvetaeva's 'Blackest of Black' (*Naicherneishii*) Pushkin," 292.

18 Tsvetaeva, "Moi Pushkin," 503. "И скоро еще подрасту."

19 Ibid., 540. "И – больше скажу: безграмотность моего младенческого отождествления стихии со стихами оказалась – прозрением." Liza Knapp interprets Tsvetaeva's final emphasis on freedom as an allusion to "Monument": "In Tsvetaeva's mind, Pushkin was not only a poet who valued and sang about 'freedom' in his 'cruel age,' but one who

applied a freedom to his poetry." Knapp, "Tsvetaeva's 'Blackest of Black' (*Naicherneishii*) Pushkin," 295.

20 Khodasevich, "Proletkul't."

21 Pushkin actually died on 29 January 1837. Dostoevsky died on 28 January 1881. The coincidence is significant for Khodasevich in writing this poem.

22 Khodasevich stopped writing poetry in 1927. For a discussion of Khodasevich's last decade, see Bethea, *Khodasevich*, 317–52.

23 "Во мне конец, во мне начало. / Мной совершенное так мало! / Но все ж я прочное звено: мне это счастие дано." Both the original and the translation can be found in Bethea, *Khodasevich*, 317.

24 The change in Khodasevich's outlook can be seen in his 1938 reflection on a long-standing debate with fellow émigré poet G.V. Adamovich. For a history of the debate and Khodasevich's reflection on it, see Bethea, *Khodasevich*, 326–31. For a detailed discussion about Khodasevich's work on Pushkin in the 1930s, see Brintlinger, *Writing a Usable Past*, 90–119. In the conclusion to her book, Brintlinger also notices that the conflation of commemoration and celebration in 1937 for the émigré community became "doubly sad," as their celebrations of the "Day of Russian Culture" were moved to the day of Pushkin's death. Twenty years after the Revolution, the prospects of "going home" and continuing their heritage in the homeland looked "more and more doubtful." Brintlinger, *Writing a Usable Past*, 166.

25 Dobrenko, *The Making of the State Reader*, 120.

26 Ibid., 117.

27 As cited in Avins, "Reaching a Reader," 273.

28 Ibid., 274.

29 There is a case to make for the idea that Berlioz is also a naive reader, albeit one without the excuses of youth or poor education. Berlioz is surprised by the apparition of Korov'iev because he knows Russian literature poorly (he fails to recognize Korov'iev as an allusion to Ivan's petty demon in *Brothers Karamazov*, and he, too, like Bezdomnyi, misses Voland as an allusion to *Faust*). As the Master points out, Berlioz was an educated, well-read individual and should have known immediately what he was facing, but, alas, he did not. The missed allusion provides an opportunity for Bulgakov to poke fun at the literary establishment while addressing the more serious question of the future of pre-revolutionary art.

30 Gasparov lays out significant parallels between Levi Matvei and Ivan Bezdomnyi. See Gasparov, "Iz nabliudenii," 209–10.

31 Bulgakov, *Master i Margarita: Polnoe Sobranie Chernovikov Romana* (hereafter *PSChR*), edited by E.Iu. Kolysheva, 2: 557. "Эти добрые люди, – заговорил арестант и, торопливо прибавив: – игемон, – продолжал: – ничему

не учились и всё перепутали, что я говорил. Я вообще начинаю опасаться, что путаница эта будет продолжаться очень долгое время. И всё из-за того, что он неверно записывает за мной … – ходит один с козлиным пергаментом и непрерывно пишет. Но я однажды заглянул в этот пергамент и ужаснулся. Решительно ничего из того, что там записано, я не говорил." All citations from *Master and Margarita* are taken from Kolysheva's edition. Translations are my own.

32 Consider the extent to which the Passion was already a clichéd genre that can evoke many allusions, not just to the Gospels. Gasparov points out important parallels between the genre in general and specifically between the Master's version of the Passion of Christ and the Passions composed by Bach. Gasparov, "Iz nabliudenii," 210.

33 Bulgakov, *PSChR*, 1: 107 and 121.

34 "Riukhin sat down and with the voice of an ill person asked for a small decanter … He drank vodka and the more he drank, the more sober he became and the more a dark malice toward Pushkin and toward fate grew in his soul." "Рюхин сел и больным голосом спросил малый графинчик … Он пил водку и чем больше пил, тем становился трезвей и тем больше темной злобы на Пушкина и на судьбу рождалось в душе." Bulgakov, *PSChR*, 1: 119.

35 Bulgakov, *PSChR*, 1: 120–7.

36 Ibid., 1: 163. "Далее: привидение – Иванушка и сцена в больнице." The date, I.VII 1933, is written just a few manuscript pages before this scene, suggesting that it was written sometime in early 1933. Bulgakov, *PSChR*, 1: 154n22.

37 The chapter is part of a notebook that seems to have been written in the second half of 1936 or 1937. Bulgakov, *PSChR*, 1: 363n1.

38 Bulgakov, *PSChR*, 1: 392.

39 Ibid., 1: 430–1.

40 Ibid., 1: 430. "Тебе хорошо!"

41 Ibid., 1: 544–6.

42 Bulgakov, *PSChR*, 2: 189–194.

43 Bulgakov, *PSChR*, 1: 544.

44 Ibid., 1: 546.

45 Ibid., 1: 431. "День разгорался над городом, край неба золотило."

46 Ibid., 1: 456. "На поэта неудержимо наваливался день."

47 The scene tends not to attract scholarly attention. Boris Miagkov explores potential allusions to Pushkin's life and work in the scene. Miagkov, *Bulgakov na patriarshikh*, 186–9. A well-researched guide to *Master and Margarita* also discusses Riukhin's interaction with the Pushkin Monument in entries on Maiakovskii and Pushkin. Lesskis and Atarova, *Putevoditel'*, 269–72, 336, and 352. See also Gasparov, "Iz nabliudenii,"

205–6 and 233–4. Basic commentary can also be found in Belobrovtseva and Kul'ius, *Roman M. Bulgakova*, 254–5.

48 Rereading the scene (end of chapter 6, "Schizophrenia, as Was Said") and having it at hand for reference will help in following the implications of the allusions as laid out in the following "Anatomy of a scene." Quotations are taken from Kolysheva's edition of Bulgakov's manuscripts as cited elsewhere, but any English-language translation of the novel should give you a sense of the scene and its allusions.

49 For the first image (called the *pushka*, "cannon"), all five *riukhi* are arranged to resemble a cannon that players then try to knock apart. "*Pushka*" also happens to be the root of "Pushkin," a joke that has been made many times in relation to the Pushkin Monument. In the contemporary context, consider Tati'iana Tolstaia's play on *pushka*/ Pushkin in *Slynx* (see chapter 5, 187). The word "*pushka*" is also used as a nickname for the larger area around the Pushkin Monument where many young people meet. Stella, "Queer Space, Pride, and Shame in Moscow," 468 and 468n37.

50 The sunrise is also sometimes interpreted as an allusion to Maiakovskii's "Jubilee" (1924), which I treat in more detail below.

51 Bulgakov, *PSChR*, 2: 592.

52 Riukhin's ignorance seems even more ironic when contrasted with Alexander Blok's performance at the 1921 Jubilee. As Sandler writes, "Because Blok died in August of that year, his public appearance was all the more memorable in retrospect, as was his eerie diagnosis of Pushkin as having died not from the bullet fired by d'Anthès but from a lack of air. It soon seemed as if Blok had explained and predicted his own imminent death, enacting a moment of prophecy of the sort Dostoevsky had exemplified." Sandler, *Commemorating Pushkin*, 90.

53 See the discussion of Pushkin's aversion to his image in the Introduction, 37–8.

54 Bulgakov, *PSChR*, 2: 591. "Мысль о том, что худшего несчастия, чем лишение разума, нет на свете? … Но это, так ведь, общая мысль."

55 Bulgakov, *PSChR*, 1: 545. "Мысль ли о том, как ужасно лишиться разума? Да, это …"

56 Pushkin, *PSS*, 1: 307. "Товарищ, верь: взойдет она, / Звезда пленительного счастья, / Россия вспрянет ото сна, / И на обломках самовластья / Напишут наши имена!"

57 Bulgakov, *PSChR*, 1: 545. "А мне не везет, нет мне счастья, не та звезда у меня."

58 Bulgakov, *PSChR*, 2: 193. "Мысль о том, что худшего несчастья, чем лишение разума, нет на свете? Да, да, конечно, и это. Но это, так ведь, общая мысль."

59 Pushkin, *PSS*, 3: 258. "На свете счастья нет, но есть покой и воля."

60 Ibid., 3: 130.

> Брожу ли я вдоль улиц шумных,
> Вхожу ль во многолюдный храм,
> Сижу ль меж юношей безумных,
> Я предаюсь моим мечтам.
>
> Я говорю: промчатся годы,
> И сколько здесь ни видно нас,
> Мы все сойдем под вечны своды –
> И чей-нибудь уж близок час.

61 For a survey of the relationship between *Alexander Pushkin* and the
Riukhin scene, see Omori, "Tvorchestvo M.A. Bulgakova," 73–6.

62 Lesley Milne interprets Bitkov's readings of Pushkin's poetry
ambivalently: "[Bitkov] has the professional attributes of a photographic
memory and total verbal recall. As a consequence, he is a walking
compendium of Pushkin's poetry, which has filled and ennobled his
being; although his prosaic mind cannot understand all of it, he responds
to it always, now with pleasure, now with perplexity." Milne, *Mikhail
Bulgakov*, 212. Given Bulgakov's context, however, it seems unlikely that
he could depict an informer, even one who has read a lot of Pushkin's
verse, as having an ennobled being. Furthermore, Bitkov does not
have a photographic memory – he substitutes "fortune" (*fortuna*) for
"happiness" (*schast'e*) when paraphrasing "'Tis time, my friend, 'tis time."
    Ellendea Proffer also reads Bitkov somewhat sympathetically: "Bitkov
tries to justify his role, but he cannot even convince himself." Proffer,
Bulgakov, 457. She cites Bitkov's description of himself as "subordinate"
(*podnevol'nyi*) and "immersed in pettiness" (*pogruzhennyi v nichtozhestvo*)
as attempts at self-justification, but this reading too ignores the
dissonance between Bitkov's lines and his recitation of "'Tis time, my
friend, 'tis time." Pushkin's poem declares that there is "will" (*vol'ia*) on
this earth, which contrasts with Bitkov's rejection of his will (*podnevol'nyi*,
"subordinate," has the same root as *vol'ia*, "will"). The "distant abode"
that Pushkin longs for is one of "labour" (*trudov*) and "pure pleasures"
(*chistykh neg*), which contrasts with Bitkov's excuse that he has been
absorbed with pettiness, especially when that pettiness refers to following
Pushkin's every move as an informer for the state. Bitkov's relief at a
vacation (*otpusk*) from his role as informant cannot be taken as something
of equal weight with Pushkin's "distant abode."
    Angela Brintlinger also finds in Bitkov a sympathetic figure, citing
his excellent memory and appreciation for Pushkin's poetry, while also

pointing out that some see in him an "ominous figure." Brintlinger, *Writing a Usable Past*, 156. Perhaps the lesson here is that Bitkov is neither sympathetic nor ominous but simply naive, posing a different sort of threat that undermines any hope that he will become a better reader in the future. That naiveté can be understood ambivalently in *Alexander Pushkin*, and points to Bulgakov's later conflation of naive reader and future poet in *Master and Margarita*.

63 Julie Curtis argues that throughout the play Bitkov develops a sensitivity to poetry that coincides with an inner moral development. In her reading of the end of the play, Bitkov is still not fully aware of the wrongs he has committed, but he does at least sense that his role has been disreputable. Despite this glimmer of hope, Curtis concludes that it "would nevertheless be wrong to read any optimism into the play on this account." Curtis, *Bulgakov's Last Decade*, 102–4.

64 Bulgakov, "Aleksandr Pushkin," 228–9. "Как его закопают, ну, тут и мою душу наконец на покаяние. В отпуск. Его в обитель дальнюю, а меня в отпуск. Ах, сколько я стихов переучил, будь они неладны … Да, стихи сочинял … И из-за тех стихов никому покоя, ни ему, ни начальству, ни мне, рабу Божьему, Степану Ильичу … я ведь за ним всюду … но не было фортуны ему … как ни напишет, мимо попал, не туда, не те, не такие …"

65 Replacing *"schast'e"* with *"fortuna"* is a telling distortion of the original, not just a lapse in memory. *"Schast'e"* indicates a feeling or state of full and complete satisfaction (happiness), whereas *"fortuna,"* a latinate cognate, implies a sense of randomness, of fate, as in the sometimes veiled or blinded Roman goddess of fate, Fortuna. Bitkov not only has imperfect recall, he has a poor understanding of the concepts in Pushkin's poetry.

66 For the textual history of *Alexander Pushkin*, see Losev's commentary on the text in Bulgakov, *Aleksandr Pushkin*, 280–7. See also Proffer, *Bulgakov*, 629n14. There is some disagreement in these sources about the dates of various events, although these discrepancies can be explained as typographical errors. Losev dates the completion of the text of the play as 9 September 1939, although every other source gives 9 September 1935 as the date of completion. Bulgakov, *Aleksandr Pushkin*, 230. Proffer writes that Elena Sergeevna signed the contract on 22 June 1940, "since Bulgakov was too ill." This too is an obvious typo since Bulgakov died on 10 March 1940. Proffer also writes that the play was approved in June of 1939, whereas Losev claims the MKhAT committee approved it on 24 October 1939. Brintlinger's analysis of *Alexander Pushkin* is thorough and goes into great detail about Bulgakov's relationship to his co-author, Veresaev, and the role of biographical writing in the aesthetic history of the play. Brintlinger, *Writing a Usable Past*, 140–61.

67 Bulgakov's last work on the scene with Riukhin and the Pushkin Monument probably took place in late November or early December. The Bulgakovs spent a month at Barvikha in late 1939 (18 November to 18 December), during which time they did not have a typewriter. The last version of the scene, typed and inserted into typescript 40, was most likely composed at Barvikha and typed up after their return to Moscow (personal correspondence with Elena Iur'evna Kolysheva on 3 August 2017).

In any event, the last scene was definitely composed after May of 1939. Bulgakov and E.S. worked on revising typescript 10.2 starting on 19 September 1938 and continued to redact this typed version of the novel until 14 May 1939 (Bulgakov, *PSChR*, 2: 7). Kolysheva also cites S.A. Ermolinskii, who notes that the line "Он не заслужил света, он заслужил покой" appeared during this time (Bulgakov, *PSChR*, 2: 7). Interpreting this line as a reworking of the fifth line of "'Tis time, my friend, 'tis time" ("На свете счастья нет, но есть покой и воля") supports the idea that Bulgakov was particularly interested in that poem in 1939 and 1940, since it plays such a prominent role in the ending of *Master and Margarita* as well as in the characterizations of Riukhin and Bitkov.

A new typescript appeared in 1939–40 based on edits made to typescript 10.2 between September 1938 and May 1939. Kolysheva provides parallel readings of these typescripts in the foreword, which notes that the new Riukhin scene appeared in the 1940 typescript but not the 1938 typescript, suggesting that it had to be inserted sometime after May 1939 (Bulgakov, *PSChR*, 2: 45). This corresponds exactly to the time when discussions about staging *Alexander Pushkin* were renewed (spring 1939) and the contract was signed (22 January 1940, about three weeks before Bulgakov's last verifiable day of work on the novel, 13 February 1940).

As this history suggests, when, exactly, Bulgakov last conceptualized the Riukhin scene is hard to pinpoint, but the fact that Bulgakov was working on it after May 1939 is indicated by the complex insertions and new moments added to the typescript between May of 1939 and February of 1940. For Kolysheva's commentary on these revisions in the typescript itself, see Bulgakov, *PSChR*, 2: 189n569, 189n578, 192n584.

68 Lesskis and Atarova, *Putevoditel'*, 352.

69 Ibid., 270.

70 Ibid., 271.

71 Sandler, *Commemorating Pushkin*, 102.

72 As cited in Lesskis and Atarova, *Putevoditel'*, 271. "я уже перестал быть поэтом. Теперь я … чиновник …"

73 Gasparov, "Iz nabliudenii," 233.

74 Lesskis and Atarova, *Putevoditel'*, 273. "Почему твоя лодка брошена раньше времени на причал?"

75 Chudakova, *Zhizneopisanie*, 479. "Маяковского прочесть как следует."

76 Riukhin's emphasis on mass reception as opposed to aesthetic reception, rumour ("*slukh*," sometimes translated as "fame") as opposed to metamorphosis, evokes an interpretation of the poem that resulted in the nineteenth-century literalization and visualization of the monument metaphor. Riukhin is unable to bring Pushkin to life, in part because he is ignorant of the possibility or lacks the motivation. Bulgakov briefly considered making the monument come to life in the sixth redaction. In this version, the monument seems to smile: "The bronze face – as it seemed to Riukhin – smiled at him with something like sympathy, or maybe curiosity." "Медное лицо – как показалось Рюхину – улыбнулось ему не то с сожалением, не то с любопытством." Bulgakov, *PSChR*, 2: 192. By deleting the lifelike response of the monument in the final redaction, Bulgakov renders Riukhin incapable of provoking a reaction. In other words, Riukhin is *unlike* Maiakovskii; he is unable to bring Pushkin to life.

77 James Rann interprets Maiakovskii's "Jubilee" as a reversal of Pushkin's demonic, mobile statue: "The statue's freedom of movement symbolizes the flexible literary inheritance that Maiakovskii thinks should constitute Pushkin's contribution to culture. This self-reflexive mobilization of Pushkin is not only an emblem of the greater flexibility Maiakovskii proposes for the reception of Pushkin but an example of it, because, rather than reiterating his mythology Maiakovskii reverses the polarity of Pushkin's binary; as Jakobson observed, 'the motif of the forced, imprisoning immobility of the statue, polemically opposed to Pushkin's myth of its sovereign rest, acquires particular vigor in Maiakovskii.' While Pushkin considers the mobile statue demonic, Maiakovskii sees immobility as unnatural." Rann, "Maiakovskii and the Mobile Monument," 776. Rann's interpretation works well within Jakobson's binary model, but it also fits with the interpretation of Pushkin's monument metaphor not as a binary but as a progression of transformation and refinement. Maiakovskii is teaching Pushkin, transforming him, performing the role of the future poet, not that of a worshipful reader.

78 "Up there in the sky / the moon / is so young that / letting her out without a chaperone / is risky." "В небе вон / луна / такая молодая, что ее / без спутников / и выпускать рискованно."

79 Sandler, *Commemorating Pushkin*, 107–8.

80 Pushkin, *PSS*, 2: 240. "Да здравствует солнце, да скроется тьма!"

81 Sandler, *Commemorating Pushkin*, 108.

82 One can track the editing of Ponyrev to Riukhin in Bulgakov, *PSChR*, 2: 182–94.

83 See 123–4 for an explanation of Riukhin's name. Its folk connotations ironically evoke the village imagery of poets like Pribludnyi and Esenin. Gasparov also provides interesting parallels between Dem'ian Bednyi and Bezymenskii that suggest Ivan's connection to a generalized image of poets of the 1920s and some of their criticisms of Bulgakov's *Days of the Turbins*. Gasparov, "Iz nabliudenii," 202–6.

84 Bulgakov, *PSChR*, 2: 547. "Трудно сказать, что именно подвело Ивана Николаевича – изобразительная ли сила его таланта или полное незнакомство с вопросом, по которому он писал."

85 Ibid., 2: 634. "Да кто же он, наконец, такой?"

86 Lovell's study of the reception history of *Master and Margarita* reveals that these gaps in Ivan's cultural literacy are replicated in the audience that first read *Master and Margarita*. Lovell, "Bulgakov as Soviet Culture," 31, 40, 46.

87 To explore in detail conflicting arguments about Ivan as a potential artist and a naive reader, see Avins, "Reaching a Reader"; Weeks, "In Defense of the Homeless"; and Kisel, "Feuilletons Don't Burn."

88 Kisel, "Feuilletons Don't Burn," 599.

89 While Bulgakov conceptualizes the problem of the newly literate mass reader through the subtext of the Pushkin Monument, Bulgakov's contemporaries were also concerned with the problem. For analyses of how Olesha, Platonov, and Zoshchenko dealt with the issue, see Kisel, "Mass Culture to Master."

4 Toporov's Petersburg Text: Rejecting the Statue (1937–2003)

1 See an explanation of this in chapter 2, 87–8.

2 Consider Bethea's argument about monumentalism and Pushkin's interest in Peter and Petersburg in *The Bronze Horseman*. Bethea, "'Mednyi vsadnik,'" 170–92.

3 Crone and Day, *My Petersburg/Myself*, 4–10.

4 Buckler, *Mapping St Petersburg*, 21–4.

5 Jakobson, "The Statue in Pushkin's Poetic Mythology," 3.

6 Ibid., 41–2.

7 This seems to be true on a personal as well as a collective level. Jonathan Brooks Platt's discussion of Iskander's "Chik and Pushkin" and Trifonov's *Disappearance* exemplifies the same phenomenon. In the early 1970s, both authors wrote stories reflecting their personal experiences of the Jubilee as children. The thirty-year retrospective on the event is a major factor in overcoming the naiveté of works produced in 1937. Platt, *Greetings, Pushkin!*, 278–87.

8 Burbank, "Editor's Note," v.

9 Alekseev, *Stikhotvorenie*, 5.

10 Sandler, *Commemorating Pushkin*, 116.

11 Brintlinger, *Writing a Usable Past*, 183.

12 This is not to say that, generally speaking, cliché itself could not be put to creative use as a device. Cliché became a tool in the hands of creative writers navigating a treacherous political environment. Carol Any makes a compelling case that cliché could be put to creative use. "Speaking in cliché became a kind of special language which people cultivated and manipulated for various purposes. Different constituencies used cliché to differing ends, but the centrality of cliché remained even when, in private conversation, it took on a shadow life and became a defamiliarization of itself." Any, "Cliché as Device."

13 Also writing about the 1937 Jubilee, Jonathan Brooks Platt takes issue with Sandler's characterization of the trauma surrounding the Jubilee. He writes, "I do not parse the diverse record of the 1937 Jubilee according to a 'surface' of totalitarian conformity and a 'depth' of traumatic truth." Platt, *Greetings, Pushkin!*, 281 and 334n4. Platt argues that the "chronotopic hybridity" he documents in various forms of cultural expression in 1937 is a unique form of innovation in and of itself, a cultural phenomenon that exists alongside, even in spite of, the terror of the Stalinist purges. Both Sandler and Platt, however, recognize the fervour of 1937 as a watershed moment in the meanings and uses of Pushkin in Soviet Russia. Sandler discusses how 1937 overshadowed subsequent anniversaries. Sandler, *Commemorating Pushkin*, 116–19. Platt remarks that the "original fervor of the Jubilee became harder and harder to recreate" and shows how, while the impulse to "chronotopic hybridity" that pervaded the 1937 Jubilee has been lost, "remnants of the Stalinist Pushkin still survive in Putin's Russia." Platt, *Greetings, Pushkin!*, 287 and 294. The 1937 Jubilee, however, also has a legacy in the story of allusion. Platt provides a compelling reading of Trifonov's *Disappearance*, in which the child Gorik becomes absorbed in a personal project for the Jubilee – the creation of a notebook that among many other things contained Pushkin's "Monument," hand-copied next to a photograph of the Pushkin Monument on Tverskoi Boulevard. Platt, *Greetings, Pushkin!*, 282–3 and 287. Gorik is ultimately humiliated. Platt focuses on Gorik's humiliation, but his discussion also highlights the role cliché played in the process. Gorik is the ideal naive reader who must come to grips with the fact that the Jubilee pushed him to perpetuate clichés and then at the same time made him feel unoriginal for doing so.

14 Nepomnyashchy, *Abram Tertz*, 22–39.

15 Tertz, *Strolls with Pushkin*, 54. "Он не играл, а жил, шутя и играя, и когда умер, заигравшись чересчур далеко, Баратынский, говорят, вместе с другими комиссарами разбиравший бумаги покойного, среди которых, например, затесался 'Медный Всадник,' восклицал: 'Можешь ты себе представить, что меня больше всего изумляет во всех этих поэмах? Обилие мыслей! Пушкин – мыслитель! Можно ли было это ожидать?' (цитирую по речи И.С. Тургенева на открытии памятника Пушкину в Москве)." Tertz, *Progulki s Pushkinym*, 15.

16 "по совести говоря, какой же он мыслитель!" Tertz, *Progulki s Pushkinym*, 16.

17 Sandler, *Commemorating Pushkin*, 301.

18 Proskurin, "Predshestvenniki Pushkina."

19 Ibid., 477.

20 Ibid.

21 Ibid., 478. "If in the work of major scholars ideological pressure interfered with an objective understanding of the material, then in 'mass' Soviet literary studies it led to evident deformations of the historical literary perspective: it forced interpreters 'not to notice' rather obvious facts or to give them an inadequate explanation." "Если в работах больших ученых идеологический прессинг мешал объективному осмыслению материала, то в 'массовом' советском литературоведении это приводило к явным деформациям историко-литературной перспективы, заставляло 'не замечать' довольно очевидных фактов или давать им неадекватное объяснение."

22 Consider Vladislav Zubok's suggestion that Lotman's school of semiotics in Tartu was an "oasis" for "Zhivago's children," the intelligentsia of the 1960s who had overcome the cultural gap between the pre-revolutionary milieu that Pasternak grew up in and the one they had grown up in during the 1930s, 1940s, and 1950s. Zubok, *Zhivago's Children*, 20, 322–3, and 431n81. Also consider Emily Johnson's discussion of how their Soviet experience conditioned Tartu semioticians' reception of Nikolai Antsiferov's *The Soul of Petersburg*. Johnson, *How St Petersburg Learned to Study Itself*, 210–13.

23 Mints, Bezrodnyi, and Danilevskii, "'Peterburgskii tekst' i russkii simvolizm," 84.

24 Kalinin, "Peterburgskii tekst," 34. See also a recent and slightly modified version of this essay: "'Peterburgskii tekst' moskovskoi filologii," *Neprikosnovennyi zapas* 2, no. 70 (http://magazines.russ .ru/nz/2010/2/ka27.html, accessed 30 August 2017). "В заключение необходимо попытаться историзировать само возникновение понятия Петербургский текст … Петербургский текст Топорова далеко выходит за рамки интерпретации петербургского периода российской истории и имеет непосредственное отношение к историческому контексту середины

1960 – начало 1970-х годов (первый вариант работы был написан в 1971 г.), связанному скорее с новым 'московским периодом.' В этом смысле Петербургский текст, но уже не как совокупность отдельных текстов, а как целостный символический конструкт, действительно призывал к 'духовному возрождению в условиях, когда ложь и зло торжествуют над истиной и добром.'"

25 While these two bibliographic notecards are undated, Toporov's interest in the Kazan Cathedral, Bronze Horseman, and "Alexandrian Pillar" reflect themes he considered in other notes and articles of this period. Furthermore, Tsiv'ian makes a convincing argument that they are connected to another occupation of Toporov in the 1990s and early 2000s: a catalogue of photographs and descriptions of the minor rivers in Petersburg and the vegetative growth in Petersburg courtyards. Tsiv'ian, "Gorod & Chelovek & Priroda," 365.

26 See the Appendix, 204–5, for the complete quotation in the original and my translation. As cited in Tsiv'ian, "Gorod & Chelovek & Priroda," 364.

27 To get a sense of how the visual structure of these theses also approximates the odic structure of "Monument," see the original and my translation of it in the Appendix, 204–5.

28 Toporov, *Peterburgskii tekst*, 662.

29 Ibid., 815.

30 Ibid.

31 The 2009 edition of Petersburg Text is part of a series entitled *Monuments of National Scholarship* (*Pamiatniki otechestvennoi nauki*).

32 Toporov, *Peterburgskii tekst*, 662.

33 See the Appendix, 205–6, for the full note. As cited in Tsiv'ian, "Gorod & Chelovek & Priroda," 365.

34 "Есть еще один карандашный набросок о том, как петербургский текст становится самодовлеющим и в каком-то смысле диктующим городу его будущее." Tsiv'ian, "Gorod & Chelovek & Priroda," 365.

35 Consider Rosenshield's concept of "backward influence" and Pelicer's idea that an allusion is most satisfactorily realized when it sheds light on the alluding text as well as the text alluded to (Introduction, 25).

36 See the Appendix, 206–7, for the full note. As published in Tsiv'ian, "Dialog vzgliadov."

37 See the Appendix, 207–8, for Dviniatina's full description of the exhibit. As published in Tsiv'ian, "Dialog vzgliadov."

38 Toporov, "O dinamicheskom kontekste."

39 Ibid., 790.

40 Jonathan Brooks Platt also engages with this interpretive strategy by employing concepts of both "horizon" and "encirclement" in his interpretations of monuments in the 1937 Jubilee. For example, see his

interpretation of images of Pushkin as a living statue. Platt, *Greetings, Pushkin!*, 75–6.

41 "Евгений, сидя на одном из 'львов сторожевых' перед домом Лобанова-Ростовского, в удалении от памятника, однако, вполне ему видимого, мог быть относительно спокоен за себя: его волновала судьба Параши, но когда он приблизился к памятнику непосредственно, его объял страх уже за себя самого, и смятенный ум его не выдержал этого испытания)." Toporov, "O dinamecheskom kontekste," 793–4.

42 "то же произошло и с пушкинским Евгением – Кругом подножия кумира/ Безумец бедный обошел." Toporov, "O dinamicheskom kontekste," 796.

43 Jakobson, "The Statue in Puškin's Poetic Mythology," in his *Puškin and His Sculptural Myth*, 1–44.

44 See the Appendix, 208–10, for the full quotation in which Toporov defines his view of the lifelike statue and the unique roles played by a naive viewer and a co-creator. Toporov, "O dinamicheskom kontekste," 790.

45 Toporov, "O dinamicheskom kontekste," 790.

46 Ibid., 778.

47 Schenker, *The Bronze Horseman*, 266.

48 Toporov's last efforts in Petersburg included the documentation of its "river text" (*rechnoi tekst*) and vegetation. In looking for the geographical roots of Petersburg in vegetation and the network of rivers and their oral histories, Toporov was exploring the material roots of the metamorphosis myth. He looked to the sky as the screen onto which monuments were projected, but at the same time he was looking for that material origin out of which (or over which) the city was formed and how that humble origin (to which it must return in the apocalyptic motifs of the Petersburg Text) would give rise to the Petersburg Text, which transcends the physical city itself. Like the statue motif in Ovid's *Metamorphoses* (see chapter 1, 47–9), Petersburg is a place that began in rough materials and rose through various stages to assume a different nature entirely: Finnish swamp > wooden city > stone city > monumental city > verbal construct (Petersburg Text). In my analysis, this was a very Pushkinian vision of metamorphosis. It should also be said that Toporov's vision did not include the opposition of nature to culture or the overcoming of nature and culture, but rather their cooperation. As Tsiv'ian writes, "The analysis of the dynamic context of monuments offered by V.N. and based on the change in perspective, that is, the situation of the viewer of the object, is also determined by *the city: the motion of the person*, against the background of *nature*, in cooperation with it, with that *nature*, which cannot be overcome by the civilizing efforts of *a person* and which will remain *to shine in eternal beauty*." "Анализ динамического контекста памятников, предложенный В.Н. и основанный на перемене точки зрения,

т. е. положения смотрящего на объект, также обусловлен *городом*: *движение человека*, происходящее на фоне *природы*, во взаимодействии с ней, с той *природой*, которую не могут преодолеть цивилизационные усилия *человека* и которая остается *сиять вечною красой*." Tsiv'ian, "Gorod & Chelovek & Priroda," 391.

49　"Со стороны Сената (на уровне земли) также нельзя найти точки, с которой статуя виделась бы целиком на фоне 'адмиральтейской' кулисы, но зато отсюда хорошо видна динамика вырастания фигуры конного всадника, как бы преодолевающей то 'материально-плотное,' что до сих пор, хотя бы частично, удерживало ее в связи с землей и творениями рук человеческих." Toporov, "O dinamicheskom kontekste," 794.

50　Toporov envisioned a similar sort of analysis for the Alexander Column. See Tsiv'ian, "Gorod & Chelovek & Priroda," 388–91.

51　Toporov, *Peterburgskii tekst*, 794.

52　Ibid., 809–10n27.

53　Toporov, "O dinamicheskom kontekste," 786.

54　My conclusions are not meant to explain Toporov's intentions. Rather, I hope to follow the example of Tat'iana Vladimirovna Tsiv'ian, who writes, "The work was cut off, the answer to these questions cannot be obtained, and the only possibility is to piece together one's own conclusions, which in no way assume to discover Toporov's intentions." "Работа оборвалась, ответа на вопросы уже не получить, и единственная возможность – надстраивать собственные умозаключения, никак не претендующие на раскрытия замысла автора." Tsiv'ian, "Gorod & Chelovek & Priroda," 376. As an author, I do not make any claims about Toporov's intentions or motivations in ending his Petersburg Text with analyses of these monuments. I point out parallels that, if they work, reveal a productive relationship between the cultural history of the Pushkin Monument and Toporov's last work on the Petersburg Text, whether or not Toporov intended it.

55　Here Bocharov plays on both meanings of the Russian word "*roman*": it can mean "novel," as well as "love affair." As cited in Tsiv'ian, "Gorod & Chelovek & Priroda," 362. "Владимир Николаевич открыл в нашей культуре такое сверхъявление, как ее *петербургский текст*. Но можно с уверенностью сказать, что он *создал* для нас его, эту мысленную реальность, что он сотворил и выстроил собственный петербургский текст в большом цикле работ, запечатлевших то, что он сам назвал в одной из этих работ своим полувековым петербургским 'романом' – и исследовательским, и душевным."

56　Tsiv'ian, "Gorod & Chelovek & Priroda," 380. See also her footnote, which describes the only instance in which Toporov allowed himself to refer to a "Moscow Text." Tsiv'ian, "Gorod & Chelovek & Priroda," 393n17.

57 Toporov, *Peterburgskii tekst*, 25–32.

58 Tsiv'ian, "Gorod & Chelovek & Priroda," 363. As Tsiv'ian writes, "как В.Н. Топоров о т к р ы л тему *петербургского текста*, так он ее и з а к р ы л … Можно предположить, что проблема будущего в связи с *петербургским текстом* возникала и перед автором концепта …"

59 Toporov, *Peterburgskii tekst*, 25. "Петербург познавал самого себя не столько из описания реалий жизни, быта, своей все более и более углубляющейся истории, сколько из русской художественной литературы."

60 In his article on Petersburg Text, David Bethea returns to Toporov's insistence that *The Bronze Horseman* is the "source" (*istok*) of Petersburg Text and seeks to identify the "heart of the *verbal*, if not the historical beginning" of the Petersburg Text. What interests Bethea here is not so much how later authors such as Gogol and Dostoevskii transformed Pushkin's work but rather analysis of a historical moment when it [*The Bronze Horseman*] "was burdened with only that measure of foresight, which Pushkin himself sanctioned." "Моя задача не в том, чтобы взглянуть на него глазами Гоголя, Достоевского или Блока; я хочу попытаться увидеть отправную точку (сердцевину *вербального*, если не исторического начала) Петербургского текста, когда она была отягчена лишь той мерой предвидения, которую санкционировал сам Пушкин." Bethea, "'Mednyi vsadnik,'" 173. Bethea too sees disagreements about where to punctuate the Petersburg Text (Vaginov? Bitov?) as one of the underlying problems of Toporov's approach. See an earlier version of this article in English and without the commentary on Toporov's Petersburg Text: Bethea, "Stabat Pater."

61 Consider also Tsiv'ian's point as cited above, that the Petersburg Text is a restricted notion: "По замыслу ее создателя, *петербургский текст* определен достаточно жестким сюжетом (жизнь, преодолевающая смерть через катартическое испытание), и термин-концепт не может быть приложен ни к какому другому городу (если только не к двойнику Петербурга)." Tsiv'ian, "Gorod & Chelovek & Priroda," 362. See also Mints, Bezrodnyi, and Danilevskii, "Peterburg skii tekst' i russkii simvolizm," 81.

62 Reynolds, "Returning the Ticket."

63 Ibid., 309.

64 Ibid., 328.

65 Bethea, *The Shape of Apocalypse*, 270.

66 Mark Griffiths shows how the elements Bethea describes in modern Russian fiction are transformed after 1991. Griffiths, "Moscow after the Apocalypse," 483.

67 Bethea, *The Shape of Apocalypse*, 270.

5 Tolstaia's *Slynx*: Disfiguring the Monument (1986–2000)

1 If, in fact, *Slynx* is to be Tolstaia's last published fiction, the novel's extensive engagement with the Pushkin Monument may be a critical factor in determining its place in her oeuvre.

2 For an engaging interpretation of aspects of apocalypse in *Slynx* that are unique to the mythic elements of Moscow and, in particular, the way that end was reimagined in post-Soviet fiction, see Griffiths, "Moscow after the Apocalypse," 483.

3 Ute Shol'ts points out that Tolstaia's *Slynx* maps elements typically associated with Petersburg onto a post-apocalpytic Moscow. Shol'ts, "Mezhdu konstruktsiei i dekonstruktsiei," 78.

4 Sandler, *Commemorating Pushkin*, 10 and 304.

5 Gillespie, "Introduction," 8.

6 Ibid., 10.

7 Ibid., 8.

8 For more on allusions to Pushkin in Tolstaia's works, see Goscilo, *TNT*, and Karen R. Smith, "Recollecting Wondrous Moments."

9 Tolstaia, "Noch'," 110. Tolstaya, "Night," 72–3.

10 Boym, "Inscriptions on the Poet's Monument," 69.

11 Ibid., 78.

12 This is difficult to translate; Alexei Petrovich's rendition of the first line of the poem comes out something like this: "To the storms, nonsensical syllables, nonsensical syllables, rummages." Tolstaia, "Noch'," 108. Jamey Gambrell's translation does the original justice: "'Apall thus tormcas tson thus ky.'" Tolstaya, "Night," 73.

13 Goscilo, *TNT*, 41.

14 Thanks to Nina Wieda for pointing this out to me.

15 Consider the theme of Pushkin's African heritage and the Pushkin Monument in Tsvetaeva's "My Pushkin." "In every black person I love Pushkin and I recognize Pushkin." "В каждом негре я люблю Пушкина и узнаю Пушкина." Tsvetaeva, "Moi Pushkin," 504.

16 Tolstaia, "Limpopo," 328, and Tolstaya, "Limpopo," 192.

17 Tolstaya, "Limpopo," 181, and Tolstaia, "Limpopo," 317–18.

18 In "Limpopo," as in "Night," Tolstaia connects Pushkin's "Winter Evening" with "Monument." Lyonechka conflates both into a series of sentences in the paragraph of his poem. "Pushkin's grave is grown over with thick goosefoot ... O'er summer's thickened goosefoot dragon-geese go flocking by. Like beasts at first they'll howl, or stamp their feathery feet and cry." "могила Пушкина заросла густой лебедою! ... Над густою лебедою гуси-лебеди летят! То как зверь они завоют, то ногами застучат!" Tolstaya, "Limpopo," 156. Tolstaia, "Limpopo," 292. Tolstaia seems to

be quoting M.A. Bulgakov's *Master and Margarita*. Sasha Riukhin also conflates the language of the Pushkin Monument and "Winter Evening" on his way back to Griboedov House from Stravinsky's clinic. Also, Karen R. Smith ("Recollecting Wondrous Moments," 504) and Goscilo (*TNT*, 184) attribute the connection between these poems in Tolstaia to their connection in Bulgakov. The visual, verbal, and performative dimensions of the Pushkin Monument facilitate Tolstaia's metapoetics of allusion and show her to be in dialogue not only with iconoclasts like Maiakovskii, Tsvetaeva, Tertz, and Toporov, but also Bulgakov.

19 Tolstaya, "Limpopo," 192. Tolstaia, "Limpopo," 329. "И гордый внук славян и ныне дикий …"

20 Pushkin, *PSS*, 3: 340. "И гордый внук славян и Финн и ныне дикий Тунгус …"

21 Tolstaya, "Limpopo," 192. Tolstaia, "Limpopo," 329. "И правда, дальше я уже ни слова не помню."

22 As cited in Tolstaia, "Siuzhet," 258. "Вот зачем, в часы заката / Уходя в ночную тьму, / С белой площади Сената / Тихо кланяюсь ему."

23 For more on Tsvetaeva's essay, see Knapp, "Tsvetaeva's 'Blackest of Black' (*Naicherneishii*) Pushkin."

24 For some examples of such appraisals, see Ute Shol'ts's summary of them in"Mezhdu konstruktsiei i dekonstruktsiei," 77–8. See also Griffiths, "Moscow after the Apocalypse," 492–3.

25 Benevolenskaia, "«*Kys'*» T. Tolstoi kak ideologicheskii roman," 135–6.

26 Ibid., 136.

27 Ute Shol'ts addresses this issue and proposes "metautopia" as a more fitting genre. Shol'ts, "Mezhdu konstruktsiei i dekonstruktsiei," 78. It is also helpful to put Shol'ts's argument in the perspective of Anindita Banerjee's idea of "heterochronotope" as answer to "the urgent need for a new descriptive term for Russian science fiction beyond the dominant binary model of utopias and dystopias." Banerjee, *We Modern People*, 160.

28 Clowes, *Imagined Geographies*, 36–7.

29 Banerjee, *We Modern People*, 2.

30 Gambrell's translation of *Kys'* as *Slynx* relays a sense of what is going on in the novel. "Slynx" combines the idea of a ferocious cat, the lynx, with the idea of a frightening mythological being that "slinks" up on you at night and tears out your spine.

31 Howell, *Apocalyptic Realism*, 3.

32 See also Dalton-Brown, "Signposting the Way to the City of Night." Dalton-Brown argues that dystopia is a reaction to utopia, which works in the context of disillusionment with the Soviet vision of a utopian future. Tolstaia's *Slynx* reacts to the nineteenth-century utopian vision of a future mass reader that can really engage with Pushkin's art and with

the myth of the Soviet reader for whom Pushkin, in Boym's formulation, is "half memorized, half unknown." Boym, "Inscriptions on the Poet's Monument," 78.

33 Howell, *Apocalyptic Realism*, 3.

34 Khagi, "One Billion Years after the End of the World," 268.

35 Ibid., 269.

36 Ibid., 268.

37 Ibid., 284.

38 Consider the publication dates for the works that address dissatisfaction with both "influence" and "intertextuality" discussed in the Introduction, 32–3.

39 Brintlinger, "The Hero in the Madhouse," 50.

40 Brintlinger suggests that Pelevin links the temporal disjunctures of 1919 and the 1990s "with a profound sense of emptiness." Brintlinger, "The Hero in the Madhouse," 53.

41 Pelevin's use of the Pushkin Monument in *Chapaev and the Void* can be read in many ways in addition to its metapoetics of allusion. Clowes effectively reads the pairing of monument and monastery as "signals of educated Russian national identity (great literary art and Orthodox Christianity)." Clowes, *Imagined Geographies*, 73. When they disappear in Moscow at the end of the novel, Clowes asserts that "Contemporary Moscow lacks the order of a productive, meaningful vision. It has lost not just the two national symbols that Petr highlights (the Pushkin Statue and Strastnoi Monastery), but layers of imperial symbols." Clowes, *Imagined Geographies*, 89. When read in this way, the Pushkin Monument metonymically stands in for Russian identity and empire, a spatial representation of the link between identity and its spatial-geographical expressions. Brintlinger reads it as a "metaphor of postrevolutionary and post-Soviet Russia … Pelevin's hero [Pustota] encapsulates the fate of the individual under the Soviets: in postrevolutionary Russia, the hero was forced into the collective, but in the postmodern world, without any meaningful collective, the hero is absent, an emptiness in and of himself." Brintlinger, "The Hero in the Madhouse," 56.

42 Pelevin, *Buddha's Little Finger*, 324.

43 Tolstaya, *The Slynx*, 29.

44 Ibid., 120. The allusion becomes one of Benedikt's favoured clichés. In one passage he relates his feeling of superiority to the serf he rents by relating that he hired the serf in order to show off – to show everyone that he was "a head above this humble servant, higher than the Alexander column, I won't dirty my hands carrying baskets." Tolstaya, *Slynx*, 78.

45 Gillespie, "Introduction," 12.

46 Tolstaya, *Slynx*, 151.

47 Ibid., 244.

48 Ibid., 245.

49 Ibid., 157–9.

50 Pushkin, *PSS*, 2: 238. "K***." Pushkin, *PSS*, 2: 239. "Если жизнь тебя обманет."

51 Tolstaya, *Slynx*, 161. Another layer of Nikita Ivanych's problematic memory is that he attributes the dedication of "Если жизнь тебя обманет" to Anna Petrovna Kern, when Pushkin actually dedicated it to Evpraksiia Nikolaevna Vul'f.

52 Chubukov provides the details of the legend as well as the historical details of Kern's death and response to the Pushkin Monument, including the passage from Modzalevskii that provides documentation for her response. Chubukov, *Vsenarodnyi pamiatnik Pushkinu*, 57–9.

53 Dostoevsky, *Notes from the Underground*, 86.

54 Tolstaya, *Slynx*, 151.

55 Tolstaia's original Russian here is "*daun*," a slang borrowing from the English "down." The word has the general connotations of "idiot" or "depressive" based on its English meaning as an adjective, but, based on its use as the last name of the English doctor who first described "*Sindrom Dauna*" or Down syndrome, it can also be interpreted as a pejorative term for a person who has Down syndrome.

56 For more on the tradition of protesting at the Pushkin Monument see Nepomnyashchy, *Abram Tertz*, 5. See also an article dedicated to the tradition on Memorial's website, *Topografiia terrora*: "Demonstratsii na Pushkinskoi ploshchadi," accessed 15 September 2017, http://topos .memo.ru/demonstracii-na-pushkinskoy-ploshchadi.

57 Tolstaya, *Slynx*, 275.

58 Griffiths, "Moscow after the Apocalypse," 491.

59 "али я тебя не холю, али ешь овса не вволю."

60 "Конь бежит, земля дрожит."

61 "Жизни мышья беготня, что тревожишь ты меня?"

62 "Свирель запела на мосту, и яблони в цвету. И ангел поднял в высоту звезду зеленую одну. И стало дивно на мосту смотреть в такую глубину, в такую высоту …"

63 Mints, Bezrodnyi, and Danilevskii, "'Peterburgskii tekst' i russkii simvolizm," 78–92.

64 Ibid., 85.

65 Ibid., 86n24. "Эти же сведения исследователь приводит и в комментарии к самому авторитетному на сегодняшний день изданию пьес Блока (см.:

Блок А. Театр. Л., 1981, с. 486), в обоих случаях ссылаясь на мемуары Бекетовой, которая, однако, ни слова не пишет о месте действия 2-го акта."

66 Mints, Bezrodnyi, and Danilevskii, "Peterburgskii tekst i russkii simvolizm," 86. "поэтому пейзаж, открывающий 2-й акт и, действительно, исполненный петербургских реалий, воспринимается именно как петербургский, но не конкретный, 'этот,' а как некий обобщенный 'образ' петербургского пейзажа."

67 Pasternak's lines comment on the lines from Blok's poem. The stanza of "The Storm" ("Metel'") that precedes the one quoted by Varvara Lukinishna posits a connection between Moscow and the "neighborhood" of the poem – it is in Moscow, beyond a "bridge": "Ни зги не видать, а ведь этот посад / Может быть в городе, в Замоскваречьи, / В Замостьи, и прочая (в полночь забредший / Гость от меня отшатнулся назад)." Immediately following the stanza quoted by Varvara Lukinishna, lines indicate a confusion of urban landscapes: "Не тот это город, и полночь не та, / И ты заблудился, ее вестовой!" In this way, the lines from this poem that are not quoted, like the lines from "Monument" that are not quoted, speak to Benedikt's mistake: "this is the wrong city" certainly applies to the relationship between Benedikt's post-Blast Moscow and the settings of Blok's and Pasternak's poetry. See Oleg Lekmanov's treatment of Pasternak's lines in his brief response to N.A. Bogomolov's 2004 monograph on Russian poetry. Lekmanov, "Mesto vstrechi izmenit' nel'zia?" Lekmanov makes a convincing argument that the line "this is the wrong city, and the midnight is wrong too" plays a crucial role both in recognizing the Moscow context of the intertextual connection between Mandel'shtam's use of the word *"zamost'ie"* and Pasternak's use of it in "The Storm," and in the initial reception of the poem among Petersburg poets such as Osip Mandel'shtam and Lev Gumilev. Both Bogomolov's monograph and Lekmanov's response to it (2004) post-date the publication of *Slynx* (2000), but their debate about the implications of both Petersburg and Moscow for Pasternak's poem illustrates the brilliance of Tolstaia's juxtaposition of these two poems in the response of a reader who seeks to find objective, one-to-one correspondences between urban realia and words like "bridge" and "neighborhood."

68 Tolstaia, "Chuzhie sny," 8. "Я не хочу простой человеческой жизни. Я хочу сложных снов …"

Conclusion: Allusion and the Naive Reader

1 Dobrenko covers in detail the developments among newly literate readers in the 1920s and scholarly attempts to study and accommodate their

experiences of reading. Particularly telling in this regard are 1) transcripts from peasant reactions to reading Pushkin and 2) the list of expectations that Dobrenko distils from comments made by mass readers in the 1920s and 1930s about what constitutes good literature. Dobrenko, *The Making of the State Reader*, 102–5 and 126–39.

2 See Toporov's note as translated in the Appendix, 208–10.

3 Ibid.

4 On this note, consider Feduta's introduction to his study of the reader in Pushkin's epoch. Feduta follows Alexander Ivanovich Beletskii's work on the theory of reading to assert that Pushkin did not need a generalized image of a reader, but rather "Bulgarin, Senkovskii, Marlinskii." Feduta, *"Kto b ni byl ty, o moi chitatel' …,"* 7.

5 In his study of print culture in the Soviet and post-Soviet eras, Stephen Lovell points simultaneously to intelligentsia hopes during glasnost that the naive reader would turn into a good one, as well as the disappointment of those hopes. He writes that, "Perestroika in the cultural sphere was, in fact, nothing less than the attempted 'massovization' of the Soviet intelligentsia. The early stages of glasnost were outstandingly successful in this respect: an enthralling public debate began on most aspects of Soviet history and society; the circulations of the major journals shot up from hundreds of thousands to millions; Soviet society did indeed seem on its way to becoming 'civilized' and 'intellectualized.' By the early 1990s, however, this cultural 'progress' had proved to be illusory." Later in his argument he drives this point home: "The Russian reader of the mid-1990s was still in a sense a cultural neophyte." Lovell, *The Russian Reading Revolution*, 72 and 155.

6 Reynolds, "Returning the Ticket," 328.

7 Stephen Blackwell's study of Nabokov's *The Gift* reveals a similar role for Zina as a good reader. Blackwell writes that, "Recognizing Zina as not merely lover or heroine but as a shaping artistic force compels us to reconsider the novel, with a sense of the ethical value of artistic reception moved to the forefront of its concerns." Blackwell, *Zina's Paradox*, 3.

8 Higgins, "Aleksei Navalny, Top Putin Critic, Arrested."

9 See Toporov's note as translated in the Appendix, 204–5.

Appendix

1 See Pushkin, "Monument," *PSS*, vol. 3, 340.

2 As cited in Tsiv'ian, "Gorod & Chelovek & Priroda," 363–5.

3 A Proto-Slavic verb, the etymological root of Russian *chuiat'*, in its meaning "to sense or to feel, to anticipate." Toporov seems to be

suggesting a connection here between the idea of the miraculous and the idea of sensitivity or sensation by positing a common Proto-Slavic root for both words.

4 As cited in Tsiv'ian, "Gorod & Chelovek & Priroda," 365.
5 As published in Tsiv'ian, "Dialog vzgliadov," 134–9.
6 As cited in Tsiv'ian, "Dialog vzgliadov," 135.
7 Toporov, "O dinamicheskom kontekste," 790.

Bibliography

Alekseev, Mikhail Pavlovich. *Stikhotvorenie Pushkina: "Ia pamiatnik sebe vozdvig":
Problemy ego izucheniia*. Leningrad: Izd-vo "Nauka," 1967.

Any, Carol. "Cliché as Device." *Conference Paper, ASEEES*, Washington, DC,
17 November 2016.

– "The Red Pushkin and the Writers' Union in 1937: Prescription and Taboo."
In *Taboo Pushkin: Topics, Texts, Interpretations*, edited by Alyssa Dinega
Gillespie, 378–401. Madison, WI: University of Wisconsin Press, 2012.

Avins, Carol. "Reaching a Reader: The Master's Audience in *The Master and
Margarita*." *Slavic Review* 45, no. 2 (Summer 1986): 272–85.

Banerjee, Anindita. *We Modern People*. Middletown, CT: Wesleyan University
Press, 2012.

Beliaev, Naum, and Igor' Shmidt. *Aleksander Mikhailovich Opekushin: 1841–1923*.
Moscow: Iskusstvo, 1954.

Belinskii, V.G. *Polnoe sobranie sochinenii v 13 tomakh*. Vol. 7. Moscow: Izd-vo
Akademii nauk SSSR, 1953–9.

Belobrovtseva, Irina, and Svetlana Kul'ius. *Roman M. Bulgakova: Kommentarii*.
Moscow: Knizhnyi klub 36.6, 2007.

Bem, A.L. "Dostoevskii – genial'nyi chitatel'." In *O Dostoevskom: Sbornik statei*.
Vol. 2, edited by A.L. Bem, 7–24. Prague: Izd-vo V.D. Kolesnikova, 1933.

Benevolenskaia, N.P. "«*Kys'*» T. Tolstoi kak ideologicheskii roman." *Izvestiia
Rossiiskogo gosudarstvennogo pedagogicheskogo universiteta im. A.I. Gertsena*
(2009): 135–6. Last accessed 8 April 2018 from https://cyberleninka.ru/
article/n/kys-t-tolstoy-kak-ideologicheskiy-roman.

Bethea, David [M.]. *Khodasevich: His Life and Art*. Princeton, NJ: Princeton
University Press, 1983.

– "'Mednyi vsadnik': Peterburgskii tekst i mifopoeticheskoe myshlenie
Pushkina." In *Sushchestvuet li peterburgskii tekst?*, edited by V.M. Markovich
and V. Shmid, 170–92. St Petersburg: Izd-vo Sankt-Peterburgskogo
universiteta, 2005.

– "Pushkin's Mythopoetic Consciousness: Apuleius, Psyche and Cupid, and the Theme of Metamorphosis in *Evgenii Onegin*." In *Alexander Pushkin: Myth and Monument*, Vol. 2 of *Two Hundred Years of Pushkin*, edited by Robert Reid and Joe Andrew, 15–37. New York: Rodopi, 2003.

– *Realizing Metaphors: Alexander Pushkin and the Life of the Poet*. Madison, WI: University of Wisconsin Press, 1998.

– *The Shape of Apocalypse in Modern Russian Fiction*. Princeton, NJ: Princeton University Press, 1989.

– "Stabat Pater: Revisiting the 'Monumental' in Peter, Petersburg, Pushkin." *Zapiski russkoi akademicheskoi gruppy v SShA (on the 300th Anniversary of St Petersburg)*, edited by Alexis Klimoff, 33 (2004): 3–21.

– "Whose Mind Is This Anyway?: Influence, Intertextuality, and the Boundaries of Legitimate Scholarship." *Slavic and East European Journal* 49, no. 1 (Spring 2005): 2–17.

Blackwell, Stephen. *Zina's Paradox: The Figured Reader in Nabokov's Gift*. New York: Peter Lang, 2000.

Bondi, Sergei M. "Pamiatnik." In *O Pushkine: Stat'i i issledovaniia*, 454–60. Moscow: Khudozh. lit., 1978.

Boym, Svetlana. "Inscriptions on the Poet's Monument." *Harvard Review* 1, no. 1 (Fall 1986): 64–81.

Brintlinger, Angela. "The Hero in the Madhouse: The Post-Soviet Novel Confronts the Soviet Past." *Slavic Review* 63, no. 1 (Spring 2004): 43–65.

– *Writing a Usable Past: Russian Literary Culture, 1917–1937*. Evanston, IL: Northwestern University Press, 2000.

Buckler, Julie. *Mapping St Petersburg: Imperial Text and Cityshape*. Princeton, NJ: Princeton University Press, 2005.

Bulgakov, Mikhail Afanas'evich. "Aleksandr Pushkin." In *Zoikina kvartira: P'esy*, edited by V.I. Losev, 5–96. St Petersburg: Azbuka Klassika, 2008.

– *Master i Margarita*. In *Polnoe Sobranie Chernovikov Romana: Osnovnoi tekst v dvukh tomakh*. Edited by E.Iu. Kolysheva. 2 vols. Moscow: Pashkov Dom, 2014.

Burbank, John. "Editor's Note." In Roman Jakobson, *Pushkin and His Sculptural Myth*, translated and edited by John Burbank, v–vi. The Hague: Mouton, 1975.

Cavendish, Philip. "Poetry as Metamorphosis: Aleksandr Pushkin's 'Ekho' and the Reshaping of the Echo Myth." *The Slavonic and East European Review* 78. no. 3 (July 2000): 439–62.

Chandler, Robert, Boris Dralyuk, and Irina Mashinski, eds. *The Penguin Book of Russian Poetry*. London: Penguin Classics, 2015.

Chubukov, Vsevolod. *Vsenarodnyi pamiatnik Pushkinu*. Moscow: Izd-vo Tverskaia, 13, 1999.

Chudakova, Marietta Omarovna. *Zhizneopisanie Mikhaila Bulgakova*. Moscow: Kniga, 1988.

Clowes, Edith. *Imagined Geographies*. Ithaca, NY: Cornell University Press, 2011.

Costello, D.P. "Pushkin and Roman Literature." *Oxford Slavonic Papers* 11 (1964): 46–55.

Crone, Anna Lisa, and Jennifer Day. *My Petersburg/Myself: Mental Architecture and Imaginative Space in Modern Russian Letters*. Bloomington, IN: Slavica, 2004.

Curtis, Julie A.E. *Bulgakov's Last Decade: The Writer as Hero*. New York: Cambridge University Press, 1987.

Dalton-Brown, Sally. "Signposting the Way to the City of Night: Recent Russian Dystopian Fiction." *Modern Language Review* 90, no. 1 (January 1995): 103–19.

Davydov, Sergei. "The Evolution of Pushkin's Political Thought." In *The Pushkin Handbook*, edited by David Bethea, 283–320. Madison, WI: University of Wisconsin Press, 2005.

– "Puškin's Easter Triptych: 'Hermit Fathers and Immaculate Women,' 'Imitation of the Italian,' and 'Secular Power.'" In *Pushkin Today*, edited by David M. Bethea, 38–58. Bloomington, IN: Indiana University Press, 1993.

Davydova, Ol'ga A. *Uvekovechennyi v bronze: Pushkiniana skul'ptura Aleksandra Opekushina*. Moscow: Izd-vo "MIK," 2016.

Dobrenko, Evgeny. *The Making of the State Reader: Social and Aesthetic Contexts of the Reception of Soviet Literature*. Translated by Jesse M. Savage. Stanford, CA: Stanford University Press, 1997.

– "Pushkin in Soviet and Post-Soviet Culture." In *The Cambridge Companion to Pushkin*, edited by Andrew Khan, 202–20. Cambridge: Cambridge University Press, 2006.

Dostoevskii/Dostoevsky, Fyodor M. *Notes from the Underground*. Translated by Michael R. Katz. New York: Norton, 2001.

– *Polnoe sobranie sochinenii v tridsati tomakh*. Vol. 30, book 1. Edited by B.G. Bazanov. Leningrad: Nauka, 1988.

– *A Writer's Diary*. Vol. 2. Translated and annotated by Kenneth Lantz. Evanston, IL: Northwestern University Press, 1994.

Esenin, Sergei A. *Polnoe sobranie sochinenii v 7 tomakh*, Vol. 2, *Stikhotvorenie*. Moscow: Nauka, 1997.

– *Polnoe sobranie sochinenii v 7 tomakh*, Vol. 7, book 1, *Avtobiografii. Darstvennye nadpisi. Fol'klornye materialy. Literaturnye manifesty*. Moscow: Nauka, 1999.

Feduta, Aleksandr Iosifovich. *"Kto b ni byl ty, o moi chitatel' …": Problema chitatelia v literature pushkinskoi epokhi*. Minsk: Limarius, 2015.

Fet, Afanasii A. *Polnoe sobranie sochinenii*. Leningrad: Sovestkii pisatel', 1959.

Fusso, Susanne. *Editing Turgenev, Dostoevsky, and Tolstoy: Mikhail Katkov and the Great Russian Novel*. DeKalb, IL: Northern Illinois University Press, 2017.

Gasparov, Boris M. "Iz nabliudenii nad motivnoi strukturoi romana M.A. Bulgakova 'Master i Margarita.'" *Slavica Hierosolymitana* 3 (1978): 198–251.

Gessen, Keith. "Kirill Medvedev: Introduction." In Kirill Medvedev, *It's No Good: Poems/Essays/Actions*, translated by Keith Gessen, Mark Krotov, Cory Merrill, and Bela Shayevich and edited by Keith Gessen, 11–21. Brooklyn, NY: n+1/ugly duckling presse, 2012.

Gillespie, Alyssa Dinega. "Bawdy and Soul: Pushkin's Poetics of Obscenity." In *Taboo Pushkin: Topics, Texts, Interpretations*, edited by Alyssa Dinega Gillespie, 185–223. Madison, WI: University of Wisconsin Press, 2012.

– "Introduction: Beyond Pushkin as Dogma." In *Taboo Pushkin: Topics, Texts, Interpretations*, edited by Alyssa Dinega Gillespie, 3–38. Madison, WI: University of Wisconsin Press, 2012.

Golburt, Luba. *The First Epoch: The Eighteenth Century and the Russian Cultural Imagination*. Madison, WI: University of Wisconsin Press, 2014.

Goscilo, Helena. *TNT: The Explosive World of Tatyana N. Tolstaya's Fiction*. New York: M.E. Sharpe, 1996.

Gribanov, Alexander. "Zametki k stat'e Iakobsona 'Statuia v poeticheskoi mifologii Pushkina.'" In *I vremia i mesto: Istoriko-filologicheskii sbornik k shestidesiatiletiiu Aleksandra L'vovicha Ospovata*, 177–86. Moscow: Novoe izd-vo, 2008.

Griffiths, Mark. "Moscow after the Apocalypse." *Slavic Review* 72, no. 3 (Fall 2013): 481–504.

Grot, Iakov. *Zhizn' Derzhavina: Po ego sochineniiam i pis'mam i po istoricheskim dokumentam*. St Petersburg: Izd-vo imperatorskoi akademii nauk, 1880.

Herman, David. "A Requiem for Aristocratic Art: Pushkin's 'Egyptian Nights.'" *Russian Review* 55, no. 4 (October 1996): 661–80.

Higgins, Andrew. "Aleksei Navalny, Top Putin Critic, Arrested as Protests Flare in Russia." *New York Times*, 26 March 2017. Accessed 11 August 2017. https://www.nytimes.com/2017/03/26/world/europe/moscow-protests-aleksei-navalny.html.

Hinds, Stephen. *Allusion and Intertext: Dynamics of Appropriation in Roman Poetry*. Cambridge: Cambridge University Press, 1998.

Hokanson, Katya. "'*Barbarus hic ego sum*': Pushkin and Ovid on the Pontic Shore." *Pushkin Review* 8–9 (2005–6): 61–75.

– "Politics and Poetry: The 'Anti-Polish' Poems and 'I Built Myself a Monument Not Made by Human Hands.'" In *Taboo Pushkin: Topics, Texts, Interpretations*, edited by Alyssa Dinega Gillespie, 283–317. Madison, WI: University of Wisconsin Press, 2012.

Horowitz, Brian. *The Myth of A.S. Pushkin in Russia's Silver Age: M.O. Gershenzon, Pushkinist*. Evanston, IL: Northwestern University Press, 1996.

Howell, Yvonne. *Apocalyptic Realism: The Science Fiction of Arkady and Boris Strugatsky*. New York: Peter Lang, 1994.

Iakubovich, Dmitrii P. "Antichnost' v tvorchestve Pushkina." In *Pushkin: Vremennik pushkinskoi komissii*, 6: 92–159. Moscow: Izd-vo AN SSSR, 1941.

Iieste, M. "Zametki k teme Pushkin i Ovidii." *Russkaia filologiia: Sbornik studencheskikh nauchnykh rabot*, edited by Z.G. Mints (1967): 171–90.

Jakobson, Roman. *Puškin and His Sculptural Myth*. Translated and edited by John Burbank. The Hague: Mouton, 1975.

Johnson, Emily D. *How St Petersburg Learned to Study Itself: The Russian Idea of Kraevedenie*. University Park, PA: The Pennsylvania State University Press, 2006.

Kahn, Andrew. "Ovid and Russia's Poets of Exile." In *A Handbook to the Reception of Ovid*, edited by John F. Miller and Carole E. Newlands, 401–15. Oxford: John Wiley & Sons, 2014.

– *Pushkin's Lyric Intelligence*. Oxford: Oxford University Press, 2008.

Kalinin, Il'ia. "Peterburgskii tekst kak produkt teoreticheskoi mifologizatsii." In *Sushchestvuet li Peterburgskii tekst*, edited by V.M. Markovich and V. Shmid, 24–34. St Petersburg: St Petersburg University Press, 2005.

Kanevskaia, Marina. "F.M. Dostoevsky's Pushkin Speech in a Cultural Context." PhD diss., Indiana University (Bloomington, IN), 1997.

Khagi, Sofya. "One Billion Years after the End of the World: Historical Deadlock, Contemporary Dystopia, and the Continuing Legacy of the Strugatskii Brothers." *Slavic Review* 72, no. 2 (Summer 2013): 267–86.

Khodasevich, Vladislav. "Proletkul't." In *Izbrannaia proza*. New York: Russica Publishers, 1982: 264–70.

Kisel, Maria. "Feuilletons Don't Burn: Bulgakov's *The Master and Margarita* and the Imagined 'Soviet Reader.'" *Slavic Review* 68, no. 3 (Fall 2009): 582–600.

– "Mass Culture to Master: Literary Metamorphoses of Early Soviet Satire." PhD diss., Northwestern University (Evanston, IL), 2008.

Knapp, Liza. "Tsvetaeva's 'Blackest of Black' (*Naicherneishii*) Pushkin." In *Under the Sky of My Africa: Alexander Pushkin and Blackness*, edited by Catharine Theimer Nepomnyashchy, Nicole Svobodny, and Liudmila A. Trigos, 279–301. Evanston, IL: Northwestern University Press, 2006.

Krein, Aleksander Z. *Rukotvornyi pamiatnik*. Moscow: Sovetskaia Rossiia, 1980.

Lachmann, Renate. *Memory and Literature: Intertextuality in Russian Modernism*. Translated by Roy Sellars and Anthony Wall. Ann Arbor: University of Michigan Press, 1997.

Lednicki, Waclaw. *Bits of Table Talk on Pushkin, Mickiewiecz, Goethe, Turgenev, and Sienkiewicz*. The Hague: Martinus Nijhoff, 1956.

– *The Bronze Horseman*. Westport, CT: Greenwood Press, 1978.

Lekmanov, Oleg. "Mesto vstrechi izmenit' nel'zia?" *Ruthenia* (June 2004). Accessed 13 September 2017. http://www.ruthenia.ru/document/533693 .html.

Lesskis, Georgii, and Kseniia Atarova. *Putevoditel' po romanu Mikhaila Bulgakova Master i Margarita*. Moscow: Raduga, 2007.

Levitt, Marcus [C]. "'Metamorfozy' Ovidiia v russkoi literature XVIII veka – Pro et contra." In *Litterarum fructus: Sbornik statei v chest' Sergeiia Ivanovicha Nikolaeva*, edited by N.Iu. Alekseeva and N.D. Kochetkova, 142–53. St Petersburg: Izd-vo Al'ians-Arkheo, 2012.

– "Pushkin's Readers, 1855–1887: The Making of a National Poet." Unpublished essay, personal correspondence, 4 April 2017.

– *Russian Literary Politics and the Pushkin Celebration of 1880*. Ithaca, NY: Cornell University Press, 1989.

– *The Visual Dominant in Eighteenth-Century Russia*. DeKalb, IL: Northern Illinois University Press, 2011.

Librovich, Sigizmund Feliksovich. *Pushkin v portretakh: Istoriia izobrazheniia poeta v zhivopisi, graviure i skul'pture*. St Petersburg: Tip. M.M. Stasiulevicha, 1890.

Loewen, Donald. *The Most Dangerous Art: Poetry, Politics, and Autobiography after the Russian Revolution*. New York: Lexington Books, 2008.

Lotman, Iuri M. *Aleksandr Sergeevich Pushkin: Biografiia pisatelia*. Leningrad: Prosveshchenie, 1983.

– *Semiosfera*. St Petersburg: Iskusstvo SPb, 2000.

– "Tekst v tekste." *Trudy po znakovym sistemam* 14 (1981): 3–18.

Lovell, Stephen. "Bulgakov as Soviet Culture." *The Slavonic and East European Review* 76, no. 1 (January 1998): 28–48.

– *The Russian Reading Revolution: Print Culture in the Soviet and Post-Soviet Eras*. New York: St Martin's Press, 2000.

Malein, Aleksander I. "Pushkin i Ovidii (otryvochnye zamechaniia)." In *Pushkin i ego sovremenniki: Materialy i issledovaniia*, 45–66. Petrograd: Imp. akad. nauk., 1916.

Martin, D.W. "The Pushkin Celebrations of 1880: The Conflict of Ideals and Ideologies." *Slavonic and East European Review* 66, no. 4 (October 1988): 505–25.

Medvedev, Kirill. *It's No Good: Poems/Essays/Actions*. Translated by Keith Gessen, Mark Krotov, Cory Merrill, and Bela Shayevich and edited by Keith Gessen. Brooklyn, NY: n+1/ugly duckling presse, 2012.

Melikhova, Aida Aleksandrovna, and Roman V. Tsekhanskii. *Strasti i nadezhdy Pushkinskoi (Strastnoi) ploshchadi i Strastnogo monastyria*. Moscow: Komissia Staraia Moskva, 2013.

Miagkov, Boris. *Bulgakov na patriarshikh*. Moscow: Algoritm, 2008.

Milne, Lesley. *Mikhail Bulgakov: A Critical Biography*. Cambridge: Cambridge University Press, 1990.

Mints, Zara G., Mikhail V. Bezrodnyi, and A.A. Danilevskii. "Peterburgskii tekst i russkii simvolizm." *Trudy po znakovym sistemam* 18 (1984): 78–92.

Modzalevskii, Boris L. "Katalog biblioteki A.S. Pushkina." In *Pushkin i ego sovremenniki: Materialy i issledovaniia* 9/10: 1–370. St Petersburg: Imp. akad. nauk., 1910.

Molok, Iurii. *Pushkin v 1937*. Moscow: NLO, 2000.

Morson, Gary Saul. "Introductory Study." In F.M. Dostoevsky, *A Writer's Diary*. Vol. 1, translated and annotated by Kenneth Lantz, 1–117. Evanston, IL: Northwestern University Press, 1993.

Mur'ianov, Mikhail F. "Iz nabliudenii nad tekstami Pushkina." *Moskovskii pushkinist* 1 (1995): 122–50.

Nepomnyashchy, Catherine Theimer. *Abram Tertz and the Poetics of Crime*. New Haven, CT: Yale University Press, 1995.

Nepomnyashchy, Catherine Theimer, and Ludmila A. Trigos. "Introduction." In *Under the Sky of My Africa: Alexander Pushkin and Blackness*, edited by Catharine Theimer Nepomnyashchy, Nicole Svobodny, and Liudmila A. Trigos, 3–45. Evanston, IL: Northwestern University Press, 2006.

Omori, Masako. "Tvorchestvo M.A. Bulgakova v sovetskom kul'turnom kontekste 1930s-x gg: Obraz A.S. Pushkina i motiv bessmertiia khudozhnika." *Novyi filologicheskii vestnik* 1, no. 28 (2014): 70–80.

Ovid. *Metamorphoses*. Translated by Stanley Lombardo. Indianapolis: Hackett, 2010.

Pelevin, Victor. *Buddha's Little Finger*. Translated by Andrew Bromfield. New York: Penguin, 1999.

Pelikan, Jaroslav. *Christianity and Classical Culture*. New Haven, CT: Yale University Press, 1993.

Pellicer, Juan Christian. "Pushkin's 'To Ovid' and Virgil's Georgics." *Pushkin Review* 14 (2011): 147–56.

Peschio, Joe. *The Poetics of Impudence and Intimacy in the Age of Pushkin*. Madison, WI: University of Wisconsin Press, 2012.

Platt, Jonathan Brooks. *Greetings, Pushkin! Stalinist Cultural Politics and the Russian National Bard*. Pittsburgh, PA: University of Pittsburgh Press, 2016.

Pokrovskii, Mikhail M. "Pushkin i antichnost.'" *Vremennik pushkinskoi komissii* 4/5: 27–56. Moscow: Izd-vo AN SSSR, 1939.

The Princeton Encyclopedia of Poetry and Poetics: Fourth Edition. Edited by Stephan Cushman, Clare Cavanagh, Jahan Ramazani, Paul Rouzer, and Roland Greene. Princeton, NJ: Princeton University Press, 2012.

Proffer, Ellendea. *Bulgakov: Life and Work*. Ann Arbor, MI: Ardis, 1984.

Proskurin, Oleg. *Poeziia Pushkina, ili podvizhnyi palimpsest*. Moscow: NLO, 1999.

– "Predshestvenniki Pushkina v XVIII i XIX vv. (Derzhavin, Zhukovskii, Batiushkov)." In *The Pushkin Handbook*, edited by David M. Bethea, 475–93. Madison, WI: University of Wisconsin Press, 2005.

– "Pushkin and Metropolitan Philaret: Rethinking the Problem." In *Taboo Pushkin: Topics, Texts, Interpretations*, edited by Alyssa Dinega Gillespie, 112–56. Madison, WI: University of Wisconsin Press, 2012.

Pushkin, Aleksander S. *Polnoe sobranie sochinenii v 10-i tomakh*. Leningrad: Izd-vo "Nauka," 1977–9.

Rann, James. "Maiakovskii and the Mobile Monument: Alternatives to Iconoclasm in Russian Culture." *Slavic Review* 71, no. 4 (Winter 2012): 766–91.

Reynolds, Andrew. "Returning the Ticket: Joseph Brodsky's 'August' and the End of the Petersburg Text?" *Slavic Review* 64, no. 2 (Summer 2005): 307–32.

Ricks, Christopher. *Allusion to the Poets*. Oxford: Oxford University Press, 2002.

Rosenshield, Gary. *Challenging the Bard*. Madison, WI: University of Wisconsin Press, 2013.

Rubins, Maria. *Crossroads of Arts, Crossroads of Cultures: Ecphrasis in Russian and French Poetry*. New York: Palgrave, 2000.

Samodelova, Elena. *Antropologicheskaia poetika S.A. Esenina: Avtorskii zhizhnetekst na perekrest'e kul'turnykh traditsii*. Moscow: Iazyki slavianskikh kul'tur, 2006.

Sandler, Stephanie. *Commemorating Pushkin*. Stanford, CA: Stanford University Press, 2004.

– *Distant Pleasures: Alexander Pushkin and the Writing of Exile*. Stanford, CA: Stanford University Press, 1989.

– "Embodied Words: Gender in Cvetaeva's Reading of Puškin." *Slavic and East European Journal* 34, no. 2 (Summer 1990): 139–57.

– "Introduction." *Slavic Review* 58, no. 2, *Special Issue: Aleksander Pushkin 1799–1999* (Summer 1999): 283–90.

Schenker, Alexander M. *The Bronze Horseman: Falconet's Monument to Peter the Great*. New Haven, CT: Yale University Press, 2003.

Scollins, Kathleen. "Pronouncing the 'New Word': The Bronze Horseman Subtext of *Crime and Punishment*." *Conference Paper, AATSEEL*, San Francisco, CA, 4 February 2017.

Sedakova, Olga. "'Non-Mortal and Mysterious Feelings': On Pushkin's Christianity." In *Pushkin's Legacy*, Vol. 3 of *Two Hundred Years of Pushkin*, edited by Robert Reid and Joe Andrew, 33–44. New York: Rodopi, 2004.

Shchegolev, Pavel E. *Duel' i smert' Pushkina: Issledovanie i materialy*. Moscow: Kniga, 1987.

Shevelenko, Irina D. "'Byvaiut strannye sblizhen'ia': Pushkin v tvorcheskom mire Tsvetaevoi 1930-kh godov." In *Pushkin i kul'tura russkogo zarubezh'ia:*

Mezhdunarodnaia nauchnaia konferentsiia, posviashchennaia 200-letiiu so dnia rozhdeniia, 1–3 iulia 1999 g, 49–63. Moscow: Russkii put', 2000.

Shmidt, Igor' Maksimilianovich. *Russkaia skul'ptura vtoroi poloviny XIX-nachala XX veka*. Moskva: Iskusstvo, 1989.

Shol'ts, Ute. "Mezhdu konstruktsiei i dekonstruktsiei: Utopicheskii ostrov v romane T. Tolstoi «Kys'»." *Vestnik Viatskogo gosudarstvennogo universiteta* 2, no. 1 (2009): 77–8. Last accessed 8 April 2018. https://cyberleninka.ru/article/v/mezhdu-konstruktsiey-i-dekonstruktsiey-utopicheskiy-ostrov-v-romane-t-tolstoy-kys.

Smith, Alexandra. "Fictionality, Theatricality, and Staging of Self: A New Look at Pushkin's 'Egyptian Nights.'" *Slavonic and East European Review* 84, no. 3 (2006): 393–418.

– "Pushkin as a Cultural Myth: Dostoevskii's Pushkin Speech and Its Legacy in Russian Modernism." In *Dostoevskii's Overcoat: Influence, Comparison, and Transposition*, edited by Joe Andrew and Robert Reid, 123–47. New York: Rodopi, 2013.

Smith, Karen R. "Recollecting Wondrous Moments: Father Pushkin, Mother Russia, and Intertextual Memory in Tatyana Tolstaya's 'Night' and 'Limpopo.'" *Studies in 20th & 21st Century Literature* 28, no. 2 (Summer 2004): 478–506.

Smoliarova, Tat'iana. "How The Bronze Horseman Was Made." In *Alexander Pushkin: Myth and Monument*, Vol. 2 of *Two Hundred Years of Pushkin*, edited by Robert Reid and Joe Andrew, 103–16. New York: Rodopi, 2003.

Solovyov, Vladimir. "The Russian National Ideal." In *A Revolution of the Spirit: Crisis of Value in Russia, 1890–1924*, edited by Bernice Glatzer Rosenthal and Martha Bohachevsky-Chomiak, 53–60. New York: Fordham University Press, 1990.

Stella, Francesca. "Queer Space, Pride, and Shame in Moscow." *Slavic Review* 72, no. 3 (Fall 2013): 458–80.

Suslov, Igor' M. *Pamiatnik Pushkinu: Putevoditel'*. Moscow: Moskovskii rabochii, 1983.

Swift, Megan. "Pushkin's 'Skazka o pope i rabotnike ego Balde' in Illustrations." *Russian Literature* 87–9 (2017): 123–46.

Tertz, Abram. *Progulki s Pushkinym*. London: William Collins Sons, 1975.

– *Strolls with Pushkin*. Translated by Catharine Theimer Nepomnyashchy and Slava I. Yastremski. New Haven, CT: Yale University Press, 1993.

Tolstaia, Tati'iana / Tolstaya, Tatyana. "Chuzhie sny." In *Izium: izbrannoe*. Moscow: Eksmo, 2012.

– "Limpopo." In *Liubish' – ne liubish': Rasskazy*, 270–328. Moscow: OLMA-PRESS, 1997.

– "Limpopo." In *Sleepwalker in a Fog*, translated by Jamey Gambrell, 133–92. New York: Alfred A. Knopf, 1992.

– "Night." In *Sleepwalker in a Fog*, translated by Jamey Gambrell, 67–76. New York: Alfred A. Knopf, 1992.

– "Noch'." In *Reka Okkervil': Rasskazy*, 102–10. Moscow: Podkova, 1999.

– "Siuzhet." In *Reka Okkervil': Rasskazy*, 251–62. Moscow: Podkova, 1999.

– *The Slynx*. Translated by Jamey Gambrell. New York: Houghton Mifflin, 2003.

Tolstoy, Leo. *Anna Karenina. The Maude Translation*. Edited by George Gibian. New York: Norton, 1970.

Toporov, Vladimir N. "O dinamicheskom kontekste 'trekhmernykh' proizvedenii izobrazitel'nogo iskusstva (semioticheskii vzgliad). Fal'konetovskii pamiatnik Petru I." In V.N. Toporov, *Peterburgskii Tekst*, 778–813. Moscow: Nauka, 2009.

– *Peterburgskii tekst*. Moscow: Nauka, 2009.

Tsiv'ian, Tat'iana Vladimirovna. "Dialog vzgliadov. Iz peterburgskikh chernovikov V.N. Toporova." In *Tekst slavianskoi kul'tury: K iubileiu Liudmily Aleksandrovny Sofronovoi*, 134–9. Moscow: Institut slavianovedenia RAN, 2011.

– "Gorod & Chelovek & Priroda." In *Rossika/Rusistika/Rossievedenie*, kn. 1, *Iazyk/Istoriia/Kul'tura*, 360–95. Moscow: Rossiisskii gosudarstvennyi gumanitarnyi universitet, 2010.

Tsvetaeva, Marina. "Moi Pushkin." In *A. Akhmatova i M. Tsvetaeva: Stikhotvoreniia, poemy, dramaturgiia, esse*, edited by L.D. Strakhova, 498–540. Moscow: Olimp, 2002.

Turgenev, Ivan Sergeevich. "Speech Delivered at the Dedication of the Monument to A.S. Pushkin in Moscow." In *The Essential Turgenev*, translated and edited by Elizabeth Cheresh Allen, 839–49. Evanston, IL: Northwestern University Press, 1994.

Vasil'eva, Zhanna. "Igry s Pushkinym: Chem interesna novaia biografia avtora samogo izvestnogo pamiatnika 'solntsu russkoi poezii.'" *Rossiiskaia gazeta*, 7 February 2017. https://rg.ru/2017/02/07/kak-opekushin-sozdaval-samyj -znamenityj-pamiatnik-pushkinu.html.

Vulikh, Nataliia V. "Ovidii." In *Pushkin: Issledovaniia i materialy*, 227–30. St Petersburg: Izd-vo "Nauka," 2004.

Wachtel, Michael. *A Commentary to Pushkin's Lyric Poetry, 1826–1836*. Madison, WI: University of Wisconsin Press, 2011.

Ware, Timothy. *The Orthodox Church*. Baltimore, MD: Penguin, 1967.

Weeks, Laura D. "In Defense of the Homeless: On the Uses of History and the Role of Bezdomnyi in *The Master and Margarita*." *Russian Review* 48, no. 1 (January 1989): 45–65.

Wood, Antony. Translation of Pushkin's "Monument." In Chandler, Dralyuk, and Mashinski, eds, *The Penguin Book of Russian Poetry*, 101–2.

Zhukovskii, Vasilii A. "Vospominanie o torzhestve 30 avgusta 1834." In
    Polnoe sobranie sochinenii v 12-i tomakh. Vol. 10, edited by A.S. Arkhangel'skii.
    St Petersburg: Izdanie A.F. Marksa, 1902.
Zoshchenko, Mikhail. "Gavrila I Pushkin." *Buzoter* no. 7 (1926): 6.
Zubok, Vladislav. *Zhivago's Children: The Last Russian Intelligentsia*. Cambridge,
    MA: Harvard University Press, 2009.

Index

1880: and censorship, 9, 77, 116; and
dedication, 14, 176; and literacy,
198, 200; and literary politics, 22,
87–8, 102, 189; and other Pushkin
celebrations, 113–14, 145–6; and
pedestal, 94, 187; and performance,
29–30, 97–8, 107–8, 111, 188
1937: and *Alexander Pushkin* (play),
132; and the built environment,
9–10, 127, 130, 160, 170; and
censorship, 184; and cliché, 30–1,
142–4; and future of poetry, 117;
and iconoclasm, 141; and literacy,
115, 200; and Maiakovskii, 136;
and *Master and Margarita*, 121–2;
and propaganda, 145–6; and
Stalinist Terror, 175, 242n13

Akhmatova, Anna Andreevna,
37, 163
Alekseev, Mikhail Pavlovich, 43–4,
58, 60, 82–3, 111, 144
Alexander Column, 31, 34–5, 51–3,
59–60, 71, 78–9, 96, 142–3, 147–51,
154–6, 159–60, 199
allusion: definition of, 15, 23–4;
density of, 129, 140, 147, 194–5,
198, 200; evolution of, 16, 37,
129; future of, 26–8, 31, 56, 62–3,

69, 80, 100, 104–5, 107, 117, 120,
140–1, 143, 147, 152, 158, 178, 180,
182; and imitation, 33, 42–4, 57,
64–5, 85, 97–100, 103, 109, 198;
and immortality, 26, 29, 37, 40–1,
44, 48, 54–7, 62, 64, 70, 72, 77, 117,
124–5, 136, 149–50, 154–5, 163–4,
168–70, 175–6, 187, 197; and intent,
33, 199; and memorization, 171;
metapoetics of, 27, 40, 58, 61, 64–6,
69, 72–3, 149–51, 153, 158, 160,
179; and monumental sculpture,
27, 32–8, 44, 96, 111, 136, 150; and
national character, 100, 109, 198;
and originality, 33, 43, 97–100,
183, 198; and patronage, 26, 41,
57, 61–6, 69; performative, 12, 14,
97, 104, 109–11, 115–16, 122, 142,
147, 152–4, 159–60, 164, 169, 185–9,
197–8, 200–2; poet and, 25, 28–9,
37, 63–4, 69, 118, 141, 164; readers
and, 15, 26, 28–9, 37, 41, 61–4,
69–71, 79, 118, 141, 164, 171, 189,
198; and "someone else's word"
(*chuzhoe slovo*), 67, 70, 89; study of,
146; as technology, 179; and time,
24, 33; and urban space, 22, 28–33,
37, 105–7, 110, 112, 129–30, 136,
141–2, 147, 158, 162, 164, 168, 181,